American Education

American Education

FOURTEENTH EDITION

Joel Spring
Queens College
City University of New York

McGraw-Hill Higher Education

Boston Burr Ridge, IL Dubuque, IA New York San Francisco St. Louis
Bangkok Bogotá Caracas Kuala Lumpur Lisbon London Madrid Mexico City
Milan Montreal New Delhi Santiago Seoul Singapore Sydney Taipei Toronto

The McGraw·Hill Companies

Higher Education

MCGRAW-HILL HIGHER EDUCATION
A DIVISION OF THE MCGRAW-HILL COMPANIES
Published by McGraw-Hill, an imprint of The McGraw-Hill Companies, Inc., 1221 Avenue of the Americas, New York, NY 10020.

This book is printed on acid-free paper.

1 2 3 4 5 6 7 8 9 0 DOC/DOC 0 9

ISBN: 978-0-07-337868-8
MHID: 0-07-337868-2

Vice President, Editor in Chief: *Michael Ryan*
Editorial Director: *Beth Mejia*
Publisher: *David S. Patterson*
Senior Sponsoring Editor: *Allison McNamara*
Executive Marketing Manager: *James Headley*
Editorial Coordinator: *Sarah Kiefer*
Senior Production Editor: *Karol Jurado*
Project Manager: *Marilyn Rothenberger*
Manuscript Editor: *Penn Street Craftspersons Associates*
Design Manager: *Ashley Bedell*
Cover Designer: *Stacy Anthony*
Production Supervisor: *Louis Swaim*
Composition: *10/12 Palatino by Laserwords*
Printing: *45# New Era Matte Plus, RR Donnelley & Sons*
Cover images: The McGraw-Hill Companies, Inc./Jill Braaten, photographer *(top left)*; © Tim Pannell/Corbis *(top right)*; The McGraw-Hill Companies, Inc./John Flournoy, photographer *(bottom left)*; The McGraw-Hill Companies, Inc. *(bottom right)*
Credits: The credits section for this book begins on page 287 and is considered an extension of the copyright page.

Library of Congress Cataloging-in-Publication Data

Spring, Joel H.
American education / Joel Spring.—14th ed.
p. cm.
ISBN-13: 978-0-07-337868-8 (alk. paper)
ISBN-10: 0-07-337868-2 (alk. paper)
1. Education—Social aspects—United States. 2. Education—Political aspects—United States. 3. Educational equalization—United States. 4. Education and state—United States.
I. Title.
LC191.4.S684 2009
370.973—dc22

2009002428

www.mhhe.com

About the Author

JOEL SPRING received his Ph.D. in educational policy studies from the University of Wisconsin. He is currently a professor at Queens College and the Graduate Center of the City University of New York. His great-great-grandfather was the first Principal Chief of the Choctaw Nation in Indian Territory and his grandfather, Joel S. Spring, was a local district chief at the time Indian Territory became Oklahoma. Joel Spring worked as a railroad conductor on the Illinois Central Railroad and for many years lived each summer on an island off the coast of Sitka, Alaska. His novel, *Alaskan Visions,* includes many of his Alaskan experiences.

Professor Spring's major research interests are history of education, globalization and education, multicultural education, Native American culture, the politics of education, and human rights education. He is the author of over 20 scholarly books with the most recent being *Pedagogies of Globalization: The Rise of the Educational Security State; How Educational Ideologies are Shaping Global Society;* and *Education and the Rise of the Global Economy.* Joel's most important textbooks are *American Education* (now in its 14th edition); *American School 1642–2004* (now in its 7th edition); and *Conflict of Interests: The Politics of American Education* (now in its 6th edition).

Professor Spring recently completed *Globalization of Education: An Introduction* and *A New Paradigm for Global School Systems: Education for a Long and Happy Life.* His book *Wheels in the Head: Educational Philosophies of Authority, Freedom, and Culture from Socrates to Human Rights* was recently translated into Chinese and published by the University of Peking Press.

Contents

A Guide with Chapter References to Discussions of No Child Left Behind Act of 2001

Title I—Improving the Academic Achievement of the Disadvantaged

1. Accountability: Standards and Testing (*Chapters 7 and 9*)
2. Schools must make "adequate yearly progress" (*Chapter 6*)
3. "Reading First" provides funds to help states and districts to establish "scientific, research-based" reading programs (*Chapter 7*)

Title II—Preparing, Training, and Recruiting High-Quality Teachers and Principals

1. Requires Schools to have "high-quality teachers" in all classrooms (*Chapter 8*)

Title III—Language Instruction for Limited English Proficient and Immigrant Children

1. Emphasizes English acquisition over bilingual instruction (*Chapter 5*)

Title V—Promoting Informed Parental Choice and Innovative Programs

1. Legislation supports public school choice and creation of charter public schools (*Chapter 6*)
2. Partnerships in Character Education funds for integrating secular character education into curricula and teaching methods of schools (*Chapter 1*)

Title VI—Flexibility and Accountability

1. Requires states to develop standards and testing programs with federal funding (*Chapter 7*)

Title VII—Indian, Native Hawaiian, and Alaska Native Education

Title VIII—Impact Aid Program

1. Federal funds for school districts impacted by federal lands such as military bases

Title IX—General Provisions

1. Boy Scouts of America Equal Access Act requires schools to allow Boy Scouts to use their facilities. Many schools banned the use of school facilities because the Boy Scouts discriminated against gay youth. (*Chapter 10*)
2. School prayer gives the U.S. Department of Education an active role in ensuring that school districts allow for school prayer within the boundaries of the law, and it requires local school districts to certify in writing that they do not prevent or interfere with participation in constitutionally protected prayer. (*Chapter 10*)

Preface

My goal is to provide an understanding of the political, social, and economic forces shaping the direction of American education. The classroom teacher's training, pedagogy, and content of instruction are directly affected by these forces. Also, I believe that the role of teachers extends beyond the classroom to participation in shaping the direction of schools in local communities, state governments, and national politics. I wanted future teachers to know that schools are not isolated from local and national events.

Of course, school policies change over time. One factor speeding up change is the discovery by national politicians that education is a good campaign issue. With the passage of the No Child Left Behind Act of 2001, American public schools must meet the demands of federal education policies and decisions by national political leaders. The classroom practices of teachers are affected by national policies.

In this fourteenth edition, I added new sections to chapters, updated topics and statistical tables, deleted dated material, and added new chapter openings as reader guides. Additions and changes to the fourteenth edition are listed below.

Changes in Fourteenth Edition

1. Chapter 1
   a. New opening to guide reader through chapter
   b. Added material on human capital goals
   c. Updated content
   d. Deleted dated material

2. Chapter 2
   a. New opening to guide reader through chapter
   b. Updated statistical tables
   c. Updated content
   d. Deleted dated material

3. Chapter 3
   a. New opening to guide reader through chapter
   b. Added new section on how courts and the U.S. Census Bureau define race
   c. Updated statistical tables
   d. Updated content
   e. Deleted dated material
4. Chapter 4
   a. New opening to guide reader through chapter
   b. New section global migration and the Immigration Act of 1965
   c. Added new section on immigration and the social construction of race
   d. Updated content
   e. Updated statistical tables
   f. Reorganized chapter sections
   g. Deleted dated material
5. Chapter 5
   a. New opening to guide reader through chapter
   b. New section on empowerment and sexism
   c. Updated content
   d. Updated statistical tables
   e. Deleted dated material
6. Chapter 6
   a. New opening to guide reader through chapter
   b. New section on charter schools and for-profit global education corporations
   c. Updated content
   d. Updated statistical tables
   e. Deleted dated material
7. Chapter 7
   a. New opening to guide reader through chapter
   b. New section on 2008 Democratic and Republican platforms
   c. Updated content
   d. Deleted dated material
8. Chapter 8
   a. New opening to guide reader through chapter
   b. New section on teacher turnover
   c. Updated content
   d. Updated statistical tables
   e. Deleted dated material
9. Chapter 9
   a. New opening to guide reader through chapter
   b. New section on cyber bullying
   c. New section on global models of curriculum and instruction
   d. Deleted dated material

PART ONE

School and Society

CHAPTER 1

The History and Goals of Public Schooling

This chapter introduces the reader to the controversies surrounding the goals of U.S. public schools. It also provides a brief history of U.S. schools by discussing educational goals from the founding of public schools in the nineteenth century to the present. The overall purpose of the chapter is to help the reader understand debates about public education. Educational goals are a product of what various people think schooling should do for the good of society. Consequently, they often reflect opinions and beliefs about how people should act and how society should be organized. Since there is wide variation in what people believe, educational goals often generate a great deal of debate. I'm sure that in reading this chapter you will find yourself taking sides on issues. For instance, some people argue that a goal of public schooling should be to reduce teenage pregnancy and to prevent the spread of AIDS. Should this involve teaching teenagers to abstain from premarital sex or should it involve teaching about the use of contraceptives? This question sparks heated debates because it goes to the heart of people's religious and moral beliefs.

It is important to understand that public schools were established to serve the public and not necessarily individual desires. The goals of public schools determine what is taught and how it will be taught. Students and parents are not asked at the schoolhouse door what they want from education. Educational goals, including the content of instruction and methods, are determined by federal, state, and local politicians, special interest groups, community organizations, and professional education organizations. Given the political control of public schools, it is not possible for the principal of a public school to design the content and methods of instruction to suit the wishes of individual parents or students. When students enter a public school they are submitting to the will of the public as determined by local, state, and federal governments.

To distinguish between educational goals I have divided them into political, social, and economic. For instance, political goals often involve teaching patriotism. But should teaching patriotism consist of saluting the flag and reciting the Pledge of Allegiance, which contains a reference to God? Some religious groups criticize flag salutes as worshiping false gods, while other people complain about the reference to God in the Pledge. Also, social goals can stimulate debates as suggested by the previous discussion about reducing teenage pregnancy. An important traditional goal of schooling is reducing crime through instruction in social values. But whose social values or morality should form the basis of instruction in public schools? Today, the economic goals of schooling primarily center on educating workers to help the U.S. economy compete in the global economy. But will this goal increase or decrease economic inequalities in society?

Throughout this chapter I have lists of questions about each set of goals. These questions do not have right or wrong answers. They are questions that reflect real debates about the role of U.S. public schools. The questions also provide insight into the historical evolution of American education. For instance, what are your answers to the following questions:

- Do you think there are public benefits from education that should override the objections of parents and other citizens regarding the teaching of particular subjects, attitudes, or values?
- Should elected representatives determine the subject matter, attitudes, and values taught in public schools?
- What should public school teachers do if they are asked to teach values that are in conflict with their own personal values?

In answering the preceding questions remember that public schools do not always operate for the general good of society. Most people assume that public schooling is good for society. However, public schools are used to advance political and economic ideologies that do not improve the condition of human beings. For instance, in the 1930s Nazis enlisted schools in a general campaign to educate citizens to believe in the racial superiority of the German people, to support fascism, and to be willing to die at the command of Hitler. Racial biology and fascist political doctrines were taught in the classroom; patriotic parades and singing took place in the schoolyard. A similar pattern occurred in South African schools in attempts to maintain a racially divided society. In the United States, racial segregation and biased content in textbooks was used to maintain a racial hierarchy.

Consequently, the reader should be aware that "education" does not always benefit the individual or society. Public and personal benefits depend on the content of instruction. To think critically about education means to think critically about the content of instruction and the potential effect of that content on society. For instance, there are constantly recurring debates about teaching the evolution of humans in contrast to the Biblical emphasis on God creating humans. Those opposed to teaching evolution claim that it has a negative effect on individual morality and society because the Biblical explanation makes humans a special creature in the eyes of God and therefore obliged to obey Scriptures. I will discuss the evolution debate in more detail later in this chapter.

In summary, this chapter will introduce readers to:

- The goals and history of U.S. public schools.
- The debates about the political, social, and economic goals of public schools.
- Questions designed to help readers formulate their own opinions about the purposes of American education.

HISTORICAL GOALS OF SCHOOLING

The historical record provides insight into current controversies surrounding public school goals. The original goals of public schools centered on citizenship training, equality of economic opportunity, and reduction of crime. These goals remain on the public school agenda. Over time, schools expanded their purposes as new problems were encountered. Most of the original goals of schooling still guide the work of educators. The multiplicity of things schools are now asked to do is a result of an accumulating historical agenda.

Therefore, a history of the evolution of public school goals provides a critical analysis of what public schools are now doing. Each of the following sections will trace the history of these goals to the present. In each section, I will list critical questions about the role of schooling in society. I have also created two time lines. Figure 1–1 indicates the approximate decades when public schools adopted particular educational goals to meet changing social and economic conditions. Figure 1–2 is a time line of events discussed in this chapter.

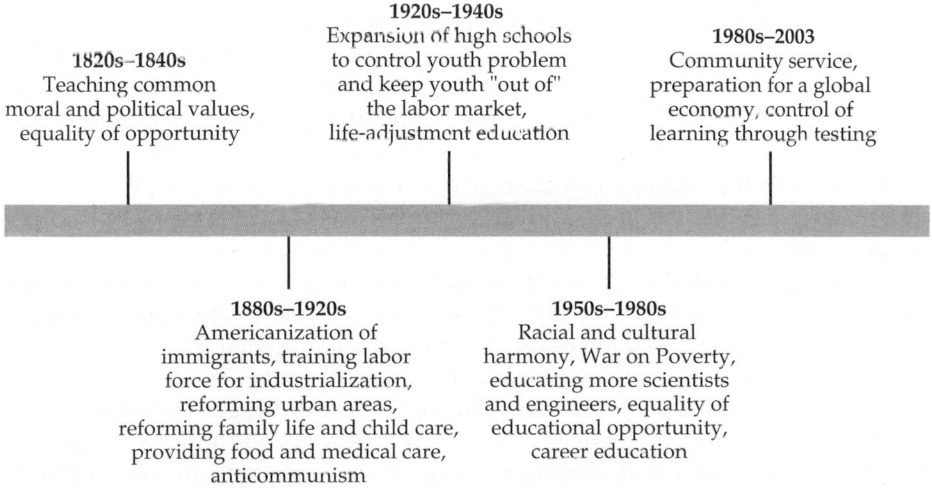

FIGURE 1–1. Goals of Public Schools in the U.S., 1820–2003

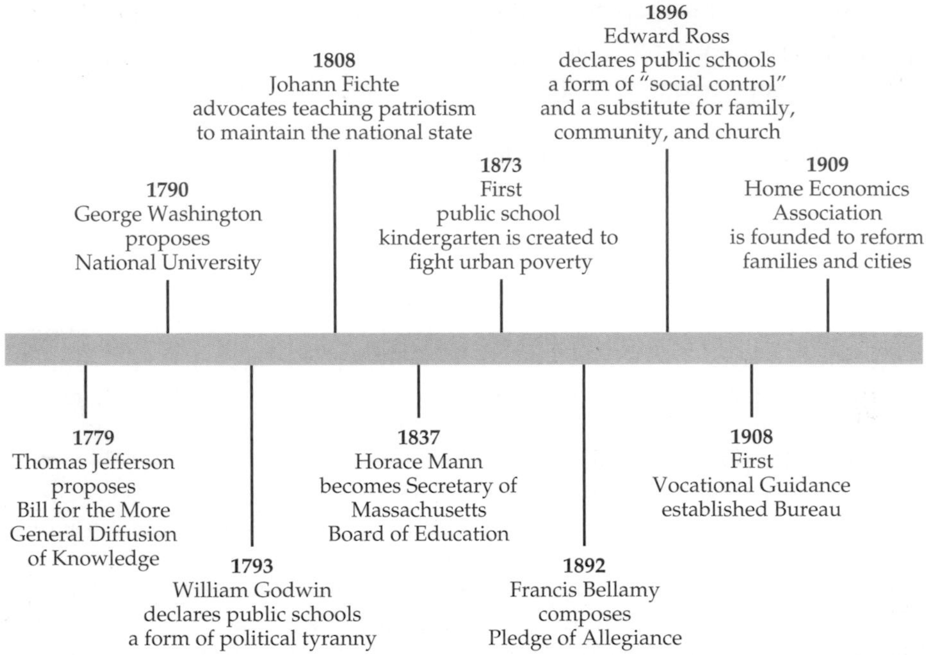

FIGURE 1–2. Time Line of Events Discussed in This Chapter

THE POLITICAL GOALS OF SCHOOLING

Before the actual establishment of public schools, public leaders argued that public schools were needed to create a national culture and to educate qualified politicians for a republican government. The role of schools in determining national culture continues into the twenty-first century, particularly as a result of increased immigration. After the American Revolution, many worried about national unity and the selection of political leaders. In his first message to Congress in 1790, President George Washington proposed a national university for training political leaders and creating a national culture. He wanted attendance by students from all areas of the country. What was hoped was that a hereditary aristocracy of the British would be replaced by an aristocracy of the educated.

Washington's proposal was criticized as elitist. Requiring a college education, some protested, would result in politicians being primarily recruited from the elite. If none but the rich had access to higher education, then the rich could use higher education as a means of perpetuating and supporting their social status.

To avoid the problem of elitism, Thomas Jefferson suggested using education to promote a *meritocracy;* a term still used to describe the affect of schools on society. A meritocracy is an educational system that gives an equal chance to all to develop their abilities and to advance in the social hierarchy. Advancement within the educational system and society is based on the merit or achievements

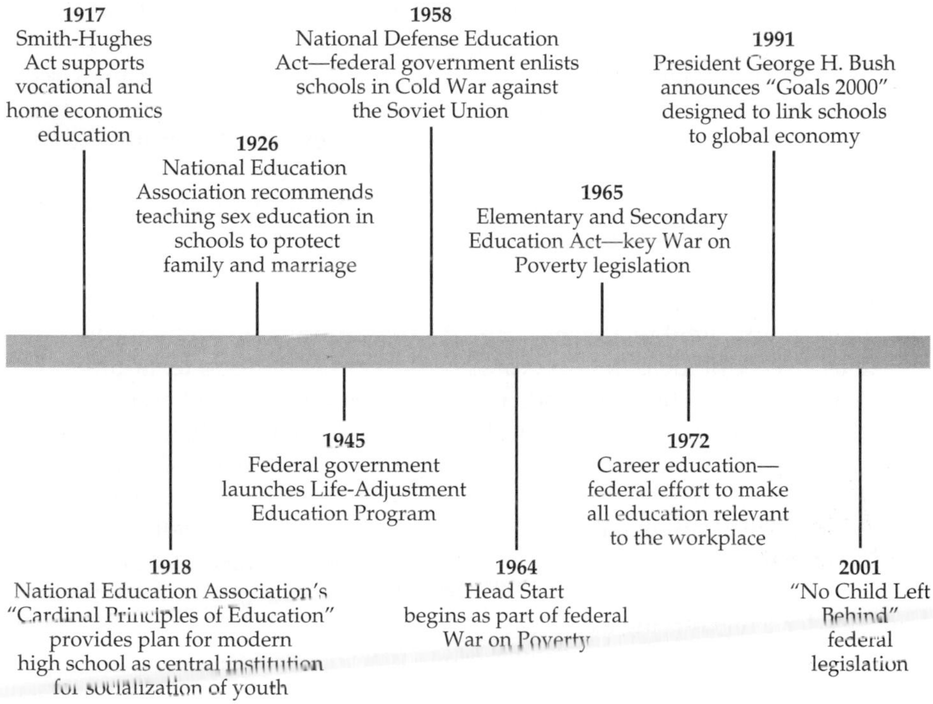

FIGURE 1–2. *(Continued)*

of the individual. For instance, consider the following situation: Students A and B are given an equal chance to attend school; student A is very successful but student B fails. Within the framework of an educational meritocracy, their success or failure in school determines their later position in society.

Jefferson was concerned with finding the best politicians through meritocratic system based on education. In the 1779 Bill for the More General Diffusion of Knowledge, Jefferson proposed three years of free education for all nonslave children. The most talented of these children were to be selected and educated at public expense at regional grammar schools. From this select group, the most talented were to be chosen for further education. Thomas Jefferson wrote in *Notes on the State of Virginia*, "By this means twenty of the best geniuses will be raked from the rubbish annually, and be instructed, at the public expense."

The details of Jefferson's plan are not as important as the idea, which has become ingrained in American social thought, that schooling is the best means of identifying democratic leadership. This idea assumes that the educational system is fair in its judgments. Fairness of selection assumes that judgment is based solely on talent demonstrated in school and not on other social factors such as race, religion, dress, and social class. Meritocracy fails if schools favor individuals from certain racial, religious, and economic groups.

Besides educating political leadership, schools were also called on to educate future citizens. However, opinions were divided on how this should be accomplished. Thomas Jefferson proposed a very limited education for the general citizenry. The three years of free education were to consist of instruction in reading, writing, and arithmetic, with reading instruction using Greek, Roman, English, and American history. Jefferson did not believe that people needed to be educated to be good citizens. He believed in the guiding power of natural reason to lead the citizen to correct political decisions. Citizens were to receive their political education from reading newspapers published under laws protecting freedom of the press. Citizens would choose between competing political ideas found in newspapers. Consequently, the important function of schools in preparing citizens was to teach reading.

Interestingly, while Jefferson wanted political opinions to be formed in a free marketplace of ideas, he advocated censorship of political texts at the University of Virginia. These contradictory positions reflect an inherent problem in the use of schools to teach political ideas. There is always the temptation to limit political instruction to what one believes are correct political ideas.

In contrast to Jefferson, Horace Mann, often called the father of public schools, wanted to instill a common political creed in all students. Mann felt that without commonly held political beliefs society was doomed to political strife and chaos. Mann developed these ideas and his reputation as America's greatest educational leader while serving as secretary of the Massachusetts Board of Education from 1837 to 1848. Originally a lawyer, Mann gave up his legal career because he believed that schooling and not law was the key to creating the good society.

Horace Mann feared that growing crime rates, social-class conflict, and the extension of suffrage would lead to violence and mob rule. Commonly held political values, Mann believed, would curtail political violence and revolution, and maintain political order. For Mann, the important idea was that all children in society attend the same type of school. This was what was meant by "common." It was a school common to all children. Within the common school, children of all religions and social classes were to share in a common education. Basic social disagreements were to vanish as rich and poor children, and children whose parents were supporters of different political parties, mingled in the schoolroom.

Within the walls of the common schoolhouse students were to be taught the basic principles of a republican form of government. Mann assumed there was general agreement about the nature of these general political values, and they could be taught without objection from outside political groups. In fact, he opposed teaching politically controversial topics because he worried that conflicting political forces would destroy the public school idea. The combination of common schooling and the teaching of a common political philosophy would establish, Mann hoped, shared political beliefs that would ensure the survival of the U.S. government. Political liberty would be possible, according to Mann's philosophy, because it would be restrained and controlled by the ideas students learned in public schools.

Is there a common set of political values in the United States? Since the nineteenth century, debates over the content of instruction have rocked the schoolhouse. Throughout the twentieth and twenty-first centuries, conservative political groups pressured local public schools to not teach left-wing ideas.

On the other hand, liberal organizations demanded schools teach their particular political doctrines.

There is a strong tradition of dissent to public schools teaching any political doctrines. Some argue that teaching of political ideas is a method of maintaining the political power of those in control of government. In the late eighteenth century, English political theorist William Godwin warned against national systems of education because they could become a means by which those controlling government could control the minds of future citizens. Writing in 1793, Godwin stated, "Their views as institutors of a system of education will not fail to be analogous to their views in their political capacity: the data upon which their instructions are founded."

Mann's political and social objectives were in part to be accomplished through socialization within the school. Simply defined, *socialization* refers to what students learn from following school rules, interacting with other students, and participating in school social events. Socialization can be contrasted with academic learning, which refers to classroom instruction, textbooks, and other forms of formal learning.

For some educational leaders, socialization is a powerful means of political control. Learning to obey school rules is socialization for obedience to government laws. Advocating the use of schools as political control, Johann Fichte, a Prussian leader in the early nineteenth century, asserted that schools should prepare students for conformity to government regulations by teaching obedience to school rules and developing a sense of loyalty to the school. He argued that students will transfer their obedience to school rules to submission to government laws. According to Fichte, loyalty and service to the school and fellow students prepares citizens for service to the country. The school, according to Fichte, is a miniature community where children learn to adjust their individuality to the requirements of the community. The real work of the school, Fichte said, is shaping this social adjustment. A well-ordered government requires citizens to go beyond mere obedience to written constitutions and laws. Fichte believed children must see the government as something greater than the individual and must learn to sacrifice for the good of the social whole.

To achieve these political goals, Fichte recommended teaching patriotic songs, national history, and literature to increase a sense of dedication and patriotism to the government. This combination of socialization and patriotic teachings, he argued, would produce a citizen more willing and able to participate in the army and, consequently, would reduce the cost of national defense.

In the United States, patriotic exercises and fostering school spirit were emphasized after the arrival in the 1890s of large numbers of immigrants from southern and eastern Europe. In 1892, Francis Bellamy wrote the Pledge of Allegiance and introduced it in the same year to educators attending the annual meeting of the National Education Association. A socialist, Bellamy wanted to include the word "equality" in the Pledge but this idea was rejected because state superintendents of education opposed equality for women and African Americans. The original Pledge of Allegiance was: "I pledge allegiance to my

Flag and to the Republic for which it stands, one nation, indivisible, with liberty and justice for all." Bellamy's Pledge of Allegiance became popular classroom practice as educators worried about the loyalty of immigrant children.

In the 1920s, the American Legion and the Daughters of the American Revolution thought that the Pledge's phrase "I pledge allegiance to my Flag" would be construed by immigrants to mean that they could remain loyal to their former nations. Consequently, "my flag" became "the flag of the United States." It was during this period that schools initiated Americanization programs which were a precursor to current debates about immigrant education. Americanization programs taught immigrant children the laws, language, and customs of the United States. Naturally, this included teaching patriotic songs and stories. With the coming of World War I, the Pledge of Allegiance, the singing of patriotic songs, participation in student government, and other patriotic exercises became a part of the American school. In addition, the development of extracurricular activities led to an emphasis on school spirit. The formation of football and basketball teams, with their accompanying trappings of cheerleaders and pep rallies, was to build school spirit and, consequently, prepare students for service to the nation.

Teaching patriotism creates problems for a society with a variety of religious, ethnic, and political groups. As mentioned earlier in the chapter, some religious groups object to pledging allegiance to a flag because they believe it is worship of a graven image. In *West Virginia State Board of Education v. Barnette* (1943), the U.S. Supreme Court ruled that expulsion from school of children of Jehovah's Witnesses for not saluting the flag was a violation of their constitutional right to freedom of religion. Some teachers view patriotic exercises as contrary to the principles of a free society. In Chapter 10, which deals with legal issues, there is a lengthy discussion of the court cases related to academic freedom and loyalty oaths as well as the conflict between patriotic requirements and students' rights.

In the 1950s, the Pledge of Allegiance underwent another transformation when some members of the U.S. Congress and religious leaders campaigned to stress the role of religion in government. In 1954, the phrase "under God" was added to the Pledge. The new Pledge referred to "one nation, under God." Congressional legislation supporting the change declared that the goal was to "acknowledge the dependence of our people and our Government upon . . . the Creator . . . [and] deny the atheistic and materialistic concept of communism." For similar reasons, Congress in 1955 added the words "In God We Trust" to all paper money.

Reflecting the continuing controversy over the Pledge, a U.S. Court of Appeals ruled in 2002 that the phrase "one nation, under God" violated the U.S. Constitution's ban on government-supported religion. The decision was later dismissed by the U.S. Supreme Court because the father in the case did not have legal custody of his daughter for whom the case was originally brought. The suit was filed by Michael Newdow, the father of a second-grade student attending California's Elk Grove Unified School District. Newdow argued his daughter's First Amendment rights were violated because she was forced to "watch and listen as her state-employed teacher in her state-run school leads her classmates in a ritual proclaiming that there is a God, and ours is 'one nation under God.'" While the issue remains unresolved, the suit raised important questions about the Pledge of Allegiance.

In reaction to the Court's decision, Anna Quindlen wrote in the July 15, 2002, edition of *Newsweek*, "His [Bellamy's] granddaughter said he would have hated the addition of the words 'under God' to a statement he envisioned uniting a country divided by race, class and, of course, religion." Another dimension of the story was that Bellamy was a socialist during a period of greater political toleration than today. In contrast to the 1890s, today it would be difficult to find a professional educational organization that would allow an outspoken socialist to write its patriotic pledge.

In recent years, community service has become a part of citizenship training. For instance, in the fall of 1998, Chicago became the nation's largest school system to require students to perform community service or service learning to receive a high school diploma. In 2008, Chicago schools stated the purpose of service learning: "GOALS: Service Learning as an educational strategy is designed to enhance social and academic learning while developing character and citizenship skills." Bruce Marchiafava, speaking for the nation's third-largest school system behind New York and Los Angeles declared, "We want students to learn the importance of community. They need to know that community is about giving, not just getting."

The immediate problem for Chicago officials was defining and identifying community service. This problem was compounded by the headache of finding enough community service activities for all the students. "If you let students work for an anti-handgun group," Marchiafava said, "do you also let them work for the NRA [the National Rifle Association, which opposes strong gun control laws]?" Are political activities community service? Does volunteer work at for-profit schools and hospitals increase profits for these institutions by decreasing labor costs? Also, who decides what is community service? What happens if the person making this decision identifies work with religious organizations as community service? Would this be a violation of the Constitution's prohibition of government aiding religion? What about objections by some people to religious groups such as the Native American Church, which uses peyote, a hallucinogenic drug, in its ceremonies? Will students be able to volunteer to work for organizations advocating the legalization of marijuana?

Chicago schools never really resolved these issues. Ambiguous regulations were adopted that give school staff the power to determine what service learning could take place with political and religious organizations. The 2006 Chicago guidelines for service learning state:

> Students may not earn Service Learning hours through the following: Religious organizations if the service involves proselytizing.
>
> Students may not earn hours for the following specific activities: Volunteer work with a political campaign without the mediation of an approved community organization or classroom instructor.

These regulations still don't answer the question of students working with the National Rifle Association, the National Organization for Reform of Marijuana Laws, or the Native American Church.

None of the issues surrounding the political goals of education are easily resolved. Can they even be achieved? For instance, consider the following questions:

- Should there be a consensus of political values in the United States and should public schools develop that consensus?
- Should the public schools develop emotional or patriotic attachments to symbols of the State through the use of songs, literature, and history?
- Should the purpose of teaching history be the development of patriotic feelings?
- Does the teaching of patriotism in schools throughout the world increase the potential for international conflict?
- Who or what government agency should determine the political values taught in public schools?

THE SOCIAL GOALS OF SCHOOLING

Solving social problems was always part of the goals of American public schools. Horace Mann believed the school was the key to social improvement. He argued that past societies failed to stop crime through the power of government laws. To stop crime, Mann reasoned, schools must instill moral values in students. Later, this approach to controlling crime was referred to as putting a police person in every child's heart. Mann even suggested that America might see the day when the training in the schoolhouse would significantly reduce the number of police required by society.

The problem for Horace Mann and later educational leaders was determining which moral values to teach in schools. His approach was to teach moral values common to most Protestant denominations. A variety of religious groups disagreed with his ideas. The Catholic Church, the largest single religious group to reject Mann's plan, established its own system of schools. Catholic Church leaders argued that education was fundamentally religious when it involved shaping behavior and that it was impossible for public schools to teach moral values that reflected the views of all religious groups. Even if the public school eliminated all religious and moral teaching, this alternative could not be accepted because education would then become irreligious.

Mann's dream of education as the key to social improvement remains alive despite conflicts over what morality should be taught in public schools. For many Americans, the school is the symbol and hope for achieving the good society. This hope is best illustrated by a story told to kindergartners in the early twentieth century about two children who bring a beautiful flower from their school class to their dirty and dark tenement apartment. Their mother placed the flower in a glass of water near a dirty window. She decides the flower needs more light to expose its beauty. The mother cleans the window allowing more light into the apartment which illuminates the dirty floors, walls, and furniture. The added light sends the mother scurrying around to clean up the now-exposed dirt. In the meantime the father, who is unemployed because of a drinking problem, returns to the apartment and is amazed to find his grim dwelling transformed into a clean and tidy house. The transformation of the apartment results in the father wanting to spend more time at home and less time at the local bar. The father's drinking problem is solved, he is able to find work, and the family lives happily ever after. This story characterizes the hope that the social influence of the school will penetrate the homes and neighborhoods of America.

This story illustrates the importance early sociologists placed on the social influence of the school. Writing in the 1890s, sociologist Edward Ross referred to education as a key mechanism for *social control.* Social control, as he used the term, referred to how a society maintained order and controlled crime and rebellion. He divided social control into external and internal. External social control involved the police and military regulating social behavior. Internal social control involved people controlling their own behaviors according to moral values. Traditionally, he argued, families, churches, and the communities taught children moral values and social responsibility. In modern society, Ross declared, the family and church were being replaced by the school as the most important institution for instilling internal values. Ross saw reliance on education for control becoming characteristic of American society. "The ebb of religion is only half a fact," Ross wrote. "The other half is the high tide of education. While the priest is leaving the civil service, the schoolmaster is coming in. As the state shakes itself loose from the church, it reaches out for the school."

Other groups advocated the expansion of the social role of the school during the same years as Edward Ross was declaring schools a central mechanism for social control. The home economics profession, currently called Family and Consumer Sciences, called upon schools to play a major role in improving the quality of American families, changing the lifestyles of women, bettering urban conditions, and reforming the American diet. Schools responded by adding home economics courses for girls and school cafeterias. Founded in 1909, the American Home Economics Association spearheaded the creation of educational goals linked to home and urban improvement projects.

Home economics courses were designed to train women to be scientific housekeepers who would free themselves from kitchen drudgery by relying on packaged and processed foods. Home economics courses taught cooking, household budgeting, sewing, and scientific methods of cleaning. The goal was providing housewives with more free time for education and working to improve municipal conditions. The family model was of wives as consumers of household products and educators and husbands as wage earners. By teaching women household budgeting, families learned to live within their means and as a result worker discontent over wages was to decline. A clean and cheerful house, it was believed, would reduce alcoholism because husbands would want to hurry home from work rather than stop at a tavern. Teaching women how to cook healthy meals would give their husbands more energy at work. And, of course, freed to receive more education, the housewives were to improve the political and cultural level of the American home.

In *Perfection Salad: Women and Cooking at the Turn of the Century,* Laura Shapiro credits home economists with the development of a distinctive American cuisine. She argues that during the latter part of the nineteenth century home economists "made American cooking American, transforming a nation of honest appetites into an obedient market for instant mashed potatoes." Jell-O and Wonder Bread, a factory-baked white bread, became symbols of American cuisine. These home economists paved the way for America's greatest contributions to global cuisine, the fast-food franchise.

School cafeterias were to reform American eating habits. Home economists made school and hospital cafeteria food healthy, inexpensive, and bland. Through the school cafeteria, home economists hoped to persuade immigrant children to abandon the diet of their parents for the new American cuisine. A founder of the home economics movement, Ellen Richards projected a liberating role for prepared food in a 1900 article titled, "Housekeeping in the Twentieth Century." In her dream home where the purchase of cheap, mass-produced furniture allowed more money for "intellectual pleasures," the pantry was filled with a large stock of prepared foods—mainly canned foods and bakery products. A pneumatic tube connected to the pantry speeded canned and packaged food to the kitchen where the wife simply heated up the meal. In addition, the meal would be accompanied by store-bought bread. Besides being unsanitary, home economists believed that homemade bread and other bakery goods required an inordinate amount of preparation time and therefore housewives should rely on factory-produced bread products. Ellen Richards dismissed the issue of taste with the comment, "I grant that each family has a weakness for the flavor produced by its own kitchen bacteria, but that is a prejudice due to lack of education." People would stop worrying about taste, she argued, when they fully realized the benefits of the superior cleanliness and consistency of factory kitchens and bakeries.

Concern about the American diet continued into the twenty-first century when in 2002 the U.S. Congress began considering the Obesity Prevention and Treatment Act that would initiate a campaign to improve the eating habits in the nation, where more than 60 percent of adults are overweight. Public schools also jumped on the campaign to control student diets. Referring to the nationwide income of $750 million earned by schools from companies that sell snack or processed food in schools, Steve O'Donoghue, a teacher at Fremont High School in California, commented, "Should schools be co-conspirators in promoting unhealthy diets? Even if we can't change a single kid's behavior, the message we send by having all these deals with junk food peddlers is that this stuff is OK." To control student diets, Fremont High School has banned junk and snack foods. However, the Center for Consumer Freedom objects to the restrictions as a denial of student freedom of choice. Who should control students' eating habits?

In addition to the family, community, health, and diets, schools were called on to exercise social control over youth. Traditionally, the high school focused on teaching academic subjects. Broader goals were established for high schools in the National Education Association's 1918 report, *The Cardinal Principles of Secondary Education.* This report set the stage for the high school to become the major public institution for the socialization of youth through school dances, athletics, student government, clubs, and other extracurricular activities. Attended by only a small portion of the population in its early years, the high school became a mass institution during the 1930s.

High school extracurricular activities aimed to control adolescent sexuality and prepare youth for future family roles. In 1926, the NEA's Committee on Character Education recommended sex education courses as a means of combating the decline of the family and regulating sexual impulses for the good of society. The recommendation defined the purpose of human life as: "The creation of one's own home and family, involving first the choice and winning of, or being won by, one's mate." Sex education was to prepare youth to fulfill this purpose. Similar to today's emphasis on sexual abstinence before marriage, these early sex education courses taught that sexual control was necessary for "proper home functioning, which includes the comfort and happiness of all, maximum development of the mates, proper child production, and effective personal and social education of children." Students were warned that sexual intercourse outside marriage should be avoided because of its potential threat to the stability of the family.

Ironically, the high school heightened the possibility of early sexual activity by bringing large numbers of youth together within one institution. High school activities created a shared experience for youth. In *From Front Porch to Back Seat: Courtship in Twentieth-Century America,* Beth Bailey argues that the high school standardized youth culture and created ritualized dating patterns. High school marriage texts and manuals built sexual boundaries around dating. According to Bailey, early high school sex education books dealt with the issue of petting, which meant anything from hand-holding to sexual acts short of actual penetration. All the books warned against promiscuous petting. High school girls were cautioned that heavy petting would lead to a decline of their dating value in the marketplace. Women were given the task of ensuring that petting did not go too far. They were warned that boys tended to sit around and talk about their sexual exploits. The worst thing that could happen to a girl was to become an object of locker room discussions. Girls were told to achieve a balance between being known as an "icicle" and a "hot number."

By the 1930s, the senior prom was the pinnacle of the high school dating experience. In *Prom Night: Youth, Schools, and Popular Culture,* Amy Best argues that as a growing number of youth attended high school, "School clubs, school dances, and student government increasingly became a significant part of the kids' lives." Proms became widespread in the 1930s as the high school became a mass institution. They were considered a poor or middle-class version of the debutante ball, which instructed youth in proper dating and mating rituals. Amy Best contends, "Proms were historically tied to a schooling project used to govern the uncontrollable youth. By enlisting you to participate in middle-class rituals like the prom, schools were able to advance a program that reigned in student's emerging and increasingly public sexualities."

By the 1940s, high schools had created a national youth culture and school youth were given the name "teenagers." After World War II, spending patterns changed as symbolized by the publication *Seventeen* magazine with its slogan "Teena means business." The word "teenager," according to Kelly Schrum, was invented by advertisers. At first advertisers experimented with "teenster" and "Petiteen," then "teenager" was popularized during the 1940s to mean a group defined by high school attendance. Defined as a major consumer market, it was believed that teenagers needed to be trained in the arts of consumption. Reflecting this trend, high school home economics courses were replaced by Family and Consumer Science courses.

Today, the sexual education of teenagers remains a controversial issue. Many people turn to the schools in efforts to exert control over adolescent sexual behavior. In recent years, the most heated value conflicts centered on AIDS education. These debates pitted those who believe in a strong moral code to control sexual behavior against those who believe in the right of free sexual activity between consenting adults. Those who believe in a strong moral code tend to support AIDS education programs that advocate sexual abstinence outside marriage and take a strong stand against homosexual activities. Those at the other end of the value spectrum emphasize educational programs that teach safe sexual procedures and advocate the dispensing of condoms in public schools.

The importance of schools in shaping social behavior continues in the twenty-first century. The 2001 federal legislation No Child Left Behind contains a section on "Partnerships in Character Education" that calls for the integration of character education into classroom instruction. At the 2002 White House Conference on Character and Community, President Bush highlighted the value of character education:

> The thing I appreciate is that you understand education should prepare children for jobs, and it also should prepare our children for life. I join you in wanting our children to not only be rich in skills, but rich in ideals. Teaching character and citizenship to our children is a high calling. It's a really high calling. And I'm grateful for your work.

While many parents and teachers support the development of good character and citizenship, there is a problem in defining its meaning. For instance, the No Child Left Behind Act refers to "integrating *secular* character education into curricula and teaching methods of schools" [my emphasis]. The use of "secular" in the legislation is to make a distinction from character education based on religious values. As examples of the elements of secular character education, the legislation provides the following:

a. Caring
b. Civic virtue and citizenship

c. Justice and fairness
d. Respect
e. Responsibility
f. Trustworthiness
g. Giving

What do these terms mean? Does "caring" mean that the individual should support a strong welfare government that guarantees all citizens health care, shelter, and adequate nutrition? Or does "caring" mean eliminating welfare programs so that the poor are forced to work and learn to be economically independent?

While public schools can't teach religion, some religiously oriented people would object to "secular character education." Christian fundamentalist groups refer to this form of character education as secular humanism. The simplest definition of secular humanism is that it comprises a set of ethical standards that place primary emphasis on a person's ability to interpret and guide his or her own moral actions. Most religions believe that good character must be grounded in religious doctrines. Many Christians believe that the sources of ethical and moral values should be the Bible and God. Secular humanism relies on the authority of human beings rather than the authority of the Scriptures. From a religious perspective, ideas like caring, respect, responsibility, and giving should be taught only in a religious context.

The controversy surrounding the goals of character education are illustrated by a 1986 legal suit brought by a group of parents against the Hawkins County School District in Tennessee for requiring students, on a threat of suspension, to read from the Holt, Rinehart and Winston basic reading series. Specifically, the parents objected to selections in the readers from *The Wizard of Oz, Rumpelstiltskin,* and *Macbeth.* The parents claimed that the textbook series contained explicit statements on secular humanism and taught values contrary to the religious beliefs of their children. In the words of presiding U.S. District Judge Thomas Gray Hull, "The plaintiffs believe that, after reading the entire Holt series, a child might adopt the views of a feminist, a humanist, a pacifist, an anti-Christian, a vegetarian, or an advocate of a 'one-world government."

Does the concept of "respect" included in the character education section of No Child Left Behind include teaching respect for households headed by gay and lesbian couples? In 1992, New York City adopted the "Children of the Rainbow" curriculum, which required elementary schools to teach tolerance toward gays and lesbians. Among the books recommended for use in classrooms were *Daddy's Roommate* and *Heather Has Two Mommies.* Both books show pictures of gay couples, including a drawing of two men in bed. Standing on top of a truck outside the school chancellor's office, Mary Cummins, the president of the local Queens district board of education, led a demonstration against the curriculum. "It is bizarre," she said, "to teach six-year-olds this [referring to the gay and lesbian content of the curriculum]. Why single out [homosexuals] for respect? Tomorrow it will be skinheads." Catholic, Pentecostal, and Baptist churches along with Orthodox Jewish synagogues protested that homosexuality is a sin and that schools should not teach respect for gay and lesbian lifestyles. Neil Lodato, a construction worker, shouted outside his daughter's school, "They should stick to teaching these babies that 1 + 1 = 2, instead of what daddy and his boyfriend are doing in the bedroom."

Should schools teach "respect" for other cultures? In *The De-Valuing of America: The Fight for Our Culture and Our Children,* William Bennett, former U.S. Secretary of Education, expresses his objections to teaching respect for other cultures. Bennett argues that U.S. cultural traditions have produced the best society on earth. Why teach respect for inferior cultures? Bennett maintains that U.S. schools should focus on transmitting the European roots of American culture.

So what does "respect" mean if it doesn't include appreciation of other lifestyles and cultures? Does it mean respect for one's own person with regard to sexual activities? The Sex Respect program began in 1983 with a curriculum guide designed to motivate teens to practice chastity. The program's current goal is "to enable each individual to progressively develop responsible behavior, positive self-esteem, and respect for others as he/she makes decisions involving the use of his/her sexual freedom." Sex Respect defines sexual freedom as the freedom to say no. In 2006, Sex Respect reported that when its founder Coleen Kelly Mast delivers her " 'save sex for marriage' message to teenagers in both public and parochial schools, the response is hand-painted posters like 'Pet your dog, not your date' [and] 'Use your will, not the pill.'"

Today, the program is being used in all 50 states and 23 foreign countries. The program's growth was made possible by Title V of the welfare-reform act of 1996 in which Congress authorized federal funds to be provided to the states in the form of block grants to promote chastity until marriage. Title V requires states to fund education that:

a. Has as its exclusive purpose, teaching the social, psychological, and health gains to be realized by abstaining from sexual activity.
b. Teaches abstinence from sexual activity outside marriage as the expected standard for all school-age children.
c. Teaches that abstinence from sexual activity is the only certain way to avoid out-of-wedlock pregnancy, sexually transmitted diseases, and other associated health problems.
d. Teaches that a mutually faithful monogamous relationship in the context of marriage is the expected standard of human sexual activity.

Both the federally funded Sex Respect program and the goals of Title V raise important questions about the meaning of respect and the goals of public schools. Should schools be involved in sex education or should this area of instruction be left to parents, the community, or religious groups? Should government legislation define a "faithful monogamous relationship in the context of marriage . . . [as] the expected standard of human sexual activity" for all people? Should public schools focus on birth control methods as opposed to abstinence from sexual activity?

Despite the fact that the historical record indicates that moral instruction has not reduced crime, controlled teenage sexuality, or ended substance abuse, society still turns to public schools as the cure for many social problems. Certainly, the school can teach subjects that will improve society without engaging in moral instruction that will light the fires of religious controversy. For instance, early home economists advocated teaching about sanitation and diseases as a means of promoting public health. High school courses can teach about the results of alcoholism and substance abuse without entering the realm of morality—for example, is smoking marijuana "evil" or just bad for your health? Social studies, history, and economics courses can study social conditions that might contribute to crime and violence. However, even in this seemingly neutral approach to social issues there is always lurking in the background the potential for conflict over moral values.

Attempts to use public schools to solve social problems will continue to raise problems about what values should dominate character education and how to reconcile secular and religious values. Consider the following questions:

- What are legitimate areas of social concern for public schools?
- Should public schools attempt to solve social problems, such as the AIDS epidemic or other epidemics, the destructive use of drugs and alcohol, teenage pregnancy, poverty, and child abuse?
- What government agency, organization, or group of individuals should decide the moral values to be taught in public schools?
- Should instruction related to social and moral issues be mandatory for all students?
- Should teachers be required to teach only the moral and social values given in the school district's curriculum?

THE ECONOMIC GOALS OF SCHOOLING

Today, the economic goals dominate public schooling as students are educated as workers for the global economy. Education is hailed as the key to economic growth. In 2008, the Partnership for 21st Century Skills issued a report with a title indicating economic education goals: *21st Century Skills, Education & Competitiveness*. The report declared, "Creating an aligned, 21st century public education system that prepares students, workers and citizens to triumph in the global skills race is the central economic competitiveness issue for the next decade."

The idea of education for economic growth and competition is not new. Since the nineteenth century, politicians and school leaders justified schools as necessary for economic development. Originally, Horace Mann proposed two major economic objectives. One was what we now call *human capital*. Simply stated, human capital theory contends that investment in education will improve the quality of workers and, consequently, increase the wealth of the community. The second was *equality of opportunity*. By going to school, everyone was to be given an equal opportunity to compete for jobs and wealth.

Horace Mann used human capital theory to justify community support of schools. For instance, why should an adult with no children be forced to pay for the schooling of other people's children? Mann's answer was that public schooling increased the wealth of the community and, therefore, even people without children economically benefitted from schools. Mann also believed that schooling would eliminate poverty by raising the wealth of the community and by preparing everyone to be economically successful.

Mann's thinking was echoed in a global context in a speech by Montana Governor Brian Schweitzer at the three-day Economic Summit on Early Childhood Investment held in September of 2007. He told the gathering of education leaders, politicians, and business groups: "We're no longer competing just with Colorado; we're competing with China. We need to challenge every single educator to create the next engineer." Linda Jacobson reported the conference for *Education Week* in an article with the descriptive human capital title: "Summit Links Preschool to Economic Success." She reported, "Hoping to win over skeptical policymakers, leaders from the business, philanthropic, and political arenas gathered here this week to strengthen their message that spending money on early-childhood education will improve high school graduation rates and help keep the United States economically strong." Preschoolers were being viewed as human resources to be educated for global economic competition.

Current discussions of human capital originated in the War on Poverty programs of the 1960s. War on Poverty programs included Head Start and Title I. The twenty-first-century's federal legislation No Child Left Behind is a renewal of Title I. The economic model of the War on Poverty in Figure 1–3 exemplifies current and past ideas about schooling and poverty. Notice that poor-quality education is one element in a series of social factors that tends to reinforce other social conditions. As you move around the inner part of the diagram, an inadequate education is linked to low-income jobs, low-quality housing, poor diet, poor medical care, health problems, and high rates of absenteeism from school and work. This model suggests eliminating poverty by improving any of the interrelated points. For instance, the improvement of health conditions will mean fewer days lost from school and employment, which will mean more income. Higher wages will mean improved housing, medical care, diet, and education. These improved conditions will mean better jobs for those of the next generation. Antipoverty programs include Head Start, compensatory education, vocation and career education, public housing, housing subsidies, food stamps, and medical care.

Today, Head Start programs are premised on the idea that some children from low-income families begin school at a disadvantage in comparison to children from middle- and high-income families. Head Start programs provide early childhood education to give poor children a head start on schooling that allows them to compete on equal terms with other children. Job-training programs are designed to end teenage and adult unemployment. Compensatory education in fields such as reading are designed to ensure the success of low-income students.

Besides the issue of poverty, human capital arguments directly influenced the organization of schools. In the twentieth and twenty-first centuries, the dominant model for linking schools to the labor market is the "sorting machine."

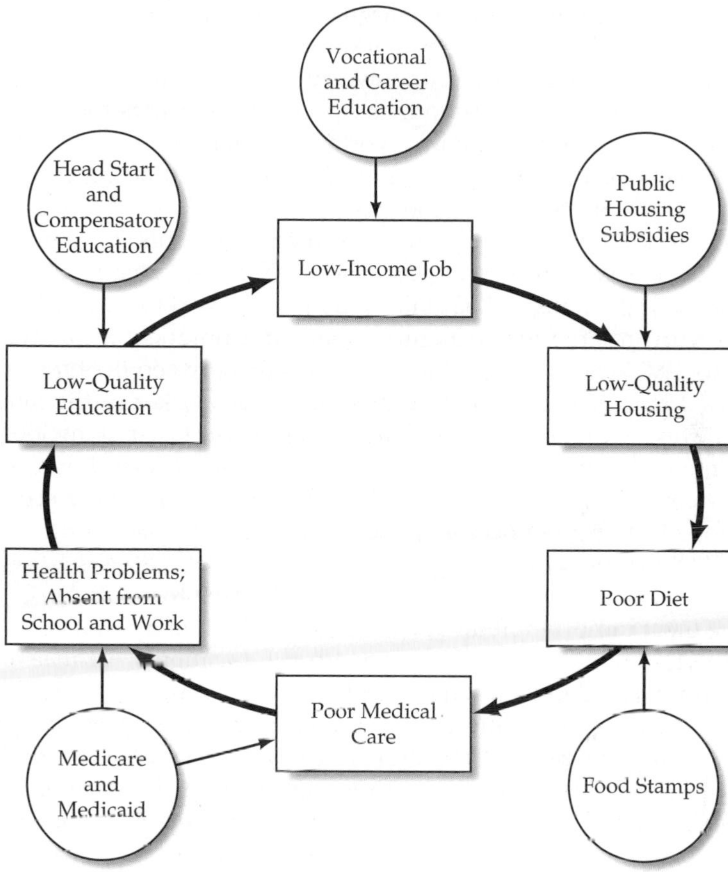

FIGURE 1–3. War on Poverty

The image of the sorting machine is that of pouring students—called human capital or human resources—into schools where they are separated by abilities and interests. Emerging from the other end of the machine, school graduates enter jobs that match their educational programs. In this model, the school counselor or other school official uses a variety of standardized tests to place the student into an ability group in an elementary school classroom and later in high school into a course of study. Ideally, a student's education will lead directly to college or a vocation. In this model, there should be a correlation among students' education, abilities, and interests and their occupations. With schools as sorting machines, proponents argue, the economy will prosper and workers will be happy because of the close tie between the schools and the labor market.

In the twenty-first century, American workers are competing in a global economy. As U.S. companies seek cheaper labor in foreign countries, American workers are forced to take reductions in benefits and wages to compete with foreign workers. The only hope, it is argued, is to train workers for jobs that pay higher wages in the global labor market.

Preparation for the global economy shifts the focus from service to a national economy to a global economy by preparing workers for international corporations and for competition in a world labor market. It is argued that the income of American workers is to rise because they will be educated for the highest-paying jobs in the world economy.

The architect of educational policies for the global economy, former Labor Secretary Robert Reich, writes in *The Work of Nations,* "Herein lies the new logic of economic capitalism: The skills of a nation's workforce and the quality of its infrastructure are what make it unique, and uniquely attractive, in the world economy." Reich draws a direct relationship between the type of education provided by schools and the placement of the worker in the labor market. He believes that many workers will be trapped in low-paying jobs unless their employment skills are improved. Reich argues, "There should not be a barrier between education and work. We're talking about a new economy in which lifelong learning is a necessity for every single member of the American workforce."

Human capital and global competitiveness are used to justify No Child Left Behind, the most important federal legislation of the twenty-first century. The opening line to the official U.S. Department of Education's *A Guide to Education and No Child Left Behind* declares, "Satisfying the demand for highly skilled workers is the key to maintaining competitiveness and prosperity in the global economy." In his 2006 State of the Union Address, President George W. Bush declared, "Keeping America competitive requires us to open more markets for all that Americans make and grow. One out of every five factory jobs in America is related to global trade . . . we need to encourage children to take more math and science, and to make sure those courses are rigorous enough to compete with other nations."

At the opening of the 2005 National Education Summit on High Schools, Kerry Killinger, CEO of Washington Mutual and vice-chair of Achieve, Inc., declared, "We face the global economy today with workers who are largely not prepared to compete for the well-paid, cutting-edge jobs that are fueling economic growth around the world. The summit is an extraordinary opportunity for states to work together to raise our academic expectations and the rigor of the preparation we give to our young people." The summit's report, *An Action Agenda for Improving America's High Schools,* proposes a core high school curriculum of four years of English and four years of math including data analysis and statistics.

Are all public school parents committed to having their children educated so that they can help U.S. businesses compete in the global economy? Did all public school parents participate in the decision to make American economic competitiveness the central educational goal? At the National Summit on High Schools, public goals for secondary schools were articulated by a combination of governors, chief executive officers of major corporations, and educational leaders. Attending the summit were 150 governors, heads of corporations, and educators. The summit was cosponsored by the National Governors Association (the self-described "collective voice of the nation's governors" founded in 1906) and Achieve, Inc. Achieve, Inc., was formed in 1996 by the National Governors Association and business leaders for the purpose of raising "academic standards and achievement so that all students graduate ready for college, work and citizenship." The list of representatives from the business community who serve as officers of Achieve, Inc., is impressive. They include Arthur F. Ryan, Chairman and CEO, Prudential Financial, Inc.; Kerry Killinger, Chairman and CEO, Washington Mutual; Craig R. Barrett, CEO, Intel Corporation; Jerry Jurgensen, CEO, Nationwide; Edward B. Rust, Jr., Chairman and CEO, State Farm Insurance; Louis V. Gerstner, Jr., Former Chairman and CEO, IBM Corporation; and Peter Sayre, Controller, Prudential Financial, Inc.

Human capital theory is the basis for the preceding economic goals for education. In schools, human capital is students, and the development of human capital simply means preparing students to be efficient workers, who, it is hoped, can find employment in their area of training. Economic growth pays for the investment in education. In the framework of human capital illustrated in Figure 1–4, an important consideration is the return on investment:

- Does investment in education produce worthwhile economic returns?
- Should governments invest in schools if there are few economic rewards?

Equality of opportunity was Horace Mann's other economic goal. The idea of equality of opportunity resolves the conflict between promises of equality

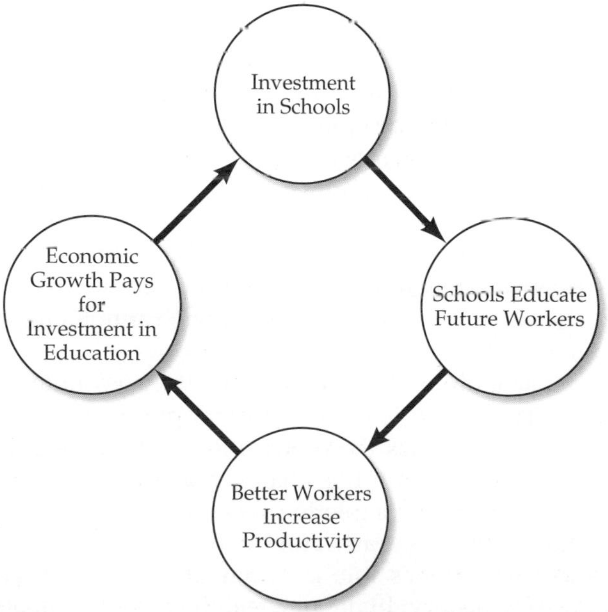

FIGURE 1–4. Human Capital Model

and the existence of a society strongly divided by economic inequalities. Equality of opportunity does not mean equal income, living conditions, or status, but rather *equality to compete for wealth.* Horace Mann envisioned schools providing children of the rich and poor an equal education so that when they graduated they would be on equal terms to compete for jobs. He believed that the idea of equality of opportunity would reduce social tensions between the rich and poor by instilling the belief in people that everyone had an equal chance to succeed. It didn't matter whether equality of opportunity actually existed because social tensions would be reduced simply by people believing that the school provided everyone with an equal chance for success.

Equality of opportunity plays an important role in human capital theory. The War on Poverty and the No Child Left Behind legislation are premised on the idea that improved schooling will provide an equal opportunity for poor children in the labor market. It also assumes that equality of opportunity will improve the efficiency of the labor market by letting talented children from poor families achieve occupations commensurate with their abilities. Allowing talented children to achieve despite family conditions will, theoretically, contribute to economic growth.

Educational inflation, however, might fly in the face of equality of opportunity and human capital arguments. Increasing the number of high school and college graduates might result in decreasing the economic value of education. It is a simple story of supply and demand. With educational inflation, the educational requirements of jobs increase while the actual skills required for the jobs do not change. This results in the declining economic value of high school and college diplomas. Educational inflation first appeared in the early 1970s when the labor market was flooded with college graduates, and scholars with doctorates were driving taxicabs and cooking in restaurants. In this situation, the occupational structure did not expand to meet the increased educational training of the labor force. The response of educational institutions was to reorganize for more specific career training and call for more limited educational aspirations. The important lesson was that the nature of the labor market was more important in determining employment than was the amount of education available to the population. Educational inflation can hinder the ability of increased schooling to end poverty. There must be an increase in the number of jobs actually requiring higher levels of education for increased schooling to effectively raise levels of income. Education alone cannot solve the problems of poverty.

As I discussed, schools are believed to benefit the economy by socializing students for work. The school is the first formal public organization encountered by the child and provides the preparation and training needed to deal with other complex social organizations. The school's attendance requirements, tardiness rules, instruction in completing tasks and following directions, and obedience to authority are preparation for the workplace.

Arguments for the school's role in socializing for the workplace can be found throughout U.S. history. In the nineteenth century, schools emphasized marching, drills, and orderliness as preparation for the modern factory. Lining up for class as well as marching in and out of the cloakroom and to the blackboard were justified as training for factory assembly lines. Today, some students are prepared for job interviews and filling out employment forms. However, there is the question of whether the school is simply educating workers who are obedient, conforming, and passive, and who are, consequently, unwilling to join or form unions to actively struggle for workers' rights.

In recent years, there has been discussion of the school's role in promoting a learning society and lifelong learning so that workers can adapt to constantly changing needs in the labor force. A learning society and lifelong learning are considered essential parts of global educational systems. Both concepts assume a world of constant technological change, which will require workers to continually update their skills. This assumption means that schools will be required to teach students how to learn so that they can continue learning throughout their lives. These two concepts are defined as follows:

- In a learning society, educational credentials determine income and status. Also, all members in a learning society are engaged in learning to adapt to constant changes in technology and work requirements.
- Lifelong learning refers to workers engaging in continual training to meet the changing technological requirements of the workplace.

In the context of education for the global economy, the larger questions include the following:

- Should the primary goal of education be human capital development?
- Should the worth of educational institutions be measured by their contribution to economic growth?
- Will the learning society and lifelong learning to prepare for technological change increase human happiness?

HUMAN CAPITAL AND THE ROLE OF BUSINESS IN AMERICAN EDUCATION

Businesses, as I just discussed, are very active in developing educational policies. Education for the global economy links schooling to the interests of the business community and international corporations. In fact, by the twenty-first century, most Americans seemed to accept business as a natural partner in the control of schools. In the 1990s, few people questioned President George Bush Senior and the National Governors Association's statement: "Parents, businesses, and community organizations will work together to ensure that schools are a safe haven for all children."

- Why would business be considered a logical partner in the preceding statement?
- Why was there no mention of unions or churches?
- Why was there no mention of participation by all the citizens who pay taxes to support schools?

The extensive and often unquestioned involvement of business in American schools has increased at a rapid rate and has made economic goals the number-one priority of public schools. Business involvement in schools raises a number of issues. It is not necessarily true that what is good for American business is good for American schools and students. The primary concern of business is the maximization of profits. Business profits depend on the quality and expense of workers. Although businesses want educated workers, they also want workers who are compliant and loyal to the company.

It can also be argued that it is in the public interest for schools to focus on the education of future workers. Doesn't everyone benefit if the economy is booming? Therefore, shouldn't public schools emphasize the development of habits that will meet the requirements of business? If you believe that the primary goal of public schools is making sure that graduates can get jobs, then your answer is "Yes!"

CONCLUSION

The school continues to be used in efforts to solve social, political, and economic problems. It is easier for politicians to blame schools for social and economic problems than to try to directly correct these problems. By relying on the school, issues are shifted from an economic and social level to a personal level. "Reform the individual rather than society" is the message of those who trust the school to end crime, poverty, broken families, drug and alcohol abuse, and myriad other social troubles.

Now the focus is on the role of the school in a global economy. This focus emphasizes the school's role in economic development. Fortunately or unfortunately, students are viewed as human resources whose primary value is their potential contribution to economic growth and productivity. But is economic expansion a worthy goal if the quality of life is not improved? Doesn't education in and of itself improve the quality of an individual's life by opening new possibilities to thinking and learning?

Suggested Readings and Works Cited in Chapter

Achieve, Inc. "About Achieve." http://www.achieve.org. This organization is composed of members of the National Governors Association and leading members of the business community dedicated to shaping the direction of U.S. schools.

——. "America's High Schools: The Front Line in the Battle for Our Economic Future." http://www.achieve.org. This document issued for the 2005 National Education Summit on High Schools stresses the importance of changing the high school curriculum to ensure the success of the U.S. in the global economy.

——. "National Education Summit on High Schools Convenes in Washington." http://www.achieve.org/node/93. This is a report on the opening of the 2005 National Education Summit on High Schools.

Achieve, Inc., and the National Governors Association. *An Action Agenda for Improving America's High Schools: 2005 National Education Summit on High Schools.* Washington, DC: Achieve, Inc., and the National Governors Association, 2005. This official report of the high school summit calls for a core high school curriculum of four years each of English and math.

BAILEY, BETH L. *From Front Porch to Back Seat: Courtship in Twentieth-Century America.* Baltimore: Johns Hopkins University Press, 1988. Bailey presents a history of twentieth-century dating, including high school dating.

BARTON, PAUL E. *High School Reform and Work: Facing Labor Market Realities.* Princeton, New Jersey: Educational Testing Service, 2006. This report highlights that the major concern of employers for entry level jobs is work attitudes. It reviews the other reports on workplace requirement reviewed in this chapter.

BENNETT, WILLIAM J. *The De-Valuing of America: The Fight for Our Culture and Our Children.* New York: Simon & Schuster, 1992. Bennett attacks multicultural education and defends the teaching of European traditions in American culture.

BEST, AMY L. *Prom Night: Youth, Schools, and Popular Culture.* New York: Routledge, 2000. Best offers a historical and sociological study of the high school prom.

BORJA, RHEA. "Pledge of Allegiance in the Legal Spotlight." *Education Week* (10 July 2002). This article details the 2002 court decision that declared the phrase "one nation, under God" a violation of the ban on a government-established religion.

Business Roundtable."About Us." http://www.businessroundtable.org. This major business organization is concerned that schools graduate students with proper job skills to help increase economic growth and improve the U.S. competitive edge in global markets.

Chicago Public Schools."Guidelines, Service Learning." http://servicelearning.cps.k12.il.us/Guidelines.html. This Web site provides information on Chicago's community service requirements for graduation.

Commission on the Reorganization of Secondary Education, National Education Association. *Cardinal Principles of Secondary Education, Bureau of Education Bulletin.* Washington, DC: U.S. Government Printing Office, 1918. Publication that outlined the goals of modern comprehensive high school.

CREMIN, LAWRENCE. *The Republic and the School.* New York: Teachers College Press, 1957. This is a good selection of Horace Mann's writings taken from his reports to the Massachusetts Board of Education and a good introduction to the social and political purposes of American education.

DELFATTORE, JOAN. *What Johnny Shouldn't Read: Textbook Censorship in America.* New Haven: Yale University Press, 1992. Delfattore discusses the Hawkins County, Tennessee, protest by Evangelical Christians over the content of school textbooks. Her book also covers other major censorship conflicts.

Democratic Leadership Council. "How a 21st Century Party Can Promote 21st Century Jobs, Panel II: Creating Higher-Skill, Higher-Wage Jobs." Democratic National Convention, Boston, Massachusetts (28 July 2004). http://www.ndol.org/print.cfm?contentid5252833. This document exemplifies the political support of educational goals tied to developing workers for the global labor market. Also, it is an example of the bipartisan support of No Child Left Behind.

EGAN, TIMOTHY. "In Bid to Improve Nutrition, Schools Expel Soda and Chips." *The New York Times on the Web* (20 May 2002). http://www.nytimes.com. Egan discusses recent attempts to wean students from snack and junk foods.

GREENBERG, DAVID. "History Lesson: The Pledge of Allegiance." http://www.slate.msn.com (28 June 2002). This article provides a history of the Pledge of Allegiance from its origin in 1892 to the present.

JACOBSON, LINDA. "Summit Links Preschool to Economic Success." *Education Week on the Web* (11 September 2007). http://www.edweek.org. Report on Economic Summit on Early Childhood Investment. Summit dealt with the topic of using preschool education to prepare future workers for global economic competition.

JOHNSON, DIRK. "Chicago Schools to Require Community Service for Graduation." *The New York Times* (1 September 1998). http://www.nytimes.com.

JEFFERSON, THOMAS. *Notes on the State of Virginia.* New York: Penguin Books, 1998.

JOHNSTON, ROBERT. "Chicago Parents Get Report Cards on Involvement." *Education Week on the Web* (8 November 2000). http://www.edweek.org. This article discusses the experiment of teachers grading parents.

KAESTLE, CARL. *Pillars of the Republic: Common Schools and American Society, 1780–1860.* New York: Hill and Wang, 1983. This is currently the best history of the common-school movement.

KATZ, MICHAEL. *The Irony of Early School Reform.* Boston: Beacon Press, 1968. This is an important study of the early relationship between social reform and education.

LAZERSON, MARVIN, and W. NORTON GRUBB. *American Education and Vocationalism: A Documentary History, 1870–1970.* New York: Teachers College Press, 1974. This good collection of documents deals with vocational education and the relationship between the school and the economy.

LEE, GORDON. *Crusade Against Ignorance: Thomas Jefferson on Education.* New York: Teachers College Press, 1961. This collection of statements by Jefferson on education has a good introductory essay.

National Association of Manufacturers. *The Skills Gap 2001.* Washington, DC: National Association of Manufacturers, 2001.

National Commission on Excellence in Education. *A Nation at Risk.* Washington, DC: U.S. Government Printing Office, 1983. The report and recommendations of this commission had a major impact on discussions about the American school.

National Education Association. *Report of the Committee on Character Education of the National Education Association.* Washington, DC: U.S. Government Printing Office, 1926. This report recommended the teaching of sex education in high schools.

"No Child Left Behind Act of 2001." Public Law 107–110 (8 January 2002). Washington, DC: U.S. Government Printing Office, 2002.

OLSON, LYNN. "Ambiguity About Preparation for Workforce Clouds Efforts to Equip Students for Future," *Education Week* (24 May 2006). Olson reports that employers are primarily interested in good work attitudes, and communication and math skills for entry-level jobs.

Partnership for 21st Century Skills. *21st Century Skills, Education & Competitiveness.* Tucson, AZ: Partnership for 21st Century Skills, 2008. Plan to prepare American schools to educate students to compete in the global economy.

PERKINSON, HENTY. *The Imperfect Panacea: American Faith in Education, 1865–1965.* New York: Random House, 1968. This is a study of attempts to use the school to solve major social problems in the United States.

QUINDLEN, ANNA. "Indivisible? Wanna Bet?" *Newsweek* (15 July 2002): 64. Quindlen argues that the phrase "under God" in the Pledge of Allegiance violates the original intention of its author Francis Bellamy and the First Amendment.

REICH, ROBERT. *The Work of Nations.* New York: Vintage Books, 1992. This is one of the major forecasts regarding the nature of work in the twenty-first century.

RODMAN, HYMAN; SUSAN LEWIS; and SARALYN GRIFFITH. *The Sexual Rights of Adolescents.* New York: Columbia University Press, 1984. This book provides information on the legal, social, and psychological aspects of adolescent sexuality.

ROSS, EDWARD A. *Social Control.* New York: Macmillan, 1906. Ross is the sociologist who declared that schools were the best instrument for controlling the public.

ROTHERHAM, ANDREW J. "How Bush Stole Education." *Blueprint Magazine* (25 March 2002). http://www.ndol.org/ndol_ci.cfm?contentid5250319&kaid5110&subid5_900023. Rotherham reports on Democratic claims that Republican President George W. Bush used ideas generated by the Democratic Party to develop No Child Left Behind legislation.

SCHRUM, KELLY. "Teena Means Business: Teenage Girls' Culture and 'Seventeen Magazine,' 1944–1950." In *Delinquents & Debutantes: Twentieth-Century American Girls' Cultures.* New York: New York University Press, 1998. This chapter discusses origin of the word "teenager" and the development of teenage commercial markets.

Sex Respect. http://www.sexrespect.com. This organization is playing a leading role in advocating abstinence via sexual education for public schools.

SHAPIRO, LAURA. *Perfection Salad: Women and Cooking at the Turn of the Century.* New York: Random House, 2001. Shapiro gives a history of the role of home economics in the development of American cuisine.

SPRING, JOEL. *Education and the Rise of the Global Economy.* Mahwah, NJ: Lawrence Erlbaum Associates, Inc., 1998. This is a study of the effect of the global economy on education in the United States and other nations and the internationalization of educational policies.

——. *Globalization and Educational Rights: An Intercivilizational Analysis.* Mahwah, NJ: Lawrence Erlbaum Associates, Inc., 2001. This book analyzes the meaning of educational rights in the context of Confucian, Islamic, Hindu, and Western civilizations.

——. *The American School: 1642–2000.* New York: McGraw-Hill Companies, Inc., 2000. This history of U.S. schools emphasizes multiculturalism and critical thinking.

——. *The Universal Right to Education: Justification, Definition, and Guidelines.* Mahwah, NJ: Lawrence Erlbaum Associates, Inc., 1998. This book provides a justification and definition of the right to education as provided for in the Universal Declaration of Human Rights.

STAGE, SARAH. "Ellen Richards and the Social Significance of the Home Economics Movement." In *Rethinking Home Economics: Women and the History of the Profession,* edited by Sarah Stage and Virginia B. Vincenti. Ithaca: Cornell University Press, 1997. This chapter outlines the social purposes of home economics education.

STAGE, SARAH, and VIRGINIA VINCENTI eds. *Rethinking Home Economics: Women and the History of a Profession.* Ithaca: Cornell University Press, 1997. This is a collection of essays on the history of home economics.

TIMPANE, MICHAEL. *Corporations and Public Education.* Report distributed by Teachers College, Columbia University, 1981. This study was conducted for the Carnegie Corporation on the growing links between public schools and business.

U. S. Department of Education. *Answering the Challenge of a Changing World: Strengthening Education for the 21st Century.* Washington, DC: U.S. Department of Education, 2006. This official government report outlines the administration's educational goals.

——. *A Guide to Education and No Child Left Behind.* Washington, DC: Education Publications Center, 2004. This is the official government guide to NCLB.

CHAPTER 2

Education and Equality of Opportunity

This chapter examines the differing models and problems associated with efforts by schools to educate for equality of opportunity. In the 1830s, Horace Mann declared schools the great balance wheel of society by providing graduates with equality of opportunity to pursue wealth. In this context, ***equality of opportunity*** **means that all members of a society are given equal chances to pursue wealth and enter any occupation or social class.** Sometimes people think equality of opportunity means equal incomes and status. Therefore, it is important to emphasize what it is not: ***Equality*** **does not mean that everyone will have equal incomes and equal status.**

I will discuss the role of schools in providing equality of opportunity by first describing the different educational models used in attempting to achieve this objective. Second, I analyze problems in schools and society in attempting to achieve equality of opportunity—namely, educational advantages and disadvantages given to the child and future worker by family income and cultural background.

In summary, this chapter will explore the continuing hope that schools can provide equality of opportunity for all people by discussing:

- The relationship between schooling and the concept of equality of opportunity.
- School models for achieving equality of opportunity including the common-schooling, sorting-machine, and testing models.
- The relationship between family income and educational achievement.
- The relationship between a student's cultural background and educational achievement.
- Discriminatory factors in the labor market that hinder the achievement of equality of opportunity including gender, race, and cultural background.
- Inequalities between schools that contribute to *inequality* of opportunity.

THE RELATIONSHIP BETWEEN SCHOOLS AND EQUALITY OF OPPORTUNITY

Equality of opportunity is based on the idea of an *un*equal society where individuals compete with each other with some becoming wealthy and some falling to the bottom of the economic scale. In Horace Mann's vision, schools will ensure that everyone receives an education that will allow them to compete for wealth on equal terms. Life is a competitive race with school being the starting point.

What about the meaning of equality of opportunity and the wording of the 1776 American Declaration of Independence, which declared "All men are created equal." In *The Pursuit of Equality in American History,* J. R. Pole argues that promoting equality of opportunity was America's way of balancing the ideal of equality with a society riddled with inequality. Since the American Revolution, the ideal of equality has been seriously compromised by the denial of women's rights, slavery, legal racial segregation, exploitation of Native Americans, and differences in wealth and status. Even many of the signers of the Declaration of Independence, including Thomas Jefferson, owned enslaved Africans and later denied U.S. citizenship to Native Americans. Did the Declaration's statement of equality exclude women since women did not gain the right to vote until the twentieth century? Apparently, given the historical circumstances, the phrase "All men are created equal" applied only to white men at the time of the signing of the Declaration. Limiting full citizenship rights to white men was highlighted by the Naturalization Act of 1790. Passed by the U.S. Congress, this legislation restricted the granting of citizenship to "free white persons" only. Under this law, Native Americans were excluded from citizenship because they were classified as domestic foreigners. Until the 1940s and 1950s, this 1790 law was used to deny citizenship to Asian immigrants.

An emphasis on equality of opportunity through schooling seemed to resolve the conflict between the use of the word "equality" and the existence of widespread inequality. Education would provide everyone with an equal chance to pursue wealth. Ideally, equality of opportunity through education would ensure that citizens occupied their particular social positions because of merit and not because of family wealth, heredity, or special cultural advantages.

Equality of opportunity can be thought of as a contest where everyone is competing for jobs and income. To provide everyone with an equal chance in the competition, all participants must begin at the same starting line. During the contest, some people will succeed and others will fail. In this concept, it is the role of the school to ensure that everyone begins the race for riches on an equal footing.

In declaring schools the great balance wheel of society, Horace Mann believed equality of opportunity would reduce tensions between the rich and poor. The poor could believe that their children had an equal chance to compete with the children of the rich. Rather than feeling antagonistic toward the wealthy, the poor could believe that they had the opportunity to join the rich. By believing schools could give everyone an equal opportunity to achieve wealth and power, one could ignore blatant social, economic, and political inequalities. Faced with obvious inequalities, people could now argue, "Hey, everyone is given a chance to get ahead. Those without money or power just didn't work hard enough. They had all the chances. They could have done well in school and gotten into a good college." This reasoning stabilized the social system by shifting the causes of inequality onto the shoulders of the individual. People seeking rectification of unequal conditions could call for more and better schools rather than demanding major political and economic changes. Schools promised to be the gateway to equal opportunity.

Can schools provide equality of opportunity to pursue wealth? How can schools be structured to provide graduates with equality of opportunity? Can they simultaneously compensate for differences in students' family income, race, ethnic background, languages spoken at home, cultural capital, and gender to provide equality of opportunity after graduation to compete for income and property? These questions are central to current discussions about school organization, curriculum, and methods of instruction.

SCHOOL MODELS FOR EQUALITY OF OPPORTUNITY

Debate over equality of opportunity is centered on three major models. These models overlap and sometimes operate simultaneously. These three models are associated with a particular historical period. However, like other things in American education, nothing ever seems to disappear; a new model or educational practice is just added onto an older one. Just as U.S. schools in the twenty-first century are a patchwork of educational goals from different historical periods, the schools are a patchwork of attempts to ensure equality of opportunity.

I call these attempts to provide equality of opportunity the common-school model, the sorting-machine model, and the high-stakes testing model. Today, all three of these models are present in public schools with the high-stakes testing model receiving the greatest attention. Interestingly, all of these models assume that schools can provide equality of opportunity. But can they?

THE COMMON-SCHOOL MODEL

In the common-school model illustrated in Figure 2–1 everyone receives an equal and common education. Theoretically, this will ensure that everyone begins the economic race on equal footing. Children from all social backgrounds attend school where they receive an education that will prepare them to compete on equal terms in the economic system. Upon graduation, all students have an equal chance to succeed; thus, competition for socioeconomic standing occurs *outside* the schoolhouse.

Nineteenth-century advocates of common schools believed that differences of social class and special advantages would disappear as everyone was

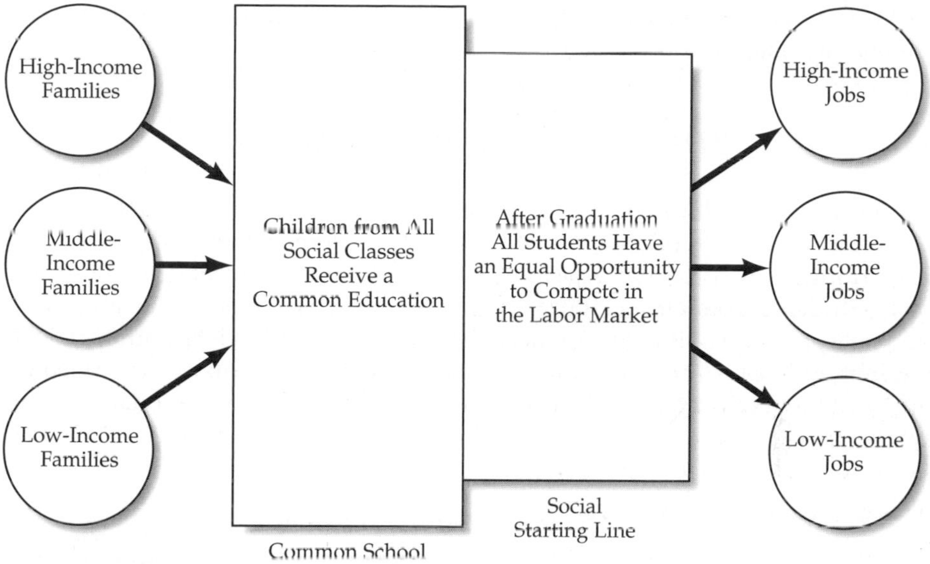

FIGURE 2–1. The Common-School Model

given an equal chance to get an equal education. During the 1830s, workingmen's parties wanted publicly supported common schools, believing that if the children of rich and poor families were mixed in the same schoolhouse there would be greater equality of opportunity. But what about before children entered schools? Would there be advantages growing up in a rich household as opposed to a poor one?

The most extreme answer to these questions came from one faction of the New York Workingman's Party. This group argued that sending students to a common school would not in itself eliminate differences in social background, because the well-to-do child would return from school to a home richly furnished and full of books, whereas the poor would return to a shanty barren of books and opportunities to learn. School, in the opinion of these workingmen, could never eliminate these differences. Their solution was that all children in New York should be removed from their families and placed in state boarding schools where they would all live in the same types of rooms, wear the same types of clothes, and eat the same food. In this milieu, education would truly allow all members of society to begin school on equal terms. This extreme solution to the problem did not receive wide support, and debates about it eventually led to the collapse of the New York Workingman's Party.

However, the common-school model continues to be plagued by differences in family backgrounds. Children with parents who read to them and expose them to a variety of cultural events are probably better prepared to learn than children whose parents are illiterate. Also, wealthy parents can provide their children with special advantages such as tutors and learning aids, while poor parents might have to struggle just to feed their children. After graduation, children might receive uneven support in pursuing a career. We will explore these issues later in this chapter.

THE SORTING-MACHINE MODEL

In the sorting-machine model, as depicted in Figure 2–2, the school attempts to overcome the influence of family background. Here, equality of opportunity is guaranteed by impartial decisions of teachers, counselors, and standardized tests. Students from all social backgrounds enter school where they are classified and placed in ability groups and tracks that will lead to jobs appropriate to student abilities. Unlike the common-school model, students receive unequal and different educations. Some students graduate with vocational training while others prepare to enter college. In this model, competition for social positions takes place *within* the school.

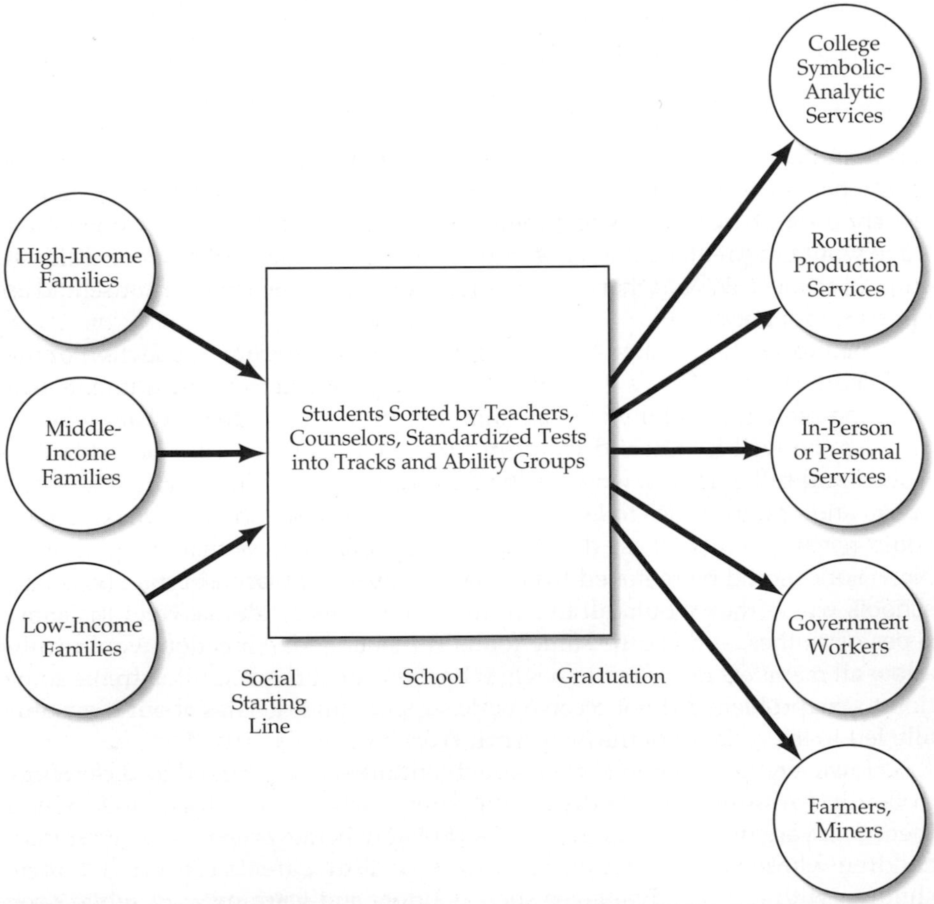

FIGURE 2–2. The Sorting-Machine Model

As it developed in the early twentieth century, students entered the first grade and were placed by their teachers in different reading and math ability groups. During junior high or what is now called middle school, students were to be tested and evaluated to find out what types of jobs they might be able to do after graduation or whether they should go on to college. An important addition to both junior or middle and high schools was the guidance counselor. Students were to meet with counselors who would help them select a future career and an educational program leading to that career.

Why did educational leaders assume that they could fairly provide equality of opportunity by sorting students according to their future positions in the job market? In part, it was a result of a belief that ability or intelligence could be scientifically determined at an early age. Intelligence testing promised to eliminate the effect of social backgrounds. Some believed intelligence tests could be an objective measure to determine what type of occupation a person should enter. Test them at the beginning of their school career and, it was argued, you could determine what type of education a child should receive and his or her future place in society. Thus, equality of opportunity would be achieved through the use of scientific testing.

Intelligence tests thus justified a hierarchical social structure based on measured intelligence. Within this framework democracy was viewed as a social system in which all people were given an equal chance to reach a level in society that corresponded to their individual level of intelligence. The French psychologist Alfred Binet, who wanted to find a method of separating children with extremely low levels of intelligence from those with normal intelligence levels, developed the first intelligence test in the early 1900s. The assumption of the test was that an inherited level of intelligence existed and could be measured independently of environmental factors such as social class, housing conditions, and cultural advantages. In the United States, the intelligence-test movement spread rapidly. Intelligence tests seemed to furnish a scientific means to achieve equality of opportunity based on individual ability.

Of course, the cultural bias of intelligence tests limits their power to be a fair means of providing equality of opportunity. In addition, there is the issue of whether an inherited native intelligence exists or whether intelligence is determined by early learning. Those believing in the existence of inheritable intelligence feel that these test results accurately reflect social-class differences. Alfred Binet contended that the reason the poor did not do well on intelligence tests was that they had lower levels of intelligence and, moreover, that was why they were poor. More recently, psychologist Arthur Jensen argued that existing tests accurately measure inherited intelligence and that differences in performance by certain racial and social groups are accurate. On the other hand, there are those who believe in the existence of inherited intelligence but feel that the questions asked on existing tests reflect the cultural and social bias of the dominant middle class in the United States. The poor, and certain racial groups, do poorly on existing tests because many test questions deal with things that are not familiar to those groups. Within this framework, the solution to the problem is the creation of an intelligence test that is free of any cultural bias.

Another approach is to reject inherited intelligence and place emphasis on the effect of the child's environment. This is the famous nurture versus nature debate. Those who see nurture as more important argue that differences in measured intelligence between social and racial groups primarily reflect differences in social conditions. The poor grow up in surroundings limited in intellectual training: an absence of books and magazines in the home; poor housing, diet, and medical care; and lack of peer-group interest in learning all might account for their poor performance on intelligence tests. This approach suggests that the school can act positively to overcome differences caused by social and cultural conditions.

Most recently, school programs try to overcome inequalities caused by differences in preparation for school learning. Early Head Start and Head Start programs are designed to counteract the supposedly inadequate learning opportunities for poor children, and compensatory education is designed to provide special instruction in reading and other skills to offset disadvantages in preparation for formal schooling.

THE HIGH-STAKES TESTING MODEL

The high-stakes testing model is a variation on the sorting-machine model (see Figure 2–3). A "high-stakes test" refers to an achievement examination that determines a person's future academic career and job opportunities. These are not tests of innate qualities, as are intelligence tests, but tests of what a person has learned. High-stakes testing begins in elementary school, where the results determine promotion from one grade to another. High-stakes tests then determine graduation from high school; admission to undergraduate, graduate, and professional schools; and professional licenses and employment credentials. In Chapter 7, I analyze the educational ramifications of high-stakes testing.

In the high-stakes testing model everyone is given an equal chance to learn, and they take the same tests to determine what they have learned. The National Education Summit on High Schools, discussed in Chapter 1, recommends that high-stakes tests be given for each course completed in the core high school curriculum, rather than a single test at graduation. Similar to the sorting-machine model, this model attempts to use scientific measurement to socially engineer equality of opportunity.

How is equality of opportunity to be achieved? Imagine a society where complete regulation of employment is based on high-stakes testing. Tests are the basis for issuing diplomas, assessment certificates for job skills, and licenses. Educational institutions become well-oiled machines processing children using a variety of tests and training to receive a particular credential for jobs ranging from child-care provider to auto mechanic to real estate salesperson to accountant to college professor. When applying for any job, people are asked to submit proof of their qualifications. This proof would be their credential. A society organized around high-stakes testing is advantageous to employers because they are presented with immediate evidence of a person's abilities to perform a job.

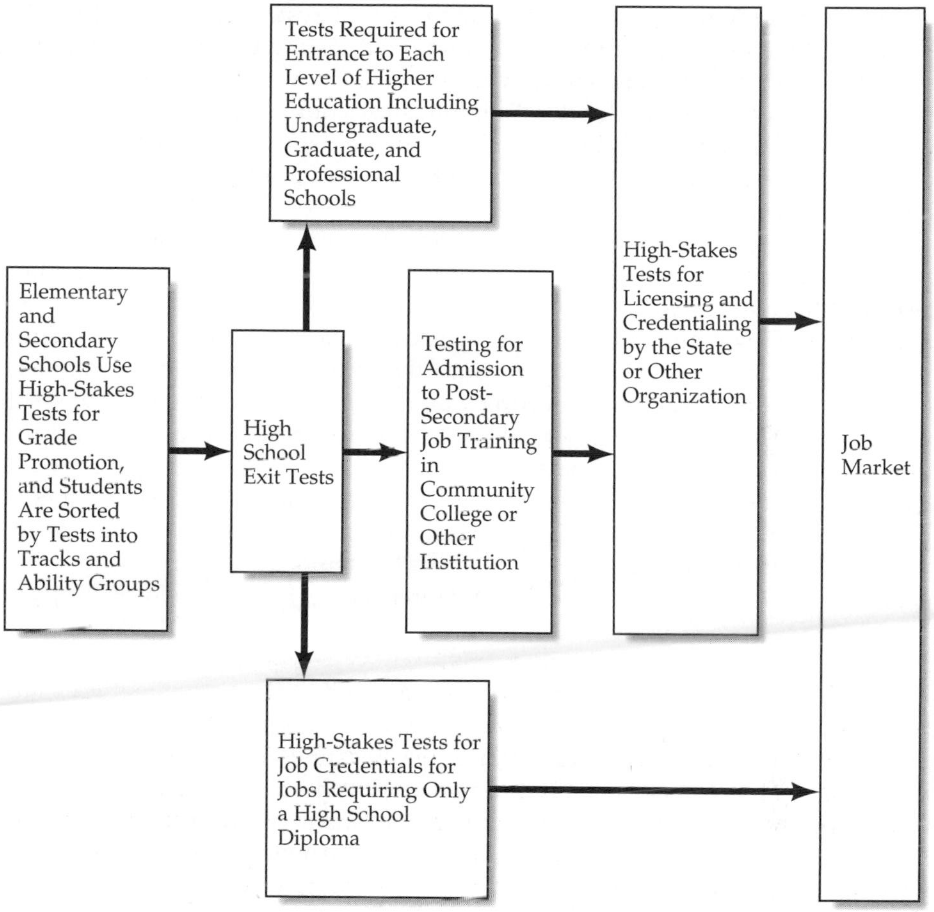

FIGURE 2-3. Equality of Opportunity: High-Stakes Testing

Throughout the twentieth century, there existed many forms of high-stakes testing used for granting licenses for careers ranging from medicine to beautician. Most of these licenses required a combination of educational achievement and state testing such as attending medical school and then taking a state examination. However, from the 1980s into the twenty-first century, the labor market has been swamped with calls for greater testing and certification. Consider the history of the licensing of teachers. In the nineteenth century, a person applying for a teaching position was simply evaluated by a local school board using whatever method it felt adequate. Then in the early twentieth century, state governments required local school systems to hire only those teachers licensed by the state. To obtain these licenses teachers had to take college courses in education. In the second half of the twentieth century, state governments began to require both college courses and the passing of a state examination. Today, the United States is rapidly on the path to requiring the passage of a national teaching examination for permanent licensing.

In the twenty-first century, most global school systems are test driven. In the United States, life-determining standardized testing begins in elementary school and extends into the workplace. Most states now require passing a state test before receiving a high school diploma. Of course, standardized testing does not end in high school but extends through a person's college career. Test centers and test courses exist for the sole purpose of preparing people to take tests. It is now a test-happy world!

In a society organized around high-stakes testing, people can undergo a variety of examinations to gain credentials that provide proof of their ability to perform a job. For instance, some employers might just be interested in a job applicant having a high school or a college diploma. Another employer might want to see a college transcript to ensure the applicant received a particular type of education, such as engineering. Another employer might want to see a diploma plus test scores qualifying the applicant for the job. Another employer might want a diploma, test scores, and a license.

In a society organized around high-stakes tests, the school becomes a crucial institution for determining economic success. To ensure equality of opportunity in the high-stakes testing model, the school must give everyone an equal chance to learn and to be tested without cultural bias. Is this possible?

EDUCATION AND INCOME

What is the relationship between education and income? This is a crucial question in considering the school's ability to provide equality of opportunity. The preceding three models assume a close relationship between education and income. Studies show that years of schooling are associated with income levels. These findings suggest that achievement in school is the road to economic success. However, a comparison of educational attainment, gender, and race suggest that other social factors affect the role of schools in determining personal income.

To demonstrate the relationship between schooling and income, I am using statistics provided by the U.S. Census Bureau and the National Center for Education Statistics. Most of these data are derived from the U.S. Census Bureau's American Community Survey 2007 and the 2000 U.S. Census; the federal government conducts a national census every 10 years with the next one to be completed in 2010. There is usually a time interval between the collection of statistics and reports. For instance, in Table 2–1 the reported statistics are for 2006 while the actual report from the National Center for Educational Statistics is dated 2008. Both the U.S. Census Bureau and the National Center for Education Statistics are constantly updating their statistical reports. Particularly useful is the annual *Digest of Education Statistics* issued by the National Center for Education Statistics and the annual U.S. Census Bureau's *Statistical Abstract: The National Data Book.* Both volumes are available on the Web sites of these federal agencies. The reader is advised to check the Web site for both government agencies for any updates to the statistics reported in this book.

While the Table 2–1 indicates a relationship between educational attainment and income, they also indicate that in the labor market gender is as important

TABLE 2–1. Median Annual Income of Year-Round, Full-Time Workers 25 Years Old and Over, by Highest level of Educational Attainment and Gender, 2006

Gender	All Workers	Less than 9th Grade	Some High School (no completion)	High School Completion (includes equivalency)	Some College, (no degree)	Bachelor's Degree	Master's Degree	Professional Degree
Male	$45,760	22,710	27,650	37,030	43,830	60,910	75,430	100,000
Female	35,100	18,130	20,130	26,740	31,950	45,410	52,440	76,240

Source: Adapted from National Center for Education Statistics, *Digest of Education Statistics 2007* (Washington, DC: U.S. Department of Education, 2008), Table 371, p. 550.

as education. Simply stated, even with equal educational attainments, men earn more than women. As Table 2–1 shows, there is a steady increase in annual median income with educational attainment. The U.S. Census Bureau provides this definition of median income as related to unrelated individuals, households, and families:

> Median income is the amount which divides the income distribution into two equal groups, half having incomes above the median, half having incomes below the median. The medians for households, families, and unrelated individuals are based on all households, families, and unrelated individuals, respectively. The medians for people are based on people 15 years old and over with income. (From Table 672—Money Income of Households—Distribution of Income and Median Income by Race and Hispanic Origin: 1999)

For men, the increase in annual median earnings from less than a ninth grade education ($22,710) to a bachelor's degree ($60,910) is $38,200. The difference for women with less than a ninth grade education ($18,130) and those with a bachelor's degree or higher ($45,410) is $27,280. As demonstrated in Table 2–2, the lifetime income for men with a professional degree is $4.8 million as compared to $1.1 million for men without a high school diploma, while for women with a professional degree the lifetime income is $2.9 million as compared to $0.7 million for women without a high school diploma.

THE BIAS OF LABOR MARKET CONDITIONS ON EDUCATIONAL ATTAINMENT, INCOME, AND GENDER

Can schools provide equality of opportunity? Are there bias factors in society that limit the ability of schools to ensure everyone an equal chance to attain wealth? Can labor market biases be corrected? According to recent studies, changes in the labor market conditions can increase equality of opportunity for women.

TABLE 2–2. Educational Attainment and Estimated Lifetime Earnings of Full-Time, Year-Round Workers by Sex and Educational Attainment, in 1999 Dollars

	Estimated Lifetime Earnings	
Educational Attainment	Women	Men
Not high school graduate	$0.7 million	$1.1 million
High school graduate	1.0	1.4
Some college	1.2	1.7
Associate's degree	1.3	1.8
Bachelor's degree	1.6	2.5
Master's degree	1.9	2.9
Doctoral degree	2.5	3.8
Professional degree	2.9	4.8

Source: This table is adapted from Figure 6 of Jennifer Day and Eric Newburger, *The Big Payoff: Educational Attainment and Synthetic Estimates of Work-Life Earnings* (Washington, DC: U.S. Census Bureau, July 2002), p. 6.

Table 2–2 shows the income differences according to educational attainment for full-time, year-round workers. First, it should be noted that incomes for both women and men rise steadily with each advance in educational attainment. Second, there is about the same percentage difference in earnings for each level of educational attainment. As shown in Table 2–2, the lifetime earnings for a female high school graduate are $1 million, while for a female with a bachelor's degree, $1.6 million. For men, a high school graduate can expect lifetime earnings of $1.4 million, and for those holding a bachelor's degree $2.5 million. Comparing women and men's earnings, a man with a high school diploma will earn $400,000 more in a lifetime than a woman with a high school diploma. A man with a bachelor's degree will earn $900,000 more in a lifetime than a woman with a bachelor's degree.

At all levels of educational attainment men earn more than women. And it is important to emphasize that these income differences are for full-time, year-round workers. In other words, the differences cannot be attributed to women working part time or taking time from work to raise children.

Several years ago, the owner of the coffee shop down the street from my house posted a notice:

> WOMEN'S INCOMES ARE 68% OF MEN'S INCOMES
> COFFEE: 68 CENTS FOR WOMEN
> 1 DOLLAR FOR MEN

I don't know where the owner got the number "68%" but it is smaller than the percentages given by the U.S. Census Bureau in a 2005 press release: "the ratio of female-to-male earnings for full-time, year-round workers was 77 cents on the dollar, up from 76 cents in 2003."

Gender discrimination in the labor market is lessening with the ratio of female-to-male earnings increasing from 2003 to 2005, which explains the lower

TABLE 2–3. Educational Attainment and Women's Estimated Lifetime Income as a Percentage of Men's Estimated Lifetime Income for Full-Time, Year-Round Workers

Educational Attainment	Women's Estimated Lifetime Income as a Percentage of Men's Estimated Lifetime Income
Not high school graduate	63%
High school graduate	71
Bachelor's degree	65
Master's degree	65
Doctoral degree	65
Professional degree	60

Source: This table is adapted from Figure 6 of Jennifer Day and Eric Newburger, *The Big Payoff: Educational Attainment and Synthetic Estimates of Work-Life Earnings* (Washington, DC: U.S. Census Bureau, 2002), p. 6.

percentage shown on the coffee shop's sign. In 2005, the coffee shop owner would have upped his price for coffee for women to 77 cents while continuing to charge men one dollar. The 2005 ratio is also larger than figures given in Table 2–3, which was compiled in 2002. In 2002, for each level of educational attainment, women earned from 60 to 72 percent of men's income.

In conclusion, the preceding statistics indicate that in the United States income is related to educational attainment but that discriminatory factors in the labor market related to gender negate some of the advantages gained through increased education; equality of opportunity depends on equality of opportunity in the labor market.

WHITE PRIVILEGE: RACE, EDUCATIONAL ATTAINMENT, AND INCOME

Like gender, race limits the effect of educational attainment on equality of opportunity in the labor market. The income differences between men and women with the same levels of education are also present when racial differences are a factor. Racial differences point to another labor market bias. Table 2–4 indicates differences in lifetime income among people of differing races with the same levels of educational attainment. I will explain the racial classifications used in Table 2–4 in the next section on "Asian" educational advantages.

At almost every level of educational attainment, "white, non-Hispanic" had higher estimated work-life earnings. The exception is for "advanced degrees" with "white, non-Hispanic" and "Asian and Pacific Islanders" having equal work-life earnings of $3.1 million. Otherwise there are significant differences. For instance, "white, non-Hispanics" with bachelor's degrees earned an estimated $2.2 million during their work-life, while "blacks" and "Hispanics" with the same educational attainment earned $1.7 and $1.8 million respectively.

TABLE 2–4. Estimated Lifetime Earnings by Educational Attainment, Race, and Hispanic Origin, in 1999 Dollars

	Estimated Lifetime Earnings			
Educational Attainment	White, Non-Hispanic	Black	Hispanic (of any race)	Asian and Pacific Islander
Not high school graduate	$1.3 million	$0.8 million	$0.9 million	$0.8 million
High school graduate	1.3	1.0	1.1	1.1
Some college	1.6	1.2	1.3	1.3
Bachelor's degree	2.2	1.7	1.8	1.7
Advanced degree	3.1	2.5	2.6	3.1

Source: This table is adapted from Figure 7 of Jennifer Day and Eric Newburger, *The Big Payoff: Educational Attainment and Synthetic Estimates of Work-Life Earnings* (Washington, D C: U.S. Census Bureau 2002), p. 7.

An interesting aspect of Table 2–4 is that percentage differences in income narrow with bachelor's and advanced degrees. This suggests that increased educational attainment will contribute to improving equality of opportunity for nonwhite groups. For instance, blacks without a high school diploma earn a lifetime income of about 72 percent of that of whites without a high school diploma ($0.8 million divided by $1.1 million). In contrast, the percentage difference is about 77 percent for a bachelor's degree and about 80 percent for an advanced degree. There is a similar decline in differences between whites and Hispanics in lifetime income with increased educational attainment. Hispanics without a high school diploma earn about 81 percent of the lifetime earnings of whites without a high school diploma and the difference between those with an advanced degree is about 83 percent.

The preceding differences are sometimes referred to as "white privilege." It is worth from $400,000 to $500,000 more to be white with a bachelor's degree! If you are black or Asian and Pacific Islander with a bachelor's degree, you will earn $500,000 less in your lifetime than will a white with a bachelor's degree. The lifetime cost for Hispanics with a bachelor's degree is $400,000.

In conclusion, comparisons of income for those with the same levels of educational attainment but of different genders and races indicate that to achieve the goal of equality of opportunity, we must remove the gender and racial biases in the labor market.

THE ASIAN ADVANTAGE: RACE, HOUSEHOLD INCOME, AND EDUCATION

White privilege appears to be negated by the high educational attainment of Asians. Today, those classified as Asian have a significantly higher median household income than whites (Table 2–5), which appears to be related to higher levels of educational attainment (Table 2–6).

TABLE 2–5. Race and Median Household Income, 2007

	White, Non-Hispanic	Black	Asian	Hispanic (of any race)
Median household income, 2007	$54,920	$33,916	$66,103	$38,679

Source: Adapted from Table 1 in Carmen DeNavas-Walt, Bernadette Proctor, and Jessica Smith, *Income, Poverty, and Health Insurance Coverage in the United States: 2007* (Washington, DC: U.S. Census Bureau, 2008), p.7.

TABLE 2–6. Educational Attainment by Race and Hispanic Origin, 2006

	White	Black	Asian and Pacific Islander	Hispanic
High school graduate of more, 2006	86.1%	80.7%	87.4%	59.3%
College graduate or more, 2006	28.4	18.5	49.7	12.4

Source: Adapted from U.S. Census Bureau, *Current Population Reports P20-550, Table 217.* Retrieved on 4 September 2008 from http://www.census.gove/compendia/statab/tables/08s0217.pdf.

The term "Asian" used in this section and the racial classifications used in Table 2–5 and the previous section require some explanation. The terms "Hispanic" and "Asian and Pacific Islander" are problematic since they cover peoples from vast and differing areas. For instance: Should the term "Hispanic" include people from Argentina who are mostly of European ancestry with those from Mexico who are mainly of Native American ancestry? Should Samoans and Koreans be placed in the same category of "Asian and Pacific Islander"? Should Hmong and Japanese be placed in the same category of "Asian"? What do "white" and "black" mean? In Chapter 4, I will discuss the complexities of defining ethnic and racial categories.

The census data used in Table 2–5 is based on self-identification. In other words, people are asked what they consider to be their race. For instance, the U.S. Census in its official "Definitions and Explanations" defines "white, non-Hispanic" as: "Respondents who selected their race as White and indicated that their origin was not one of the Hispanic origin subgroups of Mexican, Puerto Rican, Cuban, Central or South American." There are many people in these Hispanic subgroups who identify themselves as "white" because their ancestors were primarily European.

Keeping in mind the difficulties in racial classification, which will be explored in Chapter 4, Tables 2–5 and 2–6 summarize differences in median household income and educational attainment by racial categories. Tables 2–5 and 2–6 indicate that higher median household incomes of Asians than whites ($66,103 versus $54,920, respectively) might be related to higher levels of educational attainment (49.7 percent of Asians with a bachelor's degree or more versus 28.4 percent of whites, respectively). I use the term *might* in this discussion because these comparisons do not prove a causal relationship. The statistics only suggest that white privilege is overcome by Asians through higher levels of educational attainment.

In conclusion, the preceding discussions do indicate a relationship between income and educational attainment but that relationship is limited by gender and racial bias in the labor market. Schools might be able to indirectly change labor market biases by changing student attitudes regarding race and gender so that when these students enter the labor market they will work to reduce bias in employment. Otherwise, enforcement of laws against discrimination and provisions for equal pay for equal work will be needed to ensure equality of opportunity.

SOCIAL AND CULTURAL CAPITAL: CHILD-REARING AND EQUALITY OF OPPORTUNITY

As discussed earlier, nineteenth-century common-school advocates worried that schools might not be able to provide equality of opportunity because children enter school with different social experiences and knowledge; a situation that members of the New York Workingman's Party wanted to correct by placing preschool children in state residential institutions. Today, the focus is on preschool education to provide all children with similar access to social experiences and knowledge as preparation for schooling. The most well known of the federal preschool programs are Early Head Start and Head Start—which, as indicated by their names, are designed to give children from low-income families a head start on schooling so that they reach the same level of educational achievement as children from high-income families.

Do different family environments for preschool children affect children's school achievement and, consequently, the ability of schools to provide equality of opportunity? In other words, do children enter school with differing abilities as a result of dissimilar family backgrounds? Do these differences in family background continue to affect learning throughout the student's school years and do they have an effect on the level of a student's educational attainment, such as graduating from high school or college?

The key to answering the preceding questions is the concept of *social and cultural capital,* which refers to the economic value of a person's behaviors, attitudes, knowledge, and cultural experiences. For instance, education, which provides a person with particular knowledge and attitudes, is related to income and therefore has economic value when seeking employment. Also, behaviors learned in the home contribute to social capital. Experiences in the home might provide the social knowledge that will help the child to later climb the occupational ladder. Do the behaviors learned in the home prepare a child to interact with professionals and managers or do they prepare the child to feel comfortable only in social situations with blue collar workers? Visits to museums, concerts, stage performances, and similar experiences increase children's cultural capital, which might make them better prepared to interact with elite groups. In other words, what social and cultural experiences does the family provide that will help the child to succeed in school and in later employment?

In my college classes, I often use scenes from rapper Eminem's movie *8 Mile* to illustrate social and cultural capital. Eminem's goal in making the movie was to illustrate his life growing up in Detroit and his crossing cultural lines to enter the world of African American rap music. He portrays his life with his mother in a trailer park as chaotic and punctuated by emotional outbursts with short declarative sentences being shouted between family members. Living in poverty, the characters' dress and manners are what some might refer to as "white trash." Fired from a pizza parlor, Eminem finds low-paying repetitive work in a factory where the bosses shout orders and Eminem obeys authority. Watching the movie one cannot imagine Eminem ever evidencing the social capital needed to get a job as a business manager, such as a manager of a bank or company. I ask students: How could Eminem's social capital be improved so that he could get a high-paying job as a bank manager? Students immediately suggest that Eminem would need to improve his grammar, speech patterns, social manners, and dress. Also, his cultural capital appears limited to popular arts. In the end, his economic success results from adapting his social and cultural capital to that of black rappers.

Variations in social and cultural capital affect the ability of children to learn in school and to gain future employment. In *Unequal Childhoods: Class, Race, and Family Life,* Annette Lareau writes:

> Many studies have demonstrated that parents' social structural location has profound implications for their children's life chances. Before kindergarten, for example, children of highly educated parents are much more likely to exhibit "educational readiness" skills, such as knowing their letters, identifying colors, counting up to twenty, and being able to write their first names.

Lareau demonstrates that educational readiness is affected by differences in child-rearing practices. She distinguishes child-rearing practices by the terms "concerted cultivation" and "accomplishment of natural growth." Concerted cultivation is practiced by what she calls "middle class" families and accomplishment of natural growth by "working class" families.

The terms *middle class* and *working class* have a special meaning in Lareau's work. Throughout this chapter, I will be highlighting differing definitions of social class. For her purposes, a middle-class family is one where one or both parents have supervisory or managerial authority in the workplace and are required to have stringent educational credentials. In working-class families, parents' occupations are without supervisory authority and do not require a high level of educational credentials.

Differences in child-rearing between working- and middle-class families is summarized in Table 2–7. Lareau concludes that middle-class families consciously intervene (concerted cultivation) in their children's lives to develop their talents. In contrast, working-class families have a more laissez-faire attitude, allowing their children to grow without much intervention (accomplishment of natural growth) except for attending to their basic needs.

TABLE 2–7. Differences in Child-Rearing Between Working- and Middle-Class Families

	Middle-Class Concerted Cultivation	Working-Class Accomplishment and Natural Growth
General	Parents involve children in multiple organized activities, such as sports, music and dance lessons, and arts, crafts, and hobby groups	Children "hang out" with siblings, friends, and relatives while parents involve them in a minimum or organized activities
Speech	Parents reason with their children, allowing them to challenge their statements and negotiate	Parents issue directives and seldom allow their children to challenge or question these directives
Dealings with institutions	Parents criticize and intervene in institutions affecting the child, such as school, and train their children to assume a similar role	Parents display powerlessness and frustration toward institutions, such as school
Results	Children gain the social and cultural capital to deal with a variety of social situations and institutions	Children develop social and cultural capital that results in dependency on institutions and jobs where they take orders rather than manage others

Source: Adapted from Annette Lareau, *Unequal Childhoods: Class, Race, and Family Life* (Berkeley: University of California Press, 2003), p. 31.

Imagine the life of middle-class children as detailed in Table 2–7. Their parents spend time chauffeuring them from training events and competitions in organized sports, to music and dance lessons, to an art, craft, or hobby group. After-school time and weekends are packed with events as parents try to develop their children's various talents. If their children encounter any problems in these activities, parents quickly intervene and discuss the situation with the coach, trainer, or teacher. These middle-class parents influence their children's behavior through reasoned discussion in which their children learn to question their parents' arguments if they think their parents are wrong.

According to Lareau, the result of concerted cultivation is the development of the social and cultural capital that allows the children and later adults to feel comfortable and know how to act in a variety of social and institutional situations; this is a result of all those after-school activities. Middle-class children learn to interact, challenge, and reason with authority; this is learned through their interaction with their parents and the model of their parents questioning institutional authority. Their cultural capital is increased through participation in activities such as dance and music lessons and attendance at cultural institutions.

In contrast, working-class parents allow their children to spend unstructured time with their friends and relatives in their yards, in local parks, on the street, or in another home. The most frequently planned activity for children is some form of organized sports. Working-class parents tell their children what to do and don't allow the children to be sassy and talk back. When problems occur at school or other institutions their children might encounter, the parents act powerless.

Working-class accomplishment of natural growth, according to Lareau, results in social capital that does not contain the skills to interact in a variety of social and institutional situations. The children lack the verbal ability and behavioral skills needed to become managers and supervisors. They primarily assume jobs where they take orders rather than give orders. Like Eminem, they lack the verbal skills, social graces, and dress to interview for jobs as bank managers, but they do have the social capital to accept low-paying jobs where they are given orders. Without exposure to museums, art and dance lessons, and attendance at concerts and stage performances, these children do not gain the cultural capital to move easily among the social elite.

The social and cultural capital developed in middle- and working-class families has different economic value. First, middle- and working-class children have different social and cultural capital when interacting with schools. These forms of capital are needed for educational success and, consequently, have economic value when educational achievement helps people gain higher-paying jobs. Middle-class children have learned the verbal and social skills to advantage themselves when interacting with teachers and school staff. If something negative happens to them at school, their parents are quick to intervene on their behalf. The opposite is true of working-class children. Their social and cultural capital hinders their ability to succeed at school. The social and cultural capital of middle-class children increases their possibilities of gaining jobs high on the income scale while working-class children have the social and cultural capital to work in jobs low on the income scale.

In conclusion, the promise of schooling providing equality of opportunity to compete for income and wealth is seriously compromised before the child even enters the classroom. Parents develop different forms of social and cultural capital which advantage or disadvantage their children in school and in the labor market. In the next section, I will discuss how family background is related to the actual reading and math skills of children as they enter kindergarten and advantages or disadvantages them throughout their school careers.

SOCIAL AND CULTURAL CAPITAL: PRESCHOOL AND EQUALITY OF OPPORTUNITY

Valerie Lee and David Burkham's report *Inequality at the Starting Gate: Social Background Differences in Achievement as Children Begin School* confirms the fears of early common-school advocates that family background would compromise the ability of schools to provide equality of opportunity. Students entering kindergarten have significantly different reading and ability skills as measured by tests given as part of the U.S. Department of Education's Early Childhood Longitudinal Study, Kindergarten Cohort. Test results show differences that are correlated with social class and race, with social class being the most important factor.

What are the preschool family factors affecting reading and math skills of children entering kindergarten? The following could be considered a parental guide for ensuring that children have high reading and math skills as measured by tests on entering kindergarten. Lee and Burkham found the strongest correlation between family factors and reading skills on entering kindergarten to be:

1. Frequency of reading (including parents reading to their children)
2. Ownership of home computer
3. Exposure to performing arts
4. Preschool

Other factors weakly correlated with reading skills are:

5. Educational expectations of family
6. Rules limiting television viewing
7. Number of tapes, records, CDs
8. Sports and clubs
9. Arts and crafts activities

For math scores, the most strongly correlated family factors are:

1. Ownership of computer
2. Exposure to performing arts
3. Preschool

Other factors weakly correlated with math skills are:

4. Educational expectations
5. Frequency of reading (including parents reading to their children)
6. Number of tapes, records, CDs
7. Sports and clubs
8. Arts and crafts activities

Therefore, if parents were planning to prepare their child to enter kindergarten with high reading and math scores they would read to their child, own a computer, take their child to performing arts events, and send their child to preschool. In addition, they should have high expectations for their child's education; have rules governing television viewing; have a large amount of media in the home, such as tapes, records, and CDs; and involve their child in sports, clubs, and arts and crafts.

Social class is directly related to kindergarten entrance-test scores and family factors correlated with high reading and math scores. Using a different definition of social class than Annette Lareau's separation of families into middle and working class, Lee and Burkham divide families by SES, or socioeconomic status, which is determined by a combination of occupation, income, educational attainment, and wealth. They divide SES into quintiles or gradations of

20 percent. Those in the lowest SES represent the 20 percent at the bottom of the SES scale in occupation, income, education, and wealth while the highest are in the top 20 percent. Table 2–8 reports math and reading achievement at the beginning of kindergarten by SES. Test scores are those used by Lee and Burkham in analyzing the Early Childhood Longitudinal Study, Kindergarten Cohort.

As noted in Table 2–8, reading and math skills on entering kindergarten are closely related to the family SES as measured by tests in the Early Childhood Longitudinal Study: the higher the SES of the family, the higher the test scores; the lower the SES of the family, the lower the test scores.

Is there a relationship between family SES and activities that are correlated with high test scores? Table 2–9 indicates the relationship found by Lee and Burkam.

As indicated in Table 2–9, upper-SES families are more likely than lower-SES families to expose their children to factors that are correlated with high math and reading scores on entering kindergarten. No wonder children from

TABLE 2–8. Socioeconomic Status and Math and Reading Scores at the Beginning of Kindergarten

Socioeconomic Status of Family	Reading Scores	Math Scores
Highest 20%	27.2	24.1
Next-highest 20%	23.6	21.0
Middle 20%	21.3	19.1
Next-lowest 20%	19.9	17.5
Lowest 20%	17.4	15.1

Source: Adapted from Valerie E. Lee and David Burkham, *Equality at the Starting Gate: Social Background Differences in Achievement as Children Begin School* (Washington, DC: Economic Policy Institute, 2002), p. 18.

TABLE 2–9. Socioeconomic Status and Family Activity Correlated with Math and Reading Scores at the Beginning of Kindergarten

Socioeconomic Status of Family	Percent of Kindergartners with a Computer in the Home	Percent of Kindergartners Whose Parents Read to Them at Least Three Times a Week	Percent of Kindergartners Who Attend Preschool	Percent of Kindergartners Who Attend Performing Arts Events (play/concert/show)
Highest 20%	84.7%	93.9%	65.0%	48.4%
Next highest 20%	71.5	87.3	52.2	43.0
Middle 20%	54.7	80.7	41.7	38.9
Next lowest 20%	38.3	76.6	31.2	33.9
Lowest 20%	19.9	62.6	20.1	27.1

Source: Data used in creating table are from Valerie E. Lee and David Burkham, *Equality at the Starting Gate: Social Background Differences in Achievement as Children Begin School* (Washington, DC: Economic Policy Institute, 2002), pp. 24–25.

higher-SES families have higher scores on tests measuring math and reading skills when entering kindergarten. Simply stated, families provide their children with differing cultural capital needed to succeed in school. Fears that family background would hinder the ability of schools to provide equality of opportunity seem confirmed by Lee and Burkham's study.

SCHOOLING: WHY ARE THE RICH GETTING RICHER AND THE POOR GETTING POORER?

The preceding statistics suggest that middle-class families and upper-SES families provide their children with the social and cultural capital needed to succeed in school. Consequently, it is legitimate to ask about the role of schooling in reinforcing social-class differences. In other words, does family income determine educational success and, as a result, the student's future income? Also, questions are currently being raised about the possible link between education and the growing inequality of incomes: Are schools contributing to the rich getting richer and the poor getting poorer?

"America's High Schools: The Front Line in the Battle for Economic Future," a report of the 2005 National Education Summit on High Schools, warns that the global labor market, as discussed in Chapter 1, is contributing to the growing inequality of incomes in the United States. The American worker now competes with workers from other nations. The argument regarding this particular view of international labor competition is: If a company can find less expensive workers in another country, then they will move to that country. If a company needs highly educated workers and these are available in the US, then the company will remain.

The result is the increasing income of Americans with skills needed for high-paying jobs in the global economy and a decline in wages for those competing for low-wage jobs. The Summit report describes the situation: "High school, beyond the front line of international economic competition, is the dividing line between those workers whose incomes have been rising and those whose incomes have been falling."

Major American businesses involved in the National Education Summit on High Schools, as discussed in Chapter 1, acknowledge the growing disparities in income in the United States. They place the blame on schools for not educating workers for the top-paying jobs in the global economy. The Summit report warns: "In short, we run the risk of losing our middle class." The report predicts:

> The average wages of high school graduates and those individuals who never graduated high school have fallen over the last two decades; the average incomes of those who went beyond high school have risen. This demarcation promises to become even starker in the coming years, as technology and trade separate the economy into two camps—those with the skills to participate in the global economy and those who lack them. If we do not make a concerted effort to move our society beyond this boundary, we will find ourselves a

society cut in two—one side enfranchised in the modern economy, experiencing its affluence, the other lacking the means of access to the future.

Are the rich getting richer and the poor getting poorer? U.S. Census figures confirm that this is so. In Table 2–10 contains U.S. Census income by the upper limits of household income in 2007 dollars from 1980 to 2007 ranked by 20 percent groups or quintiles with a special category for those in the top 5 percent of household income.

Table 2–10 indicates that real household income for all groups increased between 1980 and 2000. However, between 2000 and 2007 real household wages for the lowest, the second, and third groups actually declined while it increased for the fourth and top 5 percent groups. This would suggest at least between 2000 and 2007 a redistribution of household income favoring those at the top. This is supported by Table 2–11, which shows that increasing inequality was evident between 1990 and 2000 with all, except the highest income, experiencing a decline in their share of total household income. The most dramatic decline was for the second 20 percent with a decline of 10 percent of the total share of household income from 9.6 percent in 1990 to 8.6 percent, while the highest 20 percent increased their share of total household income from 46.6 percent in 1990 to 50.4 percent in 2005. One could argue from these statistics that there is growing inequality between income groups.

TABLE 2–10. Income Limits for Each Fifth and Top 5 percent of Households of All Races: 1980, 1990, 2000, 2007

	Upper Limit of Each Fifth (2007 Dollars)				
Year	Lowest	Second	Third	Fourth	Lower Limit of Top 5%
2007	$20,291	$39,100	62,000	100,000	177,000
2000	21,576	39,733	62,819	98,449	174,850
1990	19,223	36,389	55,671	84,899	145,711
1980	17,915	33,598	51,509	75,418	121,371

Source: U.S. Census Bureau, "Historical Income Tables–Households–Table H-1." Retrieved on 5 September 2008 from http://www.census.gov/hhes/www/income/histinc/h01AR.html.

TABLE 2–11. Shares of Household Income in Quintiles in 2005 Dollars 1980, 1990, 2000, 2005

Year	Lowest 20%	Second 20%	Third 20%	Fourth 20%	Highest 20%
2005	3.4%	8.6%	14.6%	23.0%	50.4%
2000	3.6	8.9	14.8	23.0	49.8
1990	3.8	9.6	16.9	24.0	46.6
1980	4.2	10.2	16.8	24.7	44.1

Source: U.S. Census Bureau, "Income Table IE-1." Retrieved on 5 September 2008 from http://www.census.gov/hhes/www/income/histinc/ineqtoc.html.

Why the increase in the percentage of total household income of the upper class? The U.S. Census Bureau explains, "Increasing income inequality is believed to be related to changes taking place in the labor market and in the composition of the households in the United States." The composition of households is an important factor with a decline in married couple households and an increase in single-parent and nonfamily households, which typically have lower incomes.

On the other hand, the National Education Summit on the High School blames the failure of schools to prepare youth for competition in the global labor market. As stated before, the labor market's contribution to income inequality is the result of increasing wages paid to well-educated or highly skilled workers and declining wages for poorly educated or low-skilled workers. Workers now compete in an international labor market. U.S. companies will move if they can find cheaper labor and production costs in another country. U.S. workers must compete with the wages paid in other countries. This results in a decline in real wages for unskilled labor in the United States.

RICH AND POOR SCHOOL DISTRICTS

Ask any real estate agent in your area to name the best local school district. Most likely the real estate agent will name school districts with either wealthy households or with households with a high percentage of college graduates. Often the housing in these districts, which may vary in large cities, is beyond the purchasing power of low-income families. This is a form of economic segregation in schooling, which contributes to inequalities in educational outcomes.

Imagine that you and your spouse are setting out to buy a house and that your primary concern is settling in an area with good schools. Your dream is for your children to attend college and, thereby, gain access to high-paying jobs. Recognizing the important influence of peers on your children's academic future, you want to live in a community where most students plan to attend college. In other words, you want the best for your children. According to Horace Mann's dream, all school districts should be equal. But this is not the case when you consider expenditures per child, test scores, and college attendance. Communities in the United States are not equal in wealth and educational attainment of their students.

Many of the wealthy districts are located in suburbs near major cities. The U.S. Census Bureau's *Money Income in the United States: 2008* reports: "High-income households tended to be family households that include two or more earners residing in the suburbs of a large city." Table 2–12 shows the findings of the 2000 census on differences in income by residential areas.

However, the distribution of the population by wealth does not exactly match the amount of educational money spent per student. In fact, because of special funds for high-poverty areas, children going to schools with the highest percentage of poor children spend more per student than other schools except for schools with the lowest percentage of poor students. This is shown in Table 2–13 as reported in the National Center for Education Statistics' *The Condition of Education 2008.*

As indicated in Table 2–13, the most money per student—$10,768—is spent in school districts with the fewest students from families below the poverty level. Districts with the highest percentage of students from families below the poverty level spend $10,191 per student as compared with those in the middle level of the scale: $8,927, $8,839, and $9,419.

There are other factors beside educational expenditures that determine the educational quality of the school district, including college attendance and test scores. Some parents use reports of test scores and college attendance rates when shopping for a new home. Where do home buyers get their information on schools? They usually get the data from real estate brokers or online services. Using these sources, home buyers can collect information on schools, neighborhood characteristics, and housing for any place in the United States. Some might consider real estate agents and Web sites the best guide to quality public education in the United States.

TABLE 2–12. Differences in Median Household Income by Residence

Residence	Median Household Income (in 2000 dollars)
Suburban—metropolitan area	$50,262
Central city—metropolitan area	36,987
Rural—outside metropolitan area	32,837

Source: Adapted from U.S. Census Bureau, *Money Income in the United States: 2000* (Washington, DC: U.S. Printing Office, September 2001), p. 2.

TABLE 2–13. Total Expenditures per Student by Level of Poverty in School Districts, 2002–2003

District Poverty Level Divided into Quintiles	Total Expenditures per Student 2002–2003
Highest percentage of students from families below poverty income threshold	$10,191
Middle-highest percentage of students from families below poverty income threshold	8,927
Middle percentage of students from families below poverty income threshold	8,839
Middle-lowest percentage of students from families below poverty income threshold	9,419
Lowest percentage of students from families below poverty income threshold	10,768

Source: Adapted from Table 41.1, National Center for Education Statistics, *The Condition of Education 2006* (Washington, DC: U.S. Department of Education, 2006), p. 197.

SOCIAL CLASS AND AT-RISK STUDENTS

During the last century, many terms, including "disadvantaged," "urban," and "culturally deprived," were used to characterize students who might have academic problems. The latest descriptor is "at-risk." Many students classified as at-risk experience few academic problems. Being at-risk is only an indication of *potential* academic problems. The National Center for Education Statistics found that 35 percent of students with risk factors finished high school and enrolled in a four-year college or university within two years of high school graduation.

Poverty is high on the list of factors that put students at-risk. The report of the National Center for Education Statistics, *The Condition of Education 2002,* lists the factors that might indicate that a student is at-risk of academic failure. In this list, the Center for Education Statistics uses socioeconomic status (SES) rather than the U.S. Census Bureau's income classifications. The socioeconomic status of students is determined by parental education level, parental occupation, family income, and household items. In the following list of at-risk factors, low socioeconomic status refers to students from the bottom 25 percent of households on a socioeconomic scale. These are families in which the parents have minimum levels of educational attainment, low income, and poor job status. The report's list of at-risk factors are:

- Being in the lowest socioeconomic status.
- Changing schools two or more times from grades 1 to 8 (except for transitions to middle school or junior high school).
- Having average grades of C or lower from grades 6 to 8.
- Being in a single-parent household during grade 8.
- Having one or more older siblings who left high school before completion.
- Being held back one or more times from grades 1 to 8.

The best predictor of whether a student will drop out of school is if a student repeated a grade in elementary and middle school, conclude sociologists Karl Alexander and Doris Entwistle in "Signs of Early Exit for Dropouts Abound" in *Education Week's* special 2006 report "Diplomas Count: An Essential Guide to Graduation Policy and Rates." Studying students in Baltimore public schools revealed that 64 percent of those who repeated a grade in elementary school and 63 percent of those who repeated a grade in middle school eventually left school without a high school diploma. Russell Rumberger, in the same report, concludes from his national study that students who move twice during high school are twice as likely to drop out. A Gates Foundation survey tied dropping out to excessive absenteeism.

Raising female incomes to the level of males would appear to be one means of reducing the number of at-risk students. Poverty combined with being raised in a single-parent family appears to put a student at-risk for school failure.

POVERTY AMONG SCHOOL-AGED CHILDREN

Poverty becomes an at-risk factor when a child's parents have a low level of educational attainment. This is why socioeconomic status, which includes parents' level of educational attainment, is used to determine at-risk factors. For instance, highly educated parents might be living in poverty because of a personal choice. The poor writer or artist is a persistent occurrence in our society. While growing up in poverty, these children might benefit from a love of learning displayed by their parents. However, in many situations, poverty contributes to educational disadvantages when combined with other risk factors.

The number of children living in poverty has varied through the years. The Center for Education Statistics report *The Condition of Education 2008: Indicator 6, Family Characteristics of 5- to 17-year-olds* provides this description of changes since 1979:

> The percentage of school-age children living in families below the poverty threshold increased from 15 percent in 1979 to 21 percent in 1995, and then decreased to 16 percent in 2002. In 2006, a larger percentage of children were living in poor households than in 1979 (17 vs. 15 percent), but both were lower than the high in 1995 of 21 percent.

Poverty falls most heavily on black and Hispanic families. The report provides this comparison of white, black, and Hispanic families:

> The percentage of White children in poor households increased from 9 percent in 1979 to 12 percent in 1995, and then decreased to 10 percent in 2006. The percentage of Black children in poor households increased from 41 percent in 1979 to 44 percent in 1992, and then decreased to 33 percent in 2006. Among Hispanics, this percentage increased from 27 percent in 1979 to 40 percent in 1995, and then decreased to 26 percent in 2006.

Eligibility for free or reduced-price lunch is one measure used by schools to determine the number of students from low-income families. A major concern is the concentration of children from low-income families in a particular school. This raises the specter of economic segregation contributing to low achievement for students from low-income families. *The Condition of Education 2008* defines high-poverty schools as having "as public schools with more than 75 percent of students eligible for free or reduced price lunch."

According to *The Condition of Education 2008,* in 2005–2006, approximately 15 percent of all elementary and secondary public school students (or 7.1 million students) attended high-poverty schools. More black, Hispanic, and American Indian/Alaska Native students attended high-poverty schools than white or Asian/Pacific Islander students. About 34 percent of Hispanic, 32 percent of black, and 24 percent of American Indian/Pacific Islander students attended high-poverty schools. Only 4 percent of white and 10 percent of Asian/Pacific Islander students were enrolled in high-poverty schools.

Health insurance is a major problem for children living in poverty. According to the U.S. Census Bureau, 19.2 percent of children living in poverty are without any form of health insurance and 11.4 percent of all children are without health insurance.

THE END OF THE AMERICAN DREAM: SCHOOL DROPOUTS

Educational inequalities are reflected in graduation rates. Consider the disparity between the Detroit, Michigan, school district where only 21.7 percent of students graduate from high school to Fairfax County, Virginia, where 82.5 percent graduate or, in other words, 78.3 percent of Detroit students drop out and only 15.5 percent of Fairfax County students drop out (as reported in *Education Week's* special 2006 report "Diplomas Count: An Essential Guide to Graduation Policy and Rates"). This is a shocking contrast. Those who do not graduate from high school will often enter a low-paying job. Children attending an urban school district are more likely to drop out than students in suburban schools. According to the special report in *Education Week,* 60 percent of urban students graduate from high school as compared to 76.2 percent of suburban students.

There appears to be hope with regard to reducing school dropout rates. Indicator 23: Status Dropout Rates by Race/Ethnicity of *The Condition of Education 2008* defines what is called "status dropout rate" as "the percentage of persons in an age group who are not enrolled in school and have not earned a high school diploma or equivalent credential, such as a General Educational Development (GED) certificate." This indicator concludes that there has been a decline in status dropout rates for 16- through 24-year-olds from 15 percent in 1972 to 9 percent in 2006. However, racial disparities still exist. The report states that "for each year between 1972 and 2006, the status dropout rate was lowest for Whites and highest for Hispanics. For example, in 2006, the status dropout rate for Whites was 6 percent, compared with 11 percent for Blacks and 22 percent for Hispanics."

School dropouts are denied the dream of equality of opportunity through schooling. However conditions are improving but racial disparities continue.

TRACKING AND ABILITY GROUPING

Two methods that can separate students according to family income are tracking and ability grouping. Tracking, primarily a practice of the high school, separates students into different curricula such as college preparatory, vocational, and general. Ability grouping places students in different classes or groups within classes based on their abilities. These abilities are usually determined by a combination of a teacher assessment of the student and standardized tests.

The United States, with its emphasis on individual differences, uses ability grouping more often than most other countries. A 1991 study found that the use of ability grouping in math classes in the United States was two-thirds higher than in other countries. In lower secondary school grades, 56 percent of math classes used ability grouping. England reported the highest use of ability grouping with 92 percent of math classes grouped in the lower secondary grades.

Often, the family income of students parallels the levels of ability grouping and tracking. That is, the higher the family income of the students, the more likely it is that they will be in the higher ability groups or a college-preparatory curriculum. Conversely, the lower the family income of the students, the more likely it is that they will be in the lower ability groups or the vocational curriculum.

Sometimes teacher expectations are linked to the perceived social class of the student. The most famous study of the tendency to live up to expectations is Robert Rosenthal and Lenore Jacobson's *Pygmalion in the Classroom.* In the first part of the study, a group of experimenters was given a random selection of rats and told that certain rats came from highly intelligent stock. The rats labeled as coming from highly intelligent stock tended to do better than the other rats, though they were randomly grouped. The two psychologists tested their results in a school to see if teacher expectations would affect student performance. After giving students a standardized intelligence test, they gave teachers the names of students whom they called late bloomers and told the teachers to expect a sudden spurt of learning from them. In fact, the names of these students were selected at random from the class. A year later the intelligence tests were administered again. The scores of the supposed late bloomers were compared with those of other children who had received scores similar to the supposed late bloomers on the original test. It was found that those students who were identified to teachers as late bloomers made considerable gains in their intelligence-test scores when compared with students not designated as late bloomers.

The principal inference of this study is that teacher expectations can play an important role in determining the educational achievement of the child. This might be a serious problem in the education of children of poor and minority groups, where teachers develop expectations that these children will either fail or have a difficult time learning. Some educators, such as teacher and educational writer Miriam Wasserman, argue that teacher expectations are a major barrier to educational success for the poor and for certain minority groups.

SOCIAL REPRODUCTION

The discussion so far in this chapter would suggest that schools might play a role in maintaining differences between social classes through economic segregation. This argument is called social reproduction. Simply defined, social reproduction means that the schools reproduce the social-class structure of society. Economists Samuel Bowles and Herbert Gintis are the major proponents of the concept of social reproduction. They contend that the school causes occupational immobility. This argument completely reverses the idea that the school creates occupational mobility. Bowles and Gintis, in constructing this thesis, accept the findings that mobility rates are consistent throughout Western industrialized countries and that family background is one major factor in determining economic and social advancement. What they argue is that the school is a medium through which family background is translated into occupational and income opportunities.

This translation occurs regarding personality traits relevant to the work task; modes of self-presentation such as manner of speech and dress; ascriptive characteristics such as race, sex, and age; and the level and prestige of the individual's education. Bowles and Gintis insist that the four factors—personality traits, self-presentation, ascriptive characteristics, and level of educational attainment—are all significantly related to occupational success. They also are all related to the social class of the family. For instance, family background is directly related to the level of educational attainment and the prestige of that attainment. Here the economic level of the family determines educational attainment. Children from low-income families do not attain so high a level of education as children from rich families. From this standpoint the school reinforces social stratification and contributes to intergenerational immobility. For ascriptive characteristics such as race, the social advantages or disadvantages of a particular racial group are again related to levels of educational attainment.

As discussed in previous sections on cultural capital, personality traits and self-presentation are, according to Bowles and Gintis, important ingredients in occupational success. In *Schooling in Capitalist America,* Bowles and Gintis support these findings on cultural capital. Child-rearing, they declare, is important in developing personality traits related to entrance into the workforce. Personalities evidencing a great deal of self-direction tend to have greater success in high-status occupations. The differences in child-rearing patterns, the authors state, are reflected in the schools attended by different social classes. Schools with populations from lower-income families tend to be more authoritarian and to require more conformity than schools attended by children from higher-income families. This is often reflected in the differences between educationally innovative schools in high-income suburbs and the more traditional schools in low-income, inner-city neighborhoods. In some cases, parents place pressure on local schools either to be more authoritarian or to allow more self-direction. The nature of this pressure tends to be related to the social class of the parents.

In this manner, Bowles and Gintis argue, the child-rearing patterns of the family are reflected in the way schools treat children. Children from authoritarian families are prepared by authoritarian schools to work at low-paying jobs that do not require independent thinking and decision making. The reverse is true for children coming from upper-income families and schools; they are socialized to high-paying jobs that require independent thinking. In this manner, education reproduces social classes. One problem with the social reproduction argument is the treatment of students as passive recipients of knowledge.

CONCLUSION

Can schools provide equality of opportunity? Or does equality of opportunity depend on economic circumstances outside the power of the school? Does the school reduce social differences or heighten them through ability grouping, tracking, teacher expectations, counseling, and inequalities in school financing? Will the equalizing of school finances ensure an equal education for children from all social classes? These questions reflect the major problems confronting a public school system that professes equal educational opportunity and tries to provide an education that will guarantee equality of opportunity.

Suggested Readings and Works Cited in Chapter

Achieve, Inc., and National Governors Association. *America's High Schools: The Frontline in the Battle for Our Economic Future.* Washington, DC: Achieve, Inc., and National Governors Association, 2003. This report was issued prior to the 2005 high school summit warning that failing high schools would destroy American competitiveness in world markets.

ALEXANDER, KARL, and DORIS ENTWISTLE. "Signs of Early Exit for Dropouts Abound." In *Education Week*'s special 2006 report "Diplomas Count: An Essential Guide to Graduation Policy and Rates." Washington, DC: Education Week, 2006. This 2006 special report provides recent information on high school graduation rates and policies.

BINET, ALFRED. *The Intelligence of the Feeble-Minded.* Baltimore: Williams & Wilkins, 1916. Alfred Binet's pioneer work on developing measurements of intelligence.

BOWLES, SAMUEL, and HERBERT GINTIS. *Schooling in Capitalist America.* New York: Basic Books, 1976. This classic book by two neo-Marxist economists argues that schooling in the United States maintains the existing social-class structure for the benefit of an economic elite.

CAREY, KEVIN. *The Funding Gap 2004: Many States Still Shortchange Low-Income and Minority Students.* Washington, DC: Education Trust, 2004. Carey shows disparities in funding based on level of poverty in school districts.

DAY, JENNIFER, and ERIC NEWBURGER. *The Big Payoff: Educational Attainment and Synthetic Estimates of Work-Life Earnings.* Washington, DC: U.S. Census Bureau, July 2002. This is an important study on the relationship between income and educational attainment.

DENAVAS-WALT, CARMEN, et al., *Income, Poverty, and Health Insurance Coverage in the United States: 2007.* Washington, DC: US Census Bureau, 2008. As indicated in the title, the report provides basic economic information about the U.S. population.

GIROUX, HENRY. *Theory of Resistance: A Pedagogy for the Opposition.* South Hadley, MA: Bergin and Garvey, 1983. In this book, Giroux criticizes reproduction theorists and presents his theories of resistance.

JENSEN, ARTHUR and Frank MIELE. *Intelligence, Race, and Genetics: Conversations with Arthur R. Jensen.* Boulder, CO: Westview Press, 2002. Psychologist Arthur Jensen explains his view on the relationship between genetics and intelligence.

KOZOL, JONATHAN. *Savage Inequalities: Children in America's Schools.* New York: Crown Publishers, 1991. Kozol details the inequalities in spending per student between school districts and the resulting inequalities in the quality of education.

LAREAU, ANNETTE. *Unequal Childhoods: Class, Race, and Family Life.* Berkeley: University of California Press, 2003. This is a study of differing child-rearing methods between middle- and working-class families and their effect on the development of cultural capital.

LEE, VALERIE E., and DAVID T. BURKHAM. *Inequality at the Starting Gate: Social Background Differences in Achievement as Children Begin School.* Washington, DC: Economic Policy Institute, 2002. This book reports the impact of preschool experiences on math and reading tests at the beginning of kindergarten.

National Center for Education Statistics. *Digest of Education Statistics 2007.* Washington, DC: U.S. Department of Education, 2008. Introduction to data regarding U.S. schools.

——. *The Condition of Education 2008.* Washington, DC: U.S. Printing Office, 2008. This excellent annual report on the conditions of schools in the United States is an invaluable source for educational statistics ranging from test scores to school finance.

——. *The Condition of Education 2008: Indicator 6, Family Characteristics of 5- to 17-year-olds.* Provides data on poverty and family structures.

——. *The Condition of Education 2008: Indicator 23: Status Dropout Rates by Race/Ethnicity.* Provides data on dropout rates.

OAKES, JEANNIE. *Keeping Track: How Schools Structure Inequality.* New Haven: Yale University Press, 1985. This book explores the issue of tracking as a source of inequality.

POLE, J. R. *The Pursuit of Equality in American History,* second edition, revised and enlarged. Berkeley: University of California Press, 1993. This is the best history on the concept of equality in U.S. history and the importance of the idea of equality of opportunity.

RATTER, MICHAEL, et al. *Fifteen Thousand Hours.* Cambridge, MA: Harvard University Press, 1979. This is a study of the differences among 12 inner-city schools in London and how those differences are related to behavior and academic achievement.

REICH, ROBERT. *The Work of Nations: Preparing Ourselves for 21st-Century Capitalism.* New York: Alfred Knopf, 1991. This study by President Bill Clinton's secretary of labor outlines the educational requirements for jobs in a global economy.

ROSENTHAL, ROBERT, and LENORE JACOBSON. *Pygmalion in the Classroom: Teacher Expectation and Pupils' Intellectual Development.* New York: Irvington, 1988. The authors study the effects of teacher expectations.

SPRING, JOEL. *Education and the Rise of the Global Economy.* Mahwah, NJ: Lawrence Erlbaum, 1998. Spring studies the development of education in the context of global economics.

U.S. Census Bureau. *Current Population Reports P20-550, Table 217* . Retrieved on 4 September 2008 from http://www.census.gov. Provides data on educational attainment.

——. "Historical Income Tables–Households–Table H-1. Retrieved on 5 September 2008 from http://www.census.gov/hhes/www/income/histinc/h01AR.html. Provides data on changes in household income.

——. "Income Table IE-1." Retrieved on 5 September 2008 from http://www.census.gov/hhes/www/income/histinc/ineqtoc.html. Provides data on income inequalities in the United States.

CHAPTER 3

Equality of Educational Opportunity

Race, Gender, and Special Needs

This chapter will focus on the issue of *equality of educational opportunity*. In contrast to *equality of opportunity* to compete in the labor market, *equality of educational opportunity* refers to giving everyone an *equal chance to receive an education.* When defined as an equal chance to attend school, equal educational opportunity is primarily a legal issue. In this context, the provision of equal educational opportunity can be defined solely on the grounds of justice: If government provides a service like education, all classes of citizens should have equal access to that service.

Another aspect of equality of educational opportunity is the treatment of students in schools. Are all students given an equal chance to learn in schools? Do students of different races and gender receive equal treatment in schools? Is there equality of educational opportunity for students with special needs?

This chapter will discuss the following issues regarding equality of educational opportunity:

- The legal issues in defining race.
- The major court decisions and laws involving equality of educational opportunity for all races.
- Current racial segregation in schools.
- The struggle for equal educational opportunity for women.
- Special needs and equality of educational opportunity.

HOW COURTS AND THE U.S. CENSUS BUREAU HAVE DEFINED RACE

The problems courts have defining race is illustrated by the famous 1895 U.S. Supreme Court case *Plessy v. Ferguson,* which allowed segregation of public schools (I will discuss the details of this case in the next section). According to the lines of ancestry as expressed at that time, Plessy was one-eighth African

American and seven-eighths white. Was Homer Plessy white or black? What was the meaning of the term *white?* Why wasn't Plessy classified as white since seven-eighths of his ancestry was white and only one-eighth was black? Why did the court consider him black?

Plessy v. Ferguson highlights the principle that race is a social and legal construction. The U.S. legal system was forced to construct a concept of race because the 1790 Naturalization Law limited naturalized citizenship to immigrants who were free white persons. This law excluded Native Americans from citizenship. This limitation remained until 1952. Because of this law, U.S. courts were forced to define the meaning of white persons. Adding to the legal problem was that most southern states had adopted the so–called one drop of blood rule, which classified anyone with an African ancestor, no matter how distant, as African American. Under the one drop of blood rule, Homer Plessy was considered black.

The startling fact about the many court cases dealing with the 1790 law was the inability of the courts to rely on scientific evidence in defining white persons. Consider two of the famous twentieth-century court cases. The first, *Takao Ozawa v. United States* (1922), involved a Japanese immigrant who graduated from high school in Berkeley, California, and attended the University of California. He and his family spoke English and attended Christian churches. A key issue in *Takao Ozawa v. United States* (1922) was whether "white persons" referred to skin color. Many Japanese are fair skinned. The Court responded to this issue by rejecting skin color as a criterion. The Court stated, "The test afforded by the mere color of the skin of each individual is impracticable, as that differs greatly among persons of the same race, even among Anglo-Saxons, ranging by imperceptible gradations from the fair blond to the swarthy brunette, *the latter being darker than many of the lighter hued persons of the brown and yellow races* [my emphasis]." Rejecting the idea of skin color, the Court recognized the term *Caucasian* to define white persons—and denied citizenship.

However, the following year the U.S. Supreme Court rejected Caucasian as a standard for defining white persons in *United States v. Bhagat Singh Thind* (1923). In this case, an immigrant from India applied for citizenship as a Caucasian. According to the scientific rhetoric of the time, Thind was a Caucasian. Faced with this issue, the Court suddenly dismissed Caucasian as a definition of white persons. The Court argued, "It may be true that the blond Scandinavian and the brown Hindu have a common ancestor in the dim reaches of antiquity, but the average man knows perfectly well that there are unmistakable and profound differences between them today." Therefore, rather than relying on a scientific definition as it had in *Takao Ozawa v. United States,* the U.S. Supreme Court declared, "What we now hold is that the words 'free white persons' are words of common speech, to be interpreted in accordance with the understanding of the common man." The Court never specified who was to represent this common man. Thind was denied citizenship.

U.S. court histories are filled with disputable efforts to define race. My nineteenth-century ancestors on my father's side were denied U.S. citizenship and were recognized as having only tribal citizenship despite the fact that the majority of their ancestors were European. Until Native Americans were granted U.S. citizenship in 1924, many so-called mixed bloods were limited to tribal citizenship. The confusion over legal racial categories was exemplified by an 1853 California court case involving the testimony of immigrant Chinese witnesses regarding the murder of another Chinese immigrant by one George Hall. The California Supreme Court overturned the murder conviction of George Hall by applying a state law that disallowed court testimony from blacks, mulattos, and Native Americans. California's chief justice ruled that the law barring the testimony of Native Americans applied to all "Asiatics" since, according to theory, Native Americans were originally Asians who crossed into North America over the Bering Straits. Therefore, the chief justice argued, the ban on court testimony from Native Americans applied to "the whole of the Mongolian race."

The effect of this questionable legal construction of race was to heighten tensions among different groups of Americans. Many of those classified as African American have European and Native American citizenship. However, because of the one drop of blood rule and legal support of segregation, the possibilities for continuing assimilation and peaceful coexistence between so-called whites and blacks were delayed and replaced by a tradition of hostility between the two groups. The law reduced the chances of evolving into a peaceful multiracial society.

Today, in an effort to resolve the problems in defining a person's race, the U.S. Census Bureau is using personal self-identification. The Census Bureau asks people to select their race from a "flash card" listing six groups: "White," "Black," "American Indian," "Eskimo and Aleut," "Asian or Pacific Islander," and "Other Races." According to the Census Bureau:

> The minimum categories for race are now: American Indian or Alaska Native; Asian; Black or African American; Native Hawaiian or Other Pacific Islander; and White. Instead of allowing a multiracial category respondents [can] select one or more races when they self-identify . . . Census 2000 questionnaires also include[d] a sixth racial category: Some Other Race. There are also two minimum categories for ethnicity: Hispanic or Latino and Not Hispanic or Latino. Hispanics and Latinos may be of any race.

The Census Bureau also uses the designation "A.O.I.C.," which stands for "alone or in combination" with other races. Thus, a Census report might indicate "Black A.O.I.C." for a person who indicates that he is only black or has an ancestry of a combination of races or ethnic groups. "Black Alone" means those who claim only black ancestry; similar definitions are made for "White A.O.I.C.," "White Alone," "Asian A.O.I.C.," and "Asian Alone."

Often, Census data refers to "Hispanic (of any race)." Regarding Hispanic self-identification, the U.S. Census Bureau explains its method: "Respondents were asked to select their [Hispanic] origin (and the origin of other household members) from a 'flash card' listing ethnic origins. People of Hispanic origin, in particular, were those who indicated their origin was Mexican, Puerto Rican, Cuban, Central or South American, or some other Hispanic origin. It should be noted that people of Hispanic origin may be of any race."

Regarding its use of racial classification, the U.S. Census Bureau attached this footnote to its 2006 report on 2004 income (there is a delay in reporting because of the time required to compile and analyze data):

> 1. The 2003 CPS [Current Population Survey] asked respondents to choose one or more races. White Alone refers to people who reported White and did not report any other race category. The use of this single-race population does not imply that it is the preferred method of presenting or analyzing data. The Census Bureau uses a variety of approaches. Information on people who reported more than one race, such as "White and American Indian and Alaska Native" or "Asian and Black or African American," is available from Census 2000 through American Factfinder. About 2.6 percent of people reported more than one race in 2000.
>
> 2. Black Alone refers to people who reported Black and did not report any other race category.
>
> 3. Asian Alone refers to people who reported Asian and did not report any other race category.

By making racial definitions subjective, self-identification makes race a matter of cultural choice. Consider a person who had a great-grandmother who was Native American, while all other ancestors were of European ancestry. This person might prefer to identify with Native American as opposed to European cultures and, consequently, choose Native American from the U.S. Census Bureau's flash card. Or consider a person who has African, European, and Native American ancestry. This combination of ancestry is typical of many U.S. citizens who identify themselves as black. Should this person choose black, white, or Native American when confronted with a U.S. Census Bureau flash card? The choice will probably be based on cultural affiliation through self-identification with white, black, or Native American cultures.

EQUALITY OF EDUCATIONAL OPPORTUNITY: RACE, COURTS, AND LEGISLATION

Equal treatment by the law is the great legal principle underlying the idea of equality of educational opportunity. Everyone should receive equal treatment by the law. No one should receive special privileges or treatment because of race, gender, religion, ethnicity, or wealth. This means that if a government provides a school system, then everyone should be treated equally by that system; everyone should have equal access to that educational system.

Added in 1868, the Fourteenth Amendment to the Constitution provided for equality under the law. One of the purposes of the Fourteenth Amendment was to extend the basic guarantees of the Bill of Rights into the areas of state and local government. The clause of the amendment that emphasized the principle of equality under the law stated, "No State shall . . . deny to any person within its jurisdiction the equal protection of the laws."

At first glance, "equal protection of the laws" would suggest that if state laws created a school system, then everyone should have equal access. However, the initial interpretation by the U.S. Supreme Court in 1895 was that "equal protection" could also mean "separate but equal." Or, in other words, segregated education based on race could be legal under the Fourteenth Amendment if all the schools were equal.

The separate but equal ruling occurred in the previously mentioned 1895 U.S. Supreme Court decision *Plessy v. Ferguson.* The case involved Homer Plessy, who was one-eighth African American and seven-eighths white. He was arrested for refusing to ride in the colored coach of a train, as required by Louisiana state law. The Supreme Court's decision in this case that segregated facilities could exist if they were equal became known as the separate but equal doctrine.

The 1954 desegregation decision *Brown v. Board of Education of Topeka* overturned the separate but equal doctrine by arguing that segregated education was inherently unequal. This meant that even if school facilities, teachers, equipment, and all other physical conditions were equal between two racially segregated schools, the two schools would still be unequal because of the racial segregation.

In 1964, Congress took a significant step toward speeding up school desegregation by passing the important Civil Rights Act. About school desegregation, Title VI of the 1964 Civil Rights Act was most important because it provided a means for the federal government to force school desegregation. In its final form, Title VI required the mandatory withholding of federal funds from institutions that practiced racial discrimination. Title VI states that no person, because of race, color, or national origin, can be excluded from or denied the benefits of any program receiving federal financial assistance. It required all federal agencies to establish guidelines to implement this policy. Refusal by institutions or projects to follow these guidelines was to result in the "termination of or refusal to grant or to continue assistance under such program or activity."

Title VI of the 1964 Civil Rights Act was important for two reasons. First, it established a major precedent for federal control of American public schools, by making it explicit that the control of money would be one method used by the federal government to shape local school policies. (This aspect of the law will be discussed in more detail in Chapter 9.) Second, it turned the federal Office of Education into a policing agency with the responsibility of determining whether school systems were segregated and, if they were, of doing something about the segregated conditions.

One result of Title VI was to speed up the process of school desegregation in the South, particularly after the passage of federal legislation in 1965 that increased the amount of money available to local schools from the federal government. In the late 1960s, southern school districts rapidly began to submit school desegregation plans to the Office of Education.

In the North, prosecution of inequality in educational opportunity as it related to school segregation required a different approach from that used in the South. In the South, school segregation existed by legislative acts that required separation of the races. There were no specific laws requiring separation of the

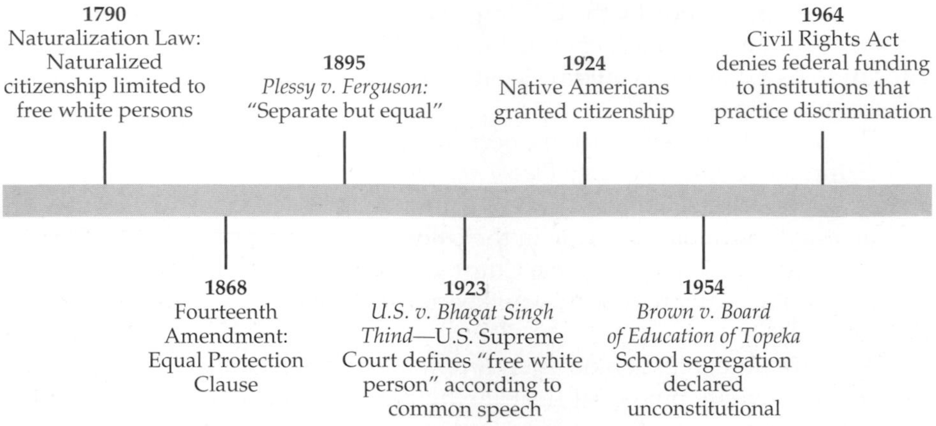

FIGURE 3–1. Time Line of Events Discussed—Equality of Educational Opportunity

races in the North. But even without specific laws, racial segregation existed. Therefore, it was necessary for individuals bringing complaints against northern school districts to prove that the existing patterns of racial segregation were the result of purposeful action by the school districts. It had to be proved that school officials intended racial segregation to be a result of their educational policies.

The conditions required to prove segregation were explicitly outlined in 1974, in the Sixth Circuit Court of Appeals case *Oliver v. Michigan State Board of Education.* The court stated, "A presumption of segregative purpose arises when plaintiffs establish that the natural, probable and foreseeable result of public officials' action or inaction was an increase or perpetuation of public school segregation." This did not mean that individual motives or prejudices were to be investigated but that the overall pattern of school actions had to be shown to increase racial segregation; that is, in the language of the court, "the question whether a purposeful pattern of segregation has manifested itself over time, despite the fact that individual official actions, considered alone, may not have been taken for segregative purposes."

Figure 3-1 presents a time line of significant events in the struggle for equality of educational opportunity.

SCHOOL SEGREGATION TODAY

School segregation for blacks and Latinos increased in recent years as indicated in Table 3–1. "Latino" is used in Table 3–1 in contrast to "Hispanic." The problems associated with the distinction between Hispanic and Latino are discussed in detail in Chapter 4. Here it suffices to say that the decision to use "Latino" was made by the source for the data—Harvard University's *The Civil Rights Project.* As indicated in Table 3–1, racial segregation increased for black students: from

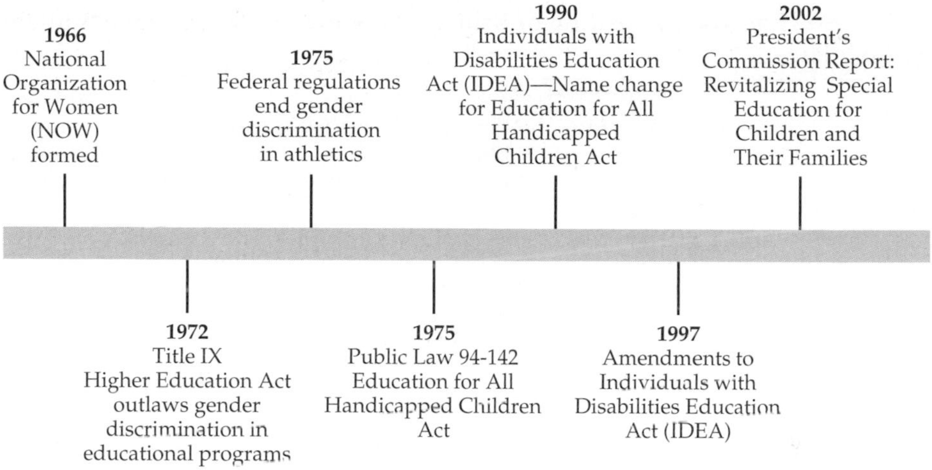

FIGURE 3–1. *(Continued)*

TABLE 3–1. Changes in School Segregation, 1991–2003

	1991–1992	2003–2004
Percentage of black students in 50–100% minority schools	66%	73%
Percentage of Latino students in 50–100% minority schools	73	77
Percentage of Native American students in 50–100% minority schools	43	52

Source: Compiled from Tables 3, 4, and 5 in Gary Orfield and Chungmei Lee, "Racial Transformation and the Changing Nature of Segregation," *The Civil Rights Project* (Cambridge: Harvard University, 2006), pp. 10–11.

66 percent of black students attending schools with 50 to 100 percent minority students in 1991–1992 to 73 percent in 2003–2004. The most segregated were Latino students with 73 percent attending schools with 50 to 100 percent minority students in 1991–1992 and 77 percent in 2003–2004.

In general, schools remain segregated with white students being the most racially isolated: The average white student attends a school where more than 78 percent of the students are white, 9 percent are black, 9 percent are Latino, 3 percent are Asian, and 1 percent are Native American (Table 3-2). As indicated in Table 3–2, the average Latino student attends schools that are 55 percent Latino and the average black student attends schools that are 53 percent black.

In 1999, Gary Orfield, head of Harvard's Civil Rights Project and a longtime advocate of school desegregation, issued a report with the ominous title, "Resegregation in American Schools." The report states, "We are clearly in a period when many policymakers, courts and opinion makers assume that

TABLE 3–2. Racial Composition of Schools Attended by the Average Student of Each Race, 2003–2004

Race	Average White Student	Average Black Student	Average Latino Student	Average Asian Student	Average Native American Student
Percentage of school that is white	78%	30%	28%	45%	44%
Percentage of school that is black	9	53	12	12	7
Percentage of school that is Latino	9	13	55	20	11
Percentage of school that is Asian	3	3	5	22	3
Percentage of school that is Native American	1	1	1	1	35

desegregation is no longer necessary. . . . Polls show that most white Americans believe that equal educational opportunity is being provided." Responding to the report, Chester Finn, a conservative critic of public schools, faulted Orfield for even worrying about school segregation. "Gary Orfield," Finn said, "must be the only American who still thinks that integration for its own sake is an important societal goal." For Finn, "The price of forced busing and other forms of social engineering is too high to pay when there are more urgent crises facing this country's schools."

In response to increased school segregation in southern states, Gary Orfield, in the summer of 2002, organized a joint conference between Harvard University's Civil Rights Project and the University of North Carolina's Center for Civil Rights. Participants reported an increase in school segregation in cities throughout the South. Experts at the conference gave the following reasons for increased segregation:

1. Recent court decisions outlawing race as a main factor in student assignment.
2. Increased residential segregation.
3. Increased role of private schools in contributing to segregation.

The continuing unequal racial treatment in schools is reflected in dropout rates. A 2004 study of high school graduation rates by Jing Miao and Walt Haney concludes: "Despite the graduation rate method used, results indicate that high school graduation rates in the U.S. have been declining in recent years and that graduation rates for black and Hispanic students lag substantially behind those of white students." This would suggest a future increasing income disparity among whites and blacks and Hispanics.

SECOND-GENERATION SEGREGATION

Second-generation segregation refers to forms of racial segregation that are a result of school practices such as tracking, ability grouping, and the misplacement of students in special education classes. Unlike segregation that existed by state laws in the South before the 1954 *Brown* decision, second-generation forms of segregation can occur in schools with balanced racial populations; for instance, all white students may be placed in one academic track and all African American or Hispanic students in another track.

Nationally, most studies examine the process of great change and no change as integration of schools results in segregation within schools. One collection of studies can be found in Ray Rist's *Desegregated Schools: Appraisals of an American Experiment*. The studies describe the subtle forms of segregation that began to occur as white and African American students were placed in integrated schools for the first time. For instance, in one recently integrated school, African American students were suspended for committing the same offenses for which white students received only a reprimand. A teacher in the school complained that, unlike African American students, when white students were sent to the principal's office, they were immediately sent back to class. In this school, equal opportunity to attend the school did not result in equal treatment within the school.

Unequal treatment of different races within the same school is one problem in integrated schools; the establishment of racial boundaries among students creates another. One study in the Rist book describes how racial boundaries were established in a high school in Memphis, Tennessee, after the students of an all–African American school were integrated with the students of an all-white school. Here, white students maintained control over most student activities. Activities in which African American students began to participate after integration were athletics and cheerleading. When this occurred, the status of these activities was denigrated by white students. On the other hand, whites could maintain control of the student government, ROTC, school clubs, and the staff of the yearbook.

This division of control among student activities reflected the rigid social boundaries that existed in the high school between the two groups. Individuals who crossed these social boundaries had to adapt to the social customs of those on the other side. For instance, African American students changed their style of dress and social conduct to be accepted by white students. African American students who crossed racial lines by making such changes found themselves accused by other African American students of "acting white" and were subsequently rejected by "unchanged" African American students. The same was true of white students who crossed racial boundaries.

The racial boundaries that continue to exist in high schools after integration reflect the racial barriers that continue in the larger society. The social life of a school often reflects the social world outside the school. Integration of a school system can help ensure equality of educational opportunity, but it cannot break down society's racial barriers. Although schools attempt to deal with this problem, its solution requires a general transformation of racial relationships in the larger society.

THE STRUGGLE FOR EQUAL EDUCATION FOR WOMEN

The reader should check the Web sites of the following organizations for current issues, policies, and the history of struggle regarding women's education: American Association of University Women (http://www.aauw.org), National Organization for Women Foundation (http://www.nowfoundation.org), and Education Equality of the Feminist Majority Foundation (http://www.feminist.org/education). These organizations are in the forefront in protecting women's rights in education.

Since the nineteenth century, the struggle for racial justice paralleled that of justice for women. Demands for equal educational opportunity pervaded both campaigns for civil rights. In the second half of the twentieth century the drive for equal educational opportunity for women was led by the National Organization for Women (NOW), which was organized in 1966. The founding document of the organization declared, "There is no civil rights movement to speak for women as there has been for Negroes and other victims of discrimination. The National Organization for Women must therefore begin to speak." In NOW's founding document, education is called "the key to effective participation in today's economy . . . [and public schools should educate a woman] to her full potential of human ability."

During its first years of activism, NOW focused on

- Eliminating discriminatory quotas against women in college and professional school admissions.
- Urging parents, counselors, and teachers to encourage women to pursue higher education and professional education.
- Eliminating discriminatory practices against women in the awarding of fellowships and loans.
- Investigating the problem of female school dropouts.

NOW's activities and that of other women's organizations turned to legal action with the passage of Title IX of the 1972 Higher Education Act. Title IX states: "No person in the United States shall, on the basis of sex, be excluded from participation in, be denied the benefits of, or be subjected to discrimination under any education program or activity receiving federal financial assistance."

The legislation applied to all educational institutions, including preschool, elementary and secondary schools, vocational and professional schools, and public and private undergraduate and graduate institutions. A 1983 U.S. Supreme Court decision, *Grove City College v. Bell,* restricted the application of Title IX to specific educational programs within institutions. In the 1987

Civil Rights Restoration Act, Congress overturned the Court's decision and amended Title IX to include *all* activities of an educational institution receiving federal aid.

Armed with Title IX, NOW and other women's organizations placed pressure on local school systems and colleges to ensure equal treatment of women in vocational education, athletic programs, textbooks and the curriculum, testing, and college admissions. Following is a brief chronological list of achievements in providing equality of educational opportunity for women:

- *1972:* Legal action against school systems with segregated courses in home economics and industrial arts.
- *1974:* With backing from NOW, more than 1,000 women's studies departments created on college campuses.
- *1975:* Federal regulations to end sex discrimination in athletics.
- *1976:* Lawsuits regarding female participation in athletics and gender-biased hiring in school administration.
- *1976:* Educational Equity Act authorizes Office of Education to prepare "non-sexist curricula and non-discriminatory vocational and career counseling, sports education, and other programs designed to achieve equity for all students regardless of sex."
- *1983:* Last all-male school in Ivy League, Columbia University, becomes coeducational.
- *1986:* FairTest organized to counter sex bias in high-stakes tests.
- *1996:* Virginia Military Institute and the Citadel become coeducational.

The struggle for equality of educational opportunity is reflected in the following changes in educational programs:

- The number of female graduates from medical school increased from 8.4 percent in 1969 to 34.5 percent in 1990.
- The percentage of doctoral and professional degrees awarded to women increased from 14.4 percent in 1971 to 36.8 percent in 1991.
- Most discrimination in vocational programs ended.
- Female participation in high school athletics increased from 7 percent in 1972 to 37 percent in 1992 and in college athletics from 15.6 percent in 1972 to 34.8 percent in 1993.

Today, some women's organizations are concerned about the growth of sex-segregated classrooms and schools. The Feminist Majority issued this statement warning about U.S Department of Education regulations that they believe weaken Title IX.

The 2006 U.S. Department of Education Changes Drastically Weaken Title IX and Should Be Rescinded

> These 2006 Title IX regulation changes allow separate facilities or classes as long as the gender that is not given the special class or school receives a "substantially equal" educational opportunity probably in a coeducational setting. "Substantially equal" is not specifically defined in the regulation and there are

> no instructions on how to learn if the single-sex activities contribute to increased sex stereotyping and sex discrimination or if they contribute to achieving any important governmental objectives such as increased academic achievement. There is also no expectation that this risky single-sex experiment show that it is any better than equitable high quality instruction designed to meet the same needs in mixed sex environments.

STUDENTS WITH DISABILITIES

By the 1960s, the civil rights movement encompassed students with disabilities. Within the context of equality of educational opportunity, students with special needs could participate equally in schools with other students only if they received some form of special help. Since the nineteenth century, many of the needs of these students have been neglected by local and state school authorities because of the expense of special facilities and teachers. In fact, many people with disabilities were forced to live in state institutions for the mentally ill or retarded. For instance, consider "Allan's story," a case history of treatment prior to the 1970s, provided by the U.S. Office of Special Education Programs:

> Allan was left as an infant on the steps of an institution for persons with mental retardation in the late 1940s. By age 35, he had become blind and was frequently observed sitting in a corner of the room, slapping his heavily callused face as he rocked back and forth humming to himself.

In the late 1970s, Allan was assessed properly for the first time. To the dismay of his examiners, he was found to be of average intelligence; further review of his records revealed that by observing fellow residents of the institution, he had learned self-injurious behavior that caused his total loss of vision. Although the institution then began a special program to teach Allan to be more independent, a major portion of his life was lost because of a lack of appropriate assessments and effective interventions.

The political movement for federal legislation to aid students with disabilities followed a path similar to the rest of the civil rights movement. First, finding themselves unable to change educational institutions by pressuring local and state governments, organized groups interested in improving educational opportunities for students with special needs turned to the courts. This was the path taken in the late 1960s by the Pennsylvania Association for Retarded Children (PARC). PARC was one of many associations organized in the 1950s to aid citizens with disabilities. These organizations were concerned with state laws that excluded children with disabilities from educational institutions because they were considered uneducable and untrainable. State organizations like PARC and the National Association for Retarded Children campaigned to eliminate these laws and to demonstrate the educability of all children. But, as the civil rights movement discovered throughout the century, local and state officials were resistant to change and relief had to be sought through the judicial system.

In *Pennsylvania Association for Retarded Children (PARC) v. Commonwealth of Pennsylvania,* a case that was as important for the rights of children with disabilities as the *Brown* decision was for African Americans, PARC objected to conditions in the Pennhurst State School and Hospital. In framing the case, lawyers for PARC focused on the legal right to an education for children with disabilities. PARC, working with the major federal lobbyist for children with disabilities, the Council for Exceptional Children (CEC), overwhelmed the court with evidence on the educability of children with disabilities. The state withdrew its case, and the court enjoined the state from excluding children with disabilities from a public education and required that every child be allowed access to an education. Publicity about the PARC case prompted other lobbying groups to file 36 cases against different state governments. The CEC prepared model legislation and lobbied for its passage at the state and federal levels.

PUBLIC LAW 94-142: EDUCATION FOR ALL HANDICAPPED CHILDREN ACT

In 1975, Congress passed Public Law 94-142, the Education for All Handicapped Children Act that guaranteed equal educational opportunity for all children with disabilities. In 1990, Congress changed the name of this legislation to Individuals with Disabilities Education Act (IDEA). The major provisions in the Public Law 94-142 were to provide for equal educational opportunity for all children with disabilities. This goal included the opportunity for all children with disabilities to attend regular school classes. As stated in the legislation, "all children with disabilities [should] have available to them . . . a free appropriate public education which emphasized special education and related services designed to meet their unique needs."

WRITING AN IEP

One of the issues confronting Congress during legislative debates was that of increased federal control over local school systems. Congress resolved this problem by requiring that an individualized education plan (IEP) be written for each student with disabilities. This reduced federal control since each IEP would be written in local school systems. IEPs are now a standard part of education programs for children with disabilities. Public Law 94-142 requires that an IEP be developed for each child jointly by the local educational agency and the child's parents or guardians. This gives the child or the parents the right to negotiate with the local school system about the type of services to be delivered.

Teachers, school administrators, and parents work together to arrive at an IEP statement. It is important that school officials and teachers understand the regulations governing the writing of IEPs. As provided for in the original legislation, an IEP includes:

1. A statement of the present levels of educational performance of such child.
2. A statement of annual goals, including short-term instructional objectives.
3. A statement of the specific educational services to be provided to such child, and the extent to which such child will be able to participate in regular educational programs.
4. The projected date for initiation and anticipated duration of such services.
5. Appropriate objective criteria and evaluation procedures and schedules for determining, on at least an annual basis, whether instructional objectives are being achieved.

WHICH CHILDREN HAVE DISABILITIES?

The National Center for Education Statistics, in *The Condition of Education 2008,* provides a listing of disability categories. The percentage of students in schools for each disability is given in Table 3–3. Below are the disabilities recognized by the federal government.

- *Autism:* A developmental disability significantly affecting verbal and nonverbal communication and social interaction, generally evident before age 3, that adversely affects a child's educational performance.
- *Deaf-Blindness:* Concomitant hearing and visual impairments, the combination of which causes severe communication and other developmental and educational problems.
- *Developmental Delay:* This term may apply to children ages 3 through 9 who are experiencing developmental delays . . . who therefore need special education and related services.
- *Emotional Disturbance:* A condition exhibiting . . . characteristics over a long period of time and to a marked degree that adversely affects a child's educational performance
- *Hearing Impairment:* An impairment in hearing, whether permanent or fluctuating, that adversely affects a child's educational performance.
- *Mental Retardation:* Significantly subaverage general intellectual functioning . . . that adversely affects a child's educational performance.
- *Multiple Disabilities:* Concomitant impairments (such as mental retardation–blindness, mental retardation, orthopedic impairment).
- *Orthopedic Impairment:* A severe orthopedic impairment that adversely affects a child's educational performance.
- *Specific Learning Disability:* A disorder in one or more of the basic psychological processes involved in understanding or in using language, spoken or written, that may manifest itself in an imperfect ability to listen, think, speak, read, write, spell, or to do mathematical calculations.

TABLE 3–3. Children (aged 3–21) with Disabilities in Public Schools, 2006–2007

Disabilities	Percentage with Disability
All disabilities	13.5%
Specific learning disabilities	5.4
Speech or language impairments	3.0
Mental retardation	1.1
Emotional disturbance	0.9
Hearing impairments	0.2
Orthopedic impairments	0.1
Other health impairments	1.2
Visual impairments	0.1
Multiple disabilities	0.3
Autism	0.5
Traumatic brain injury	0.1
Developmental delay	0.7

Source: National Center for Education Statistics, *The Condition of Education 2008* (Washington, DC: U.S. Printing Office, 2006), p. 94.

- *Speech or Language Impairment:* A communication disorder such as stuttering, impaired articulation, a language impairment, or a voice impairment that adversely affects a child's educational performance.
- *Traumatic Brain Injury:* An acquired injury to the brain caused by an external physical force, resulting in total or partial functional disability or psychosocial impairment, or both, that adversely affects a child's educational performance.
- *Visual Impairments:* An impairment in vision that, even with correction, adversely affects a child's educational performance.

INCLUSION

The 1975 Education for All Handicapped Children Act called for the integration of children with disabilities into regular classes. Similar to any form of segregation, the isolation of children with disabilities often deprives them of contact with other students and denies them access to equipment found in regular classrooms, such as scientific equipment, audiovisual aids, classroom libraries, and computers. Full inclusion, it is believed, will improve the educational achievement and social development of children with disabilities. Also, it is hoped, bias against children and adults with disabilities decreases because of the interactions of students with disabilities with other students. The integration clause of The Education for All Handicapped Children Act specified that:

> to the maximum extent appropriate, handicapped children, including children in public or private institutions or other care facilities, are educated with children who are not handicapped, and that special classes, separate schooling,

> or other removal of handicapped children from the regular educational environment occurs only when the nature or severity of the handicap is such that education in regular classes with the use of supplementary aids and services cannot be achieved satisfactorily.

The term *inclusion* is the most frequently used word to refer to the integration of children with disabilities into regular classrooms. The phrase *full inclusion* refers to the inclusion of all children with disabilities.

In 1990, advocates of full inclusion received federal support with the passage of the Americans with Disabilities Act. This historic legislation bans all forms of discrimination against the disabled. The Americans with Disabilities Act played an important role in the 1992 court decision *Oberti v. Board of Education of the Borough of Clementon School District,* which involved an 8-year-old, Rafael Oberti, classified as educable mentally retarded. U.S. District Court Judge John F. Gerry argued that the Americans with Disabilities Act requires that people with disabilities be given equal access to services provided by any agency receiving federal money, including public schools. Judge Gerry decided that Rafael Oberti could manage in a regular classroom with special aides and a special curriculum. In his decision, Judge Gerry wrote, "Inclusion is a right, not a privilege for a select few."

The 1997 Congressional amendments to this legislation, now called the Individuals with Disabilities Education Act, emphasized the importance of including children with disabilities in regular classes. In the text of the 1997 amendments, it was claimed that since the passage of the original legislation research, inclusion in regular classes improved the academic performance of children with disabilities. In the words of the Amendments, "Over 20 years of research and experience has demonstrated that the education of children with disabilities can be made more effective by . . . having high expectations for such children and ensuring their access in the general curriculum to the maximum extent possible."

During Congressional hearings leading to the passage of the 1997 Individuals with Disabilities Education Act Amendments, there were complaints that appropriate educational services were not being provided for more than one-half of the children with disabilities in the United States. Also, more than 1,000,000 of the children with disabilities in the United States were excluded entirely from the public school system and were not educated with their peers. In addition, there were complaints that many disabilities were going undetected.

The inclusion of children with disabilities in regular classrooms created a new challenge for regular teachers. Classroom teachers, according to the legislation, were to be provided with "appropriate special education and related services and aids." The legislation specified that teachers should receive extra training to help children with disabilities. In the words of the legislation, school districts must provide: "high-quality, intensive professional development for all personnel who work with such children in order to ensure that they have the skills and knowledge necessary to enable them to meet developmental goals." Also, teacher education programs were to give all student teachers training in working with students with disabilities.

INCLUSION AND NO CHILD LEFT BEHIND

On 9 December 2003, federal regulations, Title I—Improving the Academic Achievement of the Disadvantaged, from the U.S. Department of Education were posted in the *Federal Register* requiring children with disabilities be included in the state testing systems under the No Child Left Behind Act of 2001. However, states are allowed to create alternative tests and standards for students with disabilities. The scores of these students are to be utilized in determining whether a school has made adequate yearly progress. As I discuss in Chapter 6, schools not making adequate yearly progress will be targeted for improvement and parents will be allowed to choose other schools.

Inclusion is one reason given for requiring the assessment of students with the most significant cognitive disabilities to be included in state testing programs. The argument is made that teachers will expect more of students and work harder at teaching students with significant cognitive disabilities if they are included in the state testing system. "Students with disabilities," the federal regulation states, "accrue positive benefits when they are included in school accountability systems. Educators realize that these students also count, just like all other students; they understand that they need to make sure that these students learn to high levels, just like other students. When students with disabilities are part of the accountability system, educators' expectations for these students are more likely to increase."

Also, federal regulations indicate a fear that if these students are not included in the state testing programs then school administrators will attempt to raise their school's test scores by classifying more students as having disabilities. In other words, excluding students with disabilities raises the specter of school administrators cheating by over-enrolling students in these programs. As the federal regulation states: "For example, we know from research that when students with disabilities are allowed to be excluded from school accountability measures, the rates of referral of students for special education increase dramatically."

The federal regulations included the testimony of an unnamed Massachusetts state official about the benefits of including students with the most significant cognitive disabilities in its assessment. The state official claimed that these students were taught concepts not normally developed in their classes. "Some students with disabilities," the state official explained, "have never been taught academic skills and concepts, for example, reading, mathematics, science, and social studies, even at very basic levels." The official asserted his/her belief in inclusion in state testing programs under No Child Left Behind: "Yet all students are capable of learning at a level that engages and challenges them."

The federal regulation provides an emphatic endorsement of inclusion: Teachers who have incorporated learning standards into their instruction cite unanticipated gains in students' performance and understanding. Furthermore, some individualized social, communication, motor, and self-help skills can be practiced during activities based on the learning standards. Too often in the past, students with disabilities were excluded from assessments and accountability systems, and the consequence was that they did not receive the academic attention they deserved. Access and exposure to the general curriculum for students with disabilities often did not occur, and there was no systemwide measure to indicate whether or what they were learning. These regulations are designed to ensure that schools are held accountable for the educational progress of students with the most significant cognitive disabilities, just as schools are held accountable for the educational results of all other students with disabilities and students without disabilities.

AN INCLUSION SUCCESS STORY

In the 10 July 2002 issue of *Education Week,* Allison Shelley tells the story of Down syndrome student Chris Vogelberger, whose first experience with inclusion was in a third grade classroom. During the first year, his spoken-language abilities increased by two years. Now attending middle school, Chris has a full-time assistant, Debbie Beiling, whom he calls Bean.

His daily lessons are loaded onto his iMac laptop by the school's special education resource teacher. His iMac lessons are modified versions of what the teacher will be presenting in class. During class instruction, the regular teacher can focus on the rest of the class while Chris works on his laptop. At times, the teacher directly helps him begin one of the modified lessons. For instance, in science class as other students are learning about the periodic table and properties of metals and nonmetals, Chris is studying the parts of the atom. In language arts, he studies words on flash cards.

Most importantly, Chris is learning to interact with other students and other students are learning to accept him. He has developed a circle of friends. One of those friends, Dan O'Connell, told reporter Allison Shelley, "I've had a better year with him here. I started out the school year thinking that everyone would be perfect in a sense, the way that they would talk and act. But then I found out that people can really be different. You learn how to deal better with everyone."

Praising the idea of inclusion, Chris's mother said, "He will not be living in a special education world. He'll be living in our world."

THE INCLUSION DEBATE

While Chris Vogelberger's story is a model of successful inclusion, there has been sharp criticism of the concept. The lack of training of classroom teachers and the limited availability of aides and special education resources make implementing inclusion difficult. Not surprisingly, the lack of adequate funding underlies all.

One critic of inclusion is the American Federation of Teachers (AFT), one of the major teachers' unions. The AFT questioned the value of inclusion by claiming there was no research supporting the movement:

> **Whereas** inclusion is being championed as the only placement for all students with disabilities by a movement of some advocacy groups—in the face of opposition from the parents of many students with disabilities and many respected advocates for the disabled—when there is no clear evidence that inclusion is appropriate or provides an educational benefit for all students with disabilities, and no clear evidence of its benefits for the other students. (AFT, "Resolution on Inclusion of Students with Disabilities," 1994)

The AFT resolution expressed a major concern about implementation of inclusion. They criticized school administrators for "placing too many students with disabilities in individual general classrooms; placing students with disabilities in general education classrooms without services . . . refusing to assist teachers who are having problems meeting the unique needs of students with disabilities."

Also, the resolution expresses concern about the extra burden inclusion places on classroom teachers. Consequently, the union declares,

> Resolved that the AFT oppose inclusion—that is, any movement or program that has the goal of placing all students with disabilities in general education classrooms regardless of the nature or severity of their disabilities, their ability to behave or function appropriately in the classroom, or the educational benefits they and their general education peers can derive.

In contrast to the American Federation of Teachers, the National Association of State Boards of Education supports full inclusion in its report *Winners All: A Call for Inclusive Schools.* The report calls for a fundamental shift in the provision of services for students with disabilities. As the report envisions the full-inclusion process, rather than teaching in a separate classroom, special education teachers would provide their services in regular classrooms by team-teaching with the regular teacher or providing other support.

The idea of inclusion is resisted by some parents who believe that separate special education classrooms provide important benefits for their children. For instance, 20 parents of children with disabilities attending the Vaughn Occupational High School in Chicago carried signs at the board of education meeting on 7 September 1994, reading "The board's inclusion is exclusion." The parents were protesting the board's decision to send their children to neighborhood schools for inclusion in regular classrooms. Traditionally, Vaughn provided vocational training for students with disabilities. The students would hold low-level jobs at McDonald's, an airline food service company, and a glass-installation business.

The board's action regarding the Vaughn students was the result of a 1992 complaint by the Illinois state board that Vaughn students were not spending time with nondisabled peers. The state board threatened to remove all federal and state funds from the school district if the students were not included in regular classrooms. Martha Luna complained about the decision because it denied her 15-year-old son, Tony, vocational training to meet his needs. Ms. Luna stated, "I know Tony won't go to college so I don't expect that, just for him to learn everyday living and work skills."

Reflecting the American Federation of Teachers' complaint about the extra burden inclusion places on classroom teachers, a survey found that over 70 percent of practicing teachers object to including students with disabilities in their classrooms. The West Virginia Federation of Teachers released a survey of 1,121 teachers showing that 87 percent did not believe that inclusion helped general education students and 78 percent did not believe that inclusion helped students with disabilities. A survey of teachers in Howard County, Maryland, reports that 64 percent of middle-school teachers believe "that inclusion detracts from their ability to fully serve the needs of the general student population." Only 21 percent believed inclusion benefitted children with disabilities. The complaints about inclusion are occurring as the proportion of disabled students receiving their education in regular classrooms increases. In 1991, for instance, 32.8 percent of disabled students were receiving their educations in regular classrooms. By 1995, the figure had risen to 44.5 percent.

The preceding figures indicate the complications in implementing inclusion programs. Following is a list of objections by teachers to inclusion programs:

- Disabled students are moved into regular classrooms without any support services.
- Experienced teachers have never received training in teaching students with disabilities or in teaching in an inclusive classroom.
- School districts implementing inclusion policies do not provide adequate training for general education teachers.
- Education schools do not provide prospective teachers with a basic knowledge of learning disabilities or situations they are likely to confront in inclusive classrooms.
- General education teachers are often excluded from the individualized education plan (IEP) team.
- Parents of nondisabled students worry that their children's education will be compromised in inclusive classrooms.

The preceding issues contain their own solutions, which include (1) more education and training for experienced and future teachers, (2) adequate support services for teachers in inclusive classrooms, (3) teacher participation on the individualized planning team, and (4) education of parents about inclusive classrooms. Model full-inclusion schools and teacher education programs do exist that address the preceding issues. Teachers and administrators at the Zachary Taylor Elementary School, a suburban Washington, DC, community, operate a model full-inclusion school that they believe is improving the academic and social performance of disabled students and has made other students more caring and tolerant. Syracuse University, in response to the problem of inadequately prepared teachers, instructs general education and special education teachers together. At the end of four years, both groups receive dual certification. In answer to worried parents of students in general education, John McDonnell, chair of the special education department at the University of Utah, states, "There really has been no effect on the educational progress of kids without disabilities by including kids with disabilities at the classroom level."

COMMISSION ON EXCELLENCE IN SPECIAL EDUCATION

In its 2002 report, "Revitalizing Special Education for Children and Their Families," President George W. Bush's Commission on Excellence in Special Education decries the condition of special education despite over 25 years of federal involvement. The Commission lists the following problems regarding students with disabilities:

- Young people with disabilities drop out of high school at twice the rate of their peers.
- Enrollment rates of students with disabilities in higher education are still 50 percent lower than enrollment among the general population.
- Most public school educators do not feel well prepared to work with children with disabilities. In 1998, only 21 percent of public school teachers said they felt very well prepared to address the needs of students with disabilities, and another 41 percent said they felt moderately well prepared.

In addition, the Commission is particularly concerned with the classification "specific learning disabilities" whose numbers grew by 300 percent since 1976. The Commission report claims that 80 percent are classified as learning disabled because they do not know how to read. As a result, out of the total population of children with disabilities, the Commission maintains, 40 percent "are there because they weren't taught to read. The reading difficulties may not be their only area of difficulty, but it's the area that resulted in special education placement."

The Commission also worried about racial bias in special education placements particularly in the areas of mental retardation. The Commission's report contends that African American children are overrepresented among those children classified as mentally retarded and emotionally disturbed. This overrepresentation illustrates another form of second-generation segregation for children who received insufficient reading instruction.

In addressing these problems, the Commission made the unique recommendation of using federal funds designated for children with disabilities to provide parents whose children are in failing schools with vouchers that would allow them to transfer to another public school or private school. From the perspective of the Commission, vouchers would give parents greater power to control their children's educational futures. As I discuss in Chapter 6, there exists a heated debate about school voucher plans.

The Commission report reiterates the concept of equality of educational opportunity for students with disabilities and the importance of inclusion. The Commission report expresses concern about many instances of local school's segregating children with disabilities from the general population. The Commission report declares: "We affirm our commitment to the fundamental belief that children with all types of disabilities must be included to the maximum extent appropriate in their school community."

And, of course, the key to any improvement in education and the education of children with disabilities is the training of future teachers. The Commission's recommendations went beyond concerns with just the proper preparation of classroom teachers for inclusion and the education of special education teachers. The Commission called for the recruitment of candidates for teacher education with high levels of verbal ability. In addition, they suggested majoring in the subject they are planning to teach and instruction in the school curriculum they are expected to transmit.

Adequately training teachers, properly classifying students, and providing the equipment and teachers for inclusion require greater investment of local, state, and federal funds. The lack of funding continues as an ongoing problem for the education of children with disabilities. However, Chris Vogelberger's story demonstrates how the struggle for equality of educational opportunity has improved the condition of human beings. Sixty years ago, people with Down syndrome might have spent their entire lives in state institutions, cut off from the rest of society.

CONCLUSION

Unequal educational opportunities continue to plague American schools. Even though the civil rights movement was able to overturn laws requiring school segregation, second-generation segregation continues to be a problem. Differences between school districts in expenditures per student tend to increase the effects of segregation. Many Hispanic, African American, and Native American students attend schools where per-student expenditures are considerably below those of elite suburban and private schools. These reduced expenditures contribute to unequal educational opportunity that, in turn, affects a student's ability to compete in the labor market.

However, the advances resulting from the struggle for equal educational opportunity highlight the importance of political activity in improving the human condition. In and out of the classroom, teachers assume a vital role in ensuring the future of their students and society. In the areas of race, gender, and children with disabilities, there have been important improvements in education since the nineteenth century. The dynamic of social change requires an active concern about the denial of equality of opportunity and equality of educational opportunity.

Suggested Readings and Works Cited in Chapter

American Association of University Women. http://www.aauw.org. This organization plays a major role in protecting women's rights in education. The reader should check the organization's annual reports on current issues.

American Council of Education. *Gender Equity in Higher Education: 2006.* Washington, DC: American Council of Education, 2006. This is a report on gender differences in enrollment in higher education.

American Federation of Teachers. "Resolution on Inclusion Students with Disabilities." http://www.aft.org/about/resolutions/1994/inclusion.htm. This resolution describes the concerns of one of the two teachers' unions about the improper administration of inclusion programs. It also contains a description of the problems that might be encountered by administrative implementation of inclusion programs.

BALFANZ, ROBERT, and NETTIE LEGTERS. *Locating the Dropout Crisis: Which High Schools Produce the Nation's Dropouts? Where Are They Located? Who Attends Them?* Baltimore: Center for Social Organization of Schools, Johns Hopkins University, 2004. This study shows that a majority of African American and 40 percent of Hispanic students attend high schools where the majority of students do not graduate.

CAREY, KEVIN. *The Funding Gap 2004: Many States Still Shortchange Low-Income and Minority Students.* Washington, DC: Education Trust, 2004. Carey shows disparities in funding based on racial concentrations in school districts.

Commission on Excellence in Special Education. "Revitalizing Special Education for Children and Their Families, 2002." Washington, DC: Department of Education, 2002. This report of George W. Bush's commission on special education recommends the use of federal funds to support vouchers for students with disabilities.

Education Equality. Feminist Majority Foundation. http://www.feminist.org/education. This site provides links and information on the history of and current problems in achieving gender equality, including criticisms of recent political attempts to reduce the impact of Title IX on schools.

Feminist Majority Foundation. Education Equality: Threats to Title IX. Retrieved from http://www.femist.org/education/ThreatstoTitleIX.asp on 7 September 2008. This site provides a information on the continuing struggle for gender equality in the schools.

IDEA'97 Regulations. www.ideapractices.org/law/regulations/regs/SubpartA.php. These are the federal regulations issued in 1997 that regulate the education of children with disabilities.

KLUGER, RICHARD. *Simple Justice.* New York: Random House, 1975. Kluger provides a good history of *Brown v. Board of Education* and the struggle for equality.

LEE, V. E.; H. M. T.MARKS; and T. BYRD. "Sexism in Single-Sex and Coeducational Secondary School Classrooms." *Sociology of Education,* Vol. 67, no. 2 (1994): 92–120. This is an important study of sexism in single-sex classrooms.

LEMANN, NICHOLAS. *The Promised Land: The Great Black Migration and How It Changed America.* New York: Vintage Books, 1991. This is a definitive history of African American migration from the South to the urban North.

LEWIN, TAMAR. "A More Nuanced Look at Men, Women and College." *The New York Times* (12 July 2006): p. B8. http://www.nytimes.com. This review of the 2006 report by the American Council of Education shows that the gender gap in undergraduate enrollments is greater among students over 25 years old.

——. "The New Gender Divide: At Colleges, Women Are Leaving Men in the Dust." *The New York Times on the Web* (9 July 2006). http://www.nytimes.com. This important newspaper article highlights the growing disparity between female and male attainment in college.

LOPEZ, IAN F. HANEY. *White by Law: The Legal Construction of Race.* New York: New York University Press: 1996. Legal cases involved in defining the legal meaning of "white" are discussed.

LOPEZ, NANCY. *Hopeful Girls, Troubled Boys: Race and Gender Disparity in Urban Education.* New York: Routledge, 2003.

MEIER, KENNETH JOSEPH STEWART, Jr.; and ROBERT ENGLAND. *Race, Class, and Education: The Politics of Second-Generation Discrimination.* Madison: University of Wisconsin Press, 1989. This book studies the politics of second-generation segregation.

MIAO, JING, and WALT HANEY. "High School Graduation Rates: Alternative Methods and Implications." *Educational Policy Analysis Archives,* Vol. 12, no. 55 (15 October 2004). Tempe, AZ: College of Education, Arizona State University. This study concludes that there is a declining high school graduation rate among black and Hispanic students.

National Center for Education Statistics. *The Condition of Education 2008.* Washington, DC: U.S. Printing Office, 2008. This excellent annual report on the conditions of schools in the United States is an invaluable source for educational statistics ranging from test scores to school finance.

——. "Indicator 8 of Students with Disabilities in Regular Classrooms." National Center for Education Statistics. *The Condition of Education 2008.* Washington, DC: U.S. Printing Office, 2008. Data on students with disabilities in U.S. public schools is provided in this report.

National Organization for Women Foundation. http://www.nowfoundation.org. The annual reports of NOW's foundation list current educational issues involving gender equity.

"National Organization for Women's 1966 Statement of Purpose" (adopted at the Organizing Conference in Washington, DC, 29 October 1966). http://www.now.org. This historic document establishes the foundation for the participation of women in the civil rights movement.

ORFIELD, GARY. *Schools More Separate: Consequences of a Decade of Resegregation.* Cambridge: Harvard University, *The Civil Rights Project,* 2001. Details of the resegregation of American schools in the last quarter of the twentieth century are presented.

——. *The Reconstruction of Southern Education: The Schools and the 1964 Civil Rights Act.* New York: Wiley-Interscience, 1969. Orfield presents a study of the desegregation of southern schools following the passage of the 1964 Civil Rights Act.

ORFIELD, GARY, and CHUNGMEI LEE. "Racial Transformation and the Changing Nature of Segregation." Cambridge: Harvard University, *The Civil Rights Project,* 2006. This is the latest report from the Harvard Civil Rights Project on the problem of segregation in American schools.

RICHARD, ALAN. "Researchers: School Segregation Rising in South." *Education Week on the Web* (11 September 2002). http://www.edweek.org. This report discusses the rise of school segregation in the South.

RIST, RAY. *Desegregated Schools: Appraisals of an American Experiment.* New York: Academic Press, 1979. This book provides many examples of second-generation segregation.

SCHEMO, DIANA JEAN. "Report Finds Minority Ranks Rise Sharply on Campuses." *The New York Times on the Web* (23 September 2002). http://www.nytimes.com. Schemo summarizes the American Council on Education report on increased minority students on college campuses.

SCHNAIBERG, LYNN. "Chicago Flap Shows Limits of 'Inclusion,' Critics Say." *Education Week* (5 October 1994): 1, 12. This article describes parent protest about inclusion in Chicago.

SHELLEY, ALLISON. "Brave New World." *Education Week* (10 July 2002). Shelley tells the story of Down syndrome student Chris Vogelberger's inclusion in regular classes.

U.S. Census Bureau. "Current Population Survey (CPS)—Definitions and Explanations." http//www.census.gov/population/www/cps/cpsdef.html. This is a guide to the racial and other terms used in the collection of the national census.

——. "Current Population Survey 2005. Annual Social and Economic Supplement." http://www.census.gov/hhes/www/income/dinctabs.html. Data on relationship between race and income are provided.

U.S. Department of Education. "Title I—Improving the Academic Achievement of the Disadvantaged." *Federal Register,* Vol. 68, no. 236 (9 December 2003). Washington, DC: U.S. Government Printing Office, 2003. Title I outlines the regulations requiring students with disabilities to be tested under the requirements of No Child Left Behind Act of 2001.

U.S. Office of Special Education Programs. "History: Twenty-Five Years of Progress in Educating Children with Disabilities Through IDEA, 2001." www.ed.gove/offices/ osers/osep. This document provides a history of federal legislation for children with disabilities beginning with the passage of Public Law 94–142.

VIADERO, DEBRA. "VA. Hamlet at Forefront of 'Full Inclusion' Movement for Disabled." *Education Week* (18 November 1992): 1, 14. This article describes the implementation of a full-inclusion plan in a community in Virginia.

——. "NASBE Endorses 'Full Inclusion' of Disabled Students." *Education Week* (4 November 1992): 1, 30. This article discusses the report supporting full inclusion of students with disabilities. The report *Winners All: A Call for Inclusive Schools* was issued by the National Association for State Boards of Education.

——. "'Full Inclusion' of Disabled in Regular Classes Favored." *Education Week* (30 September 1992): 11. This is a report on the court case *Oberti v. Board of Education of the Borough of Clementon School District,* which involves full inclusion.

WALSH, MARK. "Judge Finds Bias in Scholarships." *Education Week* (15 February 1989): 1, 20. This article describes the court ruling that found the awarding of scholarships by using test scores to be biased against female students.

WOLF, CARMEN, et al. *Income, Poverty, and Health Insurance Coverage in the United States: 2003.* Washington, DC: U.S. Census Bureau, August 2004. The authors provide important census material on the relationship between race and income.

WOLLENBERG, CHARLES. *All Deliberate Speed: Segregation and Exclusion in California Schools, 1855–1975.* Berkeley: University of California Press, 1976. This is a good history of segregation in California. It includes a discussion of the important Court decision regarding Mexican Americans, *Mendez et al. v. Westminster School District of Orange County,* and of the segregation of Asian Americans.

CHAPTER 4

Student Diversity

This chapter focuses on the diverse cultures and languages of students attending American schools. Cultural and language conflicts in U.S. schools date back to the nineteenth century, particularly regarding Native Americans, Mexican Americans, and Asians. In the twenty-first century, there is a continuation of cultural and language issues in schools as a result of increased immigration following passage of the Immigration Act of 1965. Recent immigration patterns are part of a worldwide migration of peoples for economic and political reasons.

In exploring the issue of student diversity, I will discuss in this chapter:

- Global migration.
- The history of cultural and language conflicts in U.S. schools as represented by Mexican Americans, Asian Americans, and Native Americans.
- The effect of the 1965 Immigration Act on student diversity in U.S. schools in the twenty-first century.
- The educational experiences of immigrants in U.S. schools.
- Language issues in U.S. schools.
- Immigration and the social construction of race.

GLOBAL MIGRATION AND THE IMMIGRATION ACT OF 1965

Globalization of the labor market and the Immigration Act of 1965 are resulting in an increasingly diverse U.S. student population. This phenomenon is not limited to the United States. Most nations face multicultural educational issues as families move, searching for better economic and political conditions. With the ease of travel, there are now transnational families moving back and forth between their host countries and their countries of origin. Some ethnic-Indian families in the United States travel back frequently to India to visit relatives, and others with relatives and friends in Central and South America make similar trips. Some even maintain homes in two different countries. As a result, U.S. classrooms host transnational students, some of whom remain bilingual. There is the little girl with aunts and uncles still in India whose parents dream of eventually finding her a husband from back home. Or the Mexican boy whose family frequently takes him to Mexico where he hangs out with cousins and friends.

There is also the worldwide phenomenon of illegal immigration. Countries have a shadow population of students whose parents worry that sending their children to school might alert authorities to their illegal status. Global population movement is restricted by each country's immigration laws. Yet workers and families from Africa risk their lives crossing the Mediterranean Sea to illegally enter Spain, while thousands from many different countries face dangerous temperatures and unforgiving deserts trying to illegally enter the more prosperous United States, for example.

The greatest influx of recent immigrants into the United States resulted from the U.S. Immigration Act of 1965. In the past, restrictions were placed on the immigration of "nonwhite" populations; the use of "white" in immigration laws created many problems of interpretation for U.S. courts. Originally, the Naturalization Act of 1790, which remained in effect until 1952, restricted naturalized citizenship to "whites only." This meant that many immigrants, particularly those from Asian countries, were not allowed to receive citizenship rights; naturalized citizenship refers to those who are not born in the United States but receive citizenship after immigration by fulfilling whatever legal requirements exist.

Anti-immigration feelings were inflamed in the 1890s with the arrival in the United States of populations from Southern and Eastern Europe. Many Americans of Protestant and English ancestry objected to this wave of immigration, particularly those from Italy, Poland, and Greece who were Roman Catholic, Eastern Orthodox, or Jewish. The result was the 1924 Immigration Act, which established an annual quota limiting immigration by national origin. The quota was determined by the percentage of the total U.S. population in 1920 that was composed of each national group.

As a consequence of the 1924 Immigration Act, the depression of the 1930s, and World War II, immigration to the United States declined from the late 1920s through the early 1950s. Immigration began to increase again in the 1950s and underwent a dramatic change after passage of the 1965 Immigration Act. Before 1965, the proportion of emigrants from Europe remained approximately constant compared with those from Asia and the rest of the Americas. But after 1965, the proportion of emigrants from Europe dramatically declined and the proportion from Asia and the Americas dramatically increased.

Opening immigration to populations that had previously been discriminated against by U.S. laws raises the issue of the response of U.S. schools to non-European cultures. In the past, as illustrated by the following examples of cultural and language issues associated with Mexican American, Asian American, and Native American students, the emphasis was on deculturalization or replacing what were considered non-American cultures with an American culture and replacing the language of the home with English.

MEXICAN AMERICAN STUDENTS AND U.S. SCHOOLS

In this section, I discuss the educational experiences of Mexican Americans as the largest group in the Hispanic/Latino/Latina population. Public schools have not provided a warm haven for these students. Popular Anglo-American writers in the nineteenth century argued that the mixture of Spanish conquerors and Native Americans resulted in "wretched hybrids and mongrels [who were] in many respects actually inferior to the inferior race itself." At the time, Anglo-Americans classified Spanish as a nonwhite and inferior race. Some American leaders envisioned, as stated by representative William Brown, "the Anglo-Saxon race, like a mighty flood [spreading over] all Mexico." This flood of Anglo-Saxons, Brown hoped, would eventually cover all of Central and South America, creating republics whose "destinies will be guided by Anglo-Saxon hands."

Allowing Mexican Americans and other Hispanic Americans to become U.S. citizens was a serious issue in 1848 with the ending of the Mexican-American War and the ratification of the Treaty of Guadalupe Hidalgo. Today, few U.S. citizens are aware of the importance of this war for the territorial expansion of the United States and the disaster for Mexico in losing almost one-half of its total territory. At the war's conclusion, the United States added territory that included major parts of the future states of California, Colorado, New Mexico, Nevada, Arizona, Utah, and Texas.

The 1848 Treaty of Guadalupe Hidalgo did provide for the granting of U.S. citizenship to the former Mexican citizens who lived in the areas conquered by the United States. Despite the treaty's provisions for citizenship, citizenship rights were abridged throughout the Southwest through limitations placed on

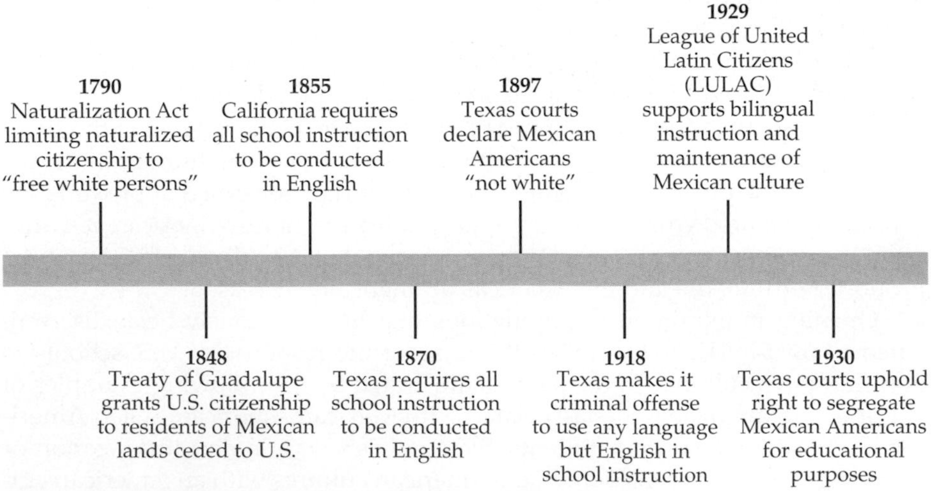

FIGURE 4–1. Key Decisions Affecting Mexican American Students in U.S. Schools

voting rights and segregation in public accommodations and schooling. Courts wrestled with the issue of racial classification. In 1897, Texas courts ruled that Mexican Americans were not white. In California, Mexican Americans were classified as Caucasian until 1930 when California's Attorney General Webb categorized them as Indians. He argued, "The greater portion of the population of Mexico are Indians." Therefore, according to the California school code, Mexican Americans were segregated based on the provision the "governing board of the school district shall have power to establish separate schools for Indian children, excepting children of Indians . . . who are the descendants of the original American Indians of the U.S." Mexican Americans were not considered "the original American Indians of the U.S."

After the conquest of Northern Mexico, state governments tried to use their school systems to replace the speaking of Spanish with English. In 1856, two years after the Texas legislature established public schools, a law was passed requiring the teaching of English as a subject. In 1870, at the height of the cowboy era, the Texas legislature passed a school law requiring English to be the language of instruction in all public schools. The same attempt to eradicate Spanish occurred in the conquered territory of California. The California Bureau of Instruction mandated in 1855 that all school classes be conducted in English. In *The Decline of the Californios: A Social History of the Spanish-Speaking California 1846–1890,* Leonard Pitt writes about the English-only requirement in public schools: "This linguistic purism went hand in hand with the nativist sentiments expressed in that year's legislature, including the suspension of the publication of state laws in Spanish."

Mexican Americans in the last half of the nineteenth century tried to escape the anti-Mexican attitudes of public school authorities by attending either Catholic schools or nonsectarian private schools. In California, some members of the Mexican community were interested in providing a bilingual education for

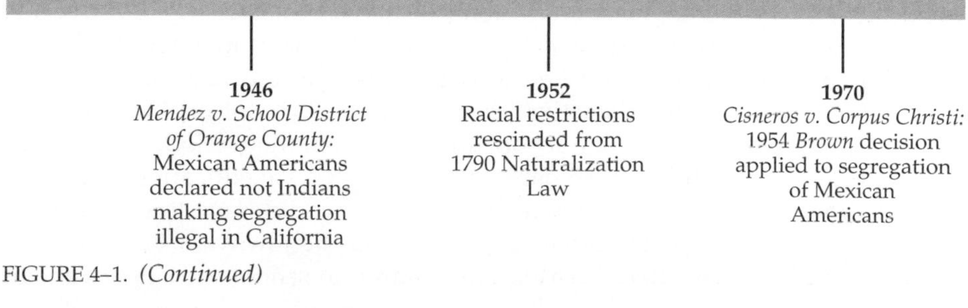

FIGURE 4–1. *(Continued)*

their children. They wanted their children to improve their ability to read and write Spanish and become acquainted with the cultural traditions of Mexico and Spain, while at the same time learning to speak English. In some places, such as Santa Barbara, California, local Mexican leaders were able to bypass the state requirement on teaching in English and were able to maintain a bilingual public school. But in most places, bilingual instruction could be had only through schools operated by the Catholic Church.

The patterns of discrimination and segregation established in the nineteenth century were accentuated during the great immigration of Mexicans into the United States in the early twentieth century. Between 1900 and 1909, a total of 23,991 Mexicans immigrated to the United States. Between 1910 and 1919 this figure increased dramatically to 173,663, and between 1920 and 1929 the number rose to 487,775.

Anglo-American attitudes about the education of the children of immigrant Mexicans involved two conflicting positions. On the one hand, farmers did not want children of their Mexican laborers to go to school because school attendance meant that they were not available for farm work. Likewise, many Mexican families were reluctant to send their children to school because of the loss of the children's contribution to the family income. On the other hand, many public officials wanted Mexican children in school so that they could be Americanized.

These conflicting positions represent the two methods by which education can be used as a method of social control. One is to deny a population the knowledge necessary to protect its political and economic rights and to economically advance in society; the other is segregation. Farmers wanted to keep Mexican laborers ignorant as a means of assuring a continued inexpensive source of labor. As one Texas farmer stated, "Educating the Mexicans is educating them away from the job, away from the dirt." Reflecting the values of the farmers in his district, one Texas school superintendent explained, "You have doubtless heard that ignorance is bliss; it seems that is so when one has to transplant onions. . . . So you see it is up to the white population to keep the Mexican on his knees in an onion patch or in new ground. This does not mix very well with education." A school principal in Colorado stated, "Never try to enforce compulsory attendance laws on the Mexicans. . . . The banks and the company will swear that the labor is needed and that the families need the money." Therefore, according to Guadalupe San Miguel, Jr., in *Let All of Them Take Heed: Mexican Americans and the Campaign for Educational Equality in Texas, 1910–1981,* one of the most discriminatory acts against the children of Mexicans was the nonenforcement of compulsory school laws. A survey of one Texas county in 1921 found only 30.7 percent of Mexican school-age children in school. In another Texas county in the 1920s, school authorities admitted that they enforced school attendance on Anglo children but not on Mexican children. San Miguel, Jr., quotes one school authority from this period: "The whites come all right except one whose parents don't appreciate education. We don't enforce the attendance on the whites because we would have to on the Mexicans." One school superintendent explained that he always asked the local school board if they wanted the Mexican children in school. Any enforcement of the compulsory education law against the wishes of the school board, he admitted, would probably cost him his job.

Those Mexican children who did attend school faced segregation and an education designed to rid them of their native language and customs. School segregation for Mexican children spread rapidly throughout Texas and California. The typical pattern was for a community with a large Mexican school population to erect a separate school for Mexican children. For instance, in 1891 the Corpus Christi, Texas, school board denied admission of Mexican children to their Anglo schools and built a separate school.

In *Chicano Education in the Era of Segregation,* Gilbert Gonzalez finds that the typical attitude in California schools was reflected in the April 1921 minutes of the Ontario, California, Board of Education: "Mr. Hill made the recommendation that the board select two new school sites; one in the southeastern part of the town for a Mexican school; the other near the Central School." Gonzalez reports that a survey conducted in the mid-1930s found that 85 percent of the districts investigated in the Southwest were segregated. In *All Deliberate Speed: Segregation and Exclusion in California Schools, 1855–1975,* Charles Wollenberg quotes a California educator writing in 1920: "One of the first demands made from a community in which there is a large Mexican population is for a separate school." A Los Angeles school official admitted that pressure from white citizens resulted in certain neighborhood schools being built to contain the majority of Mexican students.

Mexican Americans experienced many years of segregation in schools before winning a series of important legal cases. The first major case occurred in Ontario, California, in 1945, when Mexican American parents demanded that the school board grant all requests for transfer out of segregated Mexican schools. When the board refused this request, Gonzalo Mendez and William Guzman sued for violation of the Fourteenth Amendment to the Constitution. The school board responded to this suit by claiming that segregation was not based on race or national origins but on the necessity of providing special instruction. In other words, the school district justified segregation on the basis that Mexican American children required special instruction because they came from homes where Spanish was the spoken language.

In 1946, a U.S. District Court ruled in *Mendez et al. v. Westminster School District of Orange County* that the only possible argument for segregation was the special educational needs of Mexican American children. These needs involved the issue of learning English. Completely reversing the educational justification for segregation, the judge argued that "evidence clearly shows that Spanish-speaking children are retarded in learning English by lack of exposure to its use by segregation." Therefore, the court ruled segregation was illegal because it was not required by state law and because there was no valid educational justification for it.

Heartened by the *Mendez* decision, the League of United Latin American Citizens (LULAC), the Mexican American equivalent of the NAACP, forged ahead in its legal attack on segregation in Texas. With support from LULAC, a group of parents in 1948 sued the Bastrop Independent School District, charging that local school authorities had no legal right to segregate children of Mexican descent and that segregation was solely because the children were of Mexican descent. In *Delgado v. Bastrop Independent School District,* the court ruled that segregating Mexican American children was illegal and discriminatory. The ruling required that the local school district end all segregation.

Although the *Mendez* and *Delgado* decisions did hold out the promise of ending segregation of Mexican Americans, local school districts used many tactics to avoid integration, including manipulation of school district lines, choice plans, and different forms of second-generation segregation. For instance, the California State Department of Education reported in 1966 that 57 percent of the children with Spanish surnames were still attending schools that were predominantly Mexican American. In 1973, a civil rights activist, John Caughey, estimated that two-thirds of the Mexican American children in Los Angeles attended segregated schools. In *All Deliberate Speed,* Wollenberg estimates that in California by 1973 more Mexican and Mexican American children attended segregated schools than in 1947.

In Mexican American Legal Defense and Education Fund (MALDEF) case, *Cisernos v. Corpus Christi Independent School District* (1970), Mexican Americans were officially recognized by the federal courts as an identifiable group in the public schools. A central issue in the case was whether the 1954 school desegregation decision could be applied to Mexican Americans. The original *Brown* decision dealt specifically with African Americans who were segregated by state and local laws. In his final decision, Judge Owen Cox ruled that blacks and Mexican Americans were segregated in the Corpus Christi school system and that Mexican Americans were an identifiable dominated group because of their language, culture, religion, and Spanish surnames.

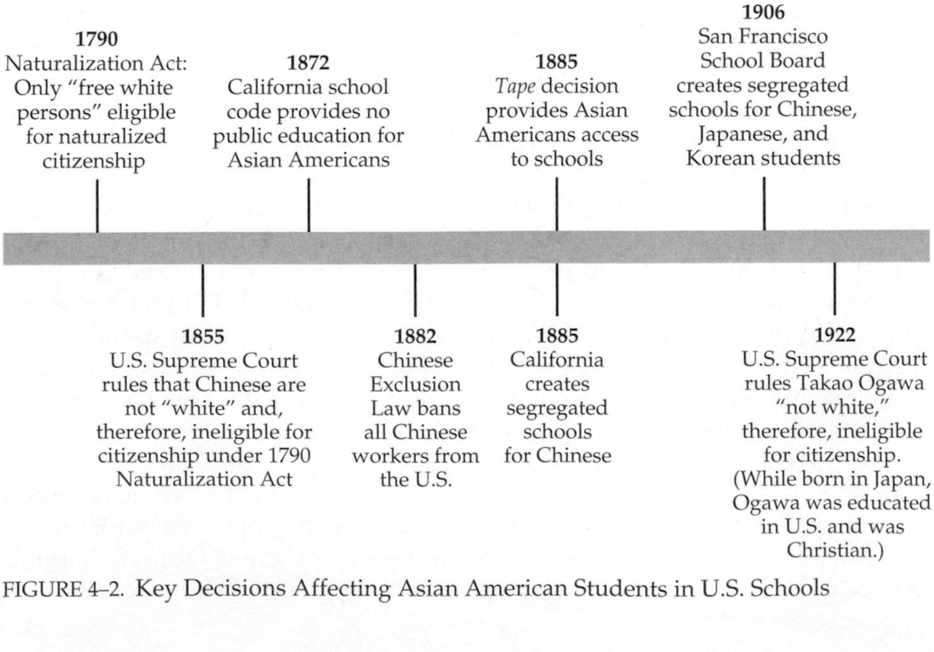

FIGURE 4–2. Key Decisions Affecting Asian American Students in U.S. Schools

Despite years of struggle, many Mexican Americans still feel their demands for equality of educational opportunity have not been met. In the fall of 1994, the Latino Education Coalition in Denver, Colorado, threatened to call a student strike if the school district did not hire more bilingual education teachers, involve Latino parents in policy decisions, and increase the number of Latino students going on to college. The threat was reminiscent of 1969, when 3,000 Latino students went on strike against the Denver school district because of high dropout rates, low academic achievement, and the district's failure to be sensitive to cultural differences. It would appear that only steady political pressure can ensure equality of educational opportunity.

ASIAN AMERICAN STUDENTS AND U.S. SCHOOLS

As with Mexican Americans, Asian Americans did not receive a warm welcome by many Anglo-American citizens. They were not eligible for citizenship because the 1790 Naturalization Law limited naturalized citizenship to "free white persons." Children born in the United States of Asian immigrant parents were U.S. citizens by birth. Figure 4–2 shows a time line of the Asian Americans' struggle in the U.S. school system.

The first Chinese immigrants arrived in California in the 1850s to join the gold rush. In search of the Golden Mountain, these first arrivals were free laborers who paid their own transportation to the gold fields of California. By 1852, there were about 20,000 Chinese immigrants in California. By the 1860s, approximately 16,000 Chinese immigrants were working in the California gold fields. But as mining profits decreased, the Chinese immigrants found themselves without enough money to return to their homeland. Searching for work,

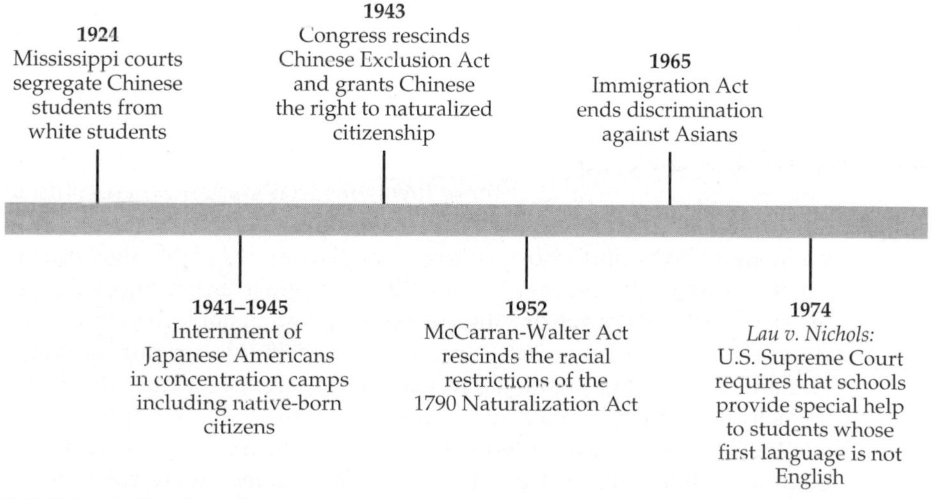

FIGURE 4–2. *(Continued)*

these Chinese immigrants were hired to build the transcontinental railroad at wages that were about one-third less than would have been paid to a white worker. In addition, Chinese workers filled low-wage jobs and built the agricultural industry in California. Racial hostility was highlighted in 1871 with the lynching of 22 Chinese men by Los Angeles mobs.

Japanese immigrated at a later date because a 1639 Japanese law forbade travel to foreign countries. Circumstances began to change in 1868 when Hawaiian planters were able to recruit 148 Japanese contract laborers and, in 1869, 100 laborers were signed up for work in the California silk industry. By 1884, the Japanese government allowed open recruitment by Hawaiian planters. Between 1885 and 1920, as many as 200,000 Japanese immigrated to Hawaii and 180,000 to the U.S. mainland. Adding to the Asian population were 8,000 Koreans who immigrated, primarily to Hawaii, between 1903 and 1920. Between 1907 and 1917, when immigration from India was restricted, 6,400 Asian Indians came to the United States. In 1907, Filipinos, who incidentally were citizens of the U.S.-captured Philippine Islands, were recruited as laborers. By 1930, there were 110,000 Filipinos settled in Hawaii and 40,000 on the mainland.

The white-only provisions of the 1790 Naturalization Law and other laws necessitated U.S. courts to deal with the racial classification of Asian Americans. In the nineteenth century, California laws simply classified as Mongolian those immigrants from northern and southern Asia, Southeast Asia, and India. Later, despite the wide-ranging cultural and language differences among these regions, European Americans used the term *Asian* in reference to immigrants and their descendants from these differing areas. Unfortunately, while *Asian American* is now commonly used in the United States, the term tends to conceal the differences between countries and peoples, such as Korea, Japan, China, Cambodia, Indonesia, and India.

Confusion over the legal status of Asians was exemplified by the 1855 case of Chan Yong. A federal district court in California ruled that under the 1790 Naturalization Act citizenship was restricted to whites only and, consequently, immigrant Chinese, such as Chan Yong, were not eligible for U.S. citizenship.

In the 1920s, laws were passed in California, Washington, Arizona, Oregon, Idaho, Nebraska, Texas, Kansas, Louisiana, Montana, New Mexico, Minnesota, and Missouri denying the right to own land to individuals who were ineligible for U.S. citizenship. The purpose of these laws was to deny land ownership to Asians.

Naturalization laws and court rulings underwent rapid change during World War II. Prior to the outbreak of hostilities against Japan, most Anglo-Americans seemed to operate from the position that all Asians were the same and that it was difficult to discern physical differences. However, during World War II, China was a U.S. ally while Japan was the enemy. Consequently, popular media, including radio, movies, newspapers, and magazines, depicted Chinese, in contrast to images presented earlier in the century, as "hardworking, brave, religious, intelligent, and practical," while Japanese were depicted as "treacherous, sly, cruel, and warlike."

As a result of wartime conditions, the ban on naturalization of Chinese was ignored and between 15,000 and 20,000 Chinese American men and women joined all branches of the military. In 1943, Congress rescinded the Chinese Exclusion Law and granted Chinese immigrants the right to become naturalized citizens but established a limited immigration quota for Chinese of only 105 each year. Naturalization rights were not extended to immigrants from India and the Philippines until 1946, with each country being given a limited quota of 100 per year.

In contrast, Japanese American citizenship status was completely ignored with the internment in concentration camps of more than 100,000 Japanese Americans during World War II. Many of these Japanese Americans were U.S. citizens because they had been born in the United States.

Why were Japanese Americans interned in concentration camps but not the descendants of other U.S. enemies, such as German and Italian Americans? Because "the Occidental eye cannot rapidly distinguish one Japanese resident from another" argued three lawyers working for the U.S. Justice Department. Adding to the demands to place Japanese citizens in concentration camps were the conclusions of the U.S. government report on the bombing of Pearl Harbor, which called the Japanese an "enemy race" and claimed that despite many generations in the United States their "racial affinities [were] not severed by migration." The report recommended the removal of all people of Japanese ancestry from coastal areas of the United States.

The citizenship issue for Asian Americans was finally resolved in 1952 when the McCarran-Walter Act rescinded the racial restrictions of the 1790 Naturalization Law. It had taken over 160 years for U.S. leaders to decide that naturalized citizenship would not be restricted to whites. The Japanese American Citizens League played an active role in eliminating the white-only provisions in immigration laws. A Japanese American Citizens League member, Harry Tagaki, commented after the passage of the McCarran-Walter Act, "The bill established our parents as the legal equal of other Americans; it gave the Japanese equality with all other immigrants, and that was a principle we had been struggling for from the very beginning."

The educational experiences of Asian Americans have paralleled their public image in the United States. By public image, I mean the representation of Asian Americans that appears in the popular press and media that is dominated by European Americans. In his study of the portrayal of Asian Americans in U.S. popular culture, Robert Lee identified five major images of Asians—"the coolie, the deviant, the yellow peril, the model minority, and the gook." As he points out, each image, including that of the model minority, has presented some threat to "the American national family."

Prior to World War II, educational discrimination and segregation resulted from images held by many European Americans of Asian Americans as coolies, the deviants, and yellow peril. The coolie image was that of the servile Asian worker who was willing to work endless hours at low wages and accept substandard living conditions; this image was considered a threat to the standard of living of the white working-class family. The deviant image was that of the Chinese opium den and Asian sexual freedom and was considered a threat to the morality of the white family. The yellow peril image was that of Asian immigrants overrunning the United States.

The image of Asians as the model minority evolved during the civil rights movement of the 1960s and 1970s. In the popular mind of European Americans, Asians were not only the model minority but also the model student. This image is strikingly different from earlier images of coolie and yellow peril. However, the model minority image was used by European Americans to criticize African Americans and Hispanics. As writer Frank Chin said in 1974 regarding the model minority image, "Whites love us because we're not black."

Ironically, the stereotype of a model minority student has caused many educators to overlook the educational problems encountered by many Asian American students in U.S. schools. Part of the problem is the tendency for non-Asians to lump all Asian Americans together. In fact, Asian Americans represent a broad spectrum of different cultures and nations including, as Valerie Ooka Pang indicates in her article "Asian American Children: A Diverse Population," "Cambodian, Chinese, East Indian, Filipino, Guamian, Hawaiian, Hmong, Indonesian, Japanese, Korean, Laotian, Samoan, and Vietnamese . . . [and] smaller Asian American groups within the category of all other Asians." According to U.S. Census classification there are 16 of these smaller Asian American groups.

Asian Americans faced many problems of educational discrimination. In *All Deliberate Speed*, Charles Wollenberg tells the story of the denial of equal educational opportunity to Asian Americans in California schools. With cries of yellow peril coming from the European American population, the state superintendent of public instruction in California, William Welcher, pointed out in 1884 that the state constitution called Chinese "dangerous to the well-being of the state" and, therefore, argued that San Francisco did not have "to undergo the expense of educating such people." Denied a public education for his daughter, Joseph Tape, an Americanized Chinese, challenged the decision in court. Judge Maguire of the municipal court ruled that since the daughter, Mamie, was an American citizen she could not be denied equal educational opportunity according to the Fourteenth Amendment to the U.S. Constitution. In addition, Judge Maguire argued that it was unjust to tax Chinese for the support of a school system that excluded Chinese children. State superintendent Welcher reacted angrily to the decision, declaring it a "terrible disaster" and asked, "Shall we abandon the education of our children to provide that of the Chinese who are thrusting themselves upon us?"

In reaction to the court decision, the California State Assembly passed legislation allowing school districts to establish segregated schools for Mongolians. This legislation empowered the San Francisco Board of Education to establish a segregated school for Asians. The courts affirmed this action in 1902, when Wong Him challenged the requirement of attending a segregated institution. Eventually, pressure from the Chinese American community brought an end to segregation. In 1921, Chinese American educator Mary Bo-Tze Lee challenged the segregation policy by showing that Chinese students scored as well as white students on IQ tests. As the Chinese population dispersed through the city, traditionally white schools were forced to open their doors to Chinese students. A study in 1947 found that formal school segregation had ended but that the original segregated Commodore Stockton school was still 100 percent Chinese.

Because Asian American students are stereotyped as model minority students, those students with educational problems are often neglected because teachers assume they will do well in school. On the other hand, many non-Asian educators resent the achievement of some Asian Americans. In 1987, *Time* called Asian Americans the "new whiz kids." *Time* reported that Asian Americans comprised 25 percent of the entering class at the University of California at Berkeley, 21 percent at the California Institute of Technology, 20 percent at the Massachusetts Institute of Technology, and 14 percent at Harvard. *Time* also reported in 1987 that because of quota systems many qualified Asian Americans were being refused admission to major universities.

The largest number of complaints centered on the admission policies of the University of California at Berkeley. *Time* quotes the cochairperson of the Asian American Task Force on University Admissions, Alameda County Superior Court Judge Ken Kawaichi, as stating that university administrators envision a campus that "is mostly white, mostly upper-class with limited numbers of African Americans, Hispanics and Asians. One day they looked around and said, 'My goodness, look at this campus. What are all these Asian people doing here?' Then they started tinkering with the system."

NATIVE AMERICAN STUDENTS AND U.S. SCHOOLS

Originally, the U.S. government attempted to destroy the languages and cultures of Native American tribes. As indicated in Figure 4–3, these policies were not reversed until the civil rights movement of the 1950s and 1960s. The initial attempt by the U.S. government to destroy the cultures and languages of Native Americans was spearheaded by Thomas McKenney, the first head of the Office of Indian Affairs. In 1819, he convinced the U.S. Congress to pass the Civilization Fund Act, which authorized the president to "employ capable persons of good moral character, to instruct them [Indians] in the mode of agriculture suited to their situation; and for teaching their children in reading, writing, and arithmetic." Reflecting on his effort to gain approval of the legislation, McKenney wrote, "I did not doubt then, nor do I now, the capacity of the Indian for the highest attainments in civilization, in the arts and religion, but I was satisfied that no adequate plan had ever been adopted for this great reformation." The Civilization Act funded Christian missionaries to educate Native Americans. Typical of missionary attitudes was Reverend James Ramsey's speech at a Choctaw school in 1846. Ramsey described his initial lecture to students and trustees in the following words: "I showed them [on a map] that the people who speak the English language, and who occupied so small a part of the world, and possessed the greatest part of its wisdom and knowledge; that knowledge they could thus see for themselves was power; and that power was to be obtained by

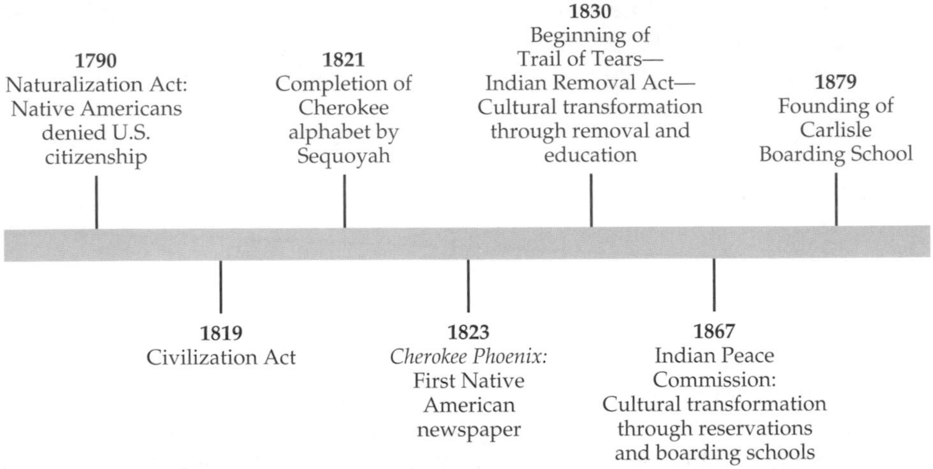

FIGURE 4–3. Key Decisions Affecting Native American Students in U.S. Schools

Christianity alone." Then he told them that the key to their success would be to continue the practice of establishing religious schools. In this way, they could share in the glory of Anglo-Saxon culture and Christianity.

In 1867, Congress created an Indian Peace Commission to deal with the warring tribes. The Peace Commission advocated using educational methods to convert Indians to Anglo-American civilization. Nathaniel Taylor, Chairman of the Peace Commission, told Crow Indians at Fort Laramie: "Upon the reservations you select, we . . . will send you teachers for your children." According to Jon Reyhner and Jeanne Eder, this promise was embodied in the Treaty of Fort Laramie with the Sioux and their allies.

The members of the Peace Commission were not entirely satisfied with the traditional attempts to educate Indians, particularly with regard to language. The Indian Peace Commission report of 1868 stated that differences in language were a major source of the continuing friction between whites and Indians; therefore, an emphasis on the teaching of English would be a major step in reducing hostilities and civilizing Native Americans. In the words of the report: "Through sameness of language is produced sameness of sentiment and thought; customs and habits are moulded [*sic*] and assimilated in the same way, and thus in process of time the differences producing trouble would have been gradually obliterated."

The first off-reservation boarding school was the Carlisle Indian School, established in Carlisle, Pennsylvania, in 1879. The founder of the school, Richard Pratt, wanted to instill the work ethic in Indian children and as he told a Baptist group, he wanted to immerse "Indians in our civilization and when we get them under [hold] them there until they are thoroughly soaked." The slogan for the Carlisle Indian School reflected the emphasis on changing the cultural patterns of Indians: "To civilize the Indian, get him into civilization. To keep him civilized, let him stay."

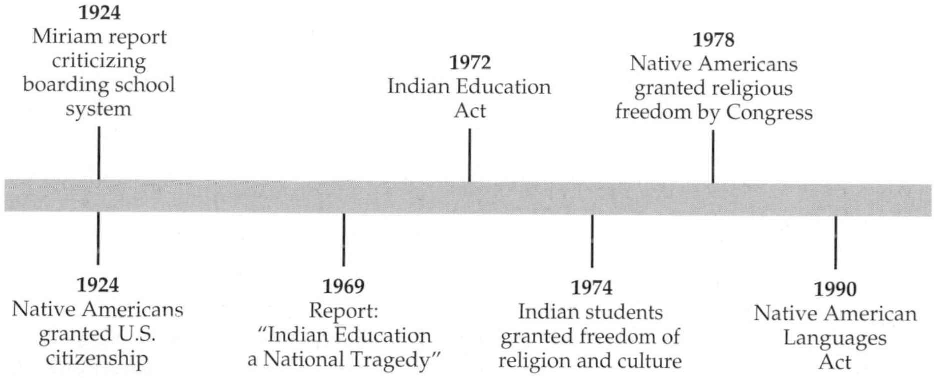

FIGURE 4–3. *(Continued)*

Pratt attacked the tribal way of life as socialistic and contrary to the values of civilization. Reflecting the values of economic individualism, Pratt complained about missionary groups who did not "advocate the disintegration of the tribes and the giving to individual Indians rights and opportunities among civilized people." He wrote to the Commissioner of Indian Affairs in 1890, "Pandering to the tribe and its socialism as most of our Government and mission plans do is the principal reason why the Indians have not advanced more and are not advancing as rapidly as they ought."

Between the founding of the Carlisle Indian School in 1879 and 1905, 25 nonreservation boarding schools were opened throughout the country. It is important to emphasize the *non*reservation location of the boarding schools because of the educational philosophy that Indian children should be removed from family and tribal influences.

Teaching English was an important issue for both nonreservation boarding schools and schools on reservations. As discussed previously, the attitude of many white educators in the latter part of the nineteenth century was that elimination of tribal languages and the learning of English would lead to the absorption and practice of white values by Indians. In the Annual Report of the Commissioner of Indian Affairs in 1887, Commissioner J.D.C. Adkins ordered the exclusive use of English at all Indian schools. Atkins pointed out that this policy was consistent with the requirement that only English be taught in public schools in territories acquired by the United States from Mexico, Spain, and Russia.

In 1889, U.S. Commissioner of Indian Affairs Thomas J. Morgan wrote a bulletin on Indian Education that outlined the goals and policies of Indian schools. The bulletin was distributed by the U.S. Bureau of Education with an introduction written by the commissioner of education, William T. Harris. In the introduction, Harris praised what he called "the new education for our American Indians," particularly the effort "to obtain control of the Indian at an early age, and to seclude him as much as possible from the tribal influences." Harris singled out the boarding school as an important step in changing the character of American Indians and argued that it was necessary to save the American

Indian, but, he wrote, "We cannot save him and his patriarchal or tribal institution both together. To save him we must take him up into our civilization."

With regard to instruction in English, Morgan stressed in the bulletin, "Only English should be allowed to be spoken, and only English-speaking teachers should be employed in schools supported wholly or in part by the Government." Also, the general principles stressed the importance of teaching allegiance to the U.S. government. As an added note, Morgan stressed the importance of bringing together the members of many different tribes in boarding schools as a means of reducing antagonisms among them.

Morgan also advocated early childhood education as a method of counteracting the influence of the Indian home. Similar to the boarding school, early childhood education would help to strip away the influences of Indian culture and language. Morgan states, "Children should be taken at as early an age as possible, before camp life has made an indelible stamp upon them."

The conditions in boarding schools lived up to Morgan's edict: "In the sweat of their faces must they eat bread." During the 1920s, a variety of investigators of Indian schools were horrified by the conditions they found. At the Rice Boarding School in Arizona, Red Cross investigators found that children were fed "bread, black coffee, and syrup for breakfast; bread and boiled potatoes for dinner; more bread and boiled potatoes for supper." In addition to a poor diet, overcrowded conditions contributed to the spread of tuberculosis and trachoma.

Using a paramilitary form of organization, boarding schools were supported by the labor of the students. As early as the fifth grade, boys and girls attended classes for half the day and worked for the other half. Children raised crops and tended farm animals to learn agricultural methods. The paramilitary organization was reflected in the constant drilling of students. The children were given little time for recreation. They were awakened at 5 A.M. and marched to the dining room, then marched back to the dormitories and classrooms. At the Albuquerque Indian School, students marched in uniforms with dummy rifles. For punishment children were flogged with ropes, and some boarding schools contained their own jails. In the 1920s, anthropologist Oliver La Farge called the Indian schools "penal institutions—where little children were sentenced to hard labor for a term of years to expiate the crime of being born of their mothers."

It was a result of the boarding schools and the long history of attempts to destroy their cultures that led Native Americans to demand control of the education of their children and restoration of their cultural heritage and languages to the curriculum. The demand for self-determination by Native Americans received consideration in government decisions after the election of John F. Kennedy in 1960. The Kennedy administration advocated Indian participation in decisions regarding federal policies. Kennedy's secretary of interior, Stewart Udall, appointed a Task Force on Indian Affairs that, in its 1961 report, recommended that Native Americans be given full citizenship and self-sufficiency.

As a result, the Rough Rock Demonstration School was created in 1966. Established on a Navajo reservation in Arizona, the school was a joint effort of the Office of Economic Opportunity and the Bureau of Indian Affairs.

One major goal of the demonstration school was for Navajo parents to control the education of their children and to participate in all aspects of their schooling. Besides tribal control, the Rough Rock Demonstration School attempted to preserve the Navajo language and culture. In contrast to the attempts to destroy Native cultures and languages that took place in the nineteenth and early twentieth centuries, the goal of learning both Navajo and English was presented for preparing children to live in both cultures.

In 1969, the U.S. Senate Committee on Labor and Public Welfare issued the report *Indian Education: A National Tragedy—A National Challenge.* The report opened with a statement condemning previous educational policies of the federal government: "A careful review of the historical literature reveals that the dominant policy of the Federal Government toward the American Indian has been one of forced assimilation . . . [because of] a desire to divest the Indian of his land." After a lengthy review of the failure of past educational policies, the report's first recommendation was for "maximum participation and control by Indians in establishing Indian education programs." In its second recommendation, the report called for maximum Indian participation in the development of educational programs in federal schools and local public schools. These educational programs were to include early childhood education, vocational education, work study, and adult literacy education.

The congressional debates resulting from the report eventually culminated in the passage of the Indian Education Act in 1972. The declared policy of the legislation was to provide financial assistance to local schools to develop programs to meet the special educational needs of Native American students. In addition, the legislation created a federal Office of Indian Education.

In 1974, the Bureau of Indian Affairs issued a set of procedures for protecting student rights and due process. In contrast to the brutal and dictatorial treatment of Indian students in the boarding schools of the late nineteenth and early twentieth centuries, each Indian student was extended the right "to make his or her own decisions where applicable." And, in striking contrast to earlier deculturalization policies, Indian students were granted "the right to freedom of religion and culture."

The most important piece of legislation supporting self-determination was the 1975 Indian Self-Determination and Education Assistance Act, which gave tribes the power to contract with the federal government to run their own education and health programs. The legislation opened with the declaration that it was "an Act to provide maximum Indian participation in the Government and education of Indian people; to provide for the full participation of Indian tribes in programs and services conducted by the federal government."

The Indian Self-Determination and Education Assistance Act strengthened Indian participation in the control of education programs. The legislation provided that a local school district receiving funds for the education of Indian students that did not have a school board composed of mostly Indians had to establish a separate local committee composed of parents of Indian students in the school. This committee was given the authority over any Indian education programs contracted with the federal government.

The principles embodied in the Indian Self-Determination and Education Assistance Act of 1975 were expanded upon in 1988 with the passage of the Tribally Controlled Schools Act. Besides the right to operate schools under a federal contract as provided in the 1975 legislation, the Tribally Controlled Schools Act provided for outright grants to tribes to support the operation of their own schools.

On 6 August 1998, President Bill Clinton issued an Executive Order for American Indian and Alaska Native Education directing a comprehensive and coordinated federal effort to improve academic performance and reduce dropout rates among Native Americans. The Executive Order emphasized that this effort would be consistent with "tribal traditions and cultures." President Clinton identified six major goals:

1. Improve reading and mathematics.
2. Increase high school completion and postsecondary attendance rates.
3. Reduce poverty and substance abuse.
4. Create strong, safe, and drug-free school environments.
5. Improve science education.
6. Expand educational technology.

FOREIGN-BORN POPULATION OF THE UNITED STATES

The post-1965 immigration entered the United States against the background of the civil rights movement. However, the largest immigration continued from Mexico. Between the late 1960s and the twenty-first century, the largest number of immigrants each year came from Mexico. In recent years, more emigrants have arrived from Asian sources, although Mexico continues to provide more than any other single country. In 1969, the order of immigrant sources to the United States was Mexico, Italy, the Philippines, Canada, and Greece. By 1973, Canada and Greece had dropped off the list, which then read Mexico, the Philippines, Cuba, Korea, and Italy. Two years later, Italy was replaced by China-Taiwan. Through the rest of the 1970s, the proportion of emigrants from Asia and the Pacific steadily increased. In 1980, the top five sources of immigrants were Mexico, Vietnam, the Philippines, Korea, and China-Taiwan. During the 1980s, the Asian population of the United States grew by 70 percent from 3.8 million in 1980 to 6.5 million in 1988. One-third of the Asian population settled in California. Asian immigrants represented many nationalities and language groups. At least 80 percent of the Asian immigrants in the 1980s came from China, Taiwan, Hong Kong, Vietnam, Cambodia, Laos, the Philippines, Japan, South Korea, and Micronesia. Most of the Asian immigrants have higher professional and educational training than earlier groups.

In 2005, the foreign-born population of the United States equaled 12 percent of the total population, or about 35.5 million people, according to the 2005 report of the U.S. Census Bureau, *American Community Survey*. Table 4–1

TABLE 4–1. Foreign-Born by World Region of Birth, 2005

World Regions	Subregions	Percentage of Foreign-Born from Region
Latin America		53.8%
Asia		26.7
Europe		13.6
Africa		3.5
Oceania		.5
Northern America		2.3

Source: Adapted from "Selected Social Characteristics in the United States: 2005," *2005 American Community Survey* (Washington, DC: U.S. Census Bureau, 2005).

indicates the world's regions from which the foreign-born originated in 2005. As indicated in Table 4–1, the majority of foreign-born citizens are from Latin America (53.8 percent) followed by Asia (26.7 percent).

Increasingly, immigrants are settling in places outside the usual gateway states like California and New York, to such regions as the Upper Midwest, New England, and the Rocky Mountain states. Rick Lyman, in a *New York Times* article on the 2005 *American Community Survey*, "Census Shows Growth of Immigrants," quotes Audrey Singer, an immigration fellow at the Brookings Institution: "What's happening now is that immigrants are showing up in many more communities all across the country than they have ever been in. So it's easy for people to look around and not just see them, but feel the impact they're having in their communities. And a lot of these are communities that are not accustomed to seeing immigrants in their schools, at the workplace, in their hospitals." For instance, the number of immigrants increased in Indiana by 34 percent; South Dakota by 44 percent; Delaware by 32 percent; Missouri by 31 percent; Colorado by 28 percent; and New Hampshire by 26 percent.

By 2005, as indicated in Table 4–2, the foreign-born population of the United States was more than 35 million people. In some urban areas, first- and second-generation immigrants outnumbered older native-born populations. For example, in New York City in the early twenty-first century, three-fifths of the population were first- and second-generation immigrants. Whereas the bulk of the immigration in the late nineteenth and early twentieth century was from Eastern and Southern Europe, the majority of the new immigrants, as indicated in Table 4–2, are from Latin America and Asia. Also, there are fewer foreign-born residents in the United States from Europe than from Latin America and Asia.

THE CHANGING POPULATION OF U.S. SCHOOLS

The changing population of the United States will result in dramatic changes in the school-age population. The meaning of majority and minority groups as legal classifications will be transformed. The majority population is often considered to be white; however, the U.S. Census Bureau projects that by

TABLE 4–2. Foreign-Born Population by Place of Birth and Citizenship Status, 2005 (in thousands [35,689 represents 35,689,000]; the term foreign-born refers to anyone who is not a U.S. citizen at birth)

Region	Foreign-Born Population (in thousands)
Total	**35,689**
Latin America	19,019
Caribbean	3,144
Central America	13,444
Mexico	10,970
Other Central America	2,474
South America	2,431
Asia	9,534
Europe	4,870
Africa	1,252
Other	1,014

Source: Adapted from U.S. Census Bureau, 2005 American Community Survey; C05006. Place of Birth for the Foreign-Born Population; and B05007, Place of Birth by Year of Entry by Citizenship Status for The Foreign-Born Population, using American FactFinder®; http://factfinder.census.gov (accessed 16 May 2008).

the year 2040 the majority of school-age children will be members of minority groups. The 2000 report of the U.S. Census Bureau projected population changes that would have the following impact on the school-age population of the United States:

I. The percentage of the school-age population that is white non-Hispanic will decrease.
   A. In 2000—65 percent.
   B. In 2020—56 percent.
   C. In 2040—less than 50 percent.
II. The Hispanic school-age population will increase.
   A. Between 2000 and 2020—60 percent increase.
   B. By 2025—nearly 25 percent of the school-age population will be Hispanic.
III. The percentage of the school-age population that is Asian and Pacific Islander will increase.
   A. In 2000—4 percent.
   B. In 2025—6.6 percent.
IV. The percentage of school-age children who are black or Native American will remain stable.

Table 4–3 provides data from the *Condition of Education 2008* on the racial and ethnic distribution of U. S. public school students. The largest percentages of Hispanic and Asian students are in the West: 36.9 percent and 7.1 percent, respectively. The second largest percentage of Hispanic students is in the South (18.8 percent), while the second largest percentage of Asian students is in the

TABLE 4–3. Percentage Distribution of the Race/Ethnicity of Public School Students Enrolled in Kindergarten Through 12th Grade, by Region, 2006

Race/Ethnicity	Region	Percentage
White	Northeast	63.8%
Black	Northeast	14.7
Hispanic	Northeast	15.3
Asian	Northeast	4.4
White	Midwest	73.4
Black	Midwest	13.2
Hispanic	Midwest	7.7
Asian	Midwest	2.6
White	South	51.5
Black	South	24.5
Hispanic	South	18.8
Asian	South	1.9
White	West	45.2
Black	West	5.1
Hispanic	West	36.9
Asian	West	7.1

Source: National Center for Education Statistics, *The Condition of Education 2000* (Washington, DC: U.S. Printing Office, 2008), pp. 86–87.

Northeast (4.4 percent). The largest percentage of white students is in the Midwest (73.4 percent), and the smallest percentage is in the South (51.5 percent). The largest percentage of black students is in the South (24.5 percent).

EDUCATIONAL EXPERIENCES OF IMMIGRANTS TO THE UNITED STATES

Immigrant groups arrive with a variety of educational backgrounds. For instance, studies of Chinese immigrants in New York City found a vast range of educational achievement. Those living in Chinatown arrived with primarily working-class backgrounds and limited exposure to formal learning. One study found that roughly 85 percent of Chinatown residents in New York, Boston, and San Francisco had not attended secondary school. The children of these immigrants often struggle in school because of language problems. On the other hand, many wealthy and well-educated Chinese immigrants, who in New York tend to live outside Chinatown, often send their children to elite universities. The educational level of immigrants reflects their social-class backgrounds. In the case of the Chinese, some come from peasant backgrounds with little access to higher education; on the other hand, some come from professional classes and are engineers and college teachers. Therefore, the educational needs of immigrants must be assessed according to their social and educational backgrounds. These backgrounds vary widely within each immigrant group and between immigrant groups. For the purposes of this discussion, I am going to focus on variations among Asian-Pacific immigrants; however, similar differences will exist among immigrants from other areas, particularly countries of the Commonwealth of Independent States.

Tables 4–4 and 4–5 indicate variations in educational attainment among foreign-born Americans. In general, the educational attainment of foreign-born Americans is less than that of native-born Americans. For instance, 40 percent of foreign-born Americans are high school graduates as compared with 60.3 percent of native-born Americans. However, these percentages should be considered according to origins of the foreign-born. As indicated in Table 4–5, Americans who were born in Europe or Asia have high school graduation rates about the same as those of native-born Americans (native, 87.5 percent; Europe, 84.9 percent; and Asia, 87.4 percent). Americans born in South America or the Caribbean have slightly lower high school graduation rates (79.3 percent and 68.6 percent, respectively). The lowest high school graduation rate is for Americans from Central America (37.7 percent). The high school graduation rate for those born in Central America is a reflection of the lack of educational opportunities in that area. Consequently, American public schools must often compensate for the limited availability of education in Central American countries.

TABLE 4–4. Population by Educational Attainment and Nativity, 2003 (as a percent of each population aged 25 and over)

Educational Attainment	Native	Foreign-Born
Less than 9th grade	4.1%	21.5%
9th to 12th grade (no diploma)	8.4	11.3
High school graduate or some college	60.3	40.0
Bachelor's degree or more	27.2	27.3

Source: U.S. Census Bureau, *The Foreign-Born Population in the United States: 2003* (Washington, DC: U.S. Printing Office, 2004), p. 5.

TABLE 4–5. Foreign-Born Population with High School Education, 2003 (aged 25 and over by world region)

World Regions	Subregions	Percentage of Foreign-Born over 25 Years of Age with High School Education
Europe		84.9%
Asia		87.4
Latin America		49.1
	Caribbean	68.6
	Central America	37.7
	South America	79.3
Other Regions		83.5

Source: Adapted from "Figure 8," U.S. Census Bureau, *The Foreign-Born Population in the United States: 2003* (Washington, DC: U.S. Census Bureau, 2004), p. 5.

The Pew Hispanic Center Report "The Improving Educational Profile of Latino Immigrants" found that the educational profile of foreign-born Latinos is improving because many are receiving an education in the United States and the quality of education in their countries of origin is improving. The report concludes: "Levels of educational achievement have improved in sending countries, and those who choose to migrate to the United States are better educated than those who stay behind." However, there remains a crisis in the education of Latino immigrants. The Pew Hispanic Center reports, "Typically, Mexican and Central American immigrants are less educated than those from the Caribbean and South America. Immigrants from Mexico and Central America are less likely to have completed either secondary education or post-secondary education than are other Latino immigrants."

The low level of educational attainment of Latino immigrants is reflected in the numbers living in poverty as indicated in Table 4–6. The highest percentage of foreign-born living in poverty are from Central America (23.6 percent), while the lowest are from Europe (8.7 percent) and Asia (11.1 percent). Certainly, this situation would be helped if the United States worked to strengthen the economies and educational systems in Central America.

LANGUAGES OF SCHOOL-AGE CHILDREN

The National Center for Education Statistics' *The Condition of Education 2008* provides a profile of language minority students in U.S. schools. Many of these students spoke English with difficulty. Judicial rulings require that schools provide special help for students with the limited English ability. As I discuss in more detail in Chapter 10, the 1974 U.S. Supreme Court decision *Lau et al. v. Nichols et al.* dealt with the refusal of the San Francisco school district to provide special help in learning English to Chinese immigrant children with limited English ability. The Court ruled that for limited-English-speaking students, schools

TABLE 4–6. People Living Below the Poverty Level by Nativity and by World Region of Birth, 2002 (in percent)

Nativity and World Region	Percentage Living Below the Poverty Level
Native	11.5%
Foreign-born	16.6
Europe	8.7
Asia	11.1
Caribbean	18.9
Central America	23.6
South America	14.5
Other regions	14.1

Source: U.S. Census Bureau, *The Foreign-Born Population in the United States: 2003* (Washington, DC: U.S. Printing Office, 2004), p. 7.

must provide aid in learning in English so that they could participate in learning in English-speaking classrooms. The Court did not specify which educational methods should be used in helping students with limited English abilities.

As indicated in Table 4–7, between 1979 and 2006, the number of school-age children (children ages 5 to 17) who spoke a language other than English at home increased from approximately 9 to 20 percent. The percentage of 5- to 17-year-old children who spoke English with difficulty increased from approximately 3 to 5 percent from 1979 to 2006.

In 2006, about 72 percent (7.8 million) of the school-age children who spoke a language other than English at home spoke Spanish followed by Indo-European (1.4 million) and Asian/Pacific (1.2 million). The National Center for Education Statistics defines Indo-European languages: "An Indo-European language other than Spanish (e.g., French, German, Portuguese, etc.)." Asian/Pacific Islander languages are defined as: "Any native language spoken by Asians or Pacific Islanders, which linguists classify variously as Sino-Tibetan, Austroasiatic, or Austronesian languages."

Table 4–8 indicates that higher percentages of children who spoke Spanish or an Asian–Pacific Islander language at home spoke English with difficulty (26.6 and 27.8 percent, respectively) than did those who spoke other Indo-European languages (19.3 percent) or other languages (18.1 percent) at home.

Are English-language learners (ELLs) being taught in segregated schools? A 2008 study "The Role of Schools in the English Language Learner Achievement Gap," released by the Pew Hispanic Center concluded that, according to *Education Week* reporter Mary Ann Zehr, "Schools that report low achievement for English-language learners also report low test scores for white and African-American students, and share characteristics associated with poor performance on standardized tests." The report found English-language learners in schools with large class sizes and high levels of students receiving free and reduced-priced lunches (indicating students from families with low incomes). The study also found that when students are not isolated in low-achieving schools they have higher test scores.

TABLE 4–7. Number and Percentage of Children Ages 5 to 17 Who Spoke a Language Other Than English at Home and Who Spoke English with Difficulty: selected years, 1979–2006

Year	Percentage of 5- to 17-Year-Olds Who Spoke a Language Other Than English at Home	Percentage of 5- to 17-Year-Olds Who Spoke English with Difficulty
1979	8.5%	2.8%
1999	16.7	5.0
2003	18.7	5.5
2006	20.3	5.2

Source: Adapted from National Center for Education Statistics, *The Condition of Education 2008* (Washington, DC: U.S. Printing Office, 2008), p. 91.

TABLE 4–8. Percentage of Children Ages 5 to 17 Who Spoke a Language Other Than English at Home and Spoke English with Difficulty, 2006

Language Spoken at Home	Percent of Total Population That Spoke a Language Other Than English at Home and Spoke English with Difficulty	Percent of Population Ages 5 to 9 That Spoke a Language Other Than English at Home and Spoke English with Difficulty	Percent of Population Ages 10 to 17 That Spoke a Language Other Than English at Home and Spoke English with difficulty
Spanish	26.6%	35.4%	21.1%
Other Indo-European	19.3	23.6	16.9
Asian/Pacific Islander	27.8	36.2	22.9
Other	18.1	21.3	15.9

Source: Adapted from National Center for Education Statistics, *The Condition of Education 2008* (Washington, DC: U.S. Printing Office, 2008), p. 92.

Zehr reports that English-learners who attend schools with even a small number of white students have higher math-test scores than do ELLs who are almost entirely isolated from such white students. And black students and white students who attend schools with even a small number of English-learners do worse on standardized math tests than black and white students who are almost entirely isolated from ELL students.

The findings of the Pew Hispanic Center report, authored by Richard Fry, highlights the importance of economic desegregation of American schools. Even English-learners are affected by the divisions between the rich and poor in American schools.

ARE U.S. TEACHERS PREPARED FOR LANGUAGE DIVERSITY?

A major problem for schools is finding teachers who are trained to teach students who have limited English proficiency (LEP). As indicated in Table 4–9, nationally only 29.5 percent of teachers of LEP students have LEP training. This figure varies between regions: in the West 47.3 percent of teachers of LEP students have training in LEP, while only 11.6 percent of teachers in the Midwest have this training. According to the National Center for Education Statistics, "When children with little or no previous exposure to the English language enter the public schools, they are often unable to profit fully from English-language-based instruction. Exceptionally high dropout rates have been reported for these students."

Another problem is the potential cultural clash between a predominantly white teaching staff and a student body with high percentages of cultural minorities. This problem is reflected in Table 4–10. While 84 percent of public school teachers are white, only 61.2 percent of students are white. While only

TABLE 4–9. Percentage of Public School Teachers with LEP Training and with LEP Students in Their Classes, by Region, 1993–1994

Region	Percentage of Teachers
Northeast	21.5%
Midwest	11.6
South	29.0
West	47.3
National	29.5

Source: National Center for Education Statistics, *Are Limited English Proficient (LEP) Students Being Taught by Teachers with LEP Training?* (December 1996), http://www.ed.gov/NCES.

TABLE 4–10. Enrollment and Teacher Characteristics in U.S. Public Elementary and Secondary Schools, Fall 2000

	Percent Distribution of Students	Percent Distribution of Teachers
White	61.2%	84%
Black	17.2	7
Hispanic	16.3	5
Asian or Pacific Islander	4.1	1
American Indian/Alaskan Native	1.2	.8

Source: National Center for Education Statistics, *Digest of Education Statistics 2002*, Tables 16 and 42, http://www.ed.gov/NCES.

7 percent of teachers are black, 17.2 percent of the students are black. As the Asian immigration increases with 4.1 percent of the student population classified as Asian or Pacific Islander, only 1 percent of the teachers are Asian or Pacific Islander. The "whiteness" of the teaching force might ensure the domination of Eurocentric culture in public schools.

IMMIGRATION AND THE SOCIAL CONSTRUCTION OF RACIAL IDENTITY

With the new immigration came a greater diversity of concepts of racial identity. These multiple concepts of racial identity demonstrate how racial concepts are socially constructed in contrast to legal or administrative definitions of race. In the 2008 book *Inheriting the City: The Children of Immigrants Come of Age*, the authors conducted a survey of racial concepts in New York City.

First- and second-generation immigrants when asked their race used a variety of descriptors, including nationality, ethnicity, culture, and language. In other words, racial identity varied among new immigrant groups. There were also variations of the concept of race within each immigrant group. In contrast, more than 90 percent of native-born African Americans and whites express a clear racial identity as black or white. The range of racial identifiers among other groups, even among nonimmigrants groups such as Puerto Ricans, is amazing and highlights variations in the social meaning of race. The majority of Puerto Ricans identify their race in either ethnic or group concepts. For instance, 30.4 percent of Puerto Ricans gave their racial identity as Puerto Rican and 26 percent as Hispanic. Other racial identities among Puerto Ricans include white, black, American, indigenous Indian, human, Latin American, Latino, mixed, and Spanish.

First- and second-generation immigrants provide a similar range of racial concepts. For instance, 95 percent of first- and second-generation Chinese immigrants gave their race as Chinese, while others gave their racial identity as American, Asian, or don't know. Some Chinese identified their race according to country of origin—there are many Chinese communities around the world—such as Vietnamese, Burmese, and Malay. In these countries, they are considered ethnic Chinese. The largest range of racial identifiers are among first- and second-generation immigrants from the Dominican Republic and South America. Among Dominicans racial identifiers include white, black, Indian, American, Dominican, Hispanic, human, Latin American, Latino, mixed, Spanish, and West Indian. Some people state that they don't know their race. For South Americans, the range was even greater and includes countries from which people originally immigrate to South America such as Japan. South Americans identified their race as white, black, Indian, Japanese, American, Asian, Colombian, Ecuadoran, Hispanic, human, Latin American, Latino, South American, and Spanish.

The variety of responses from first- and second-generation immigrants regarding race indicates the changing character of racial concepts since earlier in American history when they were defined by American law and judicial rulings. The only ones who continue to think in former legal and judicial racial concepts are native-born African Americans and whites. Table 4–11 provides a short summary of the racial identities of first- and second-generation immigrants in New York City (a more complete table of racial identities can be found in *Inheriting the City: The Children of Immigrants Come of Age.* Are U.S. citizens in transition to a society where concepts of race are less important in determining social status? One indication of this possibility are those people who give their racial identity as human.

Recognition that the term *race* is a socially constructed concept, the U.S. Census Bureau rejects any scientific or anthropological definition of race. In fact, it states that racial categories are determined by sociopolitical circumstances. It is important to note in the following statement accompanying the *2006 American Community Survey* both the recognition of the social construction of race and also that the determination of a person's race is through self-identification.

TABLE 4–11. What Does "Race" Mean? Varieties of Racial Identities Among Native and Immigrant Groups Percentage Response

Race Given	Native Black	Native White	West Indian	South American	Chinese
White		95.9%	0.2%	19.5%	0.5%
Black	99.5%	0.2	92.9	3.7	
Native American	0.2				
Chinese			0.2		95.0
Indian				0.2	
Japanese				0.2	
Vietnamese					0.2
American		1.0		3.2	0.2
Asian				0.2	3.3
Burmese					0.2
Colombian				5.2	
Dominican					
Ecuadoran				4.7	
Hispanic		0.2	0.5	36.9	
Human			0.2	0.5	0.2
Indigenous Indian				1.0	
Latin American				1.7	
Latino		0.2	0.2	4.7	
Mixed	0.2		0.5		
Peruvian				2.0	
Puerto Rican				0.7	
South American				0.5	
Spanish				5.0	
West Indian			3.9		
Malay					0.2
Other race		0.2	0.2	0.5	
Don't know		0.5	0.7	8.5	0.3
Refused to answer		1.7	0.2	0.5	

Source: Adapted from Table 3.1, "Racial Identification by Group," in Philip Kasinitz, John Mollenkopf, Mary C. Waters, and Jennifer Holdaway, *Inheriting the City: The Children of Immigrants Come of Age* (Cambridge: Harvard University Press, 2008), p. 71.

> The concept of race, as used by the Census Bureau, reflects self-identification by people according to the race or races with which they most closely identify. *These categories are socio-political constructs and should not be interpreted as being scientific or anthropological in nature. Furthermore, the race categories include both racial and national-origin groups* [author's emphasis].

Why, given its troubles in defining the concept, does the U.S. Census Bureau use these racial classifications? The answer, as it has been throughout the history of the United States, is a requirement of U.S. government policies. After admitting that race is a sociopolitical construct, the U.S. Census Bureau's 2006 Subject Definitions states:

> The racial classifications used by the Census Bureau adhere to the October 30, 1997, Federal Register Notice entitled, *"Revisions to the Standards for the Classification of Federal Data on Race and Ethnicity,"* issued by the Office of Management and Budget (OMB). These standards govern the categories used to collect and present federal data on race and ethnicity. The OMB requires five minimum categories (White, Black or African American, American Indian or Alaska Native, Asian, and Native Hawaiian or Other Pacific Islander) for race. The race categories are described below with a sixth category, "Some other race," added with OMB approval. In addition to the five race groups, the OMB also states that respondents should be offered the option of selecting one or more races.

Therefore, it is an administrative fiat of the Office of Management and Budget that requires reporting in the five racial classifications used in Table 4–11. Again, it is important to note that race is selected by the person being surveyed. Of course this raises the question of whether or not the person being surveyed knows what the Office of Management and Budget means by "White," "Black or African American," "American Indian or Alaska Native," "Asian," and "Native Hawaiian or Other Pacific Islander." The official definitions of race given by the Office of Management and Budget and the U.S. Census Bureau reflect a national origins definition of race rather than an anthropological or scientific definition. Like many of the respondents on racial identification in Table 4–11, race is considered in terms of national or regional origins. The following are the official definitions of racial categories:

> **White**—A person having origins in any of the original peoples of Europe, the Middle East, or North Africa. It includes people who indicate their race as "White" or report entries such as Irish, German, Italian, Lebanese, Near Easterner, Arab, or Polish.
> **Black or African American**—A person having origins in any of the Black racial groups of Africa. It includes people who indicate their race as "Black or African American," or provide written entries such as African American, Afro-American, Kenyan, Nigerian, or Haitian.
> **American Indian or Alaska Native**—A person having origins in any of the original peoples of North and South America (including Central America) and who maintain tribal affiliation or community attachment.
> **Asian**—A person having origins in any of the original peoples of the Far East, Southeast Asia, or the Indian subcontinent including, for example, Cambodia, China, India, Japan, Korea, Malaysia, Pakistan, the Philippine Islands, Thailand, and Vietnam. It includes "Asian Indian," "Chinese," "Filipino," "Korean," "Japanese," "Vietnamese," and "Other Asian."
> **Native Hawaiian or Other Pacific Islander**—A person having origins in any of the original peoples of Hawaii, Guam, Samoa, or other Pacific Islands.
> **Some Other Race**—Includes all other responses not included in the "White," "Black or African American," "American Indian or Alaska Native," "Asian," and "Native Hawaiian or Other Pacific Islander" race categories described above.
> **Two or More Races**—For data product purposes, "Two or More Races" refers to combinations of two or more of the following race categories:
> 1. White
> 2. Black or African American

3. American Indian and Alaska Native
4. Asian
5. Native Hawaiian and Other Pacific Islander
6. Some other race

The Office of Management and Budget and the U.S. Census Bureau provides 57 possible combinations for the category "Two or More Races" ranging from "1. White; Black or African American" to "57. White; Black or African American; American Indian and Alaska Native; Asian; Native Hawaiian and Other Pacific Islander; Some other race."

An analysis of these official definitions highlight the lack of a clear definition of race. For instance, the preceding definitions provided for "White" and "Black or African American" are regional with whites having ancestral origins in Europe, the Middle East, or North Africa and blacks having "origins in any of the Black racial groups of Africa." Even here there is some confusion because there are black-skinned groups in North Africa who might or might not under these definitions identify as white. Also, the Office of Management and Budget uses the term "racial groups" without providing a definition.

The "American Indian or Alaska Native" is even more confusing. I believe that many people in the United States associate the term "American Indian" to indigenous people living within the nation. The Canadian term for indigenous peoples living within its country's borders is First Nations. However, the Bureau of Management and Budget and the U.S. Census Bureau define American Indian as "A person having origins in any of the original peoples of North and South America (including Central America) and who maintain tribal affiliation or community attachment."

This broad definition of American Indian becomes confusing when considering the U.S. Census's category "Hispanic or Latino origin (of any race)." Imagine that you are an indigenous person from Central or South American—many people from these regions have indigenous ancestry—and you are asked your race. According to the preceding definition you might respond American Indian. However, you might be tempted to respond Hispanic or Latino since the U.S. Census Bureau states that these terms can reflect "heritage, nationality group, lineage, or country of birth of the person or the person's parents or ancestors before their arrival in the United States. People who identify their origin as Spanish, Hispanic, or Latino may be of *any race* [author's emphasis]."

The broad regional sweep of the term "Asian" as a racial category renders it somewhat meaningless. In what ways are the peoples of China and India related? Certainly not by culture and religion. For instance, Singapore with its mixed population uses racial categories that distinguish between Indians and Chinese. In fact, the term *Asian American* brings together populations that are distinctly different in languages and cultures.

Current differences in racial identity among first- and second-generation immigrant children and youth and the difficulties faced by the federal government in defining race highlight the possible movement of U.S. society to a post-racial society. Concepts of race may be disappearing to be replaced by terms such as national origin, culture, or language group.

CONCLUSION

The diversity of the student population raises important questions regarding culture and language. The history of Mexican American, Asian American, and Native American schooling highlights serious issues regarding the responsibility of the schools to preserve language and cultural traditions. Consider the following set of questions:

- Should public schools consciously attempt to eradicate the language of non-English-speaking students in a manner similar to that used with Mexican American and Native American students?
- Should public schools attempt to preserve the home language of non-English-speaking students?
- Should the public schools consciously attempt to change or Americanize the culture of immigrant students?
- Should public schools preserve the cultures of immigrant, Native American, and Mexican American students?

Suggested Readings and Works Cited in Chapter

Advisory Board for the President's Initiative on Race. *One America in the 21st. Century. Forging a New Future.* Washington, DC: U.S. Printing Office, 1998. This report predicted future of race relations in the 21st century. It is a government projection on the composition of U.S. population in the 21st century.

CHIN, FRANK, et al., eds. *Aiiieeeee! An Anthology of Asian-American Writers.* Washington, DC: Howard University Press, 1974. In this anthology, Chin criticizes the idea of Asian Americans being viewed as the model Americans.

COLEMAN, MICHAEL C. *Presbyterian Attitudes toward American Indians, 1837–1893.* Jackson: University of Mississippi Press, 1985. This is a good history of missionary attempts to change Native American cultures.

Committee on Labor and Public Welfare, U.S. Senate 91st Congress, 1st Session. *Indian Education: A National Tragedy–A National Challenge.* Washington, DC: U.S. Government Printing Office, 1969. This is the report that set the stage for recent efforts in Indian education.

DONATO, RUBEN. *The Other Struggle for Equal Schools: Mexican Americans during the Civil Rights Era.* Albany: State University of New York, 1997. This is the best study of the Mexican American civil rights movement and its impact on education.

FLORES, JUAN and GEORGE YUDICE. *Living Borders/Buscando America: Languages of Latino Self-Formation, Latinos and Education,* edited by Antonia Darder, Rodolfo D. Torres, and Henry Gutierrez. New York: Routledge, 1997. Deals with language issues among Latinos.

FOX, GEOFFREY. *Hispanic Nation: Culture, Politics, and the Constructing of Identity.* Tucson: University of Arizona Press, 1996. I relied on this book for my discussion of the meaning of *Hispanic* and *Latino/Latina.*

FRY, RICHARD. *The Role of Schools in the English Language Learner Achievement Gap.* Washington, DC: Pew Hispanic Center, 2008. Study demonstrates the effect on English-learners of attending overcrowded schools serving low-income families.

GONZALEZ, GILBERT. *Chicano Education in the Era of Segregation.* Philadelphia: Balch Institute Press, 1990. This is a history of when Chicanos were segregated in U.S. schools.

GONZALES, MANUEL. *Mexicanos: A History of Mexicans in the United States.* Bloomington: Indiana University Press, 1999. Gonzales provides a good introductory history of Mexican Americans.

LEE, ROBERT G. *Orientals: Asian Americans in Popular Culture.* Philadelphia: Temple University Press, 1999. This is an important study of the popular image of Asian Americans in the United States.

LOW, VICTOR. *The Unimpressible Race: A Century of Educational Struggle by the Chinese in San Francisco.* San Francisco: East/West Publishing, 1982. This is the book to read to understand racism and segregation of Chinese in California.

LOWELL, B. LINDSAY, and ROBERTO SURO. *The Improving Educational Profile of Latino Immigrants.* Washington, DC: Pew Hispanic Center Report, 2002. This report contains statistics on the educational attainment of Latino immigrants to the United States and finds levels of educational attainment to be increasing.

LYMAN, RICK. "Census Shows Growth of Immigrants." *The New York Times on the Web* (15 August 2006). http://www.nytimes.com. This article discusses implications of immigration findings of the *2005 American Community Survey.*

NAKANISHI, DON T., and TINA YAMANO NISHIDA, eds. *The Asian American Educational Experience.* New York: Routledge, 1995. This is an excellent collection of articles on Asian American education.

National Center for Education Statistics. *The Condition of Education 2008.* Washington, DC: U.S. Printing Office, 2008. This excellent annual report on the conditions of schools in the United States provides data on the racial/ethnic distribution of students in U.S. schools.

——. "Are Limited English Proficient (LEP) Students Being Taught by Teachers with LEP Training?" (December 1996). http://www.ed.gov/NCES. The lack of training for U.S. teachers to educate LEP students is brought to light.

PANG, VALERIE OOKA. "Asian American Children: A Diverse Population." *The Educational Forum* (Fall 1990): 49–66. This is a good discussion of diversity in the Asian American population in the United States.

PHILIP, JOHN MOLLENKOPF; MARY C. WATERS; and JENNIFER HOLDAWAY. *Inheriting the City: The Children of Immigrants Come of Age.* Cambridge: Harvard University Press, 2008. A study of immigrant youth in New York City.

PITT, LEONARD, and RAMON GUTIERREZ. *The Decline of the Californios: A Social History of Spanish-Speaking Californios, 1846–1890.* Berkeley: University of California Press, 1999. This is an important history of the resident population of California when the United States took the area from Mexico.

PRUCHA, FRANCIS PAUL. *Documents of United States Indian Policy.* Lincoln: University of Nebraska Press, 1990. This volume contains reprints of all the important laws, court cases, and reports affecting Indian education.

REYHNER, JON, and JEANNE EDER. *A History of Indian Education.* Billings: Eastern Montana College, 1989. The authors provide a short introduction to the history of Indian education.

SAN MIGUEL, GUADALUPE, JR. *"Let All of Them Take Heed": Mexican Americans and the Campaign for Educational Equality in Texas, 1910–1981.* Austin: University of Texas Press, 1987. This is a good history of the events and court cases surrounding efforts by Mexican Americans to end segregation.

SZASZ, MARGARET. *Education and the American Indian: The Road to Self-Determination, 1928–1973.* Albuquerque: University of New Mexico Press, 1974. Szasz provides a good history of the revolution in Native American education in the twentieth century.

TAKAKI, RONALD. *A Different Mirror: A History of Multicultural America.* Boston: Little, Brown and Company, 1993. This is the single-best history of multiculturalism in the United States.

——. *Strangers from a Different Shore: A History of Asian Americans.* New York: Penguin Books, 1989. Takaki writes an excellent history of Asian Americans.

U.S. Census Bureau. *American Community Survey, Puerto Rico Community Survey: 2006 Subject Definitions.* Washington, DC: U.S. Census Bureau, 2006. Definitions and problems associated with racial categories used by the Census Bureau.

——. "Population Estimates." http://www.census.gov. Population projections into the next century are listed.

——. "Selected Social Characteristics in the United States: 2005," *2005 American Community Survey.* Washington, DC: U.S. Census Bureau, 2005. This census survey contains statistics on foreign-born peoples and language spoken in the home.

——. "2005 American Community Survey; C05006. Place of Birth for the Foreign-Born Population; and B05007, Place of Birth by Year of Entry by Citizenship Status for the Foreign-Born Population, using American FactFinder." http://factfinder.census.gov (accessed: 16, May 2008). Provides data on countries of origin of immigrants to the United States.

WEINBERG, MEYER. *Asian American Education: Historical Background and Current Realities.* Mahwah, NJ. Lawrence Erlbaum Associates, Inc., 1997. Weinberg presents an excellent history of the Asian American educational experience in the United States.

WOLLENBERG, CHARLES M. *All Deliberate Speed: Segregation and Exclusion in California Schools, 1855–1975.* Berkeley: University of California Press, 1976. This is a landmark study of segregation in the education of Asian Americans, Mexican Americans, and Native Americans in California.

ZEHR, MARY ANN. "The Role of Schools in the English Language Learner Achievement Gap." *Education Week on the Web* (26 June 2008). Report on the Pew Hispanic Center study, which found that English-learners are negatively affected by attending overcrowded schools serving low-income families.

CHAPTER 5

Multicultural and Multilingual Education

This chapter will discuss issues in multicultural and multilingual education. As discussed in Chapter 4, there is a currently a global migration of peoples, which has raised issues in national school systems regarding multicultural and multilingual student populations. Most nations of the world face the issue of multicultural education because of the global movement of populations caused by the growth of an international labor market, multinational corporations, the search for better economic and political conditions, and displacement by war. As the host country of the largest number of global migrants, Americans have engaged in a broad spectrum of debates about what should be the type of multicultural and multilingual education in schools.

The issue of basic cultural differences in worldviews is part of the discussion of multicultural and multilingual education. Also, some of multicultural proposals embrace issues of racism and sexism. In this context the following issues will be discussed:

- Cultural differences in seeing and knowing the world.
- Biculturalism or the ability to move easily between two cultures.
- Dominated cultures.
- Different forms of multicultural education.
- Racism and sexism.
- Different forms of language education.
- Language rights.

CULTURAL DIFFERENCES IN KNOWING AND SEEING THE WORLD

A fundamental aspect of multicultural education is that different students have different ways of knowing and seeing the world. The pioneer work in this field is Richard Nisbett's *The Geography of Thought: How Asians and Westerners Think Differently . . . and Why.* Working with social psychologists from Japan and China,

Nisbett concluded that Japanese and Chinese students have a holistic worldview while U.S. students tend to see the world as made up of discrete categories of objects that could be defined by a set of rules. Nisbett states that Japanese and Chinese students see "the world in holistic terms. They see a great deal of the field, especially background events; they are skilled in observing relationships between events . . . Modern Westerners . . . see the world in analytic, atomistic terms; they see objects as discrete and separate from their environments."

These differences were exemplified in a number of psychological experiments. For example, in an experiment conducted at Japan's Kyoto University and at America's University of Michigan, students were shown eight colored animated scenes of underwater life with one or more "focal" fish that were brighter and larger than the others. The fish were shown swimming around plants, rocks, and bubbles. Similar to the results of many other experiments conducted by Nisbett, the results of this experiment indicate that after 20 seconds of viewing the scene, Japanese students remembered many of the details of the whole scene while the American students remembered primarily the focal fish. In other words, Japanese students looked at the whole scene while the Americans looked at the parts—particularly the most noticeable parts. In responding to questions, Japanese students began by describing the total environment ("It looked like a pond . . .) whereas the Americans began by describing the focal fish.

In another experiment, American and Chinese children were presented with a series of illustrations depicting three objects. The children were asked to place two of the objects together. One illustration showed a chicken, cow, and grass. American children grouped the chicken and cow together because they are both animals. Chinese children grouped the cow and grass together because the cow eats grass. In fact, the cow and chicken ordinarily have no experiential relationship: If a human were introduced into the illustration and children were asked to group three objects together, then one might hypothesize that both American and Chinese children would group the cow, chicken, and human together but for different reasons. The American children would put the three together because they are all animals, while the Chinese children would put the three together because the human eats chickens and drinks cows' milk.

Nisbett and two Chinese colleagues conducted a similar experiment yielding similar results using college students in the United States, Taiwan, and the People's Republic of China. They gave the participants three words and asked which two of the words were related. One set of words included *panda, monkey,* and *banana.* As the reader can guess from the previous discussion, the American college students tended to see the closest relationship between the panda and monkey because they are animals and the Chinese students grouped the monkey and banana together because monkeys eat bananas.

Differences in "seeing" a forest is one way to illustrate the differences between American and Japanese or Chinese worldviews. Americans are inclined to see a forest in taxonomic categories. Those seeing a forest through the lens of taxonomic categories, which is what many people call Western "seeing," would observe groups of trees, bushes, animals, birds, insects, moss, flowers, and so on. In contrast, those seeing the forest through a holistic lens of relationships, which is what many people might call the Asian way of seeing, would view an interrelated world of birds eating berries and insects, moss growing on trees and the earth, animals eating the moss and leaves, bees pollinating flowers, bushes sheltering animals, and so on. Of course a Westerner could understand the interdependence of the forest but, according to the preceding discussion, the Westerner would initially focus on separate objects having common characteristics.

Nisbett argues that these differences in knowing and seeing the world can be traced back to differences in the original philosophical underpinnings of Western- and what he identifies as Confucian-based societies: "Confucian-based societies" refers to communities guided by an ethical system first articulated by the Chinese scholar Confucius (551?–479? BCE). The major Confucian-based nations are identified as Korea, Japan, and China.

Nisbett asserts that Westerners developed a belief that knowledge could exist separate from human experience. He traced the belief back to ancient Greeks, who distrusted knowledge gained through the senses and favored abstract thought. The Greeks believed that they could study an object in isolation from its total environment. Isolated, Greeks tried to discern the disparate parts of the object. This approach to seeing the world, he argues, set the stage for the later Western development of the scientific method and the use of science to search for the basic matter of the universe, such as the atom, rather than focusing on how the whole universe works.

In Confucian-based societies, people see the world as made up of relationships based on some form of contact or interaction between objects. In contrast to ancient Greek thought, which favored abstract forms of human behavior, Confucius focused on a person's relationship to others. For Confucius, people were interdependent and inextricably bonded to others through emotional ties. For this reason, modern-day Confucianism maintains a sense of responsibility to others along with a holistic view of society. People in Confucian-based societies demonstrate a greater sense of social responsibility and conformity to group wishes than those in the individualistically oriented Western society.

BICULTURALISM: COLLECTIVIST AND INDIVIDUALIST SOCIETIES

An important understanding in multicultural education is that people can be bicultural in knowing and viewing the world. This is particularly important for understanding the learning processes of students who have recently arrived in the United States. In general, Americans are highly individualistic with a worldview, as demonstrated in the previously discussed experiments, that favors seeing the parts in contrast to the whole. However, people can be bicultural, switching from a holistic to a Western worldview. This is what many children from Confucian-based and other collectivist societies must learn when entering U.S. schools. They must learn to be bicultural.

There are many societies other than Confucian-based ones that have a collectivist view of social relationships. The differences between individualist and collectivist cultures center around personal orientation to self and others. In individualist cultures, behavior is primarily determined by personal attributes and feelings. People focus on their own individual freedom and personal goals. Social psychologist Eunkook M. Suh writes, "Psychological characteristics [in individualist cultures] commonly associated with mental health . . . portray the personal qualities of a highly independent, self-reliant individual who is capable of transcending the influences of others and the society."

In collectivist societies, people rely on their relationship to others to judge their own happiness. Success in a collectivist society is measured by fulfillment of one's duties and obligations toward one's in-group. In collectivist societies, Suh writes, "discussion of the individual starts with the Confucian assumption that the person exists in relationship to others. The individual is viewed as being fundamentally socially oriented, situation centered, interdependent, and inextricably bonded to others through emotional ties."

In researching the differences between Western and Confucian ways of knowing, Nisbett found that Hong Kong Chinese, who have been influenced by British schools and traditions and Chinese culture, could be prompted to think according to a Confucian or Western perspective; they are bicultural in their ways of seeing the world. Biculturalism results from what is referred to as hybridity of cultures. For example, many immigrants from collectivist cultures to the United States and Europe must undergo some adaptation to the individualist culture of the host society. Social psychologists Daphna Oyerman, Izumi Sakamoto, and Armand Lauffer write, "Hybridization involves the melding of cultural lenses or frames such that values and goals that were focused on in one context are transposed to a new context . . . Cultural hybridization may be said to occur when an individual or group is exposed to and influenced by more than one cultural context." These researchers found that some immigrant cultures in the United States retained their parental culture in their private lives while taking on the values of the host culture in their public lives. Regarding hybridization, they found that among Asian American students individualist cultural values were included in the in-group "without a loss of the social obligation that is built into collectivism."

International studies yield the following rankings between collectivist and individualist nations. These rankings also indicate that it is wrong to think of collectivist societies being Asian or Confucian when many are in South America and Africa. I suspect that high collectivist ratings for countries in South America and Africa are a result of indigenous cultures.

The Ten Most Collectivist Nations in Rank Order Beginning with the Most Collectivist

1. China
2. Colombia
3. Indonesia

4. Pakistan
5. Korea
6. Peru
7. Ghana
8. Nepal
9. Nigeria
10. Tanzania

The following list of individualist nations are primarily Western. The one exception is South Africa, which, despite the existence of indigenous peoples, might be considered to be dominated by a European culture.

The Ten Most Individualist Nations in Rank Order Beginning with the Most Individualist

1. United States
2. Australia
3. Denmark
4. Germany
5. Finland
6. Norway
7. Italy
8. Austria
9. Hungary
10. South Africa

In conclusion, American multicultural education must consider the transition of immigrant children from collectivist societies to the individualist orientation of U.S. society. This transition involves learning to be bicultural. The immigrant child from a collectivist society learns to know and view the world in individualistic terms while still being able to switch to a collectivist view. Often, the child from a collectivist society learns to think in individualistic terms when dealing with American schools and institutions but switches to a collectivist view when interacting with family and the surrounding immigrant community.

THE DIFFERENCE BETWEEN DOMINANT, DOMINATED, AND IMMIGRANT CULTURES

In multicultural education, a distinction is made between *dominant, dominated,* and *immigrant* cultures. The **dominant culture** is the prevailing culture, which is European American in the United States. This is the culture brought to the colonies and the United States by immigrants from Europe and modified by the social and political conditions in America. Traditionally, the curriculum of public schools has been based on European American traditions. In this sense, European American culture is the dominant culture of public schools.

Dominated cultures refer to groups who were forcefully incorporated into the United States. For instance, Africans were forcefully brought to the

United States as slaves, and their cultures were changed by the domination of European American culture to produce an African American culture. Similarly, Native American tribes were conquered by the United States and "Americanized." Mexicans living in the Southwest were forcefully made part of the United States with the signing in 1848 of the Treaty of Guadalupe Hidalgo and a new Mexican American culture emerged. Finally, the Spanish-American War of 1898 resulted in the forceful annexation of Puerto Rico to the United States; therefore, Puerto Ricans represent another dominated culture.

Immigrant cultures refer to the first generation of groups who freely decided to come to the United States. *First generation* refers to adults and children who are born in another county and then emigrate to the United States. European American immigrants are included in this category. Immigrants have a variety of educational, cultural, and linguistic backgrounds. The diversity of immigrant languages and cultures presents a complex problem for schoolteachers. In *The Inner World of Immigrant Children,* Cristina Igoa provides questions designed to help teachers do research into the educational background of immigrant children. I strongly recommend that all teachers of immigrant children read Igoa's invaluable book. Igoa's list of questions includes the following:

- Were the children schooled or unschooled before they came into the country?
- Was their education fragmented?
- Are the children dependent on the teacher for learning? Do they have any independent learning skills?
- Did they learn English abroad?
- How much of their own language did they learn, orally and in writing, receptively and productively?
- What is the educational attainment of their parents?

DOMINATED CULTURES: JOHN OGBU

Anthropologist John Ogbu concludes that the historical experience of dominated groups resulted in the development of a basic distrust of the major institutions in American society. For instance, a history of forced subjugation and slavery, segregation, discrimination, and harassment by police and government officials left many members of the African American community with the feeling that the government works primarily to benefit European Americans. This general distrust of institutions includes public schools. Segregation and second-generation segregation have left many African Americans feeling that public schooling is organized to keep them at the bottom rungs of America's social and economic system. Mexican Americans and Puerto Ricans encountered the hostility of segregation and second-generation segregation as well as attempts to keep them from speaking Spanish. Similarly, many Native Americans feel a strong hostility toward schools because of the deculturalization programs they experienced in government-operated boarding schools. For instance, Mick Fedullo, in his wonderful book on Indian education, *Light of the*

Feather: Pathways Through Contemporary Indian America, recounts a discussion with an Apache bilingual education teacher, Elenore Cassadore, about Apache attitudes toward schools. As she tells Fedullo, many Apache parents were sent to Bureau of Indian Affairs' boarding schools where they "came to believe that their teachers were the evil ones, and so anything that had to do with 'education' was also evil—like books." Now, she explains, they send their children to school only because of compulsory-education laws. "But they tell their kids not to take school seriously. So, to them, printed stuff is white-man stuff."

According to Ogbu, these historical conditions created a **cultural frame of reference** among dominated groups that is quite different from that of many immigrants and European Americans. Cultural frames of reference refer to the manner in which people interpret their perceptions of the world. A person's cultural frame of reference is formed, in part, by his or her family's historical experience. For instance, an African American child might not have witnessed a lynching of a black person by a white mob, but knowledge of these incidents might be passed on to the child through the recounting of family history and experience in the United States. A Mexican American child might not have experienced discrimination in employment, but he or she might frequently hear about it through family conversations. The history told by families and a person's experiences play a major role in shaping one's cultural frame of reference.

Differences in cultural frames of reference can result in differing interpretations of the same event. For instance, a European American might perceive a school as an institution that is benign and helpful. In contrast, a member of a dominated group might perceive a school as an institution not to be trusted. The actions of a disgruntled waiter in a restaurant might be interpreted through the cultural frame of reference of a European American as resulting from the waiter not feeling good about his job. On the other hand, the cultural frame of reference of African Americans, Native Americans, Mexican Americans, and Puerto Ricans might lead members of these groups to interpret the waiter's actions as hostile and prejudicial.

Also, differences in cultural frames of reference can result in differences in action in particular situations. For instance, in the preceding example, a European American might give little attention to the actions of a disgruntled waiter. On the other hand, members of a dominated group might act in a hostile manner to what they perceive to be the prejudicial actions of the waiter. Low academic achievement, Ogbu argues, results from dominated cultures holding negative feelings about schools. Ogbu identifies six ways this can occur:

1. Some members of dominated groups believe that they must act white to succeed in school. This feeling is exemplified by the previous quotation from the Apache teacher.
2. Some students from dominated cultures may fear that doing well in school will symbolize a rejection of their own culture.
3. Peer pressure against acting white might result in students actually avoiding academic achievement.

4. The feelings of hostility some students from dominated cultures might feel toward school can result in conflicts with European American administrators, teachers, and other students. Of course, these conflicts might be in response to real feelings and actions displayed by school officials and other students.
5. Conflicts with school personnel and other students can heighten distrust of school and a rejection of school rules. The open rejection of school rules leads to suspension, expulsion, and other forms of school punishment.
6. Some students from dominated cultures might begin school disillusioned about their ability to achieve. This can result in little effort being put into academic work.

These six reactions to school cause, according to Ogbu, **low academic effort syndrome** and **counteracademic attitudes** and behaviors. Low academic effort syndrome refers to lack of effort in doing schoolwork, which results from peer pressure, conflict, and disillusionment. Counteracademic attitudes and behaviors refer to actions that are hostile toward the school and its rules.

Obviously, many students from dominated groups succeed in school and they do not display a low academic effort syndrome or adopt counteracademic attitudes and behavior. Despite their success in school, many of these students still interpret their educational experience through a cultural frame of reference that is quick to note prejudice and unfair treatment. This type of cultural frame of reference can be found in Jake Lamar's autobiography *Bourgeois Blues: An American Memoir.* Although his father was a successful businessperson who could afford to live in wealthy neighborhoods in New York City and send his children to elite private schools, Jake discovered that racism was still a major factor in his life. Richard Rodriguez interprets his academic success through the cultural frame of reference of a Mexican American in his autobiography *Hunger of Memory: The Education of Richard Rodriguez.* Key to understanding the problems of students from dominated cultures is the pain Rodriguez felt as his academic success widened the gap between him and his family culture.

It is important to remember that many students of dominated cultures do succeed in school and in the economic life of the United States. Advocates of multicultural education programs argue that educational programs supporting cultural diversity can help students from dominated cultures who might be experiencing low academic effort syndrome and exhibiting counter academic attitudes and behaviors. These multicultural programs are described in the next section.

EMPOWERMENT THROUGH MULTICULTURAL EDUCATION: JAMES BANKS, SONIA NIETO, AND CRITICAL PEDAGOGY

Leaders of the multicultural education movement, such as James Banks, Christine Sleeter, Carl Grant, and Sonia Nieto, are concerned with empowering oppressed people by integrating the history and culture of dominated groups into public school curricula and textbooks. In general, their goal is to reduce prejudice, eliminate sexism, and equalize educational opportunities. **Empowerment** is concerned with ethnic studies and raising consciousness. Within this context, the term means providing the intellectual tools for creating a just society. Usually the concept of empowerment is contrasted with benevolent helping, such as welfare programs, family assistance, and other forms of aid. These programs, it is argued, keep people in a state of dependence. Empowerment gives people the ability to break out of these dependent states. Ethnic studies can empower dominated and oppressed immigrant cultures by creating an understanding of the methods of cultural domination and by helping to build self-esteem. For instance, the study of African American, Native American, Puerto Rican, Hawaiian American, and Mexican American history serves the dual purpose of building self-esteem and empowerment. In addition, the empowerment of women and people with disabilities involves, in part, the inclusion of their histories and stories in textbooks and in the curriculum.

As one aspect of social empowerment, ethnic studies have influenced textbooks and classroom instruction in the United States. The ethnic studies movement resulted in the integration of content into the curriculum dealing with dominated and immigrant cultures, women, and people with disabilities. Multicultural educator James Banks worries that many school districts consider content integration as the primary goal of multicultural education. He states, "The widespread belief that content integration constitutes the whole of multicultural education might . . . [cause] many teachers of subjects such as mathematics and science to view multicultural education as an endeavor primarily for social studies and language arts teachers."

The best example of multicultural education for empowerment is Sonia Nieto's *Affirming Diversity: The Sociopolitical Context of Multicultural Education.* Growing up as a Puerto Rican in New York City, Nieto felt the tension between the language and culture of her family and the language and culture of the school. The school made her feel that there was something deficient with her background. She states, "We learned to feel ashamed of who we were, how we spoke, what we ate, and everything else that was 'different' about us." For Nieto, the goal of multicultural education should be to bridge the gap between the culture of the family and the culture of the school so that children of immigrant and dominated families do not have to suffer the pain and shame that she experienced. In her words, "Our society must move beyond causing and exploiting students' shame to using their cultural and linguistic differences to struggle for an education that is more in tune with society's rhetoric of equal and high-quality education for all students."

Multiculturalism for social empowerment attempts to maintain cultural identity while promoting values of social justice and social action. In her book, Nieto presents a chart displaying the seven characteristics of this form of multicultural education.

1. The school curriculum is openly antiracist and antidiscriminatory. An atmosphere is created where students feel safe about discussing sexism, racism, and discrimination. In addition, the curriculum includes the history

and cultural perspectives of a broad range of people. Students are to be taught to identify and challenge racism in society.

2. Multicultural education is considered a basic part of a student's general education, which means that all students become bilingual and all students study different cultural perspectives.
3. Multiculturalism should pervade the curriculum by being included in all aspects of the curriculum and in the general life of the school, including bulletin boards, lunchrooms, and assemblies.
4. Multicultural education is considered important for all students.
5. Schools should teach social justice by preparing students to overcome racism and discrimination against various cultures.
6. Learning should emphasize the asking of the questions why, how, and what if. When these questions are asked regarding issues of social injustice they can lead to a questioning of the very foundations of political and economic institutions. This makes multicultural education a combination of content and "process."
7. Multicultural education should include critical pedagogy as the primary method of instruction. With critical pedagogy, in Nieto's words, "students and teachers are involved in a 'subversive activity' and decision making and social action skills are the basis of the curriculum."

In the framework of this approach to multicultural education, critical pedagogy helps students to understand the extent to which cultures can differ. In addition, these differences are to be affirmed and given equal treatment. Also, critical pedagogy will help students to understand cultural domination and how they can end it.

Missing from multicultural education for social empowerment is an analysis of the intersection of different cultures. It is assumed that an understanding of oppression and discrimination will provide a common theme in critical pedagogy that will prepare all students to struggle for social justice. But there are important and deep differences in values between cultures. Does social justice mean giving a person an opportunity to achieve within the framework of English or Native American values? Or does it mean creating a whole new set of values for the world?

EMPOWERMENT THROUGH MULTICULTURAL EDUCATION: RACISM

Advocates of multicultural education for empowerment include in their agenda ridding the world of racism. Racism can be defined as prejudice plus power. Racism refers to acts of oppression of one racial group toward another. One form of oppression is economic exploitation. This definition of racism distinguishes between simple feelings of hostility and prejudice toward another racial group and the ability to turn those feelings into some form of oppression. For instance, black people might have prejudicial feelings toward white people, but they have little opportunity to express those prejudicial feelings in some form of economic or political oppression of white people. On the other hand, prejudicial feelings that white people might have toward blacks can turn into racism when they become the basis for discrimination in education, housing, and the job market. Within this framework, racism becomes the act of social, political, and economic oppression of another group.

When discussions of racism occur in my multicultural education classes, white students complain of a sense of hostility from black students and, consequently, accuse black students of racism. Black students respond that their feelings represent prejudice and not racism because they lack the power to discriminate against whites. The troubling aspect of this response is the implication that if these black students had the power, they would be racist. One black student pointed out that there are situations where blacks can commit racist acts against whites. The black student used the example of the killing of white passengers by a black man on a commuter railroad several years ago. The evidence seemed to indicate that the killer was motivated by extreme hatred of whites that the newspapers labeled "black rage." This was a racist act, the black student argued, because the gun represented power.

Racism is often thought of as whites oppressing people of color. Of course, there are many problems with this definition. If one parent is black and another white, are their children considered black or white? Can one white-skinned child of this marriage be considered white while one dark-skinned child is considered black? Jake Lamar recalls how the confusion over skin color sparked the development of his racial consciousness at the age of 3. Jake was sitting at the kitchen table when his Uncle Frank commented "about how obnoxious white people were." Jake responded, "But Mommy's white." His uncle replied that his mother was not white but was "just light-skinned." Jake then said that he thought his father, brother, and himself were black while his sister and mother were white. His mother then explained that they had many white ancestors that caused the variation in skin color, but they were still "all Negroes." Thinking back on this incident, Jake Lamar reflected, "Black and white then meant something beyond pigmentation . . . so my first encounter with racial awareness was at once enlightening and confusing, and shot through with ambiguity."

Keeping in mind the complexities of racial classification and the importance of social class, certain generalities can be made about the racial attitudes of whites at the end of the twentieth century. In *Prejudice and Racism,* social psychologist James Jones summarizes the racial attitudes of some whites:

- Whites feel more negatively toward blacks than they do toward Hispanics, Asians, and legal and illegal immigrants.
- Whites perceive blacks as lazy, violent, and less intelligent than Hispanics, Asians, and legal and illegal immigrants.
- Whites believe blacks are receiving more attention from government than they deserve.
- Whites believe blacks are too demanding in their struggle for equal rights.

- High levels of anti-black racism are correlated with white attitudes that police and the death penalty make streets safe, and with opposition to assistance to the poor.
- Anti-black and anti-Hispanic racism are correlated with whites' opposition to open immigration and multilingualism.

TEACHING ABOUT RACISM

In many ways it is difficult when schools are becoming more segregated to reduce racist attitudes in the classroom. One excellent book is Beverly Tatum's *Why Are All the Black Kids Sitting Together in the Cafeteria?: A Psychologist Explains the Development of Racial Identity*. Educator and African American activist Beverly Tatum worries about the loss of white allies in the struggle against racism and the hostility she feels from white college students when teaching about racism. Reflecting on her teaching experiences, she writes, "White students . . . often struggle with strong feelings of guilt when they become aware of the pervasiveness of racism. . . . These feelings are uncomfortable and can lead white students to resist learning about race and racism." Part of the problem, she argues, is that seeing oneself as the oppressor creates a negative self-image, which results in a withdrawal from a discussion of the problem. What needs to be done, she maintains, is to counter the guilt by giving white students a positive self-image of whites fighting against racism. In other words, a self-image of whites being allies with blacks in the struggle against racism.

A popular antiracist curriculum for preschool children is the National Association for the Education of Young Children's "Anti-Bias Curriculum: Tools for Empowering Young Children." This curriculum and related methods of instruction are designed to reduce prejudice among young children regarding race, language, gender, and physical ability differences. The premise of the method is that at an early age children become aware of the connection between power and skin color, language, and physical disabilities. Cited as examples are a 2 1/2-year-old Asian child who refuses to hold the hand of a black classmate because "It's dirty" and a 4-year-old boy who takes over the driving of a pretended bus because "Girls can't be bus drivers."

According to the Anti-Bias Curriculum, research findings show that young children classify differences between people and they are influenced by bias toward others. By the age of 2, children are aware of gender differences and begin to apply color names to skin colors. Between ages 3 and 5, children try to figure out who they are by examining the differences in gender and skin color. By 4 or 5 years old, children engage in socially determined gender roles and they give racial reasons for the selection of friends. Based on these research findings, the advocates of the curriculum believe that prejudice can be reduced if there is conscious intervention to curb the development of biased concepts and activities.

Another antiracist education program is the Teaching Tolerance Project that began after a group of teenage skinheads attacked and beat to death an

Ethiopian man on a street in Portland, Oregon, in 1988. After this incident, members of the Southern Poverty Law Center decided it was time to do something about teaching tolerance. Dedicated to pursuing legal issues involving racial incidents and denial of civil rights, the law center sued, for the man's family, the two men who were responsible for teaching violent racism to the Portland skinheads. These two teachers, Tom Metzger, the head of the White Aryan Resistance, and his son, became symbols of racist teachings in the United States. In a broad sense, the Teaching Tolerance Project is designed to provide information about teaching methods and materials that will counter the type of racist teachings represented by Metzger and his son.

Similar to the Anti-Bias Curriculum, the Teaching Tolerance Project primarily defines racism as a function of psychological attitudes, in contrast to an emphasis on racism as a function of economic exploitation. On the inside cover of its magazine *Teaching Tolerance,* tolerance is defined as "the capacity for or the practice of recognizing and respecting the beliefs or practices of others." Within the context of this definition, the project members "primarily celebrate and recognize the beliefs and practices of racial and ethnic groups such as African-Americans, Latinos, and Asian-Americans."

The primary purpose of the Teaching Tolerance Project is to provide resources and materials to schools to promote "interracial and intercultural understanding between whites and nonwhites." There have also been decisions to include material dealing with cultural tolerance, homelessness, and poverty. The Teaching Tolerance Project is only one of many educational attempts to end racism in the United States. The end of racism is essential for the full provision of equality of opportunity and equality of educational opportunity in U.S. society.

EMPOWERMENT THROUGH MULTICULTURAL EDUCATION: SEXISM

In Failing at Fairness: How America's Schools Cheat Girls, Myra and David Sadker summarize current research on educational discrimination against girls. One surprising result of their research and analysis of other data was that girls are equal to or ahead of boys in most measures of academic achievement and psychological health during the early years of schooling, but by the end of high school and college, girls have fallen behind boys on these measurements. On entrance examinations to college, girls score lower than boys, particularly in science and mathematics. Boys receive more state and national scholarships. Women score lower than men on all entrance examinations to professional schools.

An explanation for the decline in test scores is that girls suffer a greater decline than boys in self-esteem from elementary school to high school. (Of course, an important general question about the following statistics is why both boys and girls decline in feelings of self-esteem.) As a measure of self-esteem, the Sadkers rely on responses to the statement, "I'm happy the way

I am." The Sadkers report that in elementary school 60 percent of girls and 67 percent of boys responded positively to the statement. By high school these positive responses declined to 29 percent for girls and 46 percent for boys. In other words, the decline in self-esteem for girls was 31 percentage points as compared with 21 percentage points for boys. Why is there less self-esteem and a greater decline in self-esteem among girls as compared with boys?

To get an answer to the question, the Sadkers asked students how their lives would be different if they suddenly were transformed into members of the opposite sex. Overall, girls responded with feelings that it wouldn't be so bad and that it would open up opportunities to participate in sports and politics. In addition, girls felt they would have more freedom and respect. Regarding self-esteem, girls expressed little regret about the consequences of the sex change. In contrast, boys expressed horror at the idea, and many said they would commit suicide. They saw themselves becoming second-class citizens, being denied access to athletics and outdoor activities, and being racked with physical problems. Concerning self-esteem, and in contrast to girls, boys expressed nothing but regret about the consequences of the sex change.

Contributing to the lack of self-esteem among girls, the Sadkers argue, are modes of classroom interaction, the representation of women in textbooks and other educational materials, and the discriminatory content of standardized tests. In one of their workshops with classroom teachers, the Sadkers illustrate classroom sex bias by asking four of the participants—two men and two women—to act like students in a middle-school social studies classroom. The lesson is about the American Revolution and it begins with an examination of homework. Acting as the teacher, David Sadker perfunctorily tells one woman that two of her answers are wrong and comments to the group on the neatness of the other woman's homework. He tells one man that two of his answers are wrong and, unlike his response to the woman with wrong answers, he urges the man to try harder and suggests ways of improving his answers. David then states to the other man that he failed to do his homework assignment. In contrast to the woman with the neat paper, this man illustrates what the Sadkers call the "bad boy role."

David Sadker then continues the lesson by discussing battles and leaders. All of the Revolutionary leaders are, of course, male. During the lesson he calls on the males 20 times each while only calling on one woman twice and completely ignoring the other woman. The one woman called on misses her question because she is given only half a second to respond. When questioning the men, David Sadker spends time giving hints and probing. At the end of this demonstration lesson, the Sadkers report, one woman commented that she felt like she was back in school. She often had the right answer but was never called on by the teacher.

What this workshop demonstration illustrates, based on the Sadkers' findings on classroom interaction, is that boys receive more and better instruction. Boys are more often called on by the teacher and boys interact more with the teacher than do girls. In a typical classroom situation, if both boys and girls have their hands raised to answer a question, the teacher is most likely to call on a boy. A teacher will spend more time responding to a boy's question than to a girl's question. In other words, girls do not receive equal educational opportunity in the classroom.

In addition, women are not so well represented as men in textbooks. The Sadkers found in 1989 elementary school language arts textbooks that there were from two to three times as many pictures of men as women. In one elementary history text, they found four times as many pictures of men as women. In one 1992 world history textbook, of 631 pages they found only 7 pages related to women. Two of those pages were devoted to a fifth grade female student who had made a peace trip to the Soviet Union.

It is most likely that the treatment received by girls in the classroom and in textbooks contributes to their low self-esteem and to their decline, as compared with boys, in performance on standardized tests from elementary school to high school. It seems logical that if less instructional time is spent with girls than boys, then boys would more rapidly advance academically. In addition, without equal representation in textbooks, girls might value themselves less and have less incentive to achieve. Less instructional time and representation in textbooks contribute to the glass ceiling of the classroom.

The lowering of self-esteem and content bias may contribute to the significant gender gap in scores on standardized college entrance examinations and entrance examinations to professional schools. For instance, on the widely used Scholastic Aptitude Test (SAT) males score 50 points higher on the math section and up to 12 points higher on the verbal section. It is important to understand that discrimination in standardized testing involves the denial of economic rewards, specifically scholarships and career opportunities.

The content bias and economic value of standardized tests were recognized in a 1989 ruling by a federal judge in New York. The judge ruled that the awarding of New York State scholarships using the SAT discriminated against female students. The case was brought to court by the Girls Clubs of America and NOW. The court argued that the scholarships were to be awarded based on academic achievement in high school and that the SAT was not constructed to test achievement but to determine college performance. The court's decision states, "The evidence is clear that females score significantly below males on the SAT while they do equally or slightly better in high schools."

In this court case, academic achievement was defined according to grades received in high school courses. Interestingly, the Sadkers argue that this apparent paradox between girls' high grades and low standardized-test scores is a result of grade inflation. This grade inflation results from female passivity and their willingness to follow classroom rules. Often, teachers formally and informally incorporate evaluations of student behavior in their academic grading practices. For girls, good behavior can result in good grades.

But the issue of grade inflation still doesn't solve the puzzle of lower performance by girls on tests like the SAT. The Sadkers suggest that one possible reason for the differences in scores between males and females is that the content of standardized tests is biased. Boys are more familiar with organized sports, financial issues, science, wars, and dates. Consequently, test items referring to these areas tend to favor boys. As an example, the Sadkers describe a gifted high school girl who lost her concentration on the preliminary SAT when she encountered an analogy question comparing "a football and a gridiron." The analogy baffled her because she had little knowledge of football.

One possible solution to teacher bias in classroom interaction, the Sadkers suggest, is to have an observer code classroom interaction so that the teacher becomes aware of any possible bias. If teachers are unconsciously favoring boys, then this observation provides the opportunity for them to change their behavior. One teacher told the Sadkers that she distributed two chips to all students. When students want to comment or ask a question, they have to give up one chip. Before the class is over, all students must use their two chips. This guarantees equal participation of all students and ensures that classroom interaction is not dominated by only a few students. In addition, the Sadkers recommend that teachers consciously search for books portraying strong female characters in a variety of occupational and social roles. They point to the work of the National Women's History Project, which since the 1970s has published materials emphasizing women's roles in history. In addition, the Sadkers recommend the use of workshops to heighten teachers' awareness of their own possible sexist behavior and to understand how to find nonsexist educational material for the classroom.

Another possible solution is single-sex education. This would eliminate the problem of female students having to compete with male students for teachers' attention. In classrooms of only girls, teachers would not tend to push girls aside and focus their instructional efforts on boys. In an all-girls school or classroom, female students might receive the equal educational opportunity denied to them in a coed classroom.

Writing in favor of girls' schools, Susan Estrich, professor of law and political science at the University of Southern California, notes that 60 percent of the National Merit Scholarship finalists are boys. Echoing the Sadkers' findings, she reports from a 1992 study of the American Association of University Women, "that even though girls get better grades (except in math), they get less from schools." While she does not dismiss efforts to equalize opportunities for girls in coed schools, she argues that currently single-sex education is working. For instance, in all-girls schools 80 percent of girls take four years of math and science, whereas in coed schools the average is two years of math and science. In Fortune 1000 companies, one-third of the female board members are graduates of women's colleges even though graduates of women's colleges represent only 4 percent of all female college graduates. In addition, graduates of women's colleges earn 43 percent of the math and 50 percent of engineering doctorates earned by all women, and they outnumber all other females in *Who's Who.*

Estrich does see the possibility of offering single-sex classes within a coed institution. She cites the example of the Illinois Math and Science Academy, which experimented with a girls-only calculus-based physics class. Instead of sitting meekly at their desks while boys command all the attention, girls are actively asking and answering questions. In an all-girls algebra class in Ventura, California, the teacher reports spending time building self-confidence along with teaching math. For Estrich, at least at this point in time, all-girls schools are a means for ending sexism in education.

There are many critics of proposals for all-female schools. One University of Michigan researcher, Valerie Lee, found that many all-girls classrooms still contained high levels of sexist behavior on the part of the teacher. In one case, a history teacher assigned a research paper and told students that she would provide "major hand-holding" to help the students. Lee argued that the offer of major hand-holding would not occur in a boys' school. In addition, she found male bashing taking place in some all-female schools.

Moreover, Lee found boys in all-male schools engaging in serious sexist comments about women. In other words, all-female schools do not do anything about the sexist attitudes of men. In fact, all-male schools might reinforce male sexist behavior. For instance, in a 1994 court case involving a suit by Shannon Faulkner to gain entrance to the all-male military college, The Citadel, one of the witnesses, a 1991 graduate of the school, reported that the word *woman* was used on campus in a derogatory manner "every day, every minute, every hour, [it was] a part of the life there."

Therefore, there is the possibility that single-sex education might result in greater academic achievement for girls while doing nothing about sexist attitudes among men. The academic gains made by women might mean little in a world dominated by sexist males. Also, the courts may not approve of single-sex public schools, because of a decision regarding all-boys African American schools in Detroit. The Court argued that the all-boys schools were a violation of the 1954 *Brown* decision that declared as unconstitutional separate but equal schools that were racially segregated.

In 1998, the American Association of University Women (AAUW) released a follow-up report to its earlier charges that public schools were shortchanging girls. The new study found that the number of girls enrolled in algebra, trigonometry, precalculus, and calculus was growing at a faster rate than the number of boys. Probably the most impressive statistic was that the differences between boys and girls was the smallest in the world on international tests in math and science. However, the report found that technology, particularly computer technology, is emerging as the new boys' club. The report found that girls have less exposure to computers inside and outside school and that girls feel less confident about using computers. The gap between boys and girls in computer knowledge and use increases from grades 8 to 11. Only 17 percent of students taking the College Board's Advanced Placement Test in computer science were women.

In reference to the technological gap between males and females, Janice Weinman, the executive director of the Washington-based AAUW said, "This is becoming the new club [computer technology] from which girls are feeling disenfranchised. Consequently, girls are not going to be appropriately prepared for the technology era of the new 21st century."

However, there are areas where girls outperform boys. More girls than boys are enrolled in advanced English, foreign language, and art courses. In addition, girls outscore boys by wide margins on reading and writing tests in middle and elementary grades.

Education Week reporter Debra Viadero provides the following summary of other findings in the AAUW study:

1. In school-to-work programs, which combine challenging academics with vocational training, girls still tend to cluster in traditional female occupations.
2. Although girls are taking more advanced-placement courses and getting better grades than boys, their scores on those exams still tend to be lower.
3. On large-scale exams, such as the National Assessment of Educational Progress, the top scorers in math and science still tend to be boys.

EDUCATING FOR ECONOMIC POWER: LISA DELPIT

Lisa Delpit is more interested in directly instructing children of dominated groups in the culture of power. She believes that advocates of multicultural education often fail to reveal to children the requirements for economic advancement. She does not reject the importance of critical thinking, but she does think children should be directly told about the standards for acceptable speech and behavior for social mobility.

Working at the University of Alaska, she criticized what she called liberal educators for primarily focusing on native culture while instructing native Alaskans. These liberal educators, she claimed, were damaging students by not preparing them for success in the broader society. She was also critical of traditional instructors for ignoring native traditions. From her perspective, native culture needed to be considered when preparing students to achieve in the real world. Delpit encountered the same issues when working with teachers of black children in Philadelphia schools. White teachers often thought they knew what was best for black students. Usually this meant some form of progressive instruction designed to enhance critical thinking and imagination. While not denying the importance of these goals, Delpit found white teachers neglecting the instruction of black students in standard English. One complaining black parent told her, "My kids know how to be black—you all teach them how to be successful in the white man's world." Several black teachers suggested to Delpit that the " 'progressive' educational strategies imposed by liberals upon black and poor children could only be based on a desire to ensure that the liberals' children get sole access to the dwindling pool of American jobs." According to Delpit, there are five important aspects that need to be addressed when preparing dominated children for access to power.

1. "Issues of power are enacted in classrooms." It is important to examine, Delpit argues, the power of teachers and government over students, textbook publishers, and curriculum developers. This examination can be considered preparation for understanding the exercise of power in the world of work.

2. "There are codes or rules for participating in power; that is, there is a 'culture of power.' " In the classroom, this means direct instruction in linguistic forms and presentation of self, including ways of talking, writing, dressing, and interacting.
3. "The rules of the culture of power are a reflection of the rules of the culture of those who have power." For Delpit, the culture of the school is the culture of the middle and upper classes. Therefore, it is important for children from dominated groups to participate in and learn school culture.
4. "If you are not already a participant in the culture of power, being told explicitly the rules of that culture makes acquiring power easier."
5. "Those with power are frequently least aware of—or least willing to acknowledge—its existence. Those with less power are often most aware of its existence." From Delpit's perspective, white liberal educators are uncomfortable admitting they are part of the culture of power. On the other hand, students from dominated groups are aware of white power and they would like the parameters of power clearly stated.

ETHNOCENTRIC EDUCATION

In ethnocentric education subjects are taught from the perspective of a particular culture. Obviously, this is what U.S. public schools have always done. The curriculum of public schools is organized around the cultural frame of reference of European Americans, while the curriculum of new ethnocentric schools is organized around the cultural frames of reference of African Americans, Native Americans, and Hispanics.

The purpose of these new ethnocentric schools is twofold. First, these schools want to overcome among some children of dominated cultures the resistance to schooling that results in low academic effort and counteracademic attitudes and behaviors. Second, these schools want to preserve the cultural traditions of each dominated group. The preservation of culture is considered important because of what are believed to be some shortcomings of European American culture. For instance, many Native Americans feel that European Americans show little respect for nature and that they are primarily concerned with the control of nature. The result of these attitudes is massive environmental destruction. What Native American culture can contribute is an understanding of how to live with nature and an attitude that shows respect for nature and desires its preservation.

There are proposals for Hispanic and Afrocentric schools that are designed to redirect resistance cultures and build student self-esteem. A major source of inspiration for ethnocentric schools comes from the work of Jawanza Kunjufu, president of the Chicago-based African American Images. African American Images serves as a publishing house for Kunjufu's books and other books and videos focused on the teaching of African American culture. African American Images also offers a model curriculum called SETCLAE: Self-Esteem Through Culture Leads to Academic Excellence. The stated goals of the curriculum are to improve academic achievement, discipline, and school climate while transmitting racial pride and enhancing students' knowledge of culture and history and its significance to contemporary living.

Kunjufu's discussion of the experience of African American students is similar to John Ogbu's. Kunjufu argues that for most African American students, being successful in school means acting white. Kunjufu exemplifies this situation by an exchange between African American students about two other academically successful African American students in his book *To Be Popular or Smart: The Black Peer Group:*

> "Girl, she thinks she's something, making the honor roll."
>
> "I know, she's beginning to act like Darryl. They both think they're white, joining the National Honor Society."

Molefi Kete Asante, chairperson of the Department of African American Studies at Temple University and one of the proponents of an Afrocentric curriculum, argues that Afrocentricity is a transforming power involving five levels of awareness. On the first four levels of this transforming experience individuals come to understand that their personality, interests, and concerns are shared by black people around the world. Afrocentricity is achieved on the fifth level when a people struggle against foreign cultures that dominate their minds. At this stage, Asante argues in his book *Afrocentricity,* "An imperative of will, powerful, incessant, alive, and vital, moves to eradicate every trace of powerlessness. Afrocentricity is like rhythms; it dictates the beat of your life."

By purging images given by white culture of African Americans as stupid and powerless, African American students can, according to the arguments of those advocating Afrocentricity, gain a new image of themselves as people of ability and power. In this sense, Afrocentricity is considered a curriculum of empowerment. In addition, the students lose the lenses that filter the world through a white Eurocentric perspective and replace them with a set of Afrocentric lenses.

Therefore, ethnocentric curriculums in the United States create a cultural battle at two levels. At one level, an ethnocentric curriculum is an attempt to give equal value to different cultural traditions. At the second level, it means purging a Eurocentric view of the world from Native American, Hispanic, and African American children's minds and replacing it with a different cultural frame of reference. The purpose of this cultural battle is to empower Native American, Hispanic, and African American children so that they believe they can succeed in the world and so that they are not self-destructive. From this perspective, getting ahead in the economic and social system is not a matter of being white but of learning to believe in oneself and one's cultural traditions.

Ethnocentric education is one method for helping children from dominated groups succeed in school. Bilingual education is another. Bilingual education, as I discuss in the next section, is particularly important for Native Americans, Mexican Americans, and Puerto Ricans because of the conscious attempt by public schools in the past to destroy their languages.

BILINGUAL EDUCATION AND ENGLISH-LANGUAGE ACQUISITION: NO CHILD LEFT BEHIND

The No Child Left Behind Act of 2001 transforms the original goals of the bilingual education movement. Bilingual education is a means for protecting minority languages while teaching English to non-English speakers. It is part of the effort to protect language and cultural rights. Some Americans object to public schools protecting minority languages and believe the primary goal should be the acquisition of English.

The No Child Left Behind Act clearly places the federal government's support on the side of English acquisition as opposed to bilingual education. One part of the legislation is titled "English Language Acquisition, Language Enhancement, and Academic Act." This part of the legislation symbolically changes the name of the federal government's Office of Bilingual Education to the Office of English Language Acquisition, Language Enhancement, and Academic Achievement for Limited English Proficient. Its shorter title is simply "The Office of English Language Acquisition." The Director of Bilingual Education and Minority Languages Affairs is now called the Director of English Language Acquisition.

To understand the significance of these changes, we need to consider the arguments *for* bilingual education. Bilingual education refers to teaching a person to be proficient in the use of two languages. For instance, Native American students can be taught to be proficient in the use of their own native languages and English, while a Mexican American or Puerto Rican child can be taught to be proficient in Spanish and English.

In addition, there are several specific types of a bilingual education, including maintenance bilingual, transitional bilingual, and two-way bilingual. As the term suggests, **maintenance bilingual** programs are designed to maintain the ability to speak, read, and write in the student's language while learning English. For instance, a student might enter school speaking only Spanish with little knowledge of English. The ability to speak Spanish does not necessarily mean that the child knows how to read and write in Spanish. Similarly, most English-speaking students entering school do not know how to read and write in English. During the early years, maintenance bilingual education programs conduct classes in the language of the student while also teaching English. Therefore, during the period when students are learning English, they are also learning the content of the curriculum, including how to read and write, in their native tongue. This avoids the problem of learning being delayed until students know English. After learning English, students continue to receive lessons in both their native languages and in English.

One of the strongest arguments for maintenance bilingual education is that students are better able to learn English if they know how to read and write in their native language. In *Affirming Diversity*, Sonia Nieto argues that children who know how to read and write in their native language will be more successful in school than children whose language is neglected by the school and who do not become literate in their native tongue.

In contrast, **transitional bilingual** does not have the goal of making the student literate in two languages. The student's native tongue is used in class until the student learns English. After the student learns English, classes are taught only in English.

Two-way bilingual programs include both English-speaking and non-English-speaking students. By conducting class in two languages, English-speaking students can learn the language of the non-English speakers, while the non-English speakers learn English. The goal is for all students to become bilingual in English and another language.

Of course, language is linked to culture. Many Mexican Americans, Puerto Ricans, and Native Americans believe that maintenance bilingual education programs are essential for the retention of their cultures. As discussed earlier in this chapter, many deculturalization programs were directed at stamping out the use of Spanish and Native American languages. In addition, a person's cultural frame of reference is directly related to attitudes regarding the use in the United States of languages other than English. The issue of cultural perspective is highlighted in Humberto Garza's comment regarding a requirement that Los Altos, California, city employees speak only English on the job. Garza is quoted by Rosalie Pedalino Porter in her book *Forked Tongue: The Politics of Bilingual Education:* "Those council people from Los Altos should be made to understand that they are advocating their law in occupied Mexico [referring to the U.S. conquest of Mexican territory, including California]. . . . They should move back to England or learn how to speak the language of Native Americans."

Garza's remarks reflect the political explosiveness of bilingual education issues. In fact, the bilingual education movement was born during the civil rights upheavals of the 1960s. At that time, Mexican Americans protested for Spanish in schools and the teaching of Mexican American history and culture. In 1968, Mexican American students boycotted four East Los Angeles high schools, demanding bilingual programs, courses in Mexican American history and culture, and the serving of Mexican American food in school cafeterias. In addition, students demanded the hiring of more Spanish-speaking teachers and the firing of teachers who seemed anti–Mexican American.

Politicians responded to Mexican American and Puerto Rican demands for the preservation of Spanish in the schools. Senator Ralph Yarborough of Texas, believing that he would lose the 1970 election to a wealthy and conservative Democrat, decided that Hispanic support was crucial for his coalition of blacks, Mexican Americans, and poor whites. To win Hispanic support, Yarborough, after being appointed to a special subcommittee on bilingual education of the Senate Committee on Labor and Public Welfare, launched a series of hearings in major Hispanic communities.

The testimony at these hearings came primarily from representatives of the Mexican American and Puerto Rican communities, and not educational experts or linguistic theorists. The hearings concluded in East Harlem, with Senator Edward Kennedy and Bronx Borough President Herman Badillo decrying the facts that there were no Puerto Rican principals and only a few Puerto Rican teachers in the New York City school system.

Yarborough supported bilingual legislation that focused on students whose "mother tongue is Spanish." The legislation included programs to impart knowledge and pride about Hispanic culture and language and to bring descendants of Mexican Americans and Puerto Ricans into the teaching profession. The legislation was clearly designed to win political support from the Hispanic community in Texas. Yarborough's efforts resulted in the passage of the previously mentioned Bilingual Education Act of 1968.

Native Americans along with Mexican Americans and Puerto Ricans welcomed the idea of bilingual education. On the other hand, some members of the Republican Party joined a movement opposing bilingual education and supporting the adoption of English as the official language of the United States. The movement for making English the official language was led by an organization, U.S. English, founded in 1983 by S. I. Hayakawa, a former Republican senator.

Some educators now argue that bilingual education is necessary for the growing Asian population in the United States. In *Myth or Reality: Adaptive Strategies of Asian Americans in California*, Henry Trueba, Li Rong, Lilly Cheng, and Kenji Ima advocate bilingual education for Asian Americans who are having difficulty learning English. They contend that many Asian immigrants are never able to enter mainstream classrooms because they never learn English. Consequently, many Asian Americans drop out of school before graduation but often go unnoticed because of the academic success of other Asian American students. According to their study, Asian immigrants who received no training in English before coming to the United States are most at risk for dropping out of school. The importance of prior training in English for academic success is highlighted by the argument "that the higher academic performance of Asians in contrast with Hispanics is consistent with the fact that 31 percent of Asians had trained in English before their arrival . . . in contrast with only 3 percent for Hispanics."

In addition, certain Asian immigrants come from areas with oral traditions and they have little exposure to written materials in their own language. This is particularly true of children from the Pacific Islands, Laotian rural groups, and Montagnards from Vietnam. This lack of exposure to a written language is a major obstacle to learning English. These students, it is argued, have difficulty differentiating between the written language forms of the classroom and oral language forms.

But even Asian American students who are successful in school continue to have language problems. At both the undergraduate and graduate levels in college, Asian Americans are predominantly in engineering, physical sciences, mathematics, and computer sciences. "Asian students," the authors write, "pursue occupations they perceive as having higher status and ones in which communicative language skills are less required." Choosing fields requiring little communicative skills limits Asian American choices in the job market.

While bilingual education remains a controversial issue, many non-English-speaking students are served primarily by English as a Second Language (ESL) programs. Although the teachers of these programs might speak the language of the students, the primary purpose of ESL classes is to teach students English so that they can learn the content of instruction in English. Unlike bilingual education programs, no attempt is made to teach reading and writing in the native language of the students.

The differences between bilingual and ESL education programs highlight the bicultural aspects of bilingualism. The general goal of ESL is the learning of English and, as a result, the gaining of knowledge about European American culture. On the other hand, Mexican Americans, Native Americans, and Puerto Ricans advocate bilingualism to retain both the student's native language and culture while learning English and European American culture.

ENGLISH LANGUAGE ACQUISITION ACT OF 2001

In 2001, a majority of Congress and President George W. Bush opposed bilingual education and stood firmly for the principle that the primary objective of U.S. schools should be the teaching of English without any attempt to preserve minority languages. The limited exception was for Native Americans and Puerto Ricans. While recognizing programs designed to maintain Native American languages and Spanish, the major thrust, the legislation states, of these programs had to be English proficiency. The legislation declares that programs authorized under this part that serve Native American (including Native American Pacific Islander) children and children in the Commonwealth of Puerto Rico may include programs . . . designed for Native American children learning and studying Native American languages and children of limited Spanish proficiency, except that an outcome of programs serving such children *shall be increased English proficiency among such children* [my emphasis].

The English Language Acquisition Act's nine major purposes clearly spell out the antibilingual education agenda: As the Office of Bilingual Education becomes the Office of English Acquisition, the goals focus on teaching English in the context of state academic standards and high-stakes testing. In fact, the first stated purpose of the legislation reads: "(1) to help ensure that children who are limited English proficient, including immigrant children and youth, attain English proficiency, develop high levels of academic attainment in English, and meet the same challenging State academic content and student academic achievement standards as all children are expected to meet." The next eight legislative purposes support this first goal, including (2) to prepare for learning core academic subjects; (3) to develop language instructional programs for limited-English-proficient students; (4) to design instructional programs that prepare limited-English-proficient children to enter all-English instruction settings; (5) to continue English instruction for limited-English-proficient children; (6) to provide language instruction programs for the parents and communities of limited-English proficient children; (7) to streamline the grant programs for English-language acquisition.

The eighth purpose gives the federal government supervisory power to ensure that states comply with the intent of the legislation. Even if a state government supports bilingual education, it is now faced with the problem of having to refuse any federal money granted under this legislation. Further, the legislation requires that state governments measure English proficiency. Specifically, the federal government will "hold State educational agencies, local educational agencies, and schools accountable for increases in English proficiency and core academic content knowledge of limited English proficient children by requiring—(A) demonstrated improvements in the English proficiency of limited English proficient children each fiscal year." The ninth and final purpose uses the language of "scientifically based research" to ensure that schools do not use bilingual education methods to teach English proficiency.

The larger question is whether politicians and the federal government should ever have been involved in the struggle to protect minority languages. The English Language Acquisition Act of 2001 replaces the goals and programs of the Bilingual Education Act of 1968. Will some future federal legislation resurrect federal involvement in bilingualism? Imagine the waste of time and money in replacing the Office of Bilingual Education with the Office of English Language Acquisition! Of course, there will continue to be a struggle between the advocates of English-only and those wanting to protect minority languages. This issue will persist in debates about American education.

GLOBALIZATION: LANGUAGE AND CULTURAL RIGHTS

The issues surrounding language and culture of the schools are present in most of the world's nations, as most nations are now multicultural and multilingual. As a result, there has been a call for international recognition of language and cultural rights. A longtime champion of these international rights, Tove Skutnabb-Kangas proposes a universal covenant protecting linguistic human rights as part of the protection of cultural rights. Key to her proposal is the definition of a mother tongue. A mother tongue, she writes, can be distinguished as "the language one learned first (the language one has established the first long-lasting verbal contacts in)" or "the language one identifies with/as a native speaker of; and/or the language one knows best."

Of fundamental importance to Tove Skutnabb-Kangas's Universal Covenant of Linguistic Human Rights is the stress on bilingual education if the student's language is not the official national language or the language of global culture and economics, which at this time is English. Bilingualism resolves the problem of maintaining the mother tongue and associated culture, while ensuring that the student has access to the world's knowledge. According to her Universal Covenant, everybody has the right to

- Identify with his/her mother tongue(s) and have this identification accepted and respected by others.
- Learn the mother tongue(s) fully, orally (when physiologically possible) and in writing.

- Profit from education mainly through the medium of their mother tongue(s) and within the state-financed educational system.
- Use the mother tongue in most official situations (including schools).

In reference to other languages, the covenant states that those "whose mother tongue is not an official language in the country where s/he is resident . . . [have the right] to become bilingual (or trilingual, if s/he has 2 mother tongues) in the mother tongue(s) and (one of) the official language(s) (according to her own choice)." Additionally, "any change . . . [in] mother tongue . . . [should be] voluntary (includes knowledge of long-term consequences) . . . [and] not imposed."

Applied to the United States, this covenant would mean that students whose mother tongues were not English would have the right to receive instruction in their mother tongues but would not have to exercise that right. In other words, students could choose to be instructed in English. The covenant also guarantees that all children will learn English, the dominant language of the United States. Essentially, students would have the right to a bilingual education if they wanted.

Some constitutions of other nations specifically recognize language rights. For instance, the Italian Constitution states, "The Republic shall safeguard linguistic minorities by means of special provisions." The Indian Constitution provides specific protection for minority language rights. The Indian Constitution states:

> 350. **Facilities for instruction in mother-tongue at primary stage:** It shall be the endeavor of every State and of every local authority within the State to provide adequate facilities for instruction in the mother-tongue at the primary stage of education to children belonging to linguistic minority groups.

Should the government be required to provide classes in a mother tongue that is spoken by only one or two students in a community? Realistically, the educational rights of minority languages can only be exercised when there is a sufficient number of students speaking a language. This is particularly a problem in a country like the United States with a high number of immigrants. Considering this problem an international agreement on language rights might state: Everyone has a right to an education using the medium of their mother-tongue within a government-financed school system when the number of students requesting instruction in that mother tongue equals the average number of students in a classroom in that government financed school system.

Of equal importance is learning the dominant or official language of society. Therefore, an addition to the right to learn minority languages might state: Everyone has the right to learn the dominant or official language of the nation. The government-financed school system will make every effort to ensure that all students are literate in the dominant or official language of the country.

Cultural rights are an important issue for indigenous peoples such as Native Americans. The United Nation's International Labor Office defines indigenous peoples as "tribal peoples in independent countries whose social, cultural and economic conditions distinguish them from other sections of the national community, and whose status is regulated wholly or partially by their own customs or traditions." In addition, the definition includes those groups who identify themselves as indigenous. This definition of indigenous includes, for example, Native Americans and Hawaiians in the United States, Aborigines in Australia, Mayans in Guatemala, Maoris in New Zealand, and Hmongs in Laos. The World Commission on Culture and Development estimates that in 1995, indigenous peoples composed 7 percent of the population of China and India (80 and 65 million, respectively). In the Americas, the largest numbers of indigenous peoples are in Peru (8.6 million) and Mexico (8 million). In Africa, the number is 25 million. The international group Worldwatch estimates that there are at least 300 million indigenous people worldwide and that between 4,000 and 5,000 of the 6,000 world languages are spoken by indigenous peoples.

A Declaration of Indigenous Peoples' Rights has been proposed to the United Nations. The declaration asserts, with regard to human rights and development,

> That the indigenous peoples have been deprived of their *human rights and fundamental freedoms,* resulting . . . in their colonization and dispossession of their lands, territories, and resources, thus preventing them from exercising, in particular, *their right to development in accordance with their own needs and interests* [my emphasis].

Regarding the right to education, the declaration asserts that indigenous children have a right to education in their own language and according to cultural practices. Article 15 states:

> Indigenous children have the right to all levels and forms of education of the State. All indigenous peoples also have this right and the right to establish and control their educational systems and institutions providing education in their own languages, in a manner appropriate to their cultural methods of teaching and learning.
> Recognition of these rights in the United States would guarantee that Native Americans would have the right to operate their own schools according to the principles of their cultures and using their languages.

CONCLUSION

The struggle over issues of language and culture will continue as dominated groups struggle for equality of opportunity and as new immigrant groups adjust to American society. On a global scale, issues of multicultural, ethnocentric, bicultural, and bilingual education will become increasingly important with the development of a global economy and the internationalization of the labor force. The United States is not the only country confronting these issues. Many European American countries have begun multicultural education programs because of the influx of foreign workers.

In the United States, conflict will continue between those who want to maintain the supremacy of English and European American traditions and dominated cultures whose members want to protect and maintain their cultural traditions. Many Native Americans, African Americans, and Hispanics reject the image of European American culture at the head of a dinner table ruling over other cultures. In addition, many immigrant groups might not be willing to give up their cultural traditions to a European American model. But whatever the conclusion of this conflict, American public schools will never be the same after the impact of the cultural and language demands of dominated groups and after the adjustment of educational programs to meet the needs of the new immigrants.

The discussion of multiculturalism generates the following set of questions:

- Should public schools teach a common culture to all students? Should that common culture be based on a Eurocentric culture?
- Should English be the official language of the United States?
- Should students have the right to learn their mother tongue and the dominant language?
- Should students have the right to receive instruction in their own culture?
- Should the major goal of instruction about different cultures be the teaching of appreciation of other cultures?
- Should public schools teach non-Eurocentric cultural traditions to maintain those cultural traditions?
- Should multicultural education attempt to change the dominant culture by incorporating values from other cultures?

Suggested Readings and Works Cited in Chapter

Advisory Board for the President's Initiative on Race. *One America in the 21st Century: Forging a New Future.* Washington, DC: U.S. Printing Office, 1998. Report predicting future of race relations in the twenty-first century.

ANYON, JEAN. *Ghetto Schooling: Political Economy of Urban Educational Reform.* New York: Teachers College Press, 1997. This book demonstrates how the combination of politics and economics creates segregated and underfunded urban schools.

ASANTE, MOLEFI KETE. *Afrocentricity.* Trenton, NJ: Africa World Press, Inc., 1988. This is an important discussion of the philosophy of Afrocentricity.

BANKS, JAMES. "Multicultural Education: Historical Development, Dimensions, and Practice." In *Review of Research in Education* 19, edited by Linda Darling-Hammond. Washington, DC: American Educational Research Association, 1993, pp. 3–50. This article is an excellent introduction to the development of the field of multicultural education.

DELPIT, LISA. *Other People's Children: Cultural Conflict in the Classroom.* New York: The New Press, 1995. Delpit provides a strong argument for utilizing a student's culture to prepare him/her for success in the economic power structure of the United States.

ESTRICH, SUSAN. "For Girls' Schools and Women's Colleges, Separate Is Better." *The New York Times Magazine* (22 May 1994): 39. Estrich argues against coeducation.

"Exit Polls on the June 2nd Vote on Proposition 227." *Los Angeles Times/Washington Edition* (4 June 1998). http://www.latimes.com. Results of voting on bilingual issue in California are provided.

FEDULLO, MICK. *Light of the Feather: Pathways Through Contemporary Indian America.* New York: William Morrow, 1992. Fedullo provides a beautiful description of the development of bicultural education among Native Americans.

HACKER, ANDREW. *Two Nations: Black and White, Separate, Hostile, Unequal.* New York: Charles Scribners' Son, 1992. This is a study of racial divisions in the United States.

HELLER, CAROL, and JOSEPH HAWKINS. "Teaching Tolerance: Notes from the Front Line." *Teachers College Record* (Spring 1994): 1–30. A history and description of the Teaching Tolerance project is presented.

IGNATIEV, N., and JOHN GARVEY. *Race Traitor.* New York: Routledge, 1996. This important book for antiracist education is based on the idea of the importance of deconstructing and reconstructing "whiteness."

IGOA, CRISTINA. *The Inner World of the Immigrant Child.* Mahwah, NJ: Lawrence Erlbaum Associates, Inc., 1995. This is an invaluable guide to instructing immigrant children and dealing with their educational and psychological problems.

KUNJUFU, JAWANZA. *To Be Popular or Smart: The Black Peer Group.* Chicago: African American Images, 1988. This is a discussion of the attitudes of African American youth regarding education.

——. *Countering the Conspiracy to Destroy Black Boys.* Chicago: African American Images, 1985. This book provides a strong argument for the necessity of an Afrocentric curriculum.

LAMAR, JAKE. *Bourgeois Blues: An American Memoir.* New York: Penguin, 1992. This powerful contemporary autobiography details the racism encountered by an upper-middle-class African American.

NISBETT, RICHARD E. *The Geography of Thought: How Asians and Westerners Think Differently . . . and Why.* York: Free Press, 2003. This is the pioneer study contrasting different ways of seeing and knowing the world.

NIETO, SONIA. *Affirming Diversity: The Sociopolitical Context of Multicultural Education.* White Plains, NY: Longman, Inc., 1992. This is a good introduction to issues in multicultural education.

OGBU, JOHN. "Class Stratification, Racial Stratification, and Schooling." In *Class, Race, & Gender in American Education,* edited by Lois Weis. Albany: State University of New York Press, 1988, pp. 163–183. In this article, Ogbu outlines his basic theory for the development of resistance to schooling among dominated cultures in the United States.

OYERMAN, DAPHNA; IZUMI SAKAMOTO; and ARMAND LAUFFER, "Cultural Accommodation: Hybridity and the Framing of Social Obligation," *Journal of Personality and Social Psychology,* Vol. 74 (1998): 1606–1616. This article explains the concept of cultural hybridity as related to different beliefs about social obligations.

PERRY, PAMELA. *Shades of White: White Kids and Racial Identities in High School.* Durham: Duke University Press, 2002. Perry performs an important study of how white high school students form their racial identities.

PORTER, ROSALIE PEDALINO. *Forked Tongue: The Politics of Bilingual Education.* New York: Basic Books, 1990. Porter attacks maintenance bilingual education programs. The book is a good introduction to the controversy surrounding bilingual education.

Public Law 107–110, 107th Congress, Jan. 8, 2002 [H.R. 1]. "No Child Left Behind Act of 2001." Washington, DC: U.S. Printing Office, 2002. This federal legislation contains the English Acquisition, Language Enhancement, and Academic Achievement Act which overturns the 1968 Bilingual Education Act.

RODRIGUEZ, RICHARD. *Hunger of Memory: The Education of Richard Rodriguez.* New York: Bantam Books, 1982. This is an important autobiography of the emotional and social struggles of a successful Mexican American student.

SAN MIGUEL, JR., GUADALUPE. *"Let All of Them Take Heed": Mexican Americans and the Campaign for Education Equality in Texas, 1910–1981.* Austin: University of Texas Lightening Source Titles, 1987. This is a landmark book on the Mexican American struggle for equality of education.

SADKER, MYRA and DAVID. *Failing at Fairness: How America's Schools Cheat Girls.* New York: Scribner's, 1995. This is the landmark study on the treatment of women in American schools.

"SETCLAE: Self-Esteem Through Culture Leads to Academic Excellence." Chicago: African American Images, 1991. This is a model Afrocentric curriculum.

SKUTNABB-KANGAS, TOVE. *Linguistic Genocide in Education or Worldwide Diversity and Human Rights?* Mahwah, NJ: Lawrence Erlbaum Associates, 2000. This publication is the most comprehensive study of language rights issues.

SPRING, JOEL. *The Universal Right to Education: Justification, Definition, and Guidelines.* Mahwah, NJ: Lawrence Erlbaum Associates, Inc., 2000. This book provides a justification for the universal right to education provided by the Universal Declaration of Human Rights. The book discusses cultural, lingual, and child rights and provides examples of human rights teaching.

——. *Globalization and Educational Rights: An Intercivilizational Analysis.* Mahwah, NJ: Lawrence Erlbaum Associates, Inc., 2000. This book discusses educational rights in the context of Confucian, Moslem, Hindu, and Western civilizations and as provided for in the constitutions of the world's nations. The book offers a statement of educational rights that could be included in national constitutions.

——. *Education and the Rise of the Global Economy.* Mahwah, NJ: Lawrence Erlbaum Associates, Inc., 1998. This book describes the process of globalization of education through colonialism and current economic policies.

SUH, EUNKOOK. "Self, the Hyphen between Culture and Subjective Well-Being." In *Culture and Subjective Well-Being,* edited by Ed Diener and Eunkook M. Suh. Cambridge: Massachusetts Institute of Technology Press, 2000. This article describes the differences between collectivist and individualist society, particularly regarding a sense of subjective well-being.

TATUM, BEVERLY DANIEL. *Why Are All the Black Kids Sitting Together in the Cafeteria?* New York: Basic Books, 1997. This landmark book on antiracist education discusses methods of creating positive antiracist models for white students.

TRUEBA, HENRY, et al. *Myth or Reality: Adaptative Strategies of Asian-Americans in California.* New York: Falmer Press, 1993. This is a study of Asian American adjustments to social life in California.

PART TWO

Power and Control in American Education

CHAPTER 6

Local Control, Choice, Charter Schools, and Home Schooling

This chapter examines the complicated question: Who controls American education? If schools are considered a major disseminator of knowledge to children and youth, then the bigger question is: Who decides what knowledge is of most worth to teach to students? These questions are directly linked to the goals of education discussed in Chapter 1. For instance, take the goal of developing human capital to ensure the United States remains competitive in the global economy. Who decides that this should be the goal of schools? Who decides what should be taught to attain this goal? Who decides how teachers should teach the knowledge considered necessary for educating workers for the global workforce?

There are several ways political control is exercised over schools. One way is through voting for representatives in the federal and state governments that legislate education policies. The second is through voting for local school boards. A third way is through parents voting with their feet by deciding to exercise choice regarding what school their children attend or if they want to keep their children out of school and educate them at home.

The first section of this chapter, "The Education Chair," asks a central question regarding the control of education: Who should decide what knowledge should be taught to public school students? Should it be national politicians, federal administrators, state politicians, state administrators, local school boards, teachers, or parents? This question is important in light of recent debates about the teaching of evolution in science courses and sexual abstinence education. Who should decide whether a student should learn evolutionary theory and/or alternative theories in science courses? Who should decide the content of instruction regarding birth control instruction and/or abstinence education?

The second section on local school boards will be followed by a discussion of the choice plans embodied in the federal legislation No Child Left Behind. This legislation not only impacts local control but it also encourages school choice, charter schools, and for-profit education. After discussing the basic provisions of No Child Left Behind, I will discuss school choice, charter schools, home schooling, and for-profit education.

THE EDUCATION CHAIR

One way of thinking about the problem of control is to imagine yourself sitting in what I will call the education chair. Imagine that at a flick of a lever this chair has the power to shape your morality, to control your behavior, and to teach you any subject. This education chair can be considered a public school that works. After all, the goals of public schooling include moral instruction, shaping behavior, and transmitting knowledge.

Now the question is, Who should control this education chair? In other words, who should decide your morality, behavior, and knowledge? You? Your parents? Your professor of education? Elected officials? How you answer this question will reflect the political values you have regarding the control of public schools.

Currently, the debate over who should control education has ranged from the business community to religious organizations to minority parents. Many groups have a stake in the outcomes of public schooling. The business community wants graduates with knowledge and behaviors that conform to its needs. Some religious organizations want schools to teach their versions of morality. In fact, a major controversy in recent years has involved fundamentalist Protestant churches accusing the public schools of teaching a morality that is destructive to their religious principles. In a similar manner, minority parents complain that public schools are damaging to their children because they teach the culture and values of the white elite.

Understanding the concept of representation is important for answering the question of who should control American education. The United States is primarily composed of representative forms of government; that is, people elect government officials to represent them on school boards, in state legislatures, and in Congress. In only a few situations, such as voting on local property taxes, are decisions made by the direct vote.

While reading this chapter, you should keep in mind the following questions:

- Who should decide what knowledge should be taught in public schools?
- Do you think public schools should let parents decide what should be taught to their children?
- Should parents receive government funding to send their children to a private secular school, a religious school, or a for-profit school?
- Do you think the government should finance only parental choice of public schools?
- Should state charter school laws finance private secular schools, religious schools, or for-profit schools?

SCHOOL BOARDS

Traditionally, community members exercise their control over public schools by electing representatives to local school boards. In turn, the school board appoints the superintendent of schools who functions as the chief executive officer of the school district. Usually, the superintendent of schools works out of the central office of the school district. School principals report directly to the central office and the superintendent.

This traditional district organization is criticized for its lack of responsiveness to the desires of parents. School board members are criticized for not representing the interests of the parents. The central office and superintendent are criticized for being bureaucratic barriers to any real change in the school district. (As I will discuss later in this chapter, home schooling, school choice, and charter schools are promoted as giving power to parents when faced with unrepresentative school boards and an entrenched bureaucratic structure in the central office.)

Boards of education are criticized for their elite membership. In other words, their membership primarily is drawn from the professional and business groups in the local community. This is not so true in rural areas, where there is often heavy representation from the farm community. Most boards of education in the United States are composed of white male professionals or businesspeople. The representation from this group on boards of education is out of proportion to their actual numbers in the population so it does not reflect the social composition of the local community.

In 2004, the National School Boards Association issued a national profile of school board members. Authored by Frederick Hess, the survey confirmed the tendency for school board members to be drawn from only a select subgroup of the entire population. Specifically, as indicated in Table 6–1, the survey concluded that school boards are less racially diverse than is the nation as a whole with membership being 85.5 percent white, 7.8 percent African American, and 3.8 percent Hispanic. In addition, as indicated in Table 6–2, a disproportionate number of school board members are male, 61.1 versus 38.9 percent female. Finally, as indicated in Tables 6–3 through 6–5, the survey concluded, "Board members have higher incomes and are better-educated than the typical American. This is especially true in large districts. Nearly half of respondents list that their occupational background is business or professional, while relatively few indicate a professional background in education."

SCHOOL CHOICE

School choice gives parents the power to vote their feet by allowing them to select a school for their children. However, there have been proposed a variety of school choice plans. Some involve parental choice of only public schools

TABLE 6–1. Racial Composition of U.S. School Boards

White	85.5%
African American	7.8
Hispanic	3.8
Other	2.3

Source: Frederick Hess, it *School Boards at the Dawn of the 21st Century* (Alexandria, VA: National School Boards Association, 2004), p. 25.

TABLE 6–2. Gender Composition of U.S. School Boards

Male	61.1%
Female	36.7

Source: Frederick Hess, it *School Boards at the Dawn of the 21st Century* (Alexandria, VA: National School Boards Association, 2004), p. 26.

TABLE 6–3. Annual Household Incomes of U.S. School Board Members

Less than $25,000	2.0%
$25,000–$74,999	38.9
$75,000–149,999	43.5
$150,000–200,000	10.8
More than $200,000	4.8

Source: Frederick Hess, it *School Boards at the Dawn of the 21st Century* (Alexandria, VA: National School Boards Association, 2004), p. 26.

TABLE 6–4. U.S. School Board Members' Professional Background

Business/professional	44.6%
Homemaker/retired	26.2
Education	13.0
Nonprofit/government	10.6
Other	5.6

Source: Frederick Hess, it *School Boards at the Dawn of the 21st Century* (Alexandria, VA: National School Boards Association, 2004), p. 27.

TABLE 6–5. Educational Attainment of U.S. School Board Members

Did not graduate high school	0.6%
High school graduate	6.2
Some college	26.2
Four-year college degree	28.7
Graduate degree	38.3

Source: Frederick Hess, it *School Boards at the Dawn of the 21st Century* (Alexandria, VA: National School Boards Association, 2004), p. 27.

while others include private schools. Those advocating parental choice of public or private schools often include the use of vouchers. Parents take a voucher from the government to the school and the school is reimbursed. Another choice is a charter school, which I will discuss in another section of this chapter. The following is a list of different types of choice plans:

1. *Public School Choice.* Under this type of choice plan, parents of students are free to choose any public school in their district or in the state. Traditionally, students are assigned to schools in their districts and if they wish to attend school in another district, then they are often required to pay tuition.
   a. Types of public school choice plans.
      i. Open enrollment among schools in a district or among districts.
      ii. Magnet schools designed to attract students and integrate schools; some restrictions are made to balance enrollment.
      iii. Alternative schools within a school district.
      iv. Public charter schools (described later in this chapter).
2. *Public-Private Choice.* Parents of students can choose between a public or private school with the tuition at the private school being paid for by a government or privately issued voucher. Traditionally, students have the choice of private and public schools without government support. Government support of private school choice, some argue, provides the opportunity for children from low-income families to attend private schools.
3. *Failing-School Choice.* Under No Child Left Behind, parents of students in schools not making adequate yearly progress can choose another school for their children. The policies surrounding this choice plan are discussed in the following section of this chapter, "National Public School Choice Plan: No Child Left Behind Act of 2001."
4. *Low-Income Private School Vouchers.* Taxpayer dollars are used to pay for all or part of the cost for students from low-income families to attend private and, often, religious schools.

The original 1960s proposal by economist Milton Friedman is very similar to the choice provisions of the No Child Left Behind Act of 2001. The National Center for Education Statistics reported in *The Condition of Education 2006* that in 2003 15 percent of public school students were attending schools of choice. Both Friedman's proposal and this recent legislation provide parents with children in low-performing schools the opportunity to send their children to another public school. Milton Friedman's original proposal called for the government to give parents monetary vouchers that could be used to purchase an education for their children at any school. Parents would give the vouchers to the school that enrolled their child. The school would then turn the voucher over to the government for reimbursement. Vouchers are another method for distributing tax dollars to schools. As a free market economist, Friedman blamed the poor quality of public schools on the lack of competition. Also, he argued that impoverished parents are often trapped in poor school systems because they cannot afford to move to the school districts with better schools.

The free market aspects of Friedman's plan appealed to many school reformers. The assumption of free market economics is that competition will produce the best products. Advocates argue that if parents can choose between schools, then schools will be forced to improve to remain competitive. Schools are like any other product in the marketplace. If a large number of parents don't choose a particular school, then that school would be forced to either change or shut down. If the school that is least attractive to parents wants to survive it will probably model itself after a school that is attractive to parents or create an entirely new educational package. Imagine the production of cars: if no one buys a particular car model, then the company must either discontinue the model or improve it.

Of course, schools differ from automobiles in that they are produced by the government and by private groups. The mix of public and private schools adds another dimension to choice plans. Should the government issue vouchers that can be redeemed only at public schools? Or should the government issue vouchers that can be redeemed at both public and private schools? The answers to these questions are reflected in the following plans:

Many supporters of religious schooling and free market advocates support the public-private model of choice. Supporters of private Catholic schools argued from the nineteenth century that it is unfair that they should pay for the education of public school students while paying for their children to attend a religious school. In addition, Catholics and Protestant fundamentalists complain that the moral values taught in public schools are destructive of the values of Christianity and that their only choice is to send their children to private religious schools. The rapid growth of private Catholic schools occurred in the nineteenth and early twentieth century, while privately operated fundamentalist Protestant schools grew rapidly in the latter half of the twentieth century.

The two teachers' unions are leading critics of school choice plans, particularly those involving private religious schools. For instance, the American Federation of Teachers declared:

> The AFT supports parents' right to send their children to private or religious schools but opposes the use of public funds to do so. The main reason for this opposition is because public funding of private or religious education transfers precious tax dollars from public schools, which are free and open to all children, accountable to parents and taxpayers alike, and essential to our democracy, to private and religious schools that charge for their services, select their students on the basis of religious or academic or family or personal characteristics, and are accountable only to their boards and clients.

In 2006, the American Federation of Teachers (AFT) issued "School Vouchers: Myths and Facts," which contained information highly critical of public-private choice plans that used vouchers. Among the many criticisms of public-private choice plans, "School Vouchers: Myths and Facts" lists the following:

> *Myth:* Vouchers will improve public education.
> *Fact:* Some voucher advocates claim that in addition to improving the education of those who leave failing schools to attend private schools, vouchers will also improve the education of those who stay behind, because the threat of competition will force their school to improve. *Despite claims to the contrary, there is no credible evidence to prove that this actually works* [my emphasis].
> *Myth:* Vouchers will save taxpayers money because the private sector can run schools more efficiently than the public sector can.
> *Fact:* Contrary to the belief that vouchers [save tax payers money] . . . voucher programs actually cost taxpayers more. Many private schools charge low tuition

rates because their costs are subsidized by other sources. Among voucher schools, in-depth studies of voucher programs point to reckless spending.

Similar to the American Federation of Teachers, the National Education Association declares in its information sheet "Vouchers" that efforts for school improvement should attempt to "reduce class size, enhance teacher quality, and provide every student with books, computers, and safe and orderly schools." The organization offers some of the following objections to public-private choice plans that use vouchers:

The Social Case Against Vouchers

- A voucher lottery is a terrible way to determine access to an education. True equity means the ability for every child to attend a good school in the neighborhood.
- Vouchers were not designed to help low-income children. Milton Friedman, the "grandfather" of vouchers, dismissed the notion that vouchers could help low-income families, saying "it is essential that no conditions be attached to the acceptance of vouchers that interfere with the freedom of private enterprises to experiment."
- A pure voucher system would only encourage economic, racial, ethnic, and religious stratification in our society. America's success has been built on our ability to unify our diverse populations.

A nagging question is whether public-private choice plans will increase racial segregation. The question is complicated because of the possibility of minority low-income families using choice plans to enter private school with a resulting integration of private education. This issue is examined by Robert Fairlie in a report for the National Center for the Study of Privatization in Education, titled "Racial Segregation and the Private/Public School Choice." He found that "At both the eighth and tenth grade levels, blacks and Hispanics are substantially less likely to attend private schools than are whites . . . [and] that white and Hispanic students enroll in private schools in response to large concentrations of black students." However, he did find that because of low levels of income, black and Hispanic families were underrepresented in the private school system. These findings led Fairlie to make two conflicting hypotheses about private school tuition vouchers. One hypothesis is that "private school tuition vouchers may lead to more segregation as families have increased opportunities to enroll their children in homogenous schools." The other is that since "racial differences in income explain a significant portion of the gap in private school [attendance] rates . . . vouchers directed towards low-income families may reduce this gap." Again, these are hypotheses with no clear-cut answer. Private school vouchers might increase segregation. On the other hand, vouchers to low-income families might increase integration of the private school system.

The choice controversy continues in a highly charged political atmosphere. In the next section, I will explain the public school choice provisions of No Child Left Behind. This public school choice plan represents a compromise between Republicans and Democrats.

NATIONAL PUBLIC SCHOOL CHOICE PLAN: NO CHILD LEFT BEHIND ACT OF 2001

The No Child Left Behind Act requires local school districts to implement a public school choice plan for parents with children in unsafe and/or failing schools. The U.S. Department of Education in its guide *Choice Provisions in No Child Left Behind* provides that students in unsafe situations be allowed to transfer to other, safer public schools. Transfers must be allowed for two reasons: (1) when a school is determined to be "persistently dangerous," and (2) when a student becomes the victim of a violent crime at a school.

The Unsafe Schools Choice Option also requires states to determine "persistently dangerous" schools by using objective criteria such as the number of times a firearm has been brought into a school, the number of fights, and so on, within the current or most recent school year. Furthermore, if a student becomes the victim of a violent criminal offense at school, the LEA (local education authority) must allow the student the choice to transfer to another public school.

Parents of students in failing schools are given the option of sending their children to another school in the same school district. A failing school is defined as one that does not make adequate yearly progress (AYP).

According to the U.S. Department of Education, a school or district achieves AYP when each group of students meets or exceeds the statewide annual objective. Further for each group, 95 percent of students enrolled must participate in the assessments on which AYP is based.

Schools not achieving adequate yearly progress are given the time line shown in Table 6–6 for school improvement. If the school fails to make adequate yearly progress two years in a row, in the following year the school must be provided with technical assistance for improvement and parents must be allowed the choice of another public school within the same public school district. In the next year, supplemental educational services such as tutoring must be provided to students along with technical assistance and public school choice. It should be noted that supplemental educational services can be from for-profit organizations.

According to the U.S. Department of Education, any school offered as a choice option must have higher academic performance than the school of origin and may not be identified for improvement. That is, students may not transfer to any schools that have been identified for improvement, corrective action, or the planning year of restructuring; or have been identified by the state as persistently dangerous. In addition, the choice option can include public charter schools within the boundaries of the local education authorities. However, local education authorities cannot disregard entrance requirements, such as evidence of specific academic ability or other skills, when identifying transfer options for students. For example, students wishing to transfer to a fine arts magnet school or to a school for gifted students would still need to meet the requirements to attend those schools.

And finally, what if no schools are available for choice by parents whose children are in unsafe schools or schools not making adequate yearly progress?

TABLE 6–6. Improvement Time Line for Schools Not Making Adequate Yearly Progress

Year	Assessment	Action Taken
1	Baseline established for measuring yearly progress	
2	Fail to make adequate yearly progress	
3	Fail to make adequate yearly progress	
4	1st year of school improvement	Technical assistance; public school choice
5	2nd year of school improvement	Technical assistance; public school choice; supplemental educational services

Source: Adapted from Cheri Pierson Yecke and Laura O. Lazo, "Sample School Timeline," *Choice Provisions in No Child Left Behind* (Washington, DC: U.S. Department of Education, 2002).

Parents must be offered the option of supplemental services such as tutoring, and/or the school system can make a cooperative agreement with another school district to receive choice students.

CHARTER SCHOOLS

Charter schools represent another method of bypassing unrepresentative school boards and educational bureaucracies. The idea was first proposed by educator Ray Budde in the 1970s and then promoted by AFT President Albert Shanker in the 1990s. Minnesota and California had the first charter school laws in 1991 and 1992, respectively. State charter school legislation mushroomed in the 1990s, and it was estimated in the report *State of the Charter Movement 2005* that there were about 1 million students enrolled in approximately 3,400 charter schools.

The No Child Left Behind Act defines a charter school as:

> (1) CHARTER SCHOOL.—The term "charter school" means a public school that—
>
> (A) in accordance with a specific State statute authorizing the granting of charters to schools, is exempt from significant State or local rules that inhibit the flexible operation and management of public schools, but not from any rules relating to the other requirements of this paragraph;
>
> (B) is created by a developer as a public school, or is adapted by a developer from an existing public school, and is operated under public supervision and direction;
>
> (C) operates in pursuit of a specific set of educational objectives determined by the school's developer and agreed to by the authorized public chartering agency;

> (D) provides a program of elementary or secondary education, or both;
> (E) is nonsectarian in its programs, admissions policies, employment practices, and all other operations, and is not affiliated with a sectarian school or religious institution;
> (F) does not charge tuition;
> (G) complies with the Age Discrimination Act of 1975, title VI of the Civil Rights Act of 1964, title IX of the Education Amendments of 1972, section 504 of the Rehabilitation Act of 1973, and part B of the Individuals with Disabilities Education Act;
> (H) is a school to which parents choose to send their children, and that admits students on the basis of a lottery, if more students apply for admission than can be accommodated;
> (I) agrees to comply with the same Federal and State audit requirements as do other elementary schools and secondary schools in the State, unless such requirements are specifically waived for the purpose of this program.

As just above, charter schools are public schools. They are different from regular public schools in that they are, as stated in section (A), "exempt from significant State or local rules." This exemption is supposed to foster innovative teaching, curriculum, and school organization. Also, as stated in section (B), a charter school can be developed as a new public school or created from "an existing public school." According to federal legislation, as stated in section (F), they cannot charge tuition. Charter schools, per sections (E) and (G), cannot be affiliated with a religious institution and they cannot discriminate on the basis of age, race, gender, religion, ethnic origin, or disability. In addition, according to section (L), charter school students must take any state-required tests.

The basic charter school structure involves a local agency applying to the state to receive a charter to operate as a school at public expense. The governmental relationship is directly between a charter school and the state agency responsible for granting charters. This allows a charter school to operate outside the control of the state educational bureaucracy and the local school board and its bureaucracy. Consequently, a charter school is free to experiment with different methods of instruction and school organization.

Charter school laws vary widely from state to state. The Charter Schools division of the U.S. Department of Education (http://www.uscharterschools.org) provides links to state laws governing charter schools. Some states allow a variety of agencies to charter schools, while others allow only a single state agency to grant charters. In some states only public schools are allowed to convert to charter schools, while in other states the establishment of new schools is also allowed. States vary in their requirements for charter school compliance with state education regulations. Most states have granted automatic waivers to most of the state education code, but in a few states, charter schools must follow most of the state education code.

In the 2004–2005 school year, there were 3,294 charter schools in the 40 states that allowed them as compared to 90,001 conventional public schools throughout the United States. Maybe as a reflection of a failure of regular public schools, charter schools enrolled a higher percentage of black, Hispanic, and American Indian/Alaska Native students than white and Asian/Pacific Islander students when compared to conventional public schools. Charter schools also had a higher percentage of students eligible for free or reduced-price lunch than conventional public schools. Charter schools were more likely than conventional public schools to be located in central cities. These figures indicate that many low-income minority parents believe that their children will received a better education in charter schools than conventional public schools.

Some charter schools even combine home schooling and distance learning. Distance learning involves instruction in the home using the Internet. Charter schools using distance learning are called Cyber Charters. The National Center for the Study of Privatization in Education lists the following characteristics of Cyber Charters:

- *Teaching and learning:* computer software, external teacher.
- *Organizational model:* computer instruction, home based setting.
- *Governance model:* cyber school, external teachers, state agencies.
- *Accountability:* fiscal, charter granting agency, testing (if required).

Three Examples of Charter Schools

The following is a description of three charter schools that are separated by philosophy and geography. They represent the startling contrasts that exist among charter schools around the country.

Located in San Diego, California, High Tech High was opened in 2000 to solve the labor shortage in high-tech industries. Executives from Qualcomm and other high-tech industries spent three years planning the school, with Qualcomm donating $3 million to the project. The long-range plan is to establish nine other High Tech Highs around the country.

High Tech High opened in September 2000 with 200 ninth and tenth grade students selected by lottery from 1,000 applications. At the school, the student's day is broken into two parts: One part focuses on independent work and the other stresses group work. Each student is given a workstation similar to what adults have in the workplace. Students develop digital portfolios that can be displayed online or on a CD-ROM.

Across the United States from High Tech High, students at the Bronx Preparatory Charter School begin each hour with a recitation of school rules. Before entering classes, students line up in the hallway with their heads aligned with that of the student they are behind. After class, the students assume the same positions with their right feet on a green tape. A teacher then marches them to their next classroom. In each classroom, the students open their identical, color-coded binders to the first page and trace the words of the school rules with their fingers while reading them aloud. "Structure creates peace of mind," said Marina Bernard Damiba, principal of the school, which educates 100 fifth and sixth graders from poor black and Hispanic families. "Remember, the kids we're teaching, this may be the only place they get it."

In 2002, *Education Week* featured a model charter school organization in Minnesota called the EdVisions Cooperative. EdVisions Cooperative is a nonprofit collective of 100 teachers and other educational professionals who operate seven charter schools in Minnesota and one in Wisconsin. The organization operates democratically to manage instruction, to evaluate instructors, to evaluate the academic program, and to hire and fire staff. Under Minnesota's charter school law, each of the EdVisions Cooperative schools receives $6,000 per student from the state.

The guiding philosophy of the EdVisions Cooperative is that teachers should have complete control over the teaching and learning that goes on in schools. In other words, traditional school administrators, such as principals, are not present in these charter schools. EdVisions claims that it saves 10 percent in normal operating costs by dispensing with the traditional administrative structure. In opposition to traditional administrative control of a school's curriculum and teaching, the selection of textbooks, and the hiring and firing of teachers, it is believed by the EdVisions Cooperative that teachers can make better decisions about these educational issues. *Education Week*'s reporter Julie Blair quotes David Greenberg, the lead teacher at El Colegio Charter School in Minneapolis and a member of the cooperative: "This model allows people to be leaders in areas in which they excel. You have control in the hands of the people who need it to deliver education to students who need it." In his former teaching job, Greenberg commented, "The most important decision I made was when to hold yearbook day. Here, we decide if we want to hire another art teacher or buy another computer." Ms. Sage-Martinson told reporter Julie Blair, "The opportunities are endless. My last job was great, but it was a dead end. I'd teach and teach and teach, but have no say in what I taught."

Are the *students* also reaping the rewards of these alternative learning centers?

ARE CHARTER SCHOOLS FAILING?

In 2006, supporters of charter schools in the U.S. Department of Education were surprised by a report issued by the National Center for Education Statistics that found that the achievement in reading and math of students in public charter schools was lower than that of students in public noncharter schools. The authors of the report, Henry Braun, Frank Jenkins, and Wendy Grigg, conclude, "After adjusting for student characteristics, charter school mean scores in reading and mathematics were lower, on average, than those of public noncharter schools. The size of these differences was smaller in reading than in mathematics." Surprisingly for those supporting charter schools as a choice for low-income and minority families, the study, *A Closer Look at Charter Schools Using Hierarchical Linear Modeling*, found no significant differences in reading achievement between students in public charter schools and charter nonpublic schools having "a central city location and serving a high-minority population." In the same locations, public noncharter school students had significantly higher math scores than students in public charter schools.

Responding to the 2006 study, U.S. Secretary of Education Margaret Spellings, a supporter of charter schools, issued the following press release:

> Many charter schools are still relatively new, and we need to examine how they improve student performance over time for a better picture of how they compare to traditional public schools. Charter schools are empowering low-income parents with new educational options and providing an important life-line for families in areas where traditional public schools have fallen short of their responsibilities.
>
> I have visited high-performing charter schools all around the country, and I have seen how they take the most at-risk students and refuse to give up on them. These schools are pioneering new classroom strategies that will help us raise achievement in all our public schools.

Similar findings are reported in a 2005 study by the National Assessment of Educational Progress, *America's Charter Schools: Results from the NAEP Pilot Study*. This report concludes that there are no significant differences between the achievement of public school and charter school students. The report states, "for students from the same racial/ethnic backgrounds, reading and mathematics performance in charter schools did not differ from that in other public schools. However, this study found lower overall mathematics performance in charter schools than in other public schools." In addition, the study finds, "in reading there was no measurable difference between the overall performance of charter school fourth-grade students as a whole and their counterparts in other public schools." A 2005 study of urban charter schools by Ron Zimmer and Richard Buddin for Rand Education also concludes "that achievement scores in charters are keeping pace, but not exceeding those in traditional public schools."

Implying that the U.S. Department of Education had hidden data showing that charter schools were not as academically effective as regular public schools, *The New York Times* reported on 16 August 2004 that charter school students were doing worse on achievement tests than comparable regular public school students. The *Times* article stated, "The findings, buried in mountains of data the Education Department released without public announcement, dealt a blow to supporters of the charter school movement, including the Bush administration." The data were unearthed by online researchers at the American Federation of Teachers, who gave it to *The New York Times*.

The American Federation of Teachers report (see Nelson et al., 2003), *Charter School Achievement on the 2003 National Assessment of Educational Progress*, given to *The New York Times* summarized the data:

- Average scores: Compared to students in regular public schools, charter school students had lower achievement both in grade 4 (six scale points lower in math, seven scale points lower in reading) and grade 8 (five points lower in math, two points lower in reading). These differences were all statistically significant, except for grade 8 reading, and translate into about a half year of schooling.

- Achievement levels: In grades 4 and 8 and both in math and reading, the percentages of charter school students performing at or above *Basic* and at or above *Proficient* were lower than the corresponding percentages for regular public school students.

Critics of charter schools said the study proved that charters were not the answer to problems facing public schools. Bella Rosenberg, assistant to the president of the American Federation of Teachers, commented, "There's just a huge distance between the sunny claims of the charter school advocates and the reality. There's a very strong accountability issue here."

Luis Huerta, a professor at Columbia University Teachers College, said that the study showed the problems faced by charter schools because of questionable financial dealings and poor performance. In 2004, California's largest charter school operator was forced to close 60 of its campuses—leaving 10,000 students stranded. Amy Stuart Wells, another professor at Columbia University Teachers College, claimed that the data "confirms what a lot of people who study charter schools have been worried about. There is a lack of accountability. They're uneven in terms of quality."

In Texas, as well, charter schools were reported as being academically behind regular public schools. Texas has one of the largest charter school programs in the country. Eight years after the program was launched as a bold educational experiment, a 2004 study by the Texas Education Agency found that only 42 percent of the students at the state's 235 independent charter campuses passed the Texas Assessment of Knowledge and Skills as compared to 67 percent in regular public schools. Criticizing the charter school movement, Ted Raab of the Texas Federation of Teachers said, "It's pretty clear the overall record of charter schools is not as good as regular public schools with comparable student populations."

Texas teacher organizations claimed the poor showing of charter schools was a result of their exemption from hiring certified teachers and class-size limits. "Charter schools already have proven some things, but many of the folks who promoted them don't want to talk about the lessons that have been learned," said Richard Kouri of the Texas State Teachers Association. The 2004 national and Texas reports followed in the wake of a scathing 2002 report on the charter school movement by the American Federation of Teachers. The report claims that charter schools contribute to racial and ethnic isolation of students by failing to educate high-cost students at the same rate as regular public schools. Consequently, these high-cost students remain in regular schools rather than transferring to charter schools. The report defines high-cost students as "low-income, English Language learners, and special education students." In addition, the report states that charter school teachers are less experienced, lower paid, and receive inferior benefits and pensions compared to regular public school teachers. The report admits that surveys show that charter school teachers "are most satisfied with education-related and colleague-related issues." On the other hand, these teachers complain about salaries and workload.

The AFT's strongest criticism was directed at charter schools operated by for-profit corporations. In the next section, I will examine these for-profit educational corporations in more detail. The AFT's criticism of for-profit charter schools includes the following:

- They enroll few students with disabilities and spend little money on special education.
- They spend more on administration and less on instruction.
- They do not innovate but use a standardized school design, curriculum, and technology package provided by the company.
- Teachers are disgruntled about the lack of professional opportunities for advancement.
- Teachers complain about not being involved in school decision making.

FOR-PROFIT COMPANIES AND CHARTERS

For-profit education companies claim to offer citizens greater control over the education of their children by expanding the notion of choice to include competition. The assumption is that competition between for-profit companies will result in better educational products and greater choice of quality schooling. Charter schools have opened their doors for investment by for-profit corporations. This is part of a general growth of corporate involvement in education ranging from the traditional textbook and testing products to actual ownership of schools. In many states, for-profit companies, meaning companies that earn a profit for their owners, can apply for state charter school status. In fact, some public school districts are now contracting for-profit companies to manage their schools. The No Child Left Behind Act allows school districts to use federal money to hire for-profit companies to provide school services. In 2004, Chicago and Boston school administrators complained that the legislation was forcing them to hire for-profit private companies to provide tutoring services to children in failing schools. The two school systems wanted to provide their own tutorial services, but that plan was rejected by the U.S. Department of Education. Some critics claim that No Child Left Behind will result in the privatization of public schools.

Clive Belfield of the National Center for the Study of Privatization in Education has provided a useful guide to for-profit companies in education. He lists as for-profit providers of school services companies that actually operate for-profit schools such as Edison and National Heritage; companies that provide curriculum and materials to home schools such as White Hat Management; and providers of supplemental services such as tutoring, summer school, music, and sports. These for-profit companies receive their earnings from public sources such as state/district charter and No Child Left Behind mandates, through tax credits, and from parents who pay directly for education-related services. Belfield identifies the major for-profit education companies as Sylvan Learning Systems, Edison Schools, Princeton Review, Kaplan, Club Z!,

In Home Tutoring Services, Brainfuse.com, Kumon North American, and EdSolutions Inc.

In 2004, six for-profit school companies formed the National Council of Education Providers to lobby for more money for charter schools and charter-friendly regulations. In 2008, the council had seven for-profit school companies. The stated goal of the organization is: "To provide quality schooling options in communities of choice through charter and non-charter public schools." The council boasts that these seven companies are serving "approximately 165,000 students across 30 states and the District of Columbia." The membership of the council in 2008 included:

Charter Schools USA, Ft. Lauderdale, FL

Connections Academy, Baltimore, MD

Edison School Inc., New York, NY

Insight Schools, Portland, OR

K12, McLean, VA

Mosaica Education, Inc., New York, NY

National Heritage Academies, Grand Rapids, MI

Stressing the important role of for-profit school companies, Michael J. Connelly, the chief executive officer of Mosaica Education, a founding member of the National Council of Education Providers, commented, "There are people who don't believe there is a role for private business in public education. And for those people, we are going to get the word out that we are not Beelzebubs. This is not a satanic plot to destroy public education."

The AFT criticizes for-profit companies for their packaged and standardized designs. In a report for the Center for Education Research, Analysis, and Innovation, Gerald Bracey writes, "An increasing number of . . . schools have been turned over to for-profit educational management organizations such as Mosaica Education. . . . Yet Mosaica and other such companies appear to have schools that resemble each other in cookie-cutter fashion, eliminating the very diversity and innovation that these charter schools' founders had envisioned."

In addition, Bracey argues, for-profit schools such as Edison, TesseracT, and Sabis provide alternative programs to existing public schools while tolerating no diversity within a school. He cites the case of an Edison school in San Francisco where half the teachers planned not to return for the 2000–2001 school year. Supposedly, teachers felt demeaned because they were required to follow a tightly controlled educational plan. "They literally give you a script with what you're supposed to say," one teacher complained.

National Heritage is one of the few education companies to actually earn a profit. The company was founded by J. C. Huizenga, a cousin of the founder of Blockbuster Video. National Heritage schools focus on the teaching of a Christian moral code along with a back-to-basics curriculum. The curriculum appeals to conservative Christians. One reason for the profitability of National Heritage is that the company avoids low-income neighborhoods and builds in affluent suburbs. In addition, Gary Miron, a research associate at the Evaluation Center at Western Michigan University, argues that the company's profitability is a result of it being "streamlined for profit."

CHARTER SCHOOLS AND FOR-PROFIT GLOBAL EDUCATION CORPORATIONS

Including companies selling products to U.S. charter schools, for-profit corporate involvement in education is now global. Take the case of the for-profit company K12, which is a member of the National Council of Education Providers described in the last section. K12 describes its offerings:

- Full-time online public schools in many states across the country.
- individual course and product sales directly to families.
- In a growing number of public schools across the country which are engaged in bringing individualized learning approaches into the traditional classroom.

The global reach of K12 came to light in 2008 when parents complained to the Arizona Virtual Academy about the unusual form of English being used in reviewers' comments about student essays. The Arizona Virtual Academy describes itself as being "Powered by K12" and advertises: **"With the Arizona Virtual Academy (AZVA),** students in **grades K–12** have a high-quality, **tuition-free,** online public school education option. Working one-on-one with a teacher, students can learn anywhere an Internet connection can be found." As a tuition-free, online public school, the Arizona Virtual Academy claims that by contracting with the for-profit K12 company students gained global connections: "AZVA students are also connected with other students who use the K12 curriculum throughout the U.S. and internationally through online discussions, clubs, and competitions."

What students and parents of the Arizona Virtual Academy weren't told is that K12 outsourced review of student essays to an India-based subsidiary, Tutors Worldwide. Students would submit their essays electronically to teachers at the Arizona Virtual Academy. The English used in India is more British-oriented as compared to American English; the reason for parental complaints. The teachers would send the essays to K12 and that company sent them over the internet to Tutors Worldwide for review. Tutors Worldwide is one of two for-profit companies that K12 contracted with for reviewing student essays. The other is Socratic Learning, Inc., located in Plano, Texas.

K12 is not the only company to use tutors outside the United States—they are cheaper to hire—to serve American school students. One such for-profit company is SMARTHINKING. This company is based in Washington, D.C., and, according to its 2008 Web site it:

> provides people, technology and training to help institutions offer their students outstanding academic support. Schools, colleges, universities, libraries,

> government agencies, textbook publishers and other education providers work with SMARTHINKING to increase student achievement and enhance learning. SMARTHINKING connects students to E-structor® Certified tutors anytime, from any Internet connection.

SMARTHINKING employs tutors in Canada, Chile, India, the Philippines, and South Africa.

I provide a detailed coverage of global for-profit education in my book, *The Globalization of Education* (Spring, 2009). The corporate structure of Educate, Inc., reflects the complex structure of global for-profit school and knowledge industries. After the 2007 purchase of Sylvan Learning Centers from Laureate Education, Inc., Educate, Inc., boasted of its ownership of Hooked on Phonics, Catapult Learning, Educate Online, and Progressus Therapy. Educate, Inc., markets its products in Europe under the Schülerhilfe brand. Involved in complex financial connections, Educate, Inc., is owned by Edge Acquisition, LLC, with Citigroup Capital Partners and Sterling Capital Partners as investors.

For-profits are undergoing a period of global expansion. For instance, the Laureate Education, Inc., has a presence in 15 countries serving 240,000 students with ownership in the United States of Walden University and 23 other universities in Asia, Europe, and the Americas. Laureate Education, Inc., claims to potential investors that the global market for for-profit higher education is increasing because of a global expansion of the middle class, expanding youth populations in Latin America and Asia, the need for educated human capital and, most importantly, the difficulties faced by governments in financing public higher education. In 2007, the company announced: "Laureate International Universities, one of the world's largest networks of private higher education institutions, and the University of Liverpool today announced the expansion of a unique partnership to leverage programs and expertise to create the next generation of international programs for students worldwide."

In September 2007, Laureate made a dramatic move to capture the Asian market when Douglas L. Becker, its chairman and chief executive officer, announced that he and his family were moving to Hong Kong to ensure the expansion of the company and to establish Asian headquarters. In an example of the international financing of for-profit education, Becker and an investor group engineered a $3.8-billion private-equity buyout of the company in June 2007. The international investor group included Harvard University; Citigroup; Microsoft cofounder Paul Allen; global philanthropist George Soros; Kohlberg Kravis Roberts & Co. (KKR); S.A.C. Capital Management, LLC; SPG Partners; Bregal Investments; Caisse de depot et placement du Quebec; Sterling Capital; Makena Capital; Torreal S.A.; and Brenthurst Funds. In reporting the move, a *Chronicle of Higher Education* article commented, "Mr. Becker devised the transformation of Laureate into an internationally focused higher-education company from its roots as a tutoring business called Sylvan Learning Systems."

The World Bank, the largest global investor in education, supports for-profit education. In 2007, the World Bank hosted a conference on Public-Private

Partnerships in Education, which included speakers not only from the World Bank but from universities from around the world, including ones in the United States, Chile, Singapore, and Venezuela. The Human Development Network is a project of the United Nations Development Program involving 144 representatives from national governments, NGOs, and research institutions. The network is designed to link those interested in a "concept of sustainable human development as an . . . approach [that] regards people's well-being as the goal of development." Expansion of educational opportunities is considered an important part of sustainable human development.

The written introduction to the conference justified public-private partnerships both from the standpoint of the existence of private schools but also from the inability of some governments to finance the expansion of educational opportunities. Encompassed under the conference's concept of public-private partnerships were "a wide range of providers, including for-profit schools (that operate as enterprises), religious schools, non-profit schools run by NGOs, public funded schools operated by private boards, and community owned schools." The inclusion of for-profit schools links the network to global learning corporations, which will be discussed later in the book.

An example of World Bank's investment in for-profit education is the SABIS International School in Lebanon. It was the first education investment by the corporation in the Middle East and North. The investment was $8 million with the intention of making it the international headquarters and the flagship of the SABIS Group of Schools. Lars Thunell, the corporation's executive vice president and CEO, said on a recent visit to the school, "Education is vital to ensuring sustainable economic growth, particularly with a rapidly growing and relatively young population across the MENA [Middle Eastern and North Africa] region. By providing high-quality services, the SABIS school is a model for further private investment in education throughout the region." In a World Bank publication, *Mobilizing the Private Sector for Public Education: A View from the Trenches,* SABIS president Carl Bistany describes that, "Since the mid-1950s SABIS has viewed 'education' as an industry and has subjected it to the rules that govern successful industries and businesses: efficiency, accountability, and optimization of resources." The company started with a school built in a small village in Lebanon in 1996 and is today a "network of 31 K–12 schools in 11 countries, with a total enrollment of 28,000 students from more than 120 nations. Seven of the 31 are charter schools in the United States, and the remaining are private schools."

The two teachers' unions are highly critical of the for-profit education movement. The NEA's report *Can Corporate Management Solve the Challenges Facing America's Public Schools?* asserts, "Corporate management of public schools has not improved students' academic performance in any of the four cities in which it's been tried." The union report concludes:

> Education is not simply another economic good or service. The learning of a nation's children is of concern to the entire nation. And while business can and should play a role in education, communities and the school boards that

represent them must retain control over the future of America's public schools. Instead of corporate takeovers, school systems should seek to fully engage their communities and build cooperation among school staff, parents, and all concerned groups and citizens.

HOME SCHOOLING

Home schooling is one answer for parents who want to take charge of their children's education. Parents can dodge the control of an unrepresentative school board and school bureaucracy by educating their children at home; however, most states do regulate home schooling to some extent. According to 2007 *Digest of Education Statistics,* in 2003 2.2 percent of students ages 5 through 17 were being home schooled, which was an increase from 1.7 percent in 1999.

The extent of state regulation and state laws are available on the Web site of the Home School Legal Defense Association (http://www.hslda.org). This organization was established to provide legal defense to home schoolers. It divides states by those with no requirements that parents contact government authorities when deciding to home school; those requiring only that parents notify appropriate government authorities; states with moderate regulation of home schoolers; and those states with extensive regulation of home schoolers. For instance in 2008, Idaho, Texas, Oklahoma, Alaska, Missouri, Illinois, Indiana, and Michigan do not require guardians of home schoolers to even contact government authorities. On the other end of the spectrum of state regulation of home schooling, North Dakota, Vermont, New York, Pennsylvania, Rhode Island, and Massachusetts have a high degree of regulation requiring, according to Home School Legal Defense Association, "parents to send notification or achievement test scores and/or professional evaluation, plus other requirements (e.g. curriculum approval by the state, teacher qualification of parents, or home visits by state officials)."

Why do families choose to home school their children? A survey conducted by the Home School Legal Defense Association cited the following reasons:

- Religious convictions—49 percent
- Positive social environment—15 percent
- Academic excellence—14 percent
- Specific needs of the child—12 percent
- Curriculum choice—5 percent
- Flexibility—5 percent

Home schooling is now a global movement. Writing for *The Washington Times,* Andrea Billups reports, "Home schooling is rapidly expanding worldwide as families abroad search for options to guide their children's education amid growing concerns over lax educational standards and increasing violence in government-run schools." The Home School Legal Defense Association claims that it has been contacted by home educators from 25 countries for information on legalization of home schooling. In fact, Christopher J. Klicka, senior lawyer at the association, traveled to Germany and Japan in the summer of 2000 to work with families to gain legal protection.

Home schooling represents a rejection of traditional arguments for public schooling. Originally, common-school reformers believed that all children should attend public schools, where they would learn to get along with others and learn a common morality and culture. Public schools were to educate good citizens. Public schools were to create a community spirit. By the twentieth century, schools required certified teachers based on the belief that good teachers needed to be trained.

Home schooling tosses all these arguments out the window. By educating their children at home, advocates reject the belief that children should obtain a common morality and culture through the public schools. In fact, many fundamentalist Christian parents, a major source of support for home schooling, feel that public schools are both immoral and irreligious. They don't want their children exposed to the values taught by public schools. Others, such as politically liberal parents, home school their children because they reject the conservative economic and political philosophy of public schools. Some choose home schooling because of what they perceive to be the factory-like instruction of public schools.

Home schooling raises the issue of parental competence as teachers. This issue came to the forefront of home-schooling concerns when the Second District Court of Appeals, in Los Angeles, ruled on 28 February, 2008 in a child-welfare case that a particular family's home-schooling arrangement required that their children be taught by a parent or tutor holding a teaching certificate. In an 18 March, 2008 *Education Week* article, "Home-School Advocates Push to Blunt, Reverse California Ruling," Linda Jacobson reported California Governor Arnold Schwarzenegger issued a statement after the ruling: "Parents should not be penalized for acting in the best interests of their children's education. This outrageous ruling must be overturned by the courts, and if the courts don't protect parents' rights then, as elected officials, we will." Home School Legal Defense Association immediately issued a statement: "We believe that the court erred in ruling . . . this is how home-schoolers have been home schooling for over 20 years."

Teachers' unions and some members of the educational establishment believe those teaching students should be certified by the government. Can you trust parents to be good teachers? Do good teachers require special training and certification?

Another frequently asked question is whether home schoolers develop social skills. The Home School Legal Defense Association provides the following answers to this question:

- Home school support groups organize field trips, teaching co-ops, and tutoring services.
- Home-schooled youngsters are active in community sports, scouting, church activities, political volunteering, community service, and more.

- Home schoolers are taken to museums, parks, libraries, and other educational institutions.

James Dobson, a columnist for *The Washington Times*, writes,

> The great advantage of home schooling, in fact, is the protection it provides to vulnerable children against the wrong kind of socialization. When children interact in large groups, the strongest and most aggressive children quickly intimidate the weak and vulnerable. I am absolutely convinced that bad things happen to immature and "different" boys and girls when they are thrown into the highly competitive world of other children.

CONCLUSION

After considering the power and politics of local school boards, choice, charter schools, privatization, and commercialization, you should again imagine that you are sitting in the education chair and answering the following questions:

- Who should control the switch?
- Should the options for throwing the switch be determined by petitioners for charter schools?
- Should the switch be controlled by parental choice?
- Should an elected school board control the switch?
- Should it be controlled by the educational bureaucracy?
- Should it be controlled by for-profit companies?

Whatever your answers, the important thing is for you to understand that the political structure of education determines the content of education that in turn directly affects what a student learns. Often, students don't question the reasons for being subjected to a particular curriculum or textbook. The content of learning in public schools is determined by a political process. But local politics of education is only one part of the process.

Suggested Readings and Works Cited in Chapter

American Federation of Teachers. "School Vouchers: Myths and Facts." Washington, DC: American Federation of Teachers, 2006. Go to the American Federation of Teachers Web site, www.aft.org, for a list of the major criticisms that the American Federation of Teachers has of public-private choice. In addition, the statement has a list of research on voucher plans.

——. "The Many Names of School Vouchers." Retrieved on 12 September 2008 from http://www.aft.org/topics/vouchers/index.htm. AFT's statement of opposition to vouchers for private schools.

ARCHER, JEFF. "Private Charter Managers Team Up." *Education Week on the Web* (4 February 2004). http://www.edweek.org. Archer's article describes the creation of the National Council of Education Providers by six for-profit education companies.

Arizona Virtual University. http://www.AZVA.org. A free online public school that pays for the services of the for-profit education company K12.

Associated Press. "Dallas Official Wants to End Edison Deal." *The New York Times on the Web* (17 August 2002). http://www.nytimes.com. Dallas superintendent complains about failure of Edison-managed schools to increase performance of students.

Belfield, Clive. *The Business of Education.* National Center for the Study of Privatization in Education. New York: Teachers College, Columbia University, 2004. You can access http://www.ncspe.org for a summary of trends in for-profit education services.

Billups, Andrea. "Home School Movement Goes Global." *The Washington Times* (19 September 2000). http://www.hslda.org.

Blair, Julie. "Doing It Their Way: Teachers Make All Decisions at Cooperative Venture." *Education Week on the Web* (27 July 2002). http://www.edweek.org. This article features Minnesota's EdVisions Cooperative, which establishes charter schools based on teacher control.

Bloomberg News. "Edison Reaches Contract on Philadelphia Schools." *The New York Times on the Web* (1 August 2002). http://www.nytimes.com. This story discusses the contract reached by Edison to manage 20 elementary and middle schools in Philadelphia.

Bracey, Gerald. "Charter Schools." This report was written for and distributed by the Center for Education Research, Analysis, and Innovation (12 October 2000). http://www.uwm.edu/Dept/CERAI.

Braun, Henry; Frank Jenkins; and Wendy Grigg. *A Closer Look at Charter Schools Using Hierarchical Linear Modeling.* Washington, DC: United States Department of Education, 2006. This study found no significant differences in achievement in reading and math between public charter schools and regular public schools.

——. *Comparing Private Schools and Public Schools Using Hierarchical Linear Modeling.* Washington, DC: U.S. Department of Education, 2006. This study found no significant differences in student achievement between public and private schools.

Braun, Henry, et al. *Comparing Private Schools and Public Schools Using Hierarchical Linear Modeling.* Washington, DC: U.S. Department of Education, July 2006. Supports the use public private school vouchers.

Center for Educational Reform. http://www.edreform.com. This Web site is an important source for information about school choice and charter schools.

——. "What the Research Reveals About Charter Schools." http://www. edreform.com. This report summarizes 53 research-based studies on charter schools.

Chubb, John E., and Terry Moe. *Politics, Markets & America's Schools.* Washington, DC: The Brookings Institution, 1990. This important study of the relationship between political control and student achievement supports choice as a means of improving student achievement.

Dobson, James. Dobson writes many articles on the advantages of home schooling for the Home Schooling Legal Defense Association. Go to http://www.hslda.org.

Edison Project. http://www.edisonproject.com. This Web site provides ongoing information about Edison school projects and financial reports.

Education Week. This excellent weekly newspaper contains news about local, state, and federal politics of education.

Fairlie, Robert. "Racial Segregation and the Private/Public School Choice." New York: National Center for the Study of Privatization in Education, 2006. This study concludes that private schools are racially segregated and that private school vouchers could either increase this segregation or reduce segregation by allowing children of low-income families to attend private schools.

Hess, Frederick. *School Boards at the Dawn of the 21st Century.* Alexandria, VA: National School Boards Association, 2004.

Home School Legal Defense Association. http://www.hslda.org. This is the best source for information on the home-schooling movement.

JACOBSON, LINDA. "Home-School Advocates Push to Blunt, Reverse California Ruling." *Education Week on the Web* (18 March 2008): http://www.edweek.org. Report of California ruling and reaction that home schooled pupils must have a certified teacher.

K12. http:www.k12.com. For-profit education company that provides lessons and curricula to public schools and individuals.

NATHAN, JOE. *Charter Schools: Creating Hope and Opportunity for American Education.* San Francisco: Jossey-Bass, 1996. Nathan describes the struggle for charter schools and provides help in organizing a charter school.

National Assessment of Educational Progress. *America's Charter Schools: Results from the NAEP 2003 Pilot Study.* Washington, DC: U.S. Department of Education, 2005. This report found no significant difference between the achievement of students in public charter schools and other public school students.

National Center for Education Statistics. "School Choice: Parental Choice of Schools." In *The Condition of Education 2006.* Washington, DC: National Center for Education Statistics, 2006. This report gives the percentage of parents exercising choice options.

——. "Charter Schools: Indicator 32." In *The Condition of Education 2007.* Washington, DC: National Center for Education Statistics, 2008. Provides statistics and information on charter schools throughout the United States.

——. "Elementary and Secondation Education Enrollment, Table 38." In *The Condition of Education 2008.* Washington, DC: National Center for Education Statistics, 2008. Table provides enrollment figures for home schoolers.

National Center for the Study of Privatization in Education. *Cyber and Home School Charter Schools: How States are Defining New Forms of Public Schooling.* New York: Teachers College, Columbia University, 2004. http://www.ncspe.org. A summary of trends in home and cyber schooling is provided.

National Council of Education Providers. "Home" and "Our Goals." http://www.educationproviders.org. Organization of seven for-profit school companies whose goal is to serve charter schools around the country.

National Education Association. "Can Corporate Management Solve the Challenges Facing America's Public Schools?" http://www.nea.org. Teachers union's concerns about private management of public schools.

——. "Five Talking Points on Vouchers." Retrieved on 12 September, 2008 from http://www.nea.org/vouchers/talkingpoints.html. NEA's opposition to school vouchers.

——. "National School Voucher Legislation Announced by Congressional Leaders and Education Secretary: Bill Will Mislead Parents and Funnel Money Away from Public Schools." Washington, DC: National Education Association, 2006. This press release can be found on http://www.nea.org and contains the National Education Association's negative response to the proposal for America's Opportunity Scholarships for Kids Act.

——. "Research Undercuts Case for Private Schools." Washington, DC: National Education Association, 2006. This press release can be found on http://www.nea.org. The organization's press release hails the study by Henry Braun et al., "Comparing Private Schools and Public Schools Using Hierarchical Linear Modeling," as proof that government money should not be used to support private school choice plans.

——. "Vouchers." Washington, DC: National Education Association, 2006. This article can be found on http://www.nea.org and lists the organization's objections to vouchers.

NELSON; HOWARD; BELLA ROSENBERG; and NANCY VAN METER. *Charter School Achievement on the 2003 National Assessment of Educational Progress.* Washington, DC: American Federation of Teachers, August 2004. This study shows poor achievement scores for charter school students in comparison to students in regular public schools.

PATRINOS, HARRY and SHOBHANA SOSALE, editors. *Mobilizing the Private Sector for Public Education: A View from the Trenches.* Washington, DC: World Bank, 2007. Articles provide an introduction to the World Bank's sponsorship of for-profit education.

Public Law 107–110, 107th Congress, Jan. 8, 2002 [H.R. 1]. "No Child Left Behind Act of 2001." Washington, DC: U.S. Printing Office, 2002. This federal legislation contains important provisions supporting public school choice and charter schools.

REID, KARLA SCOON. "Districts Spar with Ed. Dept. over Tutoring: Chicago, Boston Argue They Should Be Allowed to Help." *Education Week* (3 November 2004): 3. This article describes how Boston and Chicago were forced by No Child Left Behind to hire for-profit companies to provide tutoring services to students in failing schools instead of using their own school services.

"Rethinking Schools: An Urban Educational Journal Online." www.rethinkingschools.org. This is an important source of information on urban school reform, including school choice, charter schools, and multicultural education.

SCHEMO, DIANA JEAN. "Nation's Charter Schools Lagging Behind, U.S. Test Scores Reveal." *The New York Times on the Web* (17 August 2004). http://www.nytimes.com. This article revealed data discovered buried in the U.S. Department of Education showing that charter school students were doing worse than regular public school students on achievement tests. The article raised serious doubts about the effectiveness of charter schools.

SMARTHINKING. http://www.smarthinking.com. For-profit online education company that provides tutoring to students in schools, colleges, and government agencies. Uses tutors located in foreign countries.

SPELLINGS, MARGARET. "Press Releases: Statement by Secretary Margaret Spellings on Release of NCES [National Center for Education Statistics] Study on Charter Schools." Released on 22 August 2006 on the U.S. Department of Education Web site. http://www.ed.gov/news/pressreleases/2006/08/08222006a.html. U.S. Secretary of Education Spellings defends charter schools after a report shows students in public charter schools have significantly lower achievement scores in reading and math than those in public noncharter schools.

SPRING, JOEL. *Educating the Consumer-Citizen: A History of the Marriage of Schools, Advertising, and Media.* Mahwah, NJ: Lawrence Erlbaum Associates, 2003. Spring provides a history of the commercialization of schools and American society.

——. Globalization of Education: An Introduction. New York: Routledge, 2009. This book contains a detailed analysis of for-profit education corporations.

STUTZ, TERENCE. "Charters Score below Public Schools, Exclusive: At 235 Texas Campuses, Passing Rate Was 42 Percent." *The Dallas Morning News* (21 October 2004). http://www.dallasnews.com. Stutz gives the report by the Texas Education Agency on the poor performance of charter schools.

WALSH, MARK. "Edison Outlines Strategies to Reassure Wall Street." *Education Week on the Web* (7 August 2002). http://www.edweek.org. Walsh provides an analysis of Edison Schools, Inc.'s, financial maneuvering.

——. "Businesses Flock to Charter Frontier." *Education Week on the Web* (22 May 2002). http://www.edweek.org. This article surveys the operation of the major companies trying to make a profit from the development of charter schools, including National Heritage Academies Inc.

——. "Education Inc." *Education Week on the Web* (4 October 2000). http://www.edweek.org. This article describes Nobel Learning Communities, Inc.'s, planned investment in for-profit schools in China.

WEINER, REBECCA. "San Diego Charter School a Model for Technology Leaders." *The New York Times on the Web* (1 November 2000). http://www.nytimes.com. Weiner provides a description of the founding and operation of High Tech High charter schools.

WILGORIN, JODI. "School Days Are Rule Days in Bronx Charter Classrooms." *The New York Times on the Web* (30 October 2000). http://www.nytimes.com. Wilgorin gives a description of the Bronx Preparatory Charter School.

WYATT, EDWARD. "Union Study Finds For-Profit Schools No Better." *The New York Times on the Web* (19 October 2000). http://www.nytimes.com. The AFT disputes an Edison school report that its test scores are improving in comparison to traditional public school students.

——. "Educational Company Says Its Scores Rise." *The New York Times on the Web* (10 August 2000). http://www.nytimes.com. Edison Schools report that test scores in its schools are improving.

——. "Investors Are Seeing Profits in Nation's Demand for Education." *The New York Times on the Web* (4 November 1999). http://www.nytimes.com. This is an important article on investment in for-profit education companies.

www.uscharterschools.org. This is the official Web site on charters operated by the U.S. Department of Education.

YECKE, CHERI PIERSON, and LAURA LC AZO. *Choice Provisions in No Child Left Behind.* Washington, DC: U.S. Department of Education, 2002. This is the official government interpretation of the choice provisions of No Child Left Behind.

ZIMMER, RON, and RICHARD BUDDIN. *Charter School Performance in Urban Districts: Are They Closing the Achievement Gap?* Santa Monica: Rand Corporation, 2005. This study, available online at http://www.rand.org/education, found no significant achievement differences between students in public charter schools and those attending noncharter public schools.

CHAPTER 7

Power and Control at State and National Levels

Political Party Platforms, High-Stakes Testing, and School Violence

This chapter will examine the relationship between federal and state control of schools. There is nothing in the U.S. Constitution about education and, consequently, it is a responsibility given to state governments. State constitutions and laws contain provisions for creating and regulating public schools. However, in recent years the federal government has exercised dramatic control over schools as best represented by the federal law No Child Left Behind. One consequence of federal involvement in local education is that political candidates for federal offices often include education issues in their campaigns. Even national presidential campaigns address school issues. As a result, federal involvement in schools ranges from sex education to testing of students.

This chapter will examine the following issues:

- Source of federal influence over local school policies.
- The 2008 education platforms of the Democratic and Republican parties.
- Increasing state government influence over local schools.
- Federal and state control of local schools through high-stakes testing and academic standards.
- A case study of federal involvement in problems of school violence.

SOURCE OF FEDERAL INFLUENCE OVER LOCAL SCHOOL POLICIES

Federal influence over state education and local schools is primarily through categorical aid. Categorical aid is money provided to support specific federal programs and legislation such as No Child Left Behind. Once the state or local school district accepts federal money, then they have to accept the regulations and requirements that accompany the program. Most states and local school systems find it difficult to refuse the money provided by the federal government. Consequently, the federal government has increased its influence over local schools despite the fact that the actual amount of money from federal sources is only a small percentage of the money local schools spend on students.

The *Condition of Education 2008* reports that the percentage of total revenue for public elementary and secondary education from local sources is about 44 percent and from state sources 47 percent. Only 9 percent of total revenue for public elementary and secondary education are from the federal government. Since the 1980s, there has been a decline in the total revenue for public elementary and secondary education from local sources and an increase of funding from the federal government. The state percentage has remained the same. This shift in funding reflects the growing role of the federal government in local schools. As I discuss in the next section, the federal legislation No Child Left Behind is an example of categorical federal aid that has had a major impact on local school systems.

NO CHILD LEFT BEHIND AS CATEGORICAL FEDERAL AID

Theoretically, No Child Left Behind balances federal and state power by allowing states to determine their own academic standards and testing programs. However, using categorical aid provided by the legislation, the federal government is able to require states to implement a range of activities including creating academic standards and testing programs, public reporting of test scores, identifying and improving schools failing to meet adequate yearly progress, using particular types of reading programs, offering choice plans, and a host of other provisions in the legislation. Throughout the legislation there are requirements placed on state governments receiving funds. For instance, Part I of Title I of the legislation states:

> For any State desiring to receive a grant under this part, the State educational agency shall submit to the Secretary [U.S. Secretary of Education] a plan, developed by the State educational agency, in consultation with local educational agencies, teachers, principals, pupil services personnel, administrators (including administrators of programs described in other parts of this title), other staff, and parents.

Federal control through requirements attached to funds given to local schools began in the 1950s. During the 1950s, the debate was about whether the federal government should give money to local school systems and let them determine how to spend the money or whether the federal government should specify how the money should be used. With passage of major Cold War education legislation, the National Defense Education Act (NDEA), Congress targeted funds for specific purposes, such as improving mathematics, science, and foreign language instruction. The next major federal educational legislation, the 1965 Elementary and Secondary Education Act (ESEA), also tied education to national policy objectives; in this case it was the War on Poverty. Funds were targeted for reading and arithmetic programs that would supposedly provide equality of educational opportunity for students from low-income families.

Regulatory control is exemplified by Title VI of the 1964 Civil Rights Act, which applies to federal education legislation. Any school agency receiving federal funds must comply with Title VI, which requires the mandatory withholding of federal funds from institutions practicing racial, religious, or ethnic discrimination. Title VI states that no person, because of race, color, or national origin, can be excluded from or denied the benefits of any program receiving federal financial assistance. Also, any educational agency receiving federal funds must comply with Title IX of the 1972 amendments to the Higher Education Act. Title IX states: "No person in the United States shall, on the basis of sex, be excluded from participation in, be denied the benefits of, or be subjected to discrimination under any education program or activity receiving Federal Assistance."

The federal government, therefore, exerts considerable indirect influence over education by

- Providing federal money to support a particular educational program (categorical aid).
- Attaching federal regulations to federal programs, such as the Republican proposal requiring states to enact state testing programs as a requirement for receiving federal money.
- Using federal agents to influence educational practices or to create model programs.
- Forcing schools to comply with civil rights legislation to receive federal money.
- Funding only select educational research.

INCREASING STATE INVOLVEMENT IN SCHOOLS

Besides increasing federal power over local schools, No Child Left Behind contains provisions strengthening state control over local schools. This represents a major change since the founding of public schools in the nineteenth century. The requirements of categorical aid provided by No Child Left Behind expand the involvement of state governments in local school activities. In the early nineteenth century, state departments of education were small and confined their activities to collecting educational statistics, promoting good schools and teacher training, and inspecting local schools. In the late nineteenth and early twentieth centuries, states expanded their role with the passage of compulsory-education laws and laws requiring specific curriculum content in the schools. Over the years, these curriculum requirements expanded in many states to cover a great deal of the course content offered in local school districts. Teacher-certification requirements also increased and became more complex. Because of the enforcement requirements of these laws, state educational bureaucracies grew steadily in the twentieth century.

In the 1960s, as the federal government became more involved in schooling, federal money expanded state educational bureaucracies by funneling federal money and programs through the state government to local school districts. This widening of state power over education carried with it seeds of controversy. For some, an expanded state-controlled education enterprise signaled the collapse of local control of education. For others, state control of education appeared necessary for the improvement of schools. And, as I discussed previously, state governments attempted to equalize spending among school districts.

Then in the 1980s and 1990s, governors, including Bill Clinton in Arkansas and George W. Bush in Texas, focused their political campaigns on educational issues. The result was a state-initiated school reform movement that called for statewide testing of public school students. Since testing required academic standards for measurement, state governments entered the business of establishing academic standards for each grade level. State testing measured the success of students in achieving these academic standards. The result of the process was greater state control over the school curriculum and the actual content of instruction.

Today, most states exercise the following major functions regarding education:

- Establishing academic standards and curriculum guidelines for local school districts.
- Testing students for achievement of academic standards.
- Testing teachers as part of the licensing procedure.
- Licensing of teachers.
- Enacting laws that affect the content of instruction (these laws vary with some states requiring the teaching of patriotism, free enterprise, drivers' education, and other educational topics).
- Providing funds to local school districts.

FEDERAL AND STATE CONTROL THROUGH HIGH-STAKES TESTS AND ACADEMIC STANDARDS

High-stakes testing mandated in No Child Left Behind provides direct control over student learning, particularly if teachers teach to the test. The No Child Left Behind Act of 2001 mandates a schedule, target populations, and reporting procedures for high-stakes testing and academic standards. The test data, as discussed in Chapter 6, are used to determine which schools are making adequate yearly progress; those that are not can receive funds for school improvement and educational services, and parents of children at those schools will be allowed school choice. Theoretically, all of this test data is to spur school improvement by identifying low-performing schools and motivating teachers and school administrators to achieve state standards. The combination of state report cards for each school district and district report cards for each school results in every level of school administration and all teachers being judged by student performance.

Also, to highlight any possible discrimination of schools and school districts, states must make available to the public a list of elementary and secondary schools receiving funds for school improvement because they have, according to state standards, been failing for two years. This public list must include "the percentage of students in each school from families with incomes below the poverty level." In addition, the state must report students "by race, ethnicity, gender, disability status, migrant status, English proficiency, and status as economically disadvantaged."

CONSEQUENCES OF FEDERAL AND STATE CONTROL THROUGH HIGH-STAKES TESTING

The high-stakes testing required under No Child Left Behind is having consequences for how teachers and principals are paid, real estate prices, instructional time in the classroom, profits for corporations making the tests, and contributes to the nationalization of public schools. Student testing affects the evaluation of teachers and administrators. In 2006, the Houston Board of Education approved a $14.5 million program that rewards teachers and administrators according to the scores of their students on standardized tests. Teachers can receive up to $3,000 annually for their students' improved test scores and administrators up to $25,000 for the improved performance of students in their schools. The New York School Chancellor Joel Klein announced near the opening of the 2002–2003 school year that district superintendents would receive bonuses up to $40,000—about a quarter of their base salaries—if test scores improved in their districts. School principals were already receiving bonuses for improved scores in their schools. In March 2004, Denver teachers voted 59 percent to 41 percent for a merit pay system using student achievement test scores. The Denver plan provides several methods for teachers to gain pay raises. The most important method is for pay hikes to be based on student academic growth as measured by test scores. Denver teachers under the plan would also be able to gain salary increases by being evaluated as satisfactory, improving their education, or teaching in high-poverty schools.

High-stakes test scores are now news items that even affect the real estate market. For instance, a 26 July 2006 *Education Week* headline reveals "Scores Linked to Home Prices." In the article, economics professor Donald Haurin reports "that a 20 percent increase in a district's pass rate on the state tests translated to a 7 percent increase in the home prices in the district."

Some people worry that testing is taking away from instructional time. "Time Devoted to Testing Surprises New Teacher" is what the editors of *Education Week* titled a 5 April 2006 letter from Cindy Mulvey of La Quinta,

California. Mulvey asks, "Is it true that our students are tested more than 85 out of 180 days?" She explains her experience as a long-term third grade substitute:

> I . . . spent more time testing my 3rd graders . . . than I did instructing them. In addition to daily multiplication quizzes, the students took a weekly spelling test, a weekly Houghton Mifflin Reading test, a chapter math test every two weeks, a theme skills test once a month, a unit math test once a month, a writing-prompt test every trimester, several county and state exams, and a physical-fitness test.

Testing is a for-profit industry. McGraw-Hill and Pearson are the two largest makers of tests. An example of the testing industry was presented in 28 August 2006 article in the popular *Newsweek* magazine titled, "Test Wars: The SAT [Scholastic Aptitude Test] vs. the ACT [American College Testing Program]." The article reveals the big business aspect of high-stakes testing in the struggle between SAT and ACT to control the college entrance exam market. High school counselors are advising some students to take both tests but some colleges are dropping both tests as an entrance requirement. In 2005, 1.2 million students took the ACT compared to 1.5 million taking the SAT. The SAT suffered serious public relations problems when in October 2005 its hired, for-profit scoring company, Pearson Educational Measurement, allowed scoring sheets to be damaged by moisture. The result: 4,411 test takers had scores reported to colleges that were lower than they should have been. It was a nightmare for these students when college rejections began to arrive in the mail. Embarrassed by the scoring errors and feeling the competitive heat from the makers of the ACT, the president of the SAT's College Board, Gaston Capteron, a former business executive and two-term governor of West Virginia, is trying to increase revenue for the College Board, which is technically a nonprofit organization. The College Board is marketing new products including English and math curricula for grades 6 through 12 along with the management of schools. By 2007 it plans to open 11 College Board public schools. In 2006, the College Board reported revenues of $530 million and Caperton's annual compensation as $639,000 with a $110,000 expense account.

Current test usage places a burden on the testing industry. "All testing companies are overwhelmed by the burdens of writing, scoring, and reporting vastly more federal tests than in the past under No Child Left Behind," declares the Washington think tank Education Sector in a 2006 report. The report complains that the testing industry is overwhelmed by "trying to test vastly greater numbers of students under very tight timelines and under highly competitive conditions." In an *Education Week* article, Vaishali Honawar writes, "watchdogs of the testing industry—dominated by CTB/McGraw, Harcourt Assessment, and Pearson—warn that errors could become only too common as standardized testing in schools multiplies under federal and state mandates."

In 2004, Connecticut's state education commissioner, Betty Sternberg, warned that the testing industry would have difficulty keeping up with demand. Her concern became a reality in 2006 when officials at Harcourt Assessment, Inc., informed the state that they had reported incorrect scores for 355 Connecticut high school students. And, as previously mentioned, a major problem was caused for college applicants when Pearson Educational Measurement incorrectly scored damaged SATs and sent the incorrect scores to colleges.

Finally, many argue that if money is going to be invested in education, then there must be some means of measuring its effectiveness. Of course, tests provide the easiest measure to report. Test results can be published in local newspapers or distributed by state agencies. But accountability based on test scores can potentially contribute to greater inequality among school districts. Real estate agents, as I discussed in Chapter 2, are reporting that home buyers are arriving at their offices with lists of school test scores to use in selecting houses. And, as was previously suggested, real estate prices can be correlated with school district test scores. Though there is no proven causal relationship, school districts reporting high test scores might be the most attractive to home buyers with school-age children.

No Child Left Behind Act of 2001 essentially creates a nationalized school system with variations being allowed in academic standards and the content of state tests. However, these variations are reduced by the requirement that every other year a sample of fourth and eighth graders in each state take *national* tests administered by the National Assessment of Educational Progress. The results of these national tests are compared to the tests created by each state. In other words, the National Assessment of Educational Progress tests could have a determining effect on the construction of state tests.

What is the controlling power of standards and tests? First, state academic standards determine what will be taught in the classroom. For instance, state science standards establish the content of instruction in science. Second, state high-stakes tests ensure that teachers teach the content specified in the state's academic standards. The state tests are constructed around the state's academic standards. If students do poorly on high-stakes tests, then teachers and school administrators are blamed. Consequently, both teachers and administrators are motivated to ensure that classroom instruction complies with academic standards and provides students with the specific knowledge and skills required by the tests.

FEDERAL AND STATE MANDATED TESTS AND EQUALITY OF OPPORTUNITY

The No Child Left Behind Act of 2001 opens the door to the high-stakes testing model of equality of opportunity discussed in Chapter 2. Simply put, high-stakes testing means that there are important consequences for students and educators resulting from test performance and also, it appears, for local housing prices. For students, high-stakes tests might determine promotion between grades or graduation from high school. For teachers and school administrators, the results of student test scores can be used to measure their performance or determine their salary increases. For individual schools, test results might determine their continued existence. Low-stakes testing means that there are no significant consequences resulting from student test performance.

There is concern that standardized tests cannot be objective in measuring student learning. There are such things as test skills that can be learned. In fact, many private agencies offer courses in test-taking. Also, the wording of questions can reflect particular cultural knowledge. I remember being stumped on a question in a standardized math test because I did not know the meaning of a word. I excelled at math but missed this test item because of my limited cultural knowledge. Writing in *Education Week,* test expert W. James Popham contends:

> If you were to review the actual items in a typical standardized achievement test, you'd find many items whose correct answer depends heavily on the socioeconomic status of a child's family. There are also many items that measure the verbal, quantitative, or spatial aptitudes that children inherit at birth. Such items are better suited to intelligence tests. Clearly items dependent either on the affluence of a student's family or on a child's genetic inheritance are not suitable for evaluating schools.

The testing approach shifts the discussion from the conditions of learning to motivation to learn. By conditions of learning, I mean students having well-trained teachers, complete sets of textbooks, small classes, and school buildings in good repair. The threat of failure on high-stakes tests will, it is assumed, overcome any major obstacles to learning. According to this reasoning,

- Fear of failure will cause students to study.
- Worried about their evaluations by school administrators, teachers will focus on instruction to keep their students from performing poorly on high-stakes tests.
- Worried about their evaluations, principals will work to ensure that teachers prepare students for high-stakes tests.
- Worried about their jobs and public images, superintendents will work to ensure that each school receives high test scores by preparing principals and teachers to ready their students for testing.

PROBLEMS IN FEDERAL CONTROL: TESTING STUDENTS WITH DISABILITIES AND ENGLISH-LANGUAGE LEARNERS

The high-stakes testing of students with disabilities and of English-language learners is an important issue. A concern is that test scores for students with disabilities and English-language learners will affect calculations of adequate yearly progress and have a negative effect on local school report cards. Both the original legislation and guidelines from the U.S. Department of Education provide accommodations for these test takers. No Child Left Behind specifies that states must make "the reasonable adaptations and accommodations for students with disabilities . . . necessary to measure the academic achievement of such students relative to State academic content and State student academic achievement standards."

In 2005, the U.S. Department of Education issued guidelines based upon the requirement of "reasonable adaptations and accommodations for students with disabilities." The guidelines allow states to use modified standards and tests for students with disabilities in complying with No Child Left Behind. Secretary of Education Margaret Spellings made the following announcement:

> The new guidelines reflect the latest scientific research that shows students with disabilities—approximately 2 percent of all students—can make progress toward grade-level standards when they receive high-quality instruction and are assessed with alternate assessments based on modified achievement standards. Under the new flexibility option announced today, eligible states may implement short-term adjustments to their adequate yearly progress decisions to reflect the need for alternate assessments based on modified achievement standards; this is a separate policy from the current regulation that allows up to 1 percent of all students being tested (those with the most significant cognitive disabilities) to take an alternate assessment.

Regarding English-language learners, No Child Left Behind specifies:

> the inclusion of limited English proficient students, who shall be assessed in a valid and reliable manner and provided reasonable accommodations on assessments administered to such students under this paragraph, including, to the extent practicable, assessments in the language and form most likely to yield accurate data on what such students know and can do in academic content areas, until such students have achieved English language proficiency.

Under these provisions, immigrant English-language learners can take math and reading tests in their native languages for the first three years they attend school in the United States. This policy can be extended two years on a student-by-student basis. As of 2005, 11 states were using mathematics and reading tests in native languages.

Testing English-language learners remains a heated topic because of the potential effect on measurements of average yearly progress. In California, 10 school districts filed suit against the state for not providing reading and math tests in Spanish and other languages. They claimed that the lack of native-language tests was endangering the average annual progress measurements of their schools. Jack O'Connell, California's superintendent of instruction, responded that it was "complex and costly" to make tests in all the different languages spoken by the state's 1.6 million English-language learners. If they only create tests in Spanish and English, he said, it would be unfair to other language populations. A similar complaint was made in 2003 against the Pennsylvania state government by the Reading school district because some of its schools had not achieved adequate yearly progress because the state had not provided tests in Spanish.

There continue to be many questions about the testing of English-language learners in relationship to adequate yearly progress reports. In 2006, Tom Horne,

Arizona's superintendent of instruction, threatened to sue the federal government over the requirement to include test scores of English-language learners in determining adequate yearly progress. He claimed that the federal government made an oral agreement with him that for the first three years that English-language learners were in the country their test scores would not be used to calculate adequate yearly progress. The U.S. Department of Education approved the state's assessment system with the qualification that the approval did not end the dispute over not using the test scores of English-language learners.

Great variations between states in testing accommodations for students with disabilities and limited-English-proficient students was found 2008 when officials for the National Assessment of Educational Progress began to plan for national testing as required by No Child Left Behind. The variation in accommodations between states and cities made it difficult to plan the national testing program. *Education Week* reporter Sean Cavanagh commented, "Perhaps no topic has as thoroughly vexed officials who oversee the nation's leading test of academic progress as the wide variation among states and cities in the proportion of students with disabilities and limited English proficiency whom they exclude from taking the exam or provide with special accommodations for it." In the article, "Testing Officials Again Tackle Accommodations And Exclusions for Special Student Populations," Cavanagh quotes Andrew C. Porter, a governing-board member of National Assessment of Educational Progress: "We know what we want. We want valid state-by-state comparisons [that take exclusions and accommodations into account]. How to get them is a little less clear."

DOES FEDERALLY MANDATED HIGH-STAKES TESTING WORK?

What criteria can be used to determine the effect of high-stakes-testing? Does it simply mean improved performance on other tests? Any meaningful determination would require a longitudinal study of the impact of high-stakes testing on a person's life. Does high-stakes testing, which often leads to teachers teaching to the test, reduce students' creativity and their willingness to take risks? It is important to remember that the goal of implementing high-stakes testing is to educate people who can compete in a global labor market. How can this be measured?

There are contradictory research findings about the value of high-stakes testing. In a 2002 study, University of Arizona researchers Audrey Amrein and David Berliner report that high-stakes testing does not improve achievement and might worsen academic performance and increase dropout rates. They find little gain in performance on college entrance examinations by students in high-stakes testing states. Their study was sharply criticized by Stanford researchers Margaret Raymond and Eric Hanushek, who accuse Amrein and Berliner of faulty research methods. Raymond and Hanushek find that the average gain for fourth and eighth graders in mathematics was higher in states using high-stakes testing as compared to states not giving much weight to test scores. The Stanford study only measures performance on tests and not the long-term consequences of an educational system centered on test performance. It could be that where standardized testing is used for promotion between grades or for high school graduation students pay closer attention to learning better test-taking skills.

Contrary to the Stanford study, a 2004 report by Henry Braun of the Educational Testing Service concludes that "comparisons slightly favor the low-stakes testing states." Braun's conclusions were based on a reanalysis of an earlier study by Amrein and Berliner. In other words, students in states with high-stakes testing did not perform any better on college entrance examinations than students in states with low-stakes testing. (Recall that low-stakes testing means that there are no significant consequences resulting from student test performance.)

In 2005, Sharon Nichols, Gene Glass, and David C. Berliner's report "High-Stakes Testing and Student Achievement: Problems for the No Child Left Behind Act" concludes that high-stakes testing disproportionately affects minority students and increases dropouts. Their analyses reveals:

- States with greater proportions of minority students implement accountability systems that exert greater pressure. This suggests that any problems associated with high-stakes testing will disproportionately affect America's minority students.
- High-stakes testing pressure is negatively associated with the likelihood that eighth and tenth graders will move into twelfth grade.
- Study results suggest that increases in testing pressure are related to larger numbers of students being held back or dropping out of school.
- Increased testing pressure produced no gains in NAEP (National Assessment of Educational Progress) reading scores at the fourth or eighth grade levels.
- Prior increases in testing pressure were weakly linked to subsequent increases in NAEP math achievement at the fourth grade level.

None of these conflicting studies examines the issue that caused the movement for high-stakes testing: Does high-stakes testing improve the ability of American workers to compete in the global labor market? It would be difficult to design a research study to answer this question that includes all possible causal factors. This research problem raises another question: Should politicians impose an educational reform for which there exists no evidence—in fact, there appears to be conflicting evidence—that it will improve the skills of American workers?

DOES FEDERAL TESTING POLICY PROMOTE UNETHICAL BEHAVIOR?

"An astonishing amount of cheating is taking place on the tests . . . under the federal No Child Left Behind," asserts W. James Popham, an emeritus professor in the Graduate School of Education at UCLA, in a 2006 commentary for

Education Week. "And the cheating I'm referring to isn't coming from the kids," he continues. Popham identifies the following forms of cheating:

- School administrators erasing incorrect responses on students' answer sheets and substituting correct answers.
- Teachers allowing more time than test instructions require.
- Teachers supplying students with hints about which answers are correct.
- Test preparation sessions using actual test items.

The reasons for the cheating, he argues, are (1) possible embarrassment to school personnel when test scores are reported in local newspapers, (2) fear that the school will not meet average yearly progress standards, and (3) fear that the school will be designated for improvement.

As Popham indicates, cheating is a major problem in any situation using high-stakes exams. For instance, college entrance exams have always been closely monitored to reduce the possibility of cheating. Now professional staffs are being monitored as high-stakes testing is used to evaluate teachers and school administrators. For example, Texas has been the scene of widespread cheating. Texas administrators and teachers have been accused of erasing student answers and adding correct answers.

There are many other examples. In 1999, teachers and administrators in 32 schools in New York City were accused of erasing wrong answers and doing corrective editing on student answer sheets. A total of 47 principals, teachers, and staff members were implicated in the scandal. Examples of cheating included a seventh grade teacher who left a sheet of answers to a citywide math test near a pencil sharpener and then urged students to sharpen their pencils while she was out of the room. A fourth grade teacher discovered an essay question concerning Cubist art on the state English test and then devoted a lecture on Cubism right before the test. But these were somewhat minor compared to the corrective editing of tests by teachers and administrators. In 2000, the Houston public schools fired a teacher and reprimanded two principals after test tampering was discovered. In Austin, Texas, school officials were accused of raising state accountability ratings through test tampering. One Austin staff member was forced to resign. An elementary school teacher was fired after it was discovered the teacher had used an answer key to change student answers. In addition, Austin school officials changed student-identification numbers so that students with low scores would not be factored into the school system's accountability ratings.

In Rhode Island, state education officials were forced to cancel the administration of English and mathematics tests for 2000 when it was discovered that many teachers had kept copies of the previous year's exams to use with students as part of the test preparation. The problem was that both years' exams contained the same questions. "It became clear that the scope of the breach was extensive," said Commissioner of Education Peter J. McWalters, "and that the assessment results would be invalid." Also in 2000, officials at one of the best schools in affluent Potomac, Maryland, were accused of cheating—the school's principal resigned and a teacher was suspended. The principal was accused of allowing students extra time to complete state examinations, coaching them on questions, and changing incorrect answers. In Fairfax County, Virginia, charges were brought against a middle-school teacher for improper coaching of students for state examinations.

Finally, in 2004, the famed Bracey Report gave its annual Gold Apple award to Steve Orel, who discovered that schools in Birmingham, Alabama, when "threatened with a state takeover, had 'administratively withdrawn' 522 students just before the state tests were administered. The district acknowledged Orel's keen powers of observation by firing him."

"There's no way to tell how much cheating there actually is," claims Monty Neill, director of FairTest, a private education group opposed to the use of standardized tests, "but I get the sense nobody is looking too hard for abuses." Neill believes that because of high-stakes testing, "Schools are turning into test coaching centers, caught up in this frenzy of trying to look their best."

The future of high-stakes testing depends on the resolution of the problems associated with the cost, the effect on students from low-income families, the increasing residential segregation based on test scores, the increasing classroom time devoted to test preparation and test-taking, the emphasis on lower-order thinking, the evaluation of teachers and school administrators, and cheating. These are not minor problems. In addition, there is now in place a testing industry that depends on schools using high-stakes testing for accountability. The testing industry is a major lobbyist for state and national testing. The final resolution of the issues raised by high-stakes testing will depend on the actions of politicians, school officials, and the testing industry.

THE FEDERAL GOVERNMENT DECIDES THE READING WAR: NO CHILD LEFT BEHIND

Should the federal government mandate a particular method of instruction for American schools? You might be a fan of a particular method of teaching reading, but does this mean that you would favor federal laws requiring its use in the classroom? The No Child Left Behind Act supports one side of what is called the "reading wars." In a seemingly innocuous phrase, the "Reading First" part of the legislation alludes to "scientifically based reading research." This refers to the use of phonic methods in reading instruction. The actual wording of the legislation is:

> To provide assistance to State educational agencies and local educational agencies in establishing reading programs for students in kindergarten through grade 3 that are based on scientifically based reading research, to ensure that every student can read at grade level or above not later than the end of grade 3.

In 2004, the major figure in the whole-language movement, Ken Goodman, was so angered by the imposition of a particular method of teaching reading on the educational community that he launched his own Web site on which he gave "Ten Alarming Facts about No Child Left Behind." Number 10 in this list of claims is that it is unconstitutional to impose "a national curriculum and methodology in reading and math." I am reproducing Goodman's entire list because it reflects the anger some educators have toward No Child Left Behind. Again, for the purposes of this section of the chapter, the most important on the list is number 10.

Ten Alarming Facts About No Child Left Behind

1. The long- and short-term effects of NCLB will be devastating for American education. . . . The ultimate goal is to privatize American education. . . .
2. Within a neoconservative movement to privatize all aspects of American society, a heavily funded and well-organized campaign has created NCLB to discredit and destroy public education. . . .
3. NCLB is driving both students and teachers out of education. There is already a dramatic increase in dropouts and pushouts from high schools due to increased high-stakes testing, the narrowing of curriculum, and controls on how and what teachers may teach. . . . Many highly professional teachers are leaving teaching or taking early retirement to escape being required to conform to aspects of the law that they believe make it impossible to teach in the best interests of their pupils. . . .
4. NCLB centralizes control of every aspect of American education, including policy, methodology, curriculum, choice of textbooks, evaluation, and staffing, shifting power from local districts and states to a Washington bureaucracy. NCLB establishes a national curriculum and methodology in reading and mathematics and other fields. . . .
5. NCLB defines what is and isn't science. Through a series of panels, laws, and mandates, the federal government has defined what is science so narrowly, that 95 percent of scientific study in education has been swept aside as unscientific and decades of research has been wiped off federal websites such as ERIC. . . .
6. NCLB makes scores on mandatory tests the basis of all major decision-making in the schools, including which schools are failing. . . .
7. The law requires busing of pupils, at district expense, from non-improved schools to other schools. . . . Even Mayor Daley in Chicago is complaining about moving hundreds of kids from failing school to failing school.
8. NCLB controls who may teach and not teach and how they will be certified. Federal standards are established which take control away from states in the name of assuring qualified teachers in every class. . . .
9. Enforcement of NCLB employs blacklists. A list of who and what conforms and does not conform to NCLB criteria is being used to blacklist people, institutions, methods, and materials. . . .
10. NCLB, the federal law, is unconstitutional, as it violates the Constitution, which leaves education to the states. NCLB affects every child and teacher in every school in the United States. It establishes a national curriculum and methodology in reading and math.

It is not within the scope of this text, nor is it appropriate within this limited space, to suggest the best methods of instruction. My purpose is to make the reader aware of the political nature of this debate. Teaching reading by using phonic methods is a staple of the conservative agenda for education, while liberals tend to support whole-language methods. During the 2000 presidential campaign, candidate George W. Bush called for more federal money for reading programs. Attached to this proposal was the proviso that phonics would be the method used in federal reading programs. Bush's proposal reflected the conservative political push for phonics instruction in the schools. This was accomplished in the No Child Left Behind legislation. Prior to the 2000 presidential campaign, the California state legislature in 1997 passed a law requiring teacher trainers to sign an assurance clause, similar to a loyalty oath, that they would educate teachers to use phonics as the method for reading instruction.

Should presidential candidates and other national politicians be in the business of promoting a particular form of instruction? Should there be a public vote on methods of instruction, such as bilingual education? In fact, should there be state laws specifying instructional methodologies? Are state politicians qualified to make decisions about the best method of instruction?

What about assigning a special state committee to decide the best method for teaching mathematics? California did it in 1998, and the result was a heated political battle that caused Jack Price, the immediate past president of the National Council of Teachers of Mathematics, to conclude, "It isn't a question now of what is best for children, but who's going to win." The struggle can best be described as being between those advocating teaching math through conceptual understanding, mental computation and estimation, and cooperative work and those favoring traditional methods of memorization, paper-and-pencil computations, and drill and practice. On one side of the battle line was the California Mathematics Council, an organization of 12,000 teachers affiliated with the national math educators' council, which supported the newer conceptual approaches to teaching math. The president of the math council, Margaret DeArmond, defended the new methods because of "what kind of jobs students need in the future." On the other side, Martha Schwartz, one of the founders of the traditionalist group Mathematically Correct, argued, "We need to be much more specific and need to focus on skills."

A CASE STUDY: STUDENT VIOLENCE AND FEDERAL ACTION

There are many historical reasons why No Child Left Behind contains a section called the Safe and Drug-Free Schools and Communities Act, which gives as one purpose "to prevent violence in and around schools." Federal authorities became involved in school violence issues in the 1990s as school shootings escalated. In November 1998, five students in Burlington, Wisconsin, plotted to hold their high school principal hostage as they called 20 student victims from their classes for execution. Fortunately, the plan unraveled as the teenager with access to his father's rifles, shotguns, and handguns dropped out and another boy bragged about the scheme at a party. This gruesome plan included forcing the principal to announce over the school's intercom that all teachers were to keep their students in their classrooms while the juvenile terrorists searched through school files to find the classes of the victims. After calling their prey to the principal's office, the executioners envisioned a blood bath, including their own deaths along with those of the principal and students. A friend of the arrested conspirators described them as "the freaks" and "the Satan worshipers."

The Wisconsin conspiracy was reminiscent of shootings in the 1997–1998 school year that left 15 people dead and 42 wounded. Barry Loukatis, a 14-year-old honors student, contributed to that total when he walked into his algebra class at the Frontier Middle School in Moses Lake, Washington, dressed in black and armed with three family guns. After shooting his teacher in the back, Barry stood over a fellow student who was choking on his own blood and pronounced, "This sure beats algebra, doesn't it." In Jonesboro, Arkansas, two seventh grade students, Mitchell Johnson and Andrew Golden, successfully carried out a plan that included tripping the school fire alarm and killing five students and teachers leaving the school building. In West Paducah, Kentucky, 14-year-old Michael Carneal told his principal, "It was kind of like I was in a dream," after killing three girls and wounding five other students. In Springfield, Oregon, Kipland Kinkel was accused of killing 2 students and wounding 20 others with his father's semiautomatic rifle in a crowded school cafeteria. A Pearl, Mississippi, boy confessed to being enthralled with violent video games after randomly shooting students outside the town's high school.

In reaction to these and other scenes of school violence, U.S. Secretary of Education Richard Riley said, "We need to recognize that teaching young people coping and social skills that allow them to turn away from violence and drugs can take many forms." He recommended "character education, peer mediation, conflict resolution, and the establishment of student-run religious clubs." President Clinton chimed in, "When kids are more worried about guns and violence than math and science, we must all be committed to changing that."

The reaction to school violence provides a case study in federal influence. A central reason for federal involvement in the nineteenth century was the collection and distribution of education statistics. In keeping with this historical function, the U.S. Department of Education's National Center for Education Statistics in March 1998 issued the statistical report, "Violence and Discipline Problems in U.S. Public Schools: 1996–97." In 2000, the Federal Bureau of Investigation and the Department of Education teamed up to issue another report on school violence titled "Indicators of School Crime and Safety, 2000." This report came to the happy conclusion for schools that "more victimizations happen away from school than at school." In other words, schools are safer than the home or streets. The report found that in 1998 students were twice as likely to be victims of serious violent crime away from school than at school. During 1998, students between the ages of 12 and 18 were victims of 2.7 million crimes. In school, students were victims of 253,000 serious violent crimes including rape, sexual assault, robbery, and aggravated assault. In addition, there were 60 school-associated violent deaths between 1 July 1997 and 30 June 1998—including 47 homicides.

Overall, the FBI report actually found a decline in school crimes during the 1990s. In fact, the study states, "As the rate of victimization in schools has declined or remained constant, students also seem to feel more secure at school now than just a few years ago. The percentage of students ages 12 through 18 who reported avoiding one or more places at school for their own safety decreased between 1995 and 1999—from 9 to 5 percent. Furthermore, the percentage of students who reported that street gangs were present at their schools decreased."

The FBI report concludes, "Therefore, the data shown in this report present a mixed picture of school safety. While overall school crime rates have declined, violence, gangs, and drugs are still evident in some schools, indicating that more work needs to be done."

In 2001, the Department of Justice teamed up with the Department of Education to issue *Indicators of School Crime and Safety: 2001.* This document provided a summary of known facts about school violence. For instance, the report stated that in 1996—1997, 10 percent of all public schools reported at least one serious violent act such as murder, rape, sexual battery, suicide, use of a weapon, or robbery. Another 47 percent of public schools reported crimes such as a physical attack or fight without a weapon, theft/larceny, and vandalism.

Teachers were sometimes crime victims. Between 1995 and 1999, teachers were victims of approximately "1,708,000 nonfatal crimes at school, including 1,073,000 thefts and 635,000 violent crimes (rape or sexual assault, robbery, and aggravated and simple assault)." According to the report, there are "79 crimes per 1,000 teachers per year."

The logical next step after the collection of these statistics is for the federal government to become directly involved in funding violence prevention programs. This extends the federal government into another arena of education and adds another step in the nationalization of the public school system. Under the Safe and Drug-Free Schools and Communities Act section of No Child Left Behind funds are provided "to support programs that prevent violence in and around schools; that prevent the illegal use of alcohol, tobacco, and drugs . . . through the provision of Federal assistance to . . . States for grants to local educational agencies."

The Safe and Drug-Free Schools and Communities Act highlights the structure of the current nationalization of schools. After identifying a problem—violence and drugs—the U.S. Congress passes a law that channels money through state governments to local school systems. The federal law specifies the type of programs that will be financially supported. To get these funds, state governments must act according to federal dictates. In turn, local schools seeking the funds must follow state guidelines. Consequently, administration of these funds requires three levels of administrators—at the local, state, and federal levels.

WHAT SHOULD BE THE FEDERAL ROLE IN EDUCATION? REPUBLICAN AND DEMOCRATIC PLATFORMS 2008

The education sections of the 2008 Republican and Democratic platforms reflect the struggles over the extent and nature of federal power over local schools. Historically, the Republican Party favored state's rights over federal power. With the passage of No Child Left Behind, Republicans found themselves responsible for supporting major federal intervention in schools. However, the 2008 Republican presidential candidate John McCain believed, according to McCain's adviser and former Arizona education commissioner Lisa Keegan, "that the federal government should play a limited role in public education." In a *New York Times* article, Keegan was quoted, "Education is obviously not the issue Senator McCain spends the most time on." As I will explain, McCain's position on limited federal involvement was in sharp contrast to that of the Democratic candidate Barack Obama.

The Republican platform reflects this uneasiness with the growth of federal involvement in education: "Although the Constitution assigns the federal government no role in local education, Washington's authority over the nation's schools has increased dramatically." The platform calls for reviewing the federal role in primary and secondary education "to identify and eliminate ineffective programs, to respect the role of states, and to better meet state needs." In reference to reducing the control of federal programs over schools, the platform states, "Local educators must be free to end ineffective programs and reallocate resources where they are most needed."

The 2008 Republican Platform supports school choice including the choice of religious schools and home schooling. In contrast, the Democrats have traditionally opposed choice plans that include religious schools. The Republican platform states, "We support choice in education for all families, especially those with children trapped in dangerous and failing schools, whether through charter schools, vouchers or tax credits for attending faith-based or other nonpublic schools, or the option of home schooling." The Republican platform also wants protection of voluntary school prayer in schools and for allowing religious groups to have equal access to school facilities.

A major school controversy, as discussed in Chapter 1, is sex education. The Republican platform expresses a commitment to teaching only abstinence education that does not include the use of birth control. "We renew our call for replacing "family planning" programs for teens with increased funding for abstinence education, which teaches abstinence until marriage as the responsible and expected standard of behavior," states the platform. "Abstinence from sexual activity is the only protection that is 100 percent effective against out-of wedlock pregnancies and sexually transmitted diseases, including HIV/AIDS when transmitted sexually." In addition, the Republican platform declares, "We oppose school-based clinics that provide referrals, counseling, and related services for abortion and contraception."

Traditionally, the two teachers unions, as I will discuss in Chapter 8, have supported the Democratic Party. Consequently, the Democratic Party has been committed to recognizing and giving importance to collective bargaining agreements with school districts. In contrast, the Republican platform declares: "School districts must have the authority to recruit, reward, and retain the best and brightest teachers, and principals must have the authority to select and assign teachers without regard to collective bargaining agreements."

The Republican platform briefly refers to the human capital goals. In contrast, the education section of the Democratic platform stresses human capital goals. The title of its education section is "A World Class Education for Every Child" and its opening sentence is "In the 21st century, where the most valuable skill is knowledge, countries that out-educate us today will out-compete us tomorrow." The Democratic platform, unlike the Republican platform, expressed concern about global economic competition: "In the platform hearings, Americans made it clear that it is morally and economically unacceptable that our high-schoolers continue to score lower on math and science tests than most other students in the world and continue to drop-out at higher rates than their peers in other industrialized nations."

In sharp contrast to the wariness about federal school programs expressed in the Republican platform, the Democratic platform called for an expansion of federally funded preschool programs; a proposal that could lead to universal preschool for all children, which includes from ages 0 to 5. The Democratic platform asserts: "Our Children's First Agenda, including increases in Head Start and Early Head Start, and investments in high-quality Pre-K, will improve quality and provide learning and support to families with children ages zero to five." In addition, the Democratic platform in supporting the two teachers unions called for some form of federal funding to increase teachers' salaries and provide for better teacher training: "We will make an unprecedented national investment to provide teachers with better pay and better support to improve their skills, and their students' learning."

In response to complaints that high-stakes testing promoted rote learning and drill, the Democratic platform called for new types of tests as opposed to shifting the educational system away from the use of high-stakes testing. "We will work with our nation's governors and Educators," the platform states, "to create and use assessments that will improve student learning and success in school districts all across America by including the kinds of critical thinking, communication, and problem-solving skills that our children will need."

CONCLUSION

State and federal politicians are increasingly involved in issues of curriculum, methods of instruction, testing, and teacher certification. The trend is for more federal and state involvement in these areas. Should there be a nationalized system of schooling? A pressing issue for the future is deciding whether there should be limits to political involvement in public schooling. Should federal and state politicians determine the content and methods of instruction?

Suggested Readings and Works Cited in Chapter

AMREIN, A. L., and D. C. BERLINER. *The Impact of High-Stakes Tests on Student Academic Performance: An Analysis of NAEP Results in States with High-Stakes Tests and ACT, SAT, and AP Test Results in States with High School Graduation Exams.* Educational Policy Studies Laboratory, Education Policy Research Unit, 2002. http://www.edpolicylab.org. This study shows little gain in performance on college entrance examination by students in high-stakes-testing states.

ARCHER, JEFF. "R.I. Halts Exams in Wake of Wide-Scale Security Breaches." *Education Week on the Web* (17 March 2000). http://www.edweek.org. This is a discussion of the Rhode Island scandal over cheating on standardized tests.

ARENSON, KAREN W. "For SAT Maker, a Broader Push to the Classroom." *The New York Times on the Web* (16 August 2006). http://www.nytimes.com. This article describes the effort by the SAT maker to increase revenues and expand into other educational services.

BELLUCK, PAM. "Students Accused of Plotting Mass Slaying." *The New York Times on the Web* (17 November 1998). http://www.nytimes.com. This is the story of the plot in Burlington, Wisconsin, to kill students and the principal.

BLUMENTHAL, RALPH. "Houston Ties Teachers' Pay to Test Scores." *The New York Times on the Web* (13 January 2006). http://www.nytimes.com. This article reports on policies in Houston and other school districts to link teachers' and administrators' pay to student scores on high-stakes tests.

BRACEY, GERALD. "The 14th Bracey Report on the Condition of Public Education." *Phi Delta Kappan* (October 2004): 149–167. Bracey gives an insightful report on annual events in education. Here, the Gold Apple award is given to a whistle-blower who pointed out that school administrators in Birmingham, Alabama, cheated on state tests.

BRAUN, HENRY. "Reconsidering the Impact of High-Stakes Testing." *Education Policy Analysis Archives*, Vol. 12, no. 1 (5 January 2004). http://epaa.asu.edu/epaa/v12n1. This study finds that students in states with high-stakes testing do not perform any better than students in states with low-stakes testing on college admission examinations.

CAVANAGH, SEAN. "Testing Officials Again Tackle Accommodations and Exclusions for Special Student Populations." *Education Week on the Web* (16 July 2008). http://www.edweek.org. Discusses the wide variations between states and cities on the accommodation of English-learners and students with disabilities in tests mandated by No Child Left Behind.

CLINES, FRANCIS. "Cheating Report Renews Debate over Use of Tests to Evaluate Schools." *The New York Times on the Web* (12 June 2000). http://www.nytimes.com. This is a national report on the effect of cheating on the use of high-stakes tests.

DILLON, SAM, "McCain Calls for Limited U.S. Role in Schools." *The New York Times on the Web* (10 September 2008). http://www.nytimes.com. Republican presidential candidate John McCain believes that education is more a state and local responsibility than a federal responsibility.

Education Week. This weekly newspaper is one of the best sources of information on national educational politics. http://www.edweek.org.

GOODMAN, KEN. *Ten Alarming Facts about No Child Left Behind* (accessed Monday, 26 July 2004). http://www.sosvoice.org. The father of the whole-language movement attacks No Child Left Behind, particularly for imposing national methods for teaching reading and math.

GOODNOUGH, ABBY. "If Test Scores of Students Swell, So May Superintendents' Wallets." *The New York Times on the Web* (25 September 2002). http://www.nytimes.com. Goodnough describes bonus system for school superintendents based on student test scores.

HANEY, WALT. "The Texas Miracle in Education." *Education Policy Analysis Archives: Center for Education, Research, Analysis, and Innovation* (21 August 2000). http://epaa.asu.edu/epaa/v8n41.

HARTOCOLLIS, ANEMONA. "9 Educators Accused of Encouraging Students to Cheat." *The New York Times on the Web* (3 May 2000). http://www.nytimes.com. This article reports on the New York City cheating scandal.

HONAWAR, VAISHALI. "SAT Glitches Prompt Broader Testing Worries." *Education Week on the Web* (22 March 2006). http://www.edweek.org. After the incorrect scoring of SAT tests in 2005 and other mishaps in the testing industry, this article reports on the continuing concerns about the ability of companies to handle the demands placed on schools to use high-stakes tests.

HU, WINNIE. "9 Fired and 11 Others Face Dismissal in Cheating Scandal." *The New York Times on the Web* (12 December 1999). http://www.nytimes.com. This article reports on the New York City testing scandal.

JOHNSTON, ROBERT. "Texas Presses Districts in Alleged Test-Tampering Cases." *Education Week on the Web* (15 March 2000). http://www.edweek.org. Johnston discusses the testing scandal in Texas.

KAUFMAN, PHILLIP, et al. "Indicators of School Crime and Safety: 2000." *Education Statistics Quarterly*, February 2001. Indicators of school crime.

KAUFMAN, PHILLIP, et al. *Indicators of School Crime and Safety: 2001.* U.S. Departments of Education and Justice. NCES 2002–113/NCJ–190075. Washington, DC: 2001. This is a recent survey of school crime and violence.

KELLER, BESS. "Next Pay-Plan Decision up to Denver Voters." *Education Week on the Web* (31 March 2004). http://www.edweek.org. Denver teachers vote for merit pay plan based on student test scores.

LAWTON, MILLICENT. "Facing Deadline, Calif. Is Locked in Battle over How to Teach Math." *Education Week on the Web* (12 March 1997). http://www.edweek.org. This article discusses California's political battle over the best method for teaching math.

LESSINGER, LEON. *Every Kid a Winner: Accountability in Education.* Chicago: Science Research Associates College Division, 1970. Lessinger presents the classic justification for accountability standards in American education.

MANZO, KATHLEEN KENNEDY. "Limitations on Approved Topics for Reading Sessions Rile Teacher Trainers." *Education Week on the Web* (5 November 1997). http://www. edweek.org. This is a discussion of the California state law restricting the use of whole language methods to teach reading.

MATHEWS, JAY. "Test Wars: The SAT vs. The ACT." *Newsweek* (28 August 2006): 78–80. This article describes the struggle between SAT and ACT to control the college entrance examination market.

MULVEY, CINDY. "Time Devoted to Testing Surprises New Teacher." *Education Week on the Web* (5 April 2006). http://www.edweek.org. In a letter to the editor, a third grade teacher complains about the amount of the school year devoted to testing.

National Center for Education Statistics. *Violence and Discipline Problems in U.S. Public Schools: 1996–97.* Washington, DC: U.S. Department of Education, 1998. This is a sweeping survey of violence in U.S. schools.

———. "Changes in Sources of Public School Revenue." *The Condition of Education 2008.* Washington, DC: National Center for Education Statistics, 2008, p. 54. Provides information on percentages of revenue supporting local schools from the federal, state, and local governments.

National Commission on Excellence in Education. *A Nation at Risk.* Washington, DC: U.S. Government Printing Office, 1983. This is the report that launched the current standards and testing movement to prepare American workers for a global workforce.

NICHOLS, SHARON; GENE GLASS; and DAVID BERLINER. "High-Stakes Testing and Student Achievement: Problems for the No Child Left Behind Act." Arizona State University, Education Policy Studies Laboratory (September 2005). http://edpolicylab.org.

POPHAM, W. JAMES. "Educator Cheating on No Child Left Behind Tests: Can We Stop It." *Education Week on the Web* (19 April 2006). http://www.edweek.org. Popham argues that tests that impact teacher and administrator salaries and affect calculations of adequate yearly progress tempt teachers and school administrators to cheat in both giving tests and reporting test scores.

———. "Standardized Achievement Tests: Misnamed and Misleading." *Education Week on the Web* (19 September 2001). http://www.edweek.org. A leading expert on test making, Popham criticizes the idea that standardized tests measure only achievement.

PORTNER, JESSICA. "Clinton Releases Findings of School Violence Survey." *Education Week on the Web* (25 March 1998). http://www.edweek.org. President Clinton's comments on school violence are reported.

Public Law 107–110, 107th Congress, Jan. 8, 2002 [H.R. 1]. "No Child Left Behind Act of 2001." Washington, DC: U.S. Printing Office, 2002. This federal legislation deals with high-stakes testing, reading, and school violence among other issues.

RAYMOND, MARGARET, and ERIC HANUSHEK. "High-Stakes Research: The Campaign Against Accountability Brought Forth a Tide of Negative Anecdotes and Deeply Flawed Research." *Education Next* (Summer 2003). Available at www. education next.org. This article disputes the findings of Amrein and Berliner that found little gain in performance on college entrance examination by students in high-stakes testing states.

Report Roundup. "Test Scores Linked to Home Prices." *Education Week on the Web* (26 July 2006). http://www.edweek.org. Economist finds that a 20 percent increase in test scores in a district results in 7 percent increase in housing prices in that district.

Report of the Platform Committee. *Renewing America's Promise.* Washington, DC: Democractic National Committee, 2008. Contains education planks of the Democratic platform.

Republican Platform Committee. *2008 Republican Platform.* http:www.gopplatform2008.com/2008Platform.pdf. Contains education planks of the Republican platform.

"Resolution on Urging Reconsideration of High-Stakes Testing." Memorandum to NCTE from NCTE Committee on Resolutions, 2000 NCTE Resolutions (16 November 2000). This is the National Council of Teachers' resolution on the Test Takers Bill of Rights.

RICHARDSON, LYNDA. "Time-Zone Caper: Suspect Is Arrested in Testing Scheme." *The New York Times* (29 October 1996): 1, B17. Richardson reports on an example of one cheating scheme on high-stakes tests.

SPRING, JOEL. *Conflict of Interests: The Politics of American Education*, 5th edition. New York: McGraw-Hill Companies, Inc., 2004. This book provides an analysis of educational politics in the United States.

———. *Political Agendas for Education: From the Christian Coalition to the Green Party*, 3rd Edition. New York: Routledge, 2005. This is a concise guide to the educational platforms of the major political organizations in the United States.

TOCH, THOMAS. Margins of Error: The Testing Industry In No Child Left Behind ERQ. Washington, DC, Education Sector Reports, 2006. http://www.educationsector.org. Report on problems facing testing industry.

U.S. Department of Education. "Spellings Announces New Special Education Guideline, Details Workable, 'Common–Sense' Policy to Help States Implement No Child Left Behind." U.S. Department of Education Press Release (10 May 2005). http://www.ed.gov/news/pressreleases/2005/05/05102005.html. These are the guidelines for testing students with disabilities under the requirements of No Child Left Behind.

———. National Center for Education Statistics. Statistics of State School Systems; Revenues and Expenditures for Public Elementary and Secondary Education; and Common Core of Data Surveys (May 2001). This is a historical review of the proportion of revenues from local, state, and federal sources.

WILGORIN, JODI. "National Study Examines Reasons Why Pupils Excel." *The New York Times on the Web* (26 July 2000). http://www.nytimes.com. This is a report on the Rand Corporation study on factors that contribute to high performance on high-stakes examinations.

YARDLEY, JIM. "Critics Say a Focus on Test Scores Is Overshadowing Education in Texas." *The New York Times on the Web* (30 October 2000). http://www.nytimes.com. This is a summary of criticisms of the Texas government's emphasis on test scores as a method of improving education.

ZEHR, MARY ANN. "New Era for Testing English-Learners Begins." *Education Week on the Web* (12 July 2006). http://www.edweek.org. This is a report on 44 states that have developed English-proficiency tests aligned with state English-language-proficiency standards. These tests are required under No Child Left Behind.

———. "State Testing of English-Language Learners." *Education Week on the Web* (15 June 2005). http://www.edweek.org. Zehr reports the complaints by school districts about states not providing tests in students' native languages and the effect on calculating adequate yearly progress.

———. "U.S. Cites Problems in California Testing." *Education Week on the Web* (9 November 2005). http://www.edweek.org. Zehr reports on the U.S. Department of Education's criticism of California for accommodating English-language learners in the state's testing program.

CHAPTER 8

The Profession of Teaching

What is an American teacher? Guardian of morality and American character? Civilizer of western mining and ranching towns? Saint of freed slaves? Social worker in urban slums? Americanizer of immigrants? Protector against fascism and communism? Warrior against poverty? Champion of the global economy? As educational goals change so do the image and training of teachers.

This chapter will discuss the following issues related to the profession of teachers:

- The changing roles of teachers in the United States.
- Teachers and No Child Left Behind.
- Teacher salaries and turnover.
- Teachers' unions.

THE CHANGING ROLES OF AMERICAN TEACHERS

Today, the emphasis is on teachers as a key element in educating workers for the global economy. Protecting the U.S. role in the global economy continues the messianic vision of teachers as the saviors of society. In the nineteenth century, the development of professional teacher training paralleled the changing image of teachers from laughable weakling to the protector of American morality and character. In the 1830s, Horace Mann's declaration that common schools eliminate crime and morally reform society required the recruitment and training of moral teachers. The key was the feminization and professional training of the teaching force. Addressing the New York legislature in 1819, Emma Willard, founder of the Troy Female Seminary, whose main purpose was to educate teachers, declared the saving grace of female teachers: "Who knows how great and good a race of men may yet arise from the forming hands of mothers, enlightened by the bounty of that beloved country, to defend her liberties, to plan her future improvements and to raise her to unparalleled glory."

In 1839, Horace Mann supported establishment of a teacher-training institution in Lexington, Massachusetts. Called a **normal school,** this institution was designed primarily to train teachers for the elementary grades.

Horace Mann quickly recognized the value of recruiting women into the teaching force. He wrote in 1846: "Reason and experience have long since demonstrated that children under 10 or 12 years of age can be more genially taught and more successfully governed by a female than by a male teacher." As protectors of morality, Mann emphasized the importance of teachers being "of pure tastes, of good manners, [and] exemplary morals." He charged local school committees with the responsibility of seeing that no teacher cross the school "threshold, who is not clothed, from the crown of his head to the sole of his foot, in garments of virtue."

Others echoed the sentiment that female teachers would be the guardians of American morality. The teacher was to save western mining and cow towns from lawlessness and immorality. Through the Board of National Popular Education, Catherine Beecher recruited teachers to civilize the West. Writing in the 1840s, Beecher envisioned "that in all parts of our country, in each neglected village, or new settlement, the Christian female teacher will quietly take her station . . . teaching . . . habits of neatness, order, and thrift; opening the book of knowledge, inspiring the principles of morality, and awakening the hope of immortality." After the Civil War, female teachers rushed into the South with a mission of creating social equality and political rights for freed slaves.

However, female teachers were often demeaned and exploited. Even into the twentieth century, most school districts did not allow female teachers to marry. In addition, teaching contracts warned female teachers not to be seen in public with men other than their fathers or brothers. Female teachers were to be moral models for their communities. In addition, female teachers were paid less than male teachers. The Boston Board of Education in 1841 urged the hiring of female teachers because "as a class, they [women] never look forward, as young men almost invariably do, to a period of legal emancipation from parental control, when they are to break away from the domestic circle and go abroad into the world, to build up a fortune for themselves; and hence, the sphere of hope and of effort is narrower, and the whole forces of the mind are more readily concentrated upon present duties."

Willard S. Elsbree, in *The American Teacher: Evolution of a Profession in a Democracy,* reports that from the 1830s up to the Civil War, increasing numbers of women entered teaching. The Civil War, with its demands for military manpower, completed the evolution of elementary school teaching from a male occupation to a primarily female occupation. For example, Elsbree states that in Indiana the number of male teachers in all grades dropped from 80 percent in 1859 to 58 percent in 1864; in Ohio the number of male teachers went from 52 percent in 1862 to 41 percent in 1864. The second-class citizenship of women in the nineteenth century made it possible to keep teachers' salaries low and contributed to the continuing low status of teaching as it became professionalized.

The growth of urban centers and immigration changed the image of teachers from protector of morality to that of social welfare worker and vocational trainer. Teachers were enlisted to fight urban problems of crowding, epidemics, drugs, and crime. In addition, they were to prepare students for work in the modern factory. As the United States transformed from a rural to an industrialized nation in the late nineteenth and early twentieth centuries, teachers became workers in large educational bureaucracies. It was during this period, as I discuss later in the chapter, that teachers, following the lead of other workers, began to unionize.

Paralleling the new role of teachers as workers and defenders of industrial life, the professionalization of teaching moved from local control to the bureaucratic confines of state governments. Nineteenth-century teachers were usually certified by taking an examination administered by the employing school system or the county board of education. Licensing, or the granting of certificates to teach, was based primarily on examination and not on the number of education courses taken. Elsbree reports that in 1898 only four states had centralized certification or licensing at the state level. By 1933 42 states had centralized licensing at the state level; the primary requirement for gaining a teacher certificate was the completion of most courses in teacher education and other fields.

The centralization of certification and the dependence on teacher-education courses led to a rapid expansion of normal schools and colleges of education in the early twentieth century. State certification laws and expanded training in education completed the professionalization of teaching. Since 1933, this pattern of professionalization has continued with many normal schools becoming college and university departments of education. Course requirements in most states have generally increased and there has been a greater monitoring of teacher-education programs. From the 1920s to the 1950s, teachers were asked to promote 100 percent Americanism against the threat of fascist and communist ideas. During this period, many states required teachers to take loyalty oaths. Organizations, such as the American Legion and Daughters of the American Revolution, helped purge schools of teachers with leftist ideas. When it appeared in the 1950s that the United States was slipping behind the Soviet Union in the military arms race and conquest of space, American teachers were called on to educate a generation of students to win the technological race. As worries shifted to poverty and race relations in the 1960s, teachers became warriors in War on Poverty programs. As unemployment and high inflation gripped the nation in the 1970s and 1980s, teachers were called on to guide students into the labor market.

Now, No Child Left Behind is pushing the certification of teachers to new levels of control and hierarchy, while some age-old questions about the profession of teaching still remain:

- Should teacher education change as the goals of schooling change?
- Should teacher education be focused on the imperatives of the global economy?
- Should teachers be trained to meet the special needs of children growing up in poverty, children from differing cultural backgrounds, children with special needs, and gay/lesbian students?

- Should teacher-education programs prepare teachers for training future citizens and inculcating moral and social values?
- Who should control teacher certification?

NO CHILD LEFT BEHIND: HIGHLY QUALIFIED TEACHERS

No Child Left Behind is a new phase in the history of U.S. teachers. Under this legislation, the federal government is directly involved in determining the training and certification of teachers. No Child Left Behind requires that public school teachers be "highly qualified." This expands federal control into the area of state teacher qualifications. It has created considerable problems for veteran and rural teachers, and science teachers who teach many different subjects, such as biology, physics, and chemistry, under the general label of "science."

The legislation's Title II—Preparing, Training, and Recruiting High-Quality Teachers—proposes increasing

> student academic achievement through strategies such as improving teacher and principal quality and increasing the number of highly qualified teachers in the classroom and highly qualified principals and assistant principals in schools.

What are "highly qualified teachers"? The U.S. Department of Education defines a highly qualified teacher as:

1. Attaining a bachelor's degree or higher in the subject taught.
2. Obtaining full state teacher certification.
3. Demonstrating knowledge in the subjects taught.
   a. New elementary school teachers must demonstrate subject matter mastery by passing a rigorous state test of subject knowledge and teaching skills in reading and language arts, writing, mathematics, and other areas of the basic elementary school curriculum.
   b. New middle and high school teachers may demonstrate competency by passing a rigorous state test in each subject taught or by holding an academic major or course work equivalent to an academic major (or an advanced degree, advanced certification or credentials).
   c. Veteran teachers (those hired before the start of the 2002–2003 school year) must demonstrate competency by either meeting the requirements of new teachers or by meeting state requirements.

The Secretary of Education's *Third Annual Report* states that standards for determining a "highly qualified" teacher must:

1. Be established by the state for grade-appropriate academic subject matter knowledge and teaching skills.
2. Be aligned with challenging state academic content and student achievement standards and developed in consultation with core content specialists, teachers, principals, and school administrators.

3. Provide objective, coherent information about the teacher's attainment of core content knowledge in the academic subjects in which a teacher teaches.

States with rural schools where teachers must teach many subjects find it difficult to comply with the requirements for highly qualified teachers. For instance, Steve Larsgaard, the superintendent of the Lander County school district in Nevada, says that his district includes the tiny town of Austin with 60 students in grades K–12 and six teachers. The six teachers teach several subjects. "It's a small town of 250," Larsgaard told *Education Week* reporter Erik Robelen. "The nearest grocery store is 110 miles away. . . . Most of rural Nevada is a lot like that. Communities are spread out."

The U.S. Department of Education estimates that there are 5,000 rural school districts or about a third of all national school systems. In 2004, the U.S. Department of Education allowed teachers in rural districts who are highly qualified in one subject another three years to become qualified in the other subjects that they might teach.

For science, the U.S. Department of Education allows teachers to demonstrate competence in either the broad field of science or in a particular subject such as biology or physics. And for veteran teachers, the U.S. Department of Education allows states to develop alternative methods of demonstrating competence in subject matter areas through "high, objective, uniform state standard of evaluation" or HOUSSE. Under this alternative, veteran teachers are not required to take subject matter tests or go back to school but must demonstrate their subject matter competence in some other form.

In 2008, *Education Week* 's Vaishali Honawar reported, "Teachers meeting the 'highly qualified' standard their states set were teaching core subjects in 94 percent of the nation's classrooms in the 2006–07 school year, but poorer schools were still less likely than their wealthier counterparts to employ them." Data from the U.S. Department of Education showed that highly qualified teachers were teaching 96 percent of core-subject classes in low-poverty schools as compared with 91 percent in high-poverty schools.

As just illustrated, No Child Left Behind is leaving an indelible mark on state teacher-education requirements. It is becoming a federalized system with the U.S. Department of Education approving state plans to meet the criteria of having highly qualified teachers. These state plans are posted on the U.S. Department of Education's Web site: http://www.ed.gov/programs.

THE REWARDS OF TEACHING

Despite increasing teacher-certification requirements with No Child Left Behind, teachers' salaries still lag behind those of other white-collar workers. Why do people become teachers if the pay is low for a job that requires an extensive education and licensing? Consider teachers' salaries. In 2005, the National Education Association, a teachers' union, released a report titled

Rankings & Estimates: Rankings of the States 2004 and Estimates of School Statistics 2005. According to this report, the U.S. average public school teacher salary for 2003–2004 was $46,752. State average public school teacher salaries ranged from those in Connecticut ($57,337), District of Columbia ($57,009), and California ($56,444) at the high end to South Dakota ($33,236), Oklahoma ($35,061), and North Dakota ($35,441) at the low end.

Teachers' salaries might compare favorably to occupations that do not require a college diploma. However, they do not compare favorably with other occupations requiring a college education. Table 8–1 compares teacher salaries with those of other white-collar occupations. This comparison was released in 2007 by the American Federation of Teachers, in its report *Survey and Analysis of Teacher Salary Trends 2005.*

Why do college students pursue a teaching career when they could earn more in other occupations requiring a college education? One answer is that teachers find their greatest reward in interacting with students. In *A Place Called School,* John Goodlad reports from his survey that the top reasons given by students for entering teaching are "having a satisfying job" and liking and wanting to help children. Despite these altruistic reasons, most students in the survey faced critical comments from family members and friends. Some parents rejected the decision and refused to support their child's schooling in teacher education.

Also, in comparison with many corporate and factory jobs, teachers enjoy a great deal of autonomy in the classroom. It has been estimated that teachers make more than 200 decisions an hour in their classrooms. These decisions range from curricular and teaching problems to behavioral problems. Unlike routine work, teaching involves creative decision making. In a national survey, "Teachers' Working Conditions," Susan Choy found that "the vast majority of teachers thought that they had a good deal of control in their own classroom over practices such as evaluating and grading students, selecting teaching techniques, and determining the amount of homework to be assigned."

TABLE 8–1. Comparison of Teacher Pay with Other Professions, 2004–2005

Profession	2005 Salary
Attorney	$100,000
Full professor	97,648
Buyer	61,553
Engineer	80,122
Assistant professor	51,249
Computer systems analyst	75,709
Accountant	54,053
Teacher	47,602

Source: American Federation of Teachers, *Survey and Analysis of Teacher Salary Trends 2005.* (Washington, DC: American Federation of Teachers, 2007), p. 4.

Other ancillary rewards of teaching are attractive to many individuals. A popular reward is the time for extended vacations and travel provided by the long summer vacation and other school holidays. Second to vacation time is the security of income and position. In most states, teacher tenure laws provide a security not often found in other jobs.

WORKING CONDITIONS

Working conditions become another factor in evaluating the rewards of teaching. Teachers average a 45-hour workweek. A national study of teachers' working conditions found that full-time public school teachers at both the elementary and secondary levels are required to be at school for an average of 33 hours a week. In addition, teachers spend an average of 12 hours after and before school and on weekends grading papers, preparing lessons, meeting with parents, and performing other school-related activities. Teachers at private schools averaged about one more hour of required time at school and one more hour of after-school work. A major issue for teachers is class size. Besides affecting the quality of learning for students, class size has a direct bearing on the working conditions of teachers. Large classes result in more papers to grade and more problems in class discipline. Also, large classes affect the quality of interaction between students and teachers. If the major reason people enter teaching is the opportunity for interacting with students, then reward is enhanced through small classes.

Time pressures as another source of teacher dissatisfaction are vividly portrayed by Theodore Sizer in his description of a day in the life of high school English teacher Horace Smith. Sizer provides sympathetic insight into the life of a 28-year veteran of teaching who still cares about his work but is constantly forced to compromise his instructional ideals with the realities of public school teaching.

Sizer assures the reader that Horace's compromises are not the result of unusually poor working conditions. In fact, the reader is often reminded that Horace Smith teaches in a suburban school where conditions are far superior to those faced by teachers in central-city school systems. Sizer is also realistic. He recognizes that all jobs involve compromises between ideals and realities. But he feels the compromises required in teaching require more than ordinary adjustments to the realities of work. The compromises required in teaching not only shatter ideals but also cheat students of opportunities to learn.

Horace Smith is proud and committed to his job. His day begins at 5:45 A.M. with a brief breakfast and a 40-minute drive, bringing him to school by 7:00. He heads directly for the teachers' lounge, where he enjoys a cup of coffee and a cigarette before the beginning of his 7:30 class. The teachers' lounge is portrayed as a warm setting in which there are the smell of old cigarette smoke and a continual card game being played by groups of teachers during their off-hours. It is the one haven in the school where teachers can meet and share daily events and professional concerns.

Horace's three junior-level classes for the day are reading *Romeo and Juliet.* As a veteran teacher who has spent many years teaching *Romeo and Juliet,* he moves his classes quickly through the drama, anticipating their difficulties and avoiding distracting issues. His second-bell class is excused for an assembly, which allows him to return to his coffee cup in the teachers' lounge. His fourth-bell class is a senior advanced-placement class that is studying *Ulysses.* On this day, 13 of the 18 seniors are attending a United Nations week at a local college. Sizer describes Horace's annoyance at losing the teaching day but also his feeling of gratefulness at being able to avoid teaching, thus allowing his students time to read. Besides his five classes, Horace has a preparation period and a lunch hour.

The final bell ends the school day at 2:00 P.M. After conversations with students, Horace collects his papers, leaves his classroom at 2:30, and goes to the auditorium. Horace is a faculty adviser to the stage crew, for which he earns an extra $800 a year. For that small amount he puts in about four hours a week—and many more hours than that in the 10 days before a performance. After stopping in the auditorium, he drives to his brother-in-law's liquor store, where he works behind the counter and in the stockroom from shortly after 4:00 P.M. until 6:30.

He eats dinner at 7:15 and then spends an hour grading papers. This is followed by several phone calls from sick students wanting assignments and students wanting to talk about the upcoming stage production. Finally, Horace ends his day by drifting off to sleep after the 11:00 news.

Horace's compromises are in the shortcuts he must take to deal with his busy day. He knows that he should be assigning his students a weekly essay of a page or two. But with a total of 120 students (central-city teachers often have more than 170 students) he is realistic and assigns only one or two paragraphs. Even with these short assignments, he estimates that grading and writing comments will take 15 to 20 minutes of his time per student. This still involves roughly 30 hours of grading. Again, Horace is realistic about his time and takes shortcuts in grading to reduce the time per student to five minutes. This means that even with reducing the assignment from a short theme to one or two paragraphs, and cutting corners while grading, Horace still must devote 10 hours a week to grading.

He must also take shortcuts in class preparations. He has taught some of his classes before, whereas others require more preparation. But even when classes are studying the same material, the differences among students require separate lesson plans. Horace recognizes that he should spend many more hours on preparation but again compromises and spends only about 10 minutes per class on preparation.

His shortcuts in grading and preparation, along with his teaching, administration, and extracurricular drama work, give him a 42-hour week. If he did not cut corners there would be another 20 hours of grading and possibly another 6 hours for preparation, which would mean a 68-hour week. On top of this is the time Horace spends working in his brother-in-law's liquor store to add to his inadequate salary. And, of course, there are the three full days he spends during Christmas vacation writing letters of reference for his students.

Lost in all these commitments is the time that should be used for reading professional journals and new literature and for doing those things that renew the life of the mind. As Sizer describes the situation, Horace hides his bitterness toward the critics who demand from teachers more scholarship and intellectual involvement. And, in the end, the students are as cheated as Horace's ideals.

In *High School,* Ernest Boyer provides similar descriptions of teachers who are overwhelmed by course loads and are forced to seek outside employment to add to their meager salaries. In many ways, Boyer paints an even grimmer picture of a high school teacher's life. His teachers have five to six classes a day with three different levels in a course. The different levels mean that more of the teachers' time is required to review subject matter and prepare for class. In addition, many teachers are assigned classes for which they have had no training. For instance, a social studies teacher might be assigned a science or mathematics course, which means endless hours of preparation. Added to this is the time spent on grading papers, preparing lesson plans, and counseling students.

Boyer found that a great deal of a teacher's time is spent on clerical and administrative chores. Many of these extra duties are nothing but baby-sitting and security tasks such as supervising hallways, lunchrooms, and student activities. Boyer found widespread complaints about clerical chores resulting from endless requests from both the school administration and the central administration of the school district. Also, teachers must keep elaborate student attendance records and send written reports to school counselors.

A great deal of a teacher's time is spent counseling students. Boyer gives the average pupil-to-counselor ratio in the United States as 319 to 1. Because there is little hope for the average student to find a counselor who has enough time to deal to any great extent with personal, academic, and career problems, students often turn to teachers for help. This creates a bind for many teachers because the better and more popular teachers often have the greatest demands on their time.

A feeling of isolation among teachers was also found in the high schools visited by Boyer. Teachers spend very little time in the company of other adults. Contact with other adults usually occurs only at lunchtime or during preparation periods in the faculty lounge. This situation gives teachers few opportunities to discuss common problems, professional issues, and intellectual topics with other teachers.

Teachers are also frequently without a permanent classroom, which means they are without their own desk: Most move from room to room carrying all their material. Many schools, particularly in central cities, are poorly maintained and have dirty windows and floors. In addition, there is often a shortage of school materials, and teachers dip into their own pockets to buy supplies.

For Boyer, a teacher's working conditions are made even more intolerable by a lack of public recognition and reward. There is a lack of respect from other adults outside teaching. Most teachers even avoid mentioning to other adults the nature of their occupation. One teacher, who works as a meat cutter during the summer, was told by a fellow butcher who discovered he was a teacher, "Man, that's a dead-end job. You must be a real dummy."

Although Sizer and Boyer analyze the lives of the high school teachers, many of their conclusions also apply to elementary school teachers. Elementary school teachers also feel time pressure in their class preparations and grading. They feel the same grim climate of isolation from adults, poor physical environment, and lack of community respect. They also must seek extracurricular school and summer employment to fill the gap left by inadequate salaries. Many teachers find that contact with students, autonomy in the classroom, job security, and extended vacations compensate for poor working conditions and salaries. Personally, I enjoy teaching. I enjoy engaging students in dialogues over important questions. I enjoy students telling me that I made them think about the world in a different way. My philosophy of teaching is embodied in this book.

As discussions of teacher work continue, more requirements are being added. As part of the nationalizing trend in teacher certification and as an example of increased steps in teacher certification, a form of national certification is being proposed by the National Board for Professional Teaching Standards.

TEACHER TURNOVER

Do working conditions cause teachers to leave the profession? In 2007, the American Federation of Teachers issued the following data on teacher turnover. One striking statistic is that teachers teaching in high poverty schools are most likely to leave teaching. Table 8–2 provides percentages of teachers who either transferred to another school or left the profession.

As indicated in Table 8–2, annually 16.9 percent of teachers leave the school where they have been teaching. A large percentage (7.8 percent) transfer to another school. The largest percentage (9 percent) leave the profession, with 2.4 percent leaving for retirement. This means that 6.6 percent of teachers left the profession completely for another job, further education, and family reasons. As indicated in Table 8–3, the biggest turnover for public schools is in high-poverty schools as compared to low-poverty schools.

The difference in teacher turnover between high-poverty (21.1 percent) and low-poverty (14.2 percent) public schools highlights the very difficult time

TABLE 8–2. Percentage Distribution of 2003–2004 Public and Private K–12 Teachers Who Did Not Teach in the Same School the Following Year and Reasons for Leaving

Total turnover at end of year	16.9%
Transferred to another school	7.8
Left teaching: Total	9
Left teaching: Took another job	3.8
Left teaching: Pursued further education	0.3
Left teaching: Left for family reasons	1.2
Left teaching: Retired	2.4
Left teaching: Other	1.3

Source: Adapted from Table 31–1, American Federation of Teachers, *Survey and Analysis of Teacher Salary Trends 2005* (Washington, DC: American Federation of Teachers, 2007), p.157.

TABLE 8–3. Percentage of 2003–2004 Public K–12 Teachers Who Did Not Teach in the Same School the Following Year, by Poverty Level of School and the Reason Teachers Left

Reason Teachers left	High-Poverty School	Low-Poverty School
Total turnover	21.1%	14.2%
Transferred to another school	10.6	6.4
Took another job	3.5	3.9
Pursued further education	0.5	0.3
Left for family reasons	2.6	0.7
Retired	2.4	2.6
Other	1.5	0.4

Source: Adapted from Table 31–3, American Federation of Teachers, *Survey and Analysis of Teacher Salary Trends 2005* (Washington, DC: American Federation of Teachers, 2007), p. 158.

school officials have in recruiting and retaining teachers in public schools serving low-income families. The 21.1 percent turnover in high-poverty schools contributes to inequality of educational opportunity. An important contribution to correcting problems of unequal education is to find a means of recruiting and retaining teachers to serve students from low-income backgrounds.

TEACHERS' UNIONS AND TEACHER POLITICS

There are two teachers' unions. One is the National Education Association (NEA) and the other is the American Federation of Teachers (AFT). Both unions have traditionally been active in supporting a wide variety of measures to benefit teachers and schools. Calling her speech "Why Teachers Should Organize," Margaret Haley declared, as the first woman to ever speak from the floor of a national meeting of the NEA, "Two ideals are struggling for supremacy in American life today: one the industrial ideal, dominating thru [*sic*] supremacy of commercialism . . . the other, the ideal of democracy, the ideal of educators." Inviting teachers to organize to protect the interests of children, workers, and democracy, Haley exhorted, "It will be well indeed if the teachers have the courage of their convictions and face all that the labor unions have faced with the same courage and perseverance." Delivered in 1904, Haley's speech marked the rise of teacher unionism and the eventual founding of the rival organization—the AFT.

In 1998, echoing Haley's idealism, Mary Kimmel bemoaned the continued rivalry between the NEA and AFT: "How can students learn if they don't have a full stomach and a safe environment? I don't know how we as educators can battle foes of public education if we're still fighting against ourselves." While struggling to overcome the differences between the two teachers' unions, organized teachers fulfilled Haley's dream of becoming an important force in American education and politics. Even national politicians paid attention to the power of the teachers' unions.

Both teachers' unions, the AFT and the NEA, actively participate in national elections. They work for both presidential and congressional candidates. Over the last two decades, they have given most of their support to candidates from the Democratic Party. This has created a split between the two national political parties over teachers' unions. Overall, Republicans oppose the work of teachers' unions, while Democrats are supportive. Of course, like other aspects of American politics, these alliances can vary from state to state.

Besides working in election campaigns, both unions have full-time Washington lobbyists who try to ensure that federal legislation does not jeopardize the welfare of teachers. Also, both unions maintain lobbyists at the state level and work for candidates to the state legislature. At the local level, teachers' unions have increasingly supported and campaigned for candidates in local school board elections. The involvement of teachers' unions in national, state, and local politics has made them a powerful political force.

Despite the failure of efforts to merge the two teachers unions, they have established a partnership called the "NEAFT Partnership" with the large 'A' symbolically representing their mutual interests. The two organizations describe the necessity of this partnership:

> Because our members are on the front lines of the future of America, and because our work and our values are rooted in the well-being of the children of this nation and their families:
>
> - The AFT and NEA are committed to work together on behalf of our members and on behalf of all those whom our members serve.
> - We are committed to nurturing and improving public education above all.
> - We are determined to fight for family needs, which must be met in order to make our public schools the equalizer they have been and should be for society. This encompasses quality of life issues, such as health care for all Americans, safe neighborhoods and a caring government.

DIFFERENCES BETWEEN THE TWO UNIONS

The differences between the NEA and the AFT are a result of the historic split between professional and union organizations. As the following historical sketches show, the NEA traditionally limited its concerns to school organization and teachers. Consequently, the NEA restricts its membership to, in the words of their official description, "anyone who works for a public school district, a college or university, or any other public institution devoted primarily to education. . . . NEA also has special membership categories for . . . college students to become teachers."

On the other hand, the AFT traditionally embraced all educational workers, teachers, state and local government employees, and health workers. According to its official description, the AFT's membership includes "public and private school teachers, paraprofessional and school-related personnel, higher education faculty and professionals, employees of state and local governments, nurses and health professionals."

The AFT's commitment to a broad union movement is reflected by its membership along with 75 other unions in the 13.1-million-member AFL-CIO. The NEA remains unaffiliated with the general labor movement represented by the AFL-CIO. The following histories of the two organizations highlight the differences in labor affiliation and membership. These histories also illustrate the struggle of teachers to improve their working conditions. In reading these two brief histories, you should keep in mind the following questions:

- Should teachers organize into unions to protect and improve their working conditions, salaries, fringe benefits, and retirement funds?
- Should teachers' unions become actively involved in political campaigns and lobbying to support legislation favorable to the interests of teachers?
- Should the actions of teachers' unions reflect the interests of other unions, low- and middle-income families, children, or public schools?
- Should teachers' unions limit their activities to the welfare of teachers and other educational professionals?
- Should teachers' unions participate in general efforts to reform public schools?
- Should teachers' unions control and manage school budgets and curricula?
- Should teachers' unions attempt through collective bargaining to control class size, lengths of the school day and year, number of faculty meetings, and other school policies?
- What should be the purpose of a teachers' organization?

A BRIEF HISTORY OF THE NATIONAL EDUCATION ASSOCIATION (NEA)

Founded in 1857, the NEA adopted the goal of nationalizing the work of state education associations. This would be one of its major functions in the history of American education. The letter inviting representatives to the founding meeting states, "Believing that what state associations have accomplished for the states may be done for the whole country by a National Association, we, the undersigned, invite our fellow-teachers throughout the United States to assemble in Philadelphia."

The 1857 meeting in Philadelphia gave birth to an organization that in the nineteenth and early twentieth centuries had major influence over the shaping of American schools and contributed to the nationalizing of the American school system. From the platform of its conventions and the work of its committees came curriculum proposals and policy statements that were adopted from coast to coast. Until the 1960s, the work of the NEA tended to be dominated by school superintendents, college professors, and administrators. These educational leaders would take the proposals of the NEA back to their local communities for discussion and possible adoption.

Examples of the work of the NEA include its major role in the shaping of the modern high school. In 1892, the NEA formed the Committee of Ten on

Secondary School Studies, under the leadership of Charles Eliot, the president of Harvard University. The Committee of Ten appointed nine subcommittees with a total membership of 100 to decide the future of the American high school. The membership of these committees reflected the domination of the organization by school administrators and representatives of higher education: 53 were college presidents or professors, 23 were headmasters of private schools, and the rest were superintendents and representatives from teacher-training institutions. The work of the Committee of Ten set the stage for the creation in 1913 of the NEA Commission on the Reorganization of Secondary Education, which in 1918 issued its epoch-making report, *Cardinal Principles of Secondary Education.* This report urged the creation of comprehensive high schools offering a variety of curricula, as opposed to the establishment of separate high schools offering a single curriculum, such as college preparatory, vocational, and commercial. This report became the major formative document of the modern high school.

The NEA also influenced the standardization of teacher training in the United States. The Normal Department of the NEA began surveying the status of institutions for teacher education in 1886, and debates began within the organization about the nature of teacher education. The official historian of the NEA, Edgar B. Wesley, stated in his *NEA: The First Hundred Years:* "By 1925 the training of teachers was rather systematically standardized." The work of the Normal Department of the NEA can claim a large share of the credit for this standardization.

NEA conventions and meetings further became a central arena for the discussion of curriculum changes in elementary and secondary schools. During the 1920s and 1930s, many surveys, studies, yearbooks, and articles were published. In 1924, the Department of Superintendence began issuing what were to be successive yearbooks on various aspects of the curriculum at various grade levels. In 1943, the Society for Curriculum Study merged with the NEA Department of Supervisors and Directors of Instruction to form an enlarged department called the Association for Supervision and Curriculum Development (ASCD). The ASCD is still recognized as the major professional organization for the discussion of curriculum issues.

After the passage of the National Defense Education Act in 1958, the NEA's leadership role in the determination of national educational policy was greatly reduced as the federal government became the major springboard for national policy. The NEA became an organization whose central focus was teacher welfare and government lobbying. This shift was a result of several developments: the emergence of the leadership role of the federal government, demands within the NEA for more emphasis on teacher welfare, greater democratic control of the organization, and the success of the AFT in winning collective bargaining for its members (thus serving as a model for the NEA).

In 1962, the NEA's activities underwent a dramatic transformation when it launched a program for collective negotiations. This meant that local affiliates would attempt to achieve collective-bargaining agreements with local boards of education. This development completely changed the nature of local organizations and required a rewriting of local constitutions to include collective bargaining. Up to this point in time, local school administrators had controlled many local education associations, which used the local organizations to convey policies determined by the board and administration. Collective bargaining reversed this situation and turned the local affiliates into organizations that told boards and administrators what teachers wanted.

Collective bargaining created a new relationship between locals of the NEA and local boards of education. Traditionally, local units of the NEA might plead for the interests of their members, but they most often simply helped to carry out policies of local school boards and administrators. Teachers bargained individually with the school board over salary and working conditions. With collective bargaining, teachers voted for an organization to represent their demands before the school board. Once selected as a representative of the local teachers, the organization would negotiate with the school board over working conditions and salaries. Many school boards were caught by surprise when their usually compliant local of the NEA suddenly demanded higher wages and better working conditions for all teachers.

The NEA's early approach to collective bargaining differed from that of the union-oriented AFT. The NEA claimed it was involved in professional negotiating and not in union collective bargaining. Professional negotiation, according to the NEA, would remove negotiation procedures from labor precedents and laws and would resort to state educational associations, rather than those of labor, to mediate or resolve conflicts that could not be settled locally. All pretense of the NEA not being a union ended in the 1970s, when the NEA joined the Coalition of American Public Employees (CAPE). CAPE is a nonprofit corporation comprising the National Education Association; American Federation of State, County, and Municipal Employees; National Treasury Employees Union; Physicians National Housestaff Association; and American Nurses Association. These organizations represent about 4 million public employees. The stated purpose of CAPE is "to provide a means of marshaling and coordinating the legislative, legal, financial, and public relations resources of the member organizations in matters of common concern." The most important of these matters "is supporting legislation to provide collective-bargaining rights to all public employees, including teachers."

By the 1980s, support of collective-bargaining legislation became one of many legislative goals of the NEA; the organization by this time was also directing a great deal of its energies to lobbying for legislation and support of political candidates. The turning point for the NEA was its endorsement of Jimmy Carter in the 1976 presidential election. This was the first time the NEA had supported a presidential candidate. After this initial involvement, the NEA expanded its activity to support candidates in primary elections. In 1980, the NEA worked actively in the primaries to ensure the victory of Jimmy Carter over Edward Kennedy for the Democratic nomination. Through the 1990s, the NEA committed itself to the support of Democratic candidates for the White House.

The major topic at the 1998 NEA convention was merger with its rival, the AFT. The consideration of a merger reflected the evolution of the organization from a professional organization to a politically active union. The evolution of the NEA is an important chapter in the political history of the United States. In recent years, the NEA had emerged as the more socially concerned and militant of the two teachers' unions. By the 1990s, the NEA had become so politically active that its rival, the AFT, was accusing it of trying to be a political kingmaker.

In 2004, the NEA campaigned to amend the No Child Left Behind Act. It supported a large number of Congressional bills to provide more flexibility to use means other than test scores for evaluation. In addition, the NEA backed legislation that would ensure that civil rights laws were enforced for faith-based providers of educational services. Since the No Child Left Behind Act allowed for the use of these faith-based providers there were many questions about the discriminatory practices and doctrines of many religious organizations. The union also supported legislation providing funds and flexibility to help teachers meet the "highly qualified" requirements of the No Child Left Behind Act. The NEA wanted legislation that would "allow an academic minor, as well as a major, to meet the requirement of demonstrating subject matter competency; extend by three years (until the end of the 2008–09 school year) the time teachers in rural schools have to meet the 'highly qualified' rules."

To improve teachers' working conditions, the NEA supported an amendment restoring the Class Size Reduction program to the No Child Left Behind Act. The NEA legislation Web site stated that the amendment "would authorize a $2 billion per year program to provide funds to school districts to hire highly qualified teachers to reduce class sizes in order to improve student achievement for both regular education and special education students. Other allowable uses of funds include recruiting and training new teachers, testing new teachers for content knowledge, and providing professional development and mentoring."

In 2008, the NEA criticized high-stakes testing and No Child Left Behind and demanded a change in federal laws. During the 2008 presidential campaign, the NEA declared, "After six years of treating children as no more than test scores, No Child Left Behind has not lived up to its promise. Education policy needs a new direction." The union called for a new federal role in education. The organization asserted that the federal government should support public schools by:

- Strengthening enforcement of civil rights laws to promote access and opportunity.
- Funding past Congressional actions and current federal mandates.
- Helping create the capacity at the local and state levels for school transformation.

This declaration indicated the continuing role the NEA would have in trying to shape the nature of American Education.

A BRIEF HISTORY OF THE AMERICAN FEDERATION OF TEACHERS (AFT)

Unlike the NEA's origins as a national policymaking organization, the AFT began in the struggle by female grade-school teachers for an adequate pension law in Illinois. The first union local, the Chicago Teachers Federation, was formed in 1897 under the leadership of Catherine Goggin and Margaret Haley. Its early fights centered on pensions and teacher salaries. Because of its success in winning salary increases, its membership increased to 2,500 by the end of its first year. In 1902, with the urging of famous settlement-house reformer Jane Addams, the Chicago Teachers Federation joined the Chicago Federation of Labor, which placed it under the broad umbrella of the American Federation of Labor (AFL).

From its beginnings, the AFT placed teacher-welfare issues and improving public education in the more general context of the labor movement in the United States. In an interview titled "The School-Teacher Unionized" in the November 1905 issue of the *Educational Review,* Margaret Haley declared: "We expect by affiliation with labor to arouse the workers and the whole people, through the workers, to the dangers confronting the public schools from the same interests and tendencies that are undermining the foundations of our democratic republic." Those "same interests" referred to in Haley's speech were big business organizations, against which Haley felt both labor and educators were struggling. The early union movement was based on the belief that there was unity between the educators' struggle to gain more financial support for the schools from big business and labor's struggle with the same interests to win collective-bargaining rights. Haley went on to state, "It is necessary to make labor a constructive force in society, or it will be a destructive force. If the educational question could be understood by the labor men, and the labor question by the educators, both soon would see they are working to the same end, and should work together."

Margaret Haley's comments highlighted the union's efforts to create mutually supportive roles between teachers and organized labor. On the one hand, teachers were to work for the interests of workers by fighting for better schools and working to remove antilabor material from the classroom. Teachers would fight to provide the best education for workers' children, while organized labor would provide the resources of its organization to support the teachers' struggle for improved working conditions and greater financial support for the schools. In addition, the type of education received by children in the schools would give children the economic and political knowledge needed to continue the work of the union movement, and teachers could share their knowledge with the adult members of the labor movement. Teachers would also increase their political and economic knowledge through their association with the labor movement.

In December 1912, the newly established magazine of the union movement, the *American Teacher,* issued a statement of the beliefs of the growing union movement in education. First, the statement argued that the improvement of American education depended on arousing teachers to realize that "their professional and social standing is far too low to enable them to produce effective results in teaching." Second, it was necessary for teachers to study the relation of education "to social progress, and to understand some important social and economic movements going on in the present-day world." Third, it was believed that teachers could use their experience in teaching to adjust education to the needs of modern living. Fourth, in one of the earliest declarations for the end of sexism in education, the statement called for high-quality teaching "without sex-antagonism."

In 1915, union locals from Chicago and Gary, Indiana, met and officially formed the AFT. In 1916, this group, along with locals from New York, Pennsylvania, Oklahoma, and Washington, DC, were accepted into the AFL. At the presentation ceremony, the head of the AFL, Samuel Gompers, welcomed the AFT to "the fold and the bond of unity and fraternity of the organized labor movement of our Republic. We earnestly hope . . . that it may . . . give and receive mutual sympathy and support which can be properly exerted for the betterment of all who toil and give service—aye, for all humanity."

It was not until 1944 that the AFT exercised any organizational control over a local school system. In 1944, the AFT local in Cicero, Illinois, signed the first collective-bargaining contract with a board of education. The form of the contract was that of a regular labor-union contract. It recognized the local as the sole bargaining agent of the teachers and listed pay schedules and grievance procedures. At the annual convention of the AFT in 1946, a committee was assigned to study collective bargaining and its application to school management. In addition, material was to be collected from trade unions on the education of shop stewards and union practices. With the introduction of collective bargaining, the AFT entered a new stage in its development.

The involvement of the AFT in collective bargaining led naturally to the question of teacher strikes. Since its founding the AFT had a no-strike policy. In 1946, the use of the strike for supporting teachers' demands became a major issue at the annual convention. Those supporting the use of the strike argued it was the only means available to arouse an apathetic citizenry to the problems in American education. It was also the only meaningful leverage teachers had against local school systems. AFT members who favored retention of the no-strike policy argued that teachers were in a public service profession and that work stoppage was a violation of public trust. In addition, it was argued that a strike deprived children of an education and was counter to the democratic ideal of a child's right to an education.

The AFT maintained its no-strike policy in the face of growing militancy among individual locals. In 1947, the Buffalo, New York, Teachers Federation declared a strike for higher salaries. The strike was considered at the time the worst teacher work stoppage in the history of the country. Other local unions supported the strikers, with local drivers delivering only enough fuel to the schools to keep the pipes from freezing. The Buffalo strike was important because it served as a model for action by other teachers around the country.

School superintendents, school board associations, and state superintendents of education condemned these actions by local teachers. The national AFT maintained its no-strike policy and adopted a posture of aid and comfort but not official sanction. As William Edward Eaton states in his *The American Federation of Teachers, 1916–1961,* "Even with a no-strike policy, the AFT had emerged as the leader in teacher work stoppages."

The event that sparked the rapid growth of teacher militancy in the 1960s, and contributed to the NEA's rapid acceptance of collective bargaining, was the formation of the New York City local of the AFT, the United Federation of Teachers (UFT). In the late 1950s, the AFT decided to concentrate on organizing teachers in New York City and to provide special funds for that purpose. After the organization of the UFT in 1960, there was a vote for a strike over the issues of a dues checkoff plan, the conducting of a collective-bargaining election, sick pay for substitutes, 50-minute lunch periods for teachers, and changes in the salary schedules. On 7 November 1960, the UFT officially went on strike against the New York City school system. The union declared the strike effective when 15,000 of the city's 39,000 teachers did not report to school and 7,500 teachers joined picket lines around the schools. In the spring of 1961, the UFT won a collective-bargaining agreement with the school system and became one of the largest and most influential locals within the AFT.

During the 1960s, teachers increasingly accepted the idea of collective bargaining and the use of the strike. This was reflected in the rapid growth of membership in the AFT. In 1966, the membership of the AFT was 125,421. By 1981, the membership had more than quadrupled to 580,000. This increased membership plus the increased militancy of the NEA heralded a new era in the relationship among American teachers' organizations and the managers of American education. With the coming of age of the strike and collective bargaining, teachers in the NEA and AFT proved themselves willing to fight for their own welfare and the welfare of American public schools.

In 2008, the AFT joined the NEA in criticizing No Child Left Behind. The AFT was particularly concerned about schools serving low-income families. The AFT's 2008 resolution on No Child Left Behind is:

> WHEREAS, efforts to radically reform the No Child Left Behind Act (the failed reiteration of the Elementary and Secondary Education Act), were unsuccessful; and
> WHEREAS, teachers and other personnel, especially in low-income urban and rural school districts, are being unduly criticized and blamed when schools do not make so-called "adequate yearly progress"; and
> WHEREAS, AFT members are rightly angry and frustrated by those aspects of NCLB that have impeded, not helped, their work; and
> WHEREAS, we will soon elect a new president and a new Congress that we hope will listen to the voice of educators,
> RESOLVED, that the American Federation of Teachers, drawing on the collective wisdom of the educators it represents, move immediately to develop a proposal that builds on the intent of ESEA to ensure that our nation's most vulnerable students get the excellent education that they deserve.

The two teachers' unions will continue to play important roles in American education. I strongly recommend visiting their Web sites (www.nea.org and www.aft.org) to examine their current reports and resources.

SHOULD TEACHERS STRIKE?

In 2006, an *Education Week* headline read "Labor Disputes Heating Up in Urban Districts, After Respite." In the article, reporter Vaishali Honawar warns:

> After a lengthy period of relative harmony, teachers in several big-city districts are raising the stakes in collective bargaining battles. Teachers in San Francisco and Oakland, Calif., have threatened to go on strike later this month, following strike-authorization votes by union members in both districts late last month. In Detroit, meanwhile, 1,500 teachers in more than 50 schools called in sick March 22.

Strikes occur when a local teachers' union is unable to reach an agreement with the board of education regarding salary and working conditions. The steps leading up to striking begin with union representatives bargaining with a board of education over a new contract that will bind both sides to a particular wage scale and work rules. The wage scale includes salary and benefits such as health and dental insurance. Work rules involve length of school day, teaching load, class size, and a host of other work-related issues.

Conflict between the two sides is generated when the board of education wants to maintain existing salary scale and benefits and increase teachers' workload, while the union wants higher salaries and improved working conditions. Both sides will usually claim to be representing the interests of the students and community. When the bargaining process fails to reach a mutually acceptable contract, union members might authorize a strike. For instance, a recent strike in Yonkers, New York, occurred when the union rejected attempts by the administration to increase teachers' workloads by extending class time.

During a strike, the local teachers' union organizes picket lines around schools. Union members are assigned times and places for picketing. The purpose of the picket line is to keep members of other unions from entering the school. Theoretically, a union member is not supposed to cross the picket line of another union. For instance, truck drivers, usually members of the Teamster's Union, are not supposed to cross teachers' union picket lines to deliver goods to the school.

Picket lines also serve as a barrier to other teachers who refuse to strike. Teachers crossing picket lines are called "scabs." Conflict among teachers over a strike can result in years of hostile feelings. I have known situations where even 10 years after a strike union members still refuse to talk to "scabs" in faculty meeting rooms.

One of the questions frequently asked organizers for the NEA is, If we form a faculty union, will we have to go on strike? The NEA's answer is: "No. A strike can only be authorized by the faculty. State or national union officers or staff members cannot under any circumstances authorize or declare a strike. Faculty would have to vote on any strike action if they ever felt compelled to do so. In some states, a strike is an illegal activity."

While many states outlaw strikes by public employees, teachers' unions in those states still conduct strikes. I was involved in an illegal strike in Ohio where the final agreement between the two sides ruled out any criminal action against union members. On the other hand, there are cases where union leaders are arrested and jailed, and the local union heavily fined by the state.

Should teachers strike? On the one hand, some argue that teachers' strikes are sometimes necessary to improve the quality of education provided to students. Teacher welfare is directly related to student welfare. High pay and good working conditions attract and retain the best teachers. On the other hand, some argue that strikes only benefit teachers. Students lose valuable time at school while teachers are on strike. Communities are forced to raise taxes to pay for increased salaries that might result from a strike. Working parents' lives are disrupted when children are forced out of school by a strike. These conflicting concerns raise the following questions:

1. Do teacher strikes endanger the public welfare by denying an education to children and disrupting the employment of parents by requiring them to take charge of their own children during strike periods?
2. Should teachers worry only about fulfilling their instructional duties without concern for their wages or working conditions?
3. Do teachers' unions improve school instruction by improving teacher morale and creating conditions that foster good teaching?
4. Would you strike as a teacher?
5. Are there any salary or work-related issues that you might be willing to strike for?

CONCLUSION

The profession of teaching has changed greatly since the nineteenth century model of teachers as paragons of morality. The changes in the profession parallel changes in the goals of U.S. schools. Essentially, the changes were from a moral to a global model. Teacher issues and concerns range from teacher education and licensing to high-stakes tests and classroom conditions.

Teachers are not passively manipulated by policymakers. Teachers' unions are a powerful force in American politics and in the formulation of educational policies. Unions protect the wages and working conditions and allow for the voice of teachers in national and local educational policy decisions.

Suggested Readings and Works Cited in Chapter

The best sources of current information about the teachers' unions can be found on their Web sites. The NEA site is www.nea.org. The AFT site is www.aft.org. The information used in this chapter on recent NEA and AFT policies was taken from these sites.

AHMAD, NASHIAH. "Strikes Hit Two Washington State Districts." *Education Week on the Web* (18 September 2002). http://www.edweek.org. Ahmad reviews teacher strikes at the opening of the 2002–2003 school year.

American Federation of Teachers. "Resolution 2008: No Child Left Behind." http://www.aft.org/about/resolutions/2008/nclb.htm. Resolution expresses concern that No Child Left Behind has done little to help schools serving low-income students.

——. "Standards, 2004." http://www.aft.org/topics/sbr/index.htm. The AFT recalls its history of support of the standards movement, its accomplishments, and its future needs.

——. *Survey and Analysis of Teacher Salary Trends 2005.* Washington, DC: American Federation of Teachers, 2007. Provides data and analysis of teacher salaries and teacher turnover.

——. "Teacher Salaries Remain Stagnant but Health Insurance Costs Soar, AFT Releases Annual State-by-State Teacher Salary Survey, 2004." http://www.aft.org/salary/index.htm. The annual teacher salary report is provided here.

BERUBE, MAURICE. *Teacher Politics: The Influence of Unions.* Westport, CT: Greenwood Press, 1988. This is a very good introduction to the politics of teachers' unions.

BORROWMAN, MERLE. *The Liberal and Technical in Teacher Education: A Historical Survey of American Thought.* New York: Teachers College Press, 1956. This is the classic study of the debates that have surrounded the development of teacher education in the United States. The book provides the best introduction to the history and issues regarding teacher education.

BOYER, ERNEST L. *High School.* New York: Harper and Row, 1983. This study, conducted for the Carnegie Foundation for the Advancement of Teaching, contains important descriptions of the work life of teachers and recommendations for the reform of teaching.

EATON, WILLIAM E. *The American Federation of Teachers, 1916–1961.* Carbondale: Southern Illinois University Press, 1975. This is a good history of the development of the AFT.

ELSBREE, WILLARD S. *The American Teacher: Evolution of a Profession in a Democracy.* New York: American Book, 1939. This is still the best history of the profession of teaching in the United States. Unfortunately it traces the professionalization of teaching only to the 1930s.

GOODLAD, JOHN. *Teachers for Our Nation's Schools.* San Francisco: Jossey-Bass Publishers, 1990. This study of teacher education in the United States contains surveys and recommendations for the teaching profession.

——. *A Place Called School.* New York: McGraw-Hill, 1984. This detailed study of American schools contains surveys and recommendations about the profession of teaching.

HERBST, JURGEN. *And Sadly Teach: Teacher Education and Professionalization in American Culture.* Madison: University of Wisconsin, 1989. This is a good source on the professionalization of teaching.

HOFFMAN, NANCY. *Woman's "True" Profession: Voices from the History of Teaching.* New York: Feminist Press, 1981. This is an important collection of essays on the history of women in teaching.

HONAWAR, VAISHALI. "Labor Disputes Heating Up in Urban Districts, After Respite." *Education Week on the Web* (5 April 2006). http://www.edweek.org. The increasing conflict between teachers' unions and big-city school administrations is reported.

——."Teachers Achieving 'Highly Qualified' Status on the Rise: Poorer Schools Still Not Getting Their Share, State Data Shows." *Education Week on the Web* (11 June 2008).

http://www.edweek.org. Report on numbers of highly qualified teachers teaching core subjects.

LORTIE, DAN. *Schoolteacher: A Sociological Study.* Chicago: University of Chicago Press, 1975. This is the most complete study of the social interactions and world of the American teacher.

MANN, HORACE. "Fourth Annual Report (1840)." In *The Republic and the School: Horace Mann on the Education of Free Men,* ed. Lawrence Cremin. New York: Teachers College Press, 1958. This report contains Horace Mann's ideas about teachers.

MILLER, JANET. *Creating Spaces and Finding Voices: Teachers Collaborating for Empowerment.* White Plains, NY: Longman, Inc., 1990. This book explores the role of teachers as researchers.

MURPHY, MARJORIE. *Blackboard Unions: The AFT & NEA.* Ithaca: Cornell University Press, 1992. This is a good introduction to teacher unionism.

National Education Association. "NEA Unveils Education Plan to Reshape Federal Role in Education" (2 July 2008). http://www.nea.org. NEA criticizes high-stakes testing and No Child Left Behind. It calls for a new role for the federal government in education.

——. *Rankings & Estimates: Rankings of the States 2004 and Estimates of School Statistics 2005.* Washington, DC: National Education Association, 2005. This report, available on the Web at http://www.nea.org, provides rankings and statistics on teachers' salaries.

——. *Assessment of Diversity in America's Teaching Force: A Call to Action.* Washington, DC: National Collaborative on Diversity in the Teaching Force, October 2004. This report criticizes the lack of diversity in the teaching force and calls for methods to improve recruitment.

——. "Frequently Asked Questions." http://www.nea.org/he/bargain/faq.html. This NEA Web page answers questions dealing with collective bargaining and strikes.

——. "Legislation to Amend the NCLB Act" (2004). NEA Legislation. http://www. nea .org/lac. The NEA calls for amendments to No Child Left Behind to reduce class size, support teachers, and add more flexibility to assessment methods.

PAIGE, ROD. "Paige's Remarks at the National Press Club" (18 March 2003). Go to the U.S. Department of Education Web site: http://www.ed.gov/news/speeches/2003/03/03182003.html.

ROBELEN, ERIK. "Federal Rules for Teachers Are Relaxed." *Education Week on the Web* (24 March 2004). http://www.edweek.org. This article discusses problems of enforcing in rural areas and with veteran teachers the highly qualified teacher provision of No Child Left Behind.

SCHUBERT, WILLIAM H., and WILLIAM C. AYERS, eds. *Teacher Lore: Learning from Our Own Experience.* White Plains, NY: Longman, 1992. This is a collection of analyses by teachers of their own teaching.

SIZER, THEODORE. *Horace's Compromise: The Dilemma of the American High School.* Boston: Houghton Mifflin, 1984. This study of the American high school contains important insights into the problems encountered by teachers.

Task Force on Teaching as a Profession. *A Nation Prepared: Teachers for the 21st Century.* New York: Carnegie Corporation of New York, 1986. This important report calls for the restructuring of the teaching profession and the establishment of a national certification board.

U.S. Department of Education. "Highly Qualified Teachers For Every Child." Available on the Department of Education Web site: http://www.ed.gov. Issued in 2006, these are guidelines for achieving the "highly qualified teacher" requirements of No Child Left Behind.

——. "Teacher Quality: Ensuring Excellence in Every Classroom." http://www.ed.gov/offices/OIIA/stmresources/march/teacherquality.html. The department provides a Web guide to alternative certification and Troops to Teachers programs.

——. *Meeting the Highly Qualified Teachers Challenge: The Secretary's Third Annual Report on Teacher Quality.* Washington, DC: U.S. Department of Education Office of Postsecondary Education, 2004. This report describes the meaning of highly qualified teachers as given in No Child Left Behind.

URBAN, WAYNE. *Why Teachers Organized.* Detroit, MI: Wayne State University, 1982. This excellent history of teachers' unions argues that the primary reason for the formation of these unions was protection of wages and seniority.

WESLEY, EDGAR. *NEA: The First Hundred Years.* New York: Harper and Brothers, 1957. This is the main source of information, in addition to original sources, about the early years of the NEA.

CHAPTER 9

Textbooks, Curriculum, E-Learning, Cyber Bullying, and Global Models of Curriculum and Instruction

Should biology courses teach evolutionary and biblical theories on the origin of life? Should public groups be allowed to censor school textbooks? Should state agencies censor material quoted in high-stakes tests? Who should determine the content of state academic standards? Should student access to the Internet be censored? Is Bible history an appropriate course in the public school? How should teachers teach?

All of the preceding questions deal with content of what is taught and allowed in schools and methods of instruction. In this chapter, I will examine

- The question of censorship of textbooks and student publications.
- The control of knowledge in textbooks and in e-learning.
- The control of knowledge in the curriculum.
- The political nature of methods of instruction.

CENSORSHIP ISSUES

Censorship is a very difficult issue for schools. Should children in public schools be exposed to ideas and values that are contrary to the beliefs of their families? The issue is similar to the question asked in Chapter 6: Who should decide what knowledge should be taught to public school students? In the context of this chapter, the question is: Who should decide what knowledge should be censored in public schools?

In 2008, a community controversy erupted when the Clovis, New Mexico, high school's yearbook, contained a spread on the school's lesbians couples. Bending to the will of citizens who objected to the featuring of lesbians in the yearbook, the superintendent apologized to the school board and promised strict censorship of the yearbook in future years. Clovis yearbook's editor-in-chief,

Maggie Chavez, told *The Clovis News Journal* that the lesbian spread was meant to be "not so much in your face, so much as 'hey, this is happening, you should take notice of it.'"

In a written commentary in *Education Week,* Thomas Panarese, a high school yearbook adviser in Fredericksburg, Virginia, worried that "yearbooks are quickly becoming the new free-speech battleground." He cited a 2007 incident at Conifer High School outside of Denver, Colorado, where the yearbook contained a spread featuring students drinking and using illegal drugs. Panarese reported that:

> A certain segment of the Clovis community thought that the photos of the lesbian couples were morally objectionable. *The Clovis News Journal* quoted one local pastor as calling for administrative oversight that would "reflect the kind of morality of the majority of the community." A disgruntled member of a group called the Christian Citizenship Team echoed that sentiment, adding: "I don't have a child in school but I'm appalled. If I were the parents of those kids, I'd own that school. Those are minors."

As an adviser to a yearbook, Panarese supported the staff of the Clovis yearbook. He asserted that as schools become more diverse school publications will reflect this diversity.

Disputes like that in Clovis are a constant in public education. The People for the American Way, a self appointed watchdog over school censorship, reports the following causes of demands for censorship of school textbooks and library books:

- Sexual content 44 percent of the time.
- Offensive language or profanity 24 percent of the time.
- Anti-Christian or endorsement of another religion 18 percent of the time.
- Objections to historical interpretations, environmentalism, feminism, discussions of government, and other issues 14 percent of the time.

People for the American Way, a politically liberal group claiming a membership of 277,000, was created to combat the influence of the religious right on textbooks. When in 2003 a school district in Arkansas banned all *Harry Potter* books for promoting witchcraft, People for the American Way issued the following press release:

> People for the American Way Foundation joined today with the American Booksellers Foundation for Free Expression and other groups to file a brief in federal court in support of parents challenging a school board's decision to remove all *Harry Potter* books from the school library shelves. The decision by the Cedarville, Arkansas, school board, which requires written parental permission before students can check out the books, disregarded a 15–0 decision by the board's Library Committee. The episode was triggered by a parent's complaint that the books promote witchcraft and sorcery as well as the ideas that "magic will solve your problems" and that "parents/teachers/rules are stupid or something to be ignored."

The American Library Association reports that Robie H. Harris's *It's Perfectly Normal: Changing Bodies, Growing Up, Sex, and Sexual Health* tops its list of most frequently challenged books in a study released in 2005. It should be noted that the following list contains a perennial favorite of adolescent literature, *The Catcher in the Rye,* first published in 1951 and the *Captain Underpants* series, which is popular with elementary-school-age children. Also on the list is the very popular *Forever* by children's author Judy Blume.

American Library Association's List of Most Challenged Books

1. *It's Perfectly Normal* by Robie H. Harris for homosexuality, nudity, sex education, religious viewpoint, abortion, and being unsuited to age group.
2. *Forever* by Judy Blume for sexual content and offensive language.
3. *The Catcher in the Rye* by J. D. Salinger for sexual content, offensive language, and being unsuited to age group.
4. *The Chocolate War* by Robert Cormier for sexual content and offensive language.
5. *Whale Talk* by Chris Crutcher for racism and offensive language.
6. *Detour for Emmy* by Marilyn Reynolds for sexual content.
7. *What My Mother Doesn't Know* by Sonya Sones for sexual content and being unsuited to age group.
8. *Captain Underpants* series by Dav Pilkey for antifamily content, being unsuited to age group, and violence.
9. *Crazy Lady!* by Jane Leslie Conly for offensive language.
10. *It's So Amazing! A Book about Eggs, Sperm, Birth, Babies, and Families* by Robie H. Harris for sex education and sexual content.

Since 1982, the American Library Association has sponsored a "Banned Books Week," which it describes as celebrating "the freedom to choose or the freedom to express one's opinion even if that opinion might be considered unorthodox or unpopular and . . . the importance of ensuring the availability of . . . unorthodox or unpopular viewpoints to all who wish to read them."

Certainly, families holding strong religious or other beliefs might object to the Association's definition of intellectual freedom. Should children have intellectual freedom or be exposed to institutions that follow the American Library Association's guidelines for intellectual freedom? The American Library Association's seventh edition of its *Intellectual Freedom Manual* gives the following as "essential" conditions for intellectual freedom:

1. All individuals have the right to hold any belief on any subject and to convey their ideas in any form they deem appropriate.
2. Society makes an equal commitment to the right of unrestricted access to information and ideas regardless of the communication medium used, the content of the work, and the viewpoints of both the author and receiver of information. Freedom to express oneself through a chosen mode of communication, including the Internet, becomes virtually meaningless if access to that information is not protected. Intellectual freedom implies a circle, and that circle is broken if either freedom of expression or access to ideas is stifled.

Besides books, high-stakes examinations have been censored. In 2002, it was revealed that officials in the New York State Department of Education had altered literary quotes in the English Regents examination. Passing this examination is required for high school graduation in New York State. Consequently, all New York seniors were required to read the same altered passages. The modification of literary passages in the exam was uncovered by Jeanne Heifetz, the mother of a Brooklyn, New York, high school student. She found that state officials "sanitized" passages from the works of noted authors such as Isaac Bashevis Singer, Anton Chekhov, and William Maxwell. The so-called sanitization of literary passages removed practically any reference to race, religion, ethnicity, sex, nudity, and alcohol. For instance, Bashevis Singer's works focus on the Jewish experience. Quotes from his texts on the exam eliminated all mentions of Judaism. "Most Jewish women" was changed to "most women." The entire line "Jews are Jews and Gentiles are Gentiles" was removed from an excerpt. Similarly, removed from a passage taken from Annie Dillard's memoir *An American Childhood* were all racial references from a description of her childhood trip to a library in a black neighborhood that had few white visitors. The purpose of Dillard's description was to highlight racial issues. The following changes were made in other passages used on New York State's English Regents exam:

- In a speech by U.N. Secretary Kolfi Annan, "fine California wine and seafood" changed to "fine seafood."
- In Anton Chekov's "The Upheaval," portion deleted about wealthy woman strip-searching household staff to find a missing brooch.
- In Carol Saline's "Mothers and Daughters," "went out to bar" changed to "went out."
- In Ernesto Galarza's "Barrio Boy," "skinny" changed to "thin" and "fat" to "heavy" in describing boys.
- In Frank Conroy's "Stop-Time," deleted sentence where boys declare intent to kill a snake (potential violence).

The changes were defended by Roseanne De Fabio, the New York Education Department's assistant commissioner for curriculum, instruction, and assessment. She admitted, "We do shorten the passages and alter the passages to make them suitable for testing situations." The passages were changed using the department's "sensitivity review guidelines." The purpose, she said, was to ensure that no students were "uncomfortable in a testing situation. Even the most wonderful writers don't write literature for children to take on a test."

In response to the revelations about the New York Regents exam, Cathy Popkin, Lionel Trilling Professor in the Humanities at Columbia University, wrote, "I implore you to put a stop to the scandalous practice of censoring literary texts, ostensibly in the interest of our students. It is dishonest. It is dangerous. It is an embarrassment. It is the practice of fools." Author Frank Conroy wondered, "Who are these people who think they have a right to 'tidy up' my prose? The New York State Political Police? The Correct Theme Authority?"

The following are other examples of complaints against books used in schools:

- J. K. Rowling's *Harry Potter* series of children's literature was criticized for promoting witchcraft and the occult. Some people complained the books are the work of the Devil himself.
- Madeleine L'Engle's *A Wrinkle in Time* was criticized for allegedly teaching demon worship and mysticism.
- Ernest Hemingway's short story "The Killers" was found objectionable because it contains the word "nigger."
- Mark Twain's *The Adventures of Huckleberry Finn* was criticized for racial stereotypes and offensive language.

Censorship of school books can't simply be dismissed as the work of extremists or concerned bureaucrats. There are reasonable objections that can be raised about the content of instruction in public schools. After all, parents must send their children to a public school if they can't afford a private school. What should parents do if they are offended by the books their children are required to read?

Parental objections also include methods of instruction. Some parents want their children to be taught by methods that emphasize independent thinking, critical thinking, and self-motivated learning. Other parents want an emphasis on rote learning and authoritarian instructional methods. Usually, fundamentalist Christian parents stress obedience to the authority of God and the Bible.

Religious objections to textbooks and instructional methods open the constitutional question of separation of religion and government. Some religious groups argue that public schools do not teach students to rely on the authority of God. Consequently, these religious groups maintain public schools are violating religious beliefs protected by the Constitution. In addition, some groups claim teaching evolutionary theory in science classes is a violation of religious rights. Court cases and legal decisions touching on these issues will be discussed in detail in Chapter 10.

Efforts at censorship of books and methods of instruction raise important issues regarding the role of public schools in a democratic society. Democracy depends on the free exchange of ideas and the diversity of ideas. On the other hand, education is compulsory. In the following sections I discuss the politics of textbooks, national standards, and methods of instruction. These topics raise the following set of questions:

- Should children in public schools be forced to read books approved by the school board that are objectionable to the children's parents?
- Should children in public schools be taught by methods of instruction approved by the school board but found objectionable by students' parents?
- Who should decide what knowledge is most worth teaching in public schools?
- Who should decide the content of textbooks and tests?

- What type of curriculum should be used in public schools?
- What methods of instruction should be used in public schools?
- Would you approve of your children reading any book?
- What curriculum and methods of instruction would you want for your children?

There is no correct answer to any of these questions, but they do highlight the dilemmas facing a government-operated school system in a society based on freedom of thought. In thinking about these questions remember that attendance at public schools is compulsory unless parents can afford a private school. In addition, the majority of voters elect school boards. This raises the issue of whether minority opinions should be overruled by the majority.

TEXTBOOKS

Textbook content is highly politicized because of state adoption policies in California and Texas, state laws, and pressures from various interest groups. Of course, textbooks do not have that appearance. Usually, textbooks seem bland and boring compendiums of facts containing no political messages. In part, this appearance is caused by the wish of textbook publishers to avoid controversy. But embedded in the blandness are facts and ideas that are the product of a whole host of political debates and decisions.

Texas and California's textbook hearings are extremely important for publishers. They are 2 of 22 states in which government committees select textbooks for public schools. Texas represents 8 percent of the $2.2 billion national market in textbooks, while California represents 12 percent. Consequently, these two states exert enormous influence over the content of textbooks used throughout the United States. As Carol Jones, the field director of the Texas chapter of Citizens for a Sound Economy, commented, "The bottom line is that Texas and California are the biggest buyers of textbooks in the country, and what we adopt in Texas is what the rest of the country gets." Her organization examines textbooks to ensure accuracy and any information that lends a liberal political slant.

In 2003, the Texas State School Board was sued for rejecting the textbook, *Environmental Science: Creating a Sustainable Future* (6th edition) by David D. Chiras. The Board had rejected the book for "promoting radical policies" and being "anti–free enterprise, and anti-American." In its place, the Board chose a science textbook partially financed by a group of mining companies according to the suit filed by Trial Lawyers for Public Justice, a Washington-based public-interest law firm. The suit claimed that the Board's actions violated the free-speech rights of Texas schoolchildren.

The suit reflected the continuing censorship issues surrounding the actions of the Texas State School Board, which plays a major role in determining the content of American textbooks. For instance, during the hot summer of 2002, the Texas State School Board began public hearings to select textbooks in history and social studies for its 4 million students. These were subject areas that were bound to attract comments from all sides of the political spectrum. Texas's textbook hearings were notorious for their strident demands by opposing interest groups to add and delete material from textbooks. At the opening of the hearings, there already seemed to be agreement among board members not to select for advanced-placement classes Pearson Prentice Hall's history text *Out of Many: A History of the American People* despite its being among the best sellers. The problem was two paragraphs dealing with prostitution in late-nineteenth-century cattle towns. "It makes it sound that every woman west of the Mississippi was a prostitute," said Grace Shore, the Republican chairwoman of the Texas State Board of Education. "The book says that there were 50,000 prostitutes west of the Mississippi. I doubt it, but even if there were, is that something that should be emphasized? Is that an important historical fact?"

During the hearings, *Out of Many: A History of the American People* was criticized not only for its section "Cowgirls and Prostitutes" but also for its mention of Margaret Sanger and the development of contraception, and the gay rights movement. Complaining about the book's content, Peggy Venable, director of the Texas chapter of Citizens for a Sound Economy, said, "I don't mean that we should sweep things under the rug. But the children should see the hope and the good things about America."

Texas textbook selection is governed by state laws that require the promotion of democracy, patriotism, and free enterprise. These innocent-sounding terms are open to dispute. Is a discussion of the possible value of federal government farm subsidies a violation of the requirement to promote "free enterprise"? Is any criticism of the actions of the federal government a violation of the requirement to promote "patriotism"?

Also at stake in 2002 was approval of science textbooks. Contrary to expectations that science texts would not be as controversial as history books, the issue of global warming caused a major uproar. Science textbooks were condemned for saying that there was a scientific consensus that the earth's climate was changing because of global warming. This claim was labeled as "anti-technology," "anti-Christian," and "anti-American." The Board rejected Jane L. Person's *Environmental Science: How the World Works and Your Place in It* because of statements such as "Destruction of the tropical rain forest could affect weather over the entire planet" and "Most experts on global warming feel that immediate action should be taken to curb global warming." To gain acceptance by the Texas Board, the statements were changed to: "Tropical rain forest ecosystems impact weather over the entire planet" and "In the past, the earth has been much warmer than it is now, and fossils of sea creatures show us that the sea level was much higher than it is today. So does it really matter if the world gets warmer?"

One text that did win approval was financed by a consortium of mining companies. Titled *Global Science: Energy, Resources, Environment,* the book was praised before the Texas Board by Duggan Flanakin, formerly of the U.S. Bureau of Mines and currently a member of the Texas Policy Foundation. The book was also commended by Ms. Shore, chair of the Texas Board and co-owner of

TEC Well Service. TEC is a producer of gas and oil and repairs and deepens oil wells. From Ms. Shore's perspective, the oil and gas industries "always get a raw deal" in environmental science textbooks.

In 2004, the Texas Education Agency approved a 122-page publishing guide for elementary, middle, and high school textbooks in language, fine arts, physical education, and health education. (The guidelines were developed in 2002 and amended in 2003 and 2004.) The guidelines inform publishers of what can and what cannot be used in textbooks in Texas. The official title is *Proclamation 2002 of the State Board of Education Advertising for Bids on Instructional Materials: Contains Amendments Dated July 11, 2003; September 12, 2003; and February 27, 2004.* In the controversial area of birth control and abstinence education, the guide informs publishers that the state high school health curriculum requires texts that will

- Analyze the importance of abstinence from sexual activity as the preferred choice of behavior in relationship to all sexual activity for unmarried persons of school age.
- Discuss abstinence from sexual activity as the only method that is 100 percent effective in preventing pregnancy, sexually transmitted diseases, and the sexual transmission of HIV or acquired immune deficiency syndrome, and the emotional trauma associated with adolescent sexual activity.

California has been the scene of struggles over another seemingly innocuous subject area, namely, mathematics. In 2000, Brian Hoey, publisher of the College Preparatory Mathematics Program, announced that his company would be withdrawing its textbooks from consideration by the California school system. Hoey complained, "Why would I want to submit my books when [decision makers] are on record as opposing them? The deck is stacked against any math program that isn't in a traditional format." This shocked the textbook publishing world because in 1999 a federal panel had stated that the companies' books were "exemplary." At issue was a new California law that requires that math instruction emphasize basic skills and repeated drills as opposed to concepts and problem solving using real-life situations.

In contrast to California, some schools around the country are adopting math textbooks from Singapore because they *don't* emphasize basic skills and drill. Singapore's books are without the eye-catching graphics used in U.S. texts. These plain books, according to Yoram Sagher, a mathematics professor at the University of Illinois at Chicago, insist "on full understanding, and an avoidance of mindless rituals that lead to a solution." Felicity Messner Ross, a middle-school math teacher in Baltimore, said, "I think these books really empower students as problem-solvers."

The reality is that very few administrators are willing to select for their schools textbooks that could cause controversy in the community. Often a local school superintendent walks a thin political line. Certainly, the desire to protect their jobs would cause administrators to avoid controversial situations. Recognizing this situation, publishers know that they will have a difficult time selling controversial books to local schools. In the words of the president of People for the American Way, Arthur Kropp, "To avoid controversy, publishers may downplay or eliminate ideas criticized by the censorship groups. They've caved into Far Right pressure in the past."

The question of who should control knowledge in a democratic society can be asked specifically about curriculum, instruction, and textbooks. The battles that happen, particularly over the curriculum and the content of textbooks, are often unnoticed by the public. In fact, I encounter very few public school students who are aware that political decisions determine the contents of their textbooks.

CURRICULAR STANDARDS AND THE POLITICAL NATURE OF KNOWLEDGE

Like many other areas of education, the No Child Left Behind Act of 2001 directly impacts national discussions of academic standards. My concern is the role of academic standards in the control of knowledge. As discussed in Chapter 7, academic or curricular standards prescribe what a student should know about a particular subject for each grade level. Advocates of academic standards argue that standards are necessary to ensure that teachers instruct students in what the state educational agency considers the important parts of each subject. In addition, high-stakes state tests linked to state standards ensure that students have learned the subject matter prescribed by the state. It is also argued that academic standards can be used to force teachers to teach more material. In turn, this will require the student to learn more.

The No Child Left Behind Act requires that states create academic standards. The opening section of the legislation declares as its first purpose: "(1) ensuring that high-quality academic assessments, accountability systems, teacher preparation and training, curriculum, and instructional materials are aligned with challenging State academic standards so that students, teachers, parents, and administrators can measure progress against common expectations for student academic achievement."

The problem in creating national standards is determining what knowledge is of most worth to teach. And basic to answering this question is the other question of who should determine what knowledge is of most worth. In addition, knowledge is not politically neutral or agreed upon by all scholars. In any discipline there is wide disagreement over what is truth. Walk down the halls of any university and you will encounter many different theories competing for dominance in a particular discipline. For instance, in psychology there are a variety of competing theories of human behavior and research methods. In areas such as history and political science, what is considered truth is often relative to the political beliefs of a particular professor. Since it is impossible to teach all things to all elementary and secondary students, some selection of content must be made. Among all the competing theories in a discipline, some decision must be made about what knowledge is of most worth to teach.

Consider the ongoing issue of the place of evolutionary theory in the academic standards for science. The No Child Left Behind Act mandates that states measure students' scientific knowledge by 2008. In a report accompanying the legislation, it is suggested that the intent of the law was for state science curricula to "help students to understand the full range of scientific views that exist." The report specifically mentions evolutionary theory as a controversial scientific theory. Those wanting evolutionary theory to be presented to science students as controversial also want students to learn about biblical statements on the origin of life and theories associated with intelligent design.

In 2006, political candidates considered moderate regarding the issue of evolution in the state curriculum claimed a victory in the state primary election of the Kansas State Board of Education. The previous year, the Board selected Bob L. Corkins as the state's new commissioner of education. Corkins is considered conservative on the inclusion of evolution in the state curriculum. The struggle over the inclusion of evolution in the Kansas science curriculum began in 1999 when a majority of state board of education members removed the teaching of evolutionary theory and discussion of the origin of the universe from the state's science standards. This gave school districts the option to exclude or include evolutionary theory in the local curriculum. The catch was that state standards determined the content of state high-stakes tests, so questions about evolutionary theory would not appear on state science examinations. This meant that science teachers would not be motivated by the threat of testing to teach evolutionary theory. A political furor resulted from the Kansas State Board's decision. Five seats on the 10-member school board came up for election in November 2000. The major focus of election rhetoric was on the evolutionary theory issue.

The decision of the Kansas State Board of Education received the widespread support by many members of the religious right. On the other hand, scientists complained that evolutionary theory was an important part of biological science. According to the National Academy of Science, evolutionary theory has become the "central unifying concept of biology."

In 2001, a newly elected Kansas Board of Education voted 7 to 3 to restore evolutionary theory to the state's science standards. In the same year, the Alabama State Board of Education unanimously decided to include in its state's science standards a disclaimer clause declaring evolutionary theory as "controversial." The disclaimer states:

> It [the theory of evolution] is controversial because it states that natural selection provides the basis for the modern scientific explanation for the diversity of living things. Since natural selection has been observed to play a role in influencing small changes in the population, it is assumed, based on the study of artifacts, that it produces large changes, even though this has not been directly observed.

In 2006, Ohio's state board of education voted to remove requirements from its state science curricular standards that encouraged students to "critically analyze" evolution. Board member Martha W. Wise, leader of the campaign to remove the language from the curricular standards, proclaimed, "This was a win for science, a win for students, and a win for the state of Ohio." The issue arose in 2002 when Ohio became a battleground for the struggle over evolutionary theory in state science standards.

In Cobb County, Georgia's second-largest school district, the school board in 2002 adopted a policy requiring teachers to provide students with a "balanced education" by giving equal weight to Biblical and evolutionary theories on the origin of life. Insurance salesman and minister, Russell Brock, told the school board, "To deny there is a God is to stand on a building and deny there is a building."

The debate over science standards and evolutionary theory raises a number of questions:

- Should curricular standards be determined by state governments?
- Should politicians determine the content of the curriculum or should that be done by academic experts? (For example, should a scientist, as opposed to an elected member of the state board of education, determine the appropriate content of biology instruction?)

Science seems like a relatively neutral area compared to creating state curricular standards for history. Consider the following questions:

1. What should be the boundary of school history? Should history taught in schools include political history, economic history, social history, and intellectual history?
2. Should U.S. history be taught from the perspective of European Americans?

Defining the boundaries of history often reflects political values. Conservatives believe that school history should focus on political history to help the student understand the operation of the U.S. government and to build patriotism. On the other hand, liberals believe that social history is important so that students understand the sources of social inequality and learn how to be political activists. Again, I want to remind the reader that neither the conservative nor liberal position represents truth. What is important to understand is that the determination of the boundaries of school history does involve political values.

This is also true with respect to the perspective to be used in the teaching of history. Teaching history from the viewpoint of Native Americans and African Americans does not cast U.S. institutions in a very positive light. For instance, it would be very difficult to use history for building patriotism if students were required to read Dee Brown's *Bury My Heart at Wounded Knee: An Indian History of the American West.* Told from the perspective of Native Americans, this history presents the U.S. government as a treacherous institution not to be trusted and the U.S. military as a band of savages involved in massacres and mutilations.

Again, the issue is not which view of history is correct, but the fact that there are different perspectives. With national standards, decisions about the boundaries and interpretations of history would be decided by political forces. These issues came to the forefront in discussions about standards for world history. How should the role of Western nations be portrayed in world history? John J. Patrick, the director of the Social Studies Development Center at Indiana University, argues, "We're not interested in a history that is Eurocentric. We're interested in global history." In contrast, Mary Bicouvaris, 1989 National Teacher of the Year, implored the National Council for History Standards not to discard all emphasis on Western nations. "Why are we turning away from the rise of the West?" she asked. "Is there a contempt for the rise of the West?"

While the goal in establishing academic standards is improving student achievement, the process opens the door to ideological control of the curriculum by politicians and special interest groups. Knowledge is not politically neutral.

CENSORSHIP OF THE INTERNET AND E-LEARNING

The wiring of American schools raises questions about student access to the world's knowledge. Here is a wonderful means of learning that is as significant as the earlier development of printed books. However, should students be allowed access to *all* the world's knowledge? Should public schools allow students to access pornography, bomb-building plans, prescriptions for terrorism, or the proclamations of racial hate groups?

These questions plague educators and noneducators as Internet use increases. Eighty-seven percent of Americans from the ages of 12 to 17 use the Internet according to a 2005 study by the Pew Internet & American Life Project. Some school districts are requiring students to use the Internet. In fact, a 2006 bill submitted to the Michigan state legislature would require online courses as a requirement for high school graduation. The bill envisions students taking online courses under teacher supervision, test-prep tutorials practiced at home, or a course conducted with online tools. On another side of the issue, 2006 legislation passed by the Virginia state legislature requires all public K–12 schools to teach Internet safety as part of regular instruction. The bill's author, State Delegate William H. Fralin, says the legislation is necessary because many parents don't have the skills to teach their own children about Internet safety. He admits, "I don't know enough about the Internet to prevent my kids from getting into trouble."

Naturally, the idea of e-learning is tied to the educational requirements of the global economy. Referring to the bill making Internet courses part of high school graduation requirements, Michigan's chief academic officer Jeremy M. Hughes said, "We thought of this as a skill that people would need to have to continue to be lifelong learners." Writing in *Education Week,* Peter J. Stokes, author of the government-sponsored essay, "How E-Learning Will Transform Education," hopes that e-learning "can help us more effectively develop the 'knowledge workers' required to sustain the growth of the new economy—workers, after all, who must possess a fluent understanding of both the ideas and communications systems of the modern workplace."

E-learning has also contributed to the growth of for-profit education. The University of Phoenix, the largest private university in the world, relies on e-learning through distance learning. So does the for-profit Walden University. For many adult workers, it is easier and more convenient to sit at home and join class discussions through chat rooms, answer questions by e-mail, download assignments including reading materials, and take Internet examinations than to go to a classroom at a prescribed time. Flexibility, resources, and interaction are the key ingredients to good distance learning.

There is a fear among some that the Internet provides too easy of an access for students to "objectionable" Web sites. The federal Children's Internet Protection Act of 2000 was designed to force schools to use Internet filters. The legislation makes it a crime for commercial Web sites to make pornography available to students. In addition, it requires libraries and schools receiving federal technology funding to equip their computers with Internet filters. Specifically, the law requires the use of technological measures that block or filter Internet access to "visual depictions" that are "harmful to minors." It also requires schools to have a plan for monitoring students' online activities. The law does contain a provision that allows the disabling of filters for adults conducting "bona fide research or other lawful purposes."

In 2003, the U.S. Supreme Court ruled that the law was constitutional. The suit against the law was brought by the American Library Association, which claimed that the law was a violation of the First Amendment because it required public libraries to turn over decisions about content to companies that develop Web filters. Chief Justice William H. Rehnquist said in his decision, "Because public libraries have traditionally excluded pornographic material from their other collections, Congress could reasonably impose a parallel limitation on its Internet assistance programs." A dissenting opinion was put forward by Justices David H. Souter and Ruth Bader Ginsburg, which stated, "government's funding conditions engage in overkill to a degree illustrated by their refusal to trust even a library's staff with an unblocked [computer] terminal."

The problem is that filters often block access to nonpornographic sites. A supporter of the law, Heather Cirio, a spokeswoman for the conservative Family Research Council, contends, "We should make sure the computers purchased with tax dollars contain filters that would protect children from obscene and pornographic materials." But Peacefire, an opponent of filtering, tested five filters on a randomly selected list of 1,000 Web sites and reported that 20 to 80 percent of the blocked sites were blocked in error. In other words, filters often block sites that were not intended to be blocked and thereby reduce the promise of the Internet to provide access to the world's knowledge. "Candidly," said Mark Uncapher of the Information Technology Association of America, "there's no silver bullet for filtering."

There are also problems involving student use of Web sites. Jean O'Brien, a student at Westlake High School near Cleveland, Ohio, created a home-based Web site containing a photo of his high school band instructor. The student's Web site described that band teacher as "an overweight middle-age man who doesn't like to get haircuts . . . [and who] likes to involve himself in everything you do." As a result, O'Brien was suspended from school for 10 days. A student in McKinney, Texas, was suspended for setting up on the school computer a Web site called C.H.O.W. or Chihuahua Haters of the World. A student in Statesboro, Georgia, was arrested for posting on his personal Web site terrorist threats against his school principal. According to Ann Besson of the American Civil Liberties Union, the Internet is creating a whole new generation of educational censorship issues. "These Web cases," she said, "have become somewhat analogous to the student newspaper cases of the past, where the school tries to say, 'You can't talk about condoms in the school newspaper.' Except that with Web sites, people tend to become more alarmed because people outside the school find out about them."

Some school districts allow students an appeal process when their access to an Internet site is blocked. For instance, Clark County, Nevada, students can ask a teacher for access to a blocked site. The teacher then notifies the school's network authority. If the school administration and the network authority composed of nine members consider the Web site appropriate, then it is unblocked. "We realized that no filtering software is perfect," commented Karlene Lee, the district's director of technology services.

Other school districts are adopting tough policies regarding Web usage. Utah's Salt Lake City school district will suspend students for "improper" use of the Internet. Students are not allowed access to any Web site that mentions birth control, condoms, or abortion.

The e-learning revolution has created the promise of new methods of learning and greater access to knowledge along with a whole host of problems associated with teacher training, costs, and censorship. E-learning also creates another arena for the development of for-profit education corporations. But researchers using data from the California and U.S. Departments of Education reported in 2002 that the use of the Internet has no measurable impact on student achievement. University of Chicago researcher Austan Goolsbee concluded, "We haven't found any evidence that it [Internet access] is [providing academic benefits]." Despite these difficulties, e-learning will probably become an essential part of public schooling.

CYBER BULLYING

In 2006, nonprofit organization Fight Crime: Invest in Kids claimed "that a third of teenagers and one in six children from 6 to 11 have had mean, embarrassing or threatening things said about them online." The organization is composed of 3,000 police chiefs, sheriffs, prosecutors, other law enforcement leaders, and violence survivors. Cyber bullying has become widespread among students with the rapid growth in the use of text messaging, instant messaging and the Internet. The organization highlighted the story of Vermont teenager Kylie Kenney, who was harassed by a Web site calling for her death and threatening and embarrassing phone calls from other students. Kenney stated, "No child should have to endure the cyber bullying I endured. I was scared, hurt and confused. I didn't know why it was happening to me. I had nowhere to turn except to my mom. I am speaking out now because I want other kids who are bullied online or on their cell phones to know that they should tell their parents or other adults." The organization's report included these other findings:

- 10 percent of the teens and 4 percent of the younger children were threatened online with physical harm.
- 16 percent of the teens and preteens who were victims told no one about it. About half of children ages 6 to 11 told their parents. Only 30 percent of older kids told their parents.
- Preteens were as likely to receive harmful messages at school (45 percent) as at home (44 percent). Older children received 30 percent of harmful messages at school and 70 percent at home.
- 17 percent of preteens and 7 percent of teens said they were worried about bullying as they start a new school year.

Fight Crime: Invest in Kids recommends relying upon parents to stop cyber bullying. The organization issued the following guidelines, which I have shortened and changed to fit in this book. A complete list of recommendations can be found at http://www.fightcrime.org/cyberbullying/10stepslong.pdf.

Ten Steps for Families to Stop Cyber Bullying

1. Kids should tell an adult, parent, teacher, or the police if they have been cyber bullied or know other kids who have received any messages or postings that are mean, embarrassing or threatening to themselves or other students.
2. Parents should insist that every school utilize antibullying programs, particularly Olweus.
3. Parents should insist that all schools work with local law enforcement to curb cyber bullying.
4. Parents should discuss cyber bullying and bullying with their kids.
5. E-mails, chats, text messages including instant messages and Web pages sent or posted by bullies should be saved as evidence.
6. Parents should instruct their kids: One, don't respond to bullying messages.
7. Kids should not give out ANY private information such as full names, addresses, phone numbers, personal identification numbers, passwords, school names, or names of family members or friends. Kids should not say anything in a chat room or post anything to a Web site that they would not want to be made public. Kids should use a screen name different from their e-mail address.
8. If children are cyber bullied, families should file complaints with the Internet service provider, cell phone company, or Web site. Cyber bullying is typically a violation of the "terms of use" and violators are subject to adverse action.

A preventive program recommended by Fight Crime: Invest in Kids is The Olweus Bullying Prevention Program operated out of Clemson University.

The program claims to have achieved a 30 to 70 percent reduction in students' reports of bullying. This program coordinates efforts between students and teachers to reduce bullying including cyber bullying. Check out the Olweus Web site: http://www.clemson.edu/olweus/content.html.

Cyber bullying raises a new level of concern about controlling the content of the Internet and cell phone usage among students. It links the parents, school staff, and police in an effort to stop the harassment of children and youth.

CONFLICTING CURRICULUM GOALS

As exemplified by the political issues surrounding state standards, the American public school curriculum is a battleground. Business groups, radical reformers, religious organizations, welfare associations, left-wing and right-wing politicians, and many other groups want the public schools to teach subjects that will serve their interests. Since the nineteenth century, the curriculum varied with changes in the political, economic, and social climates, and continues to do so now.

In *The Struggle for the American Curriculum, 1893–1958,* Herbert M. Kliebard identifies four types of curricula that have vied for dominance in American public schools. Each of these curricula still receives support from issues generated by particular social, economic, and political factors:

1. Social efficiency
2. Humanism
3. Social meliorism
4. Developmentalism

The **social-efficiency** curriculum has the greatest influence in American schools. Backed by those who want the schools primarily to serve the needs of the economy, it is designed to prepare students for the workforce. Often, social-efficiency curricula emphasize vocational subjects and are associated with the educational goals of human capital.

In sharp contrast to the advocate of social efficiency, the **humanist** wants the curriculum to introduce students to the cultural traditions of society. A humanist spurns the idea of a vocational curriculum and favors the development of general intellectual skills. Often the humanist wants the curriculum to be organized around standard academic subjects like literature, history, foreign languages, the arts, and science.

The **social meliorist** wants the curriculum to cause social improvement and change. Social meliorism reflects the reform element in American education. At the most extreme, the social meliorist will ask for courses to solve each new social problem. Sometimes this means educating students to bring about general political and economic changes. But more often it means the advocacy of courses to solve problems such as alcoholism, drug abuse, AIDS, and traffic accidents.

In many ways, **developmentalism** is the most radical of the four curricular types. The developmentalist wants the curriculum organized around the psychological development of the child. This means a curriculum focused on the needs of the individual child as opposed to the focus of social-efficiency educators, humanists, and social meliorists, respectively, on economic needs, the passing on of culture, and social reform. Of the four curricular types, developmentalism has had the least influence on the public school curriculum. The child-centered curriculum of the developmentalist is often rejected by supporters of the other types of curricula for being anti-intellectual and failing to give the student the necessary skills to function in society and the world of work.

In the twenty-first century, No Child Left Behind represents a combination of social-efficiency, humanist, and social meliorist curricular goals. Based on a human-capitalist model, the social-efficiency model strives to educate workers for new jobs in a rapidly changing technological society. Workers must now be prepared to continually update their skills with each technological advancement. Humanism receives support because of its contribution by teaching students how to learn and general intellectual skills. Humanists advocate that all students be required to take a core curriculum emphasizing traditional academic subjects. Social meliorists hope to save low-income children from low-performing and unsafe schools.

The current blend of social-efficiency, humanistic, and social meliorism curricula marks a sharp contrast to the traditional divisions. In the early part of the twentieth century, humanists resisted the growing vocationalization of U.S. schools by trying to preserve the teaching of Greek and Latin in the schools. They argued, in the tradition of the liberal arts, that the purpose of education should be the training of the mind and, because of that training, the development of character. For humanists, the study of classical languages, literature, and history would give students the mental tools and character to be moral and successful.

Social-efficiency educators in the early twentieth century, however, argued that the school should provide individualized training based on a person's future destination in the labor force. The worth of all public school courses, they argued, should be judged by their contribution to a person's social worth in the world of work. Therefore, social-efficiency educators called for abandoning the long-standing tradition of teaching Latin and Greek for more vocational courses.

By the 1920s, the battle lines were clearly drawn between the humanists and social-efficiency advocates. Neither side could claim victory, but the social-efficiency philosophy did replace many traditional humanist components of the curriculum. In the 1930s, a new group of humanists working under the label of **essentialist** reacted against the too-specialized curriculum of the social-efficiency advocates and declared the need for a common core curriculum. While essentialists did not base their proposals for a core curriculum on a traditional classical education, they emphasized the importance of teaching a common cultural tradition. Unlike earlier humanists who looked to the past, essentialists examined the cultural requirements of the present.

While the humanist argument for a core curriculum was being modified by the practical outlook of the essentialist of the 1930s, social meliorists were calling for major transformations in the public school curriculum. Since the early days of the common-school movement of the 1830s and 1840s, public schools had been viewed as a source of social change and improvement. The depression of the 1930s sparked widespread concern with social and economic conditions. Many Americans began to believe that the only hope lay in basic changes in the economic organization of the society.

Influenced by these arguments, a group of educators calling themselves **social reconstructionists** argued for the teaching of subjects that would prepare the individual to be an active participant in the economic transformation of society. Often this meant a stress on social studies courses designed to give students the skills to analyze political and economic conditions. In contrast to the social meliorist who accepted the basic structure of society and wanted to reform the individual, the social reconstructionist envisioned social improvement as a product of individual empowerment. For political radicals, social reconstructionism offered the hope that public schools could be used to make fundamental changes in society.

Social meliorists were prominent in calls for changes in the curriculum that would prepare minorities and poor people for more equal participation in the economy. For social meliorists of the 1960s, a major goal of education became the elimination of poverty and racism. These changes in the curriculum were designed to provide the children of the poor with equal access to education by improving their basic skills. Combined with desegregation, these curricular changes were to end poverty and racism.

In the late 1960s, the social unrest sparked by the Vietnam War dimmed the hopes of social meliorists. Campus protests and disruptions alarmed conservatives and created demands for the restoration of law and order. Republicans attacked the curricular changes of the social meliorists as unproven social experimentation. War protesters, however, linked antiwar activities with greater demands for cultural freedom. Included in these demands was greater educational freedom for students to pursue their own interests. In addition, the financial cost of the war and energy problems in the 1970s caused unemployment and economic stagnation.

Thus, in the late 1960s and early 1970s, a confused period of curricular change occurred with conservatives demanding more discipline in the schools, cultural and antiwar protesters demanding more freedom in the schools, and social-efficiency advocates demanding changes in the curriculum to solve the problems of unemployment and economic stagnation. The result in the 1970s was that conservatives and social-efficiency advocates joined forces to emphasize, as a solution to both discipline and economic problems, career-education courses, expanded vocational offerings, and closer linkages between the curriculum and the needs of the labor market. Mostly, those seeking greater educational freedom established private alternative schools outside the organization of the public schools. Although many reasons might be given for the short life of these schools, certainly financial problems made it difficult for them to compete with public schools.

In the twenty-first century, social efficiency dominates official discussions about the curriculum. The curriculum is organized, as I discussed in Chapter 1, to provide students with the skills needed to compete in the global labor market. The emphasis is on human capital education.

THE GLOBAL MODELS OF CURRICULUM AND INSTRUCTION

Currently, global discussions of education are dominated by four conflicting models: human capital, progressive, religious, and Indigenous. For instance, goals and methods of religious education are often in conflict with human capital and progressive models. The American educational system should be thought of as nested in a global system of education. For instance, many countries operated according to the human capital model; a model much discussed so far in this book regarding the American educational goals. The following is the world model of human capital education:

Human Capital World Model

1. National standardization of the curriculum.
2. Standardized testing for promotion, entrance, and exiting from different levels of schooling.
3. Performance evaluation of teaching based on standardized testing of students.
4. Mandated textbooks.
5. Scripted lessons.
6. Teaching of world languages, particularly English.
7. The goal of education is educating workers to compete in the global economy.
8. The value of education is measured by economic growth and development.

The reader will note the similarities between No Child Left Behind and the human capital world model regarding standardization of the curriculum, standardized testing, mandated textbooks, the importance of English, and the goals of educating workers and economic growth. In contrast, the progressive education world model emphasizes education for social change and justice.

Progressive Education World Model

1. Teacher professionalism and autonomy.
2. Learning based on students' interests and participation.
3. Active learning.
4. Protection of local languages.
5. Education for ensuring social justice.
6. Education for active participation in determining social and political change.

There are major differences between the human capital and progressive education models. In schools, the human capital model assumes control of teachers' behaviors through a prescribed national curriculum and reliance on standardized testing with the goal of educating workers for the global economy. The progressive model assumes that instruction will involve active learning based on students' interests and participation with a high degree of teacher autonomy in lesson planning with the goal of educating citizens who will actively address issues of social justice.

Both the human capital and progressive education models are part of the Western educational tradition, which became part of the global flow of educational ideas. A criticism of both models is that they support a secular society whose goals are either economic development or economic equity. Missing, for some, are spiritual and religious goals and values. Globally, there are large numbers of religious schools serving Christian, Buddhist, Islamic, Hindu, and other religious communities. Some provide religious instruction after school hours or on religious days, while others operate full-time schools. Religious schools offer instruction that emphasizes spirituality in contrast to the economic and secular emphasis of human capital and progressive education world models. Therefore, I will call these religious world educational models.

Religious Education World Models

1. Study of traditional religious texts.
2. Study and practice of religious rites.
3. Emphasis on spirituality.
4. Emphasis on instilling moral and ethical standards.
5. Rejection of secularism.

In its 13 September 2007 news release announcing ratification of the Declaration on Rights of Indigenous Peoples, the United Nations estimated that there are 370 million Indigenous peoples existing around the globe in areas of the South Pacific, Asia, Europe, and, of course, including the numerous Indigenous nations of Africa and North and South America. Who are the Indigenous peoples of the world?

One definition emphasizes long-term occupancy of a particular geographical area. For instance, the Indigenous nations of Canada emphasize "long-term occupancy" by choosing the self-identifier "First Nations." However, some groups that today identify themselves as Indigenous were previously imperialistic powers with empires that dominated other peoples and lands, such as the Aztecs, Mayans, and Incas of the Americas. Are these nations or the peoples that dominated the long-term occupiers? One resolution of who is Indigenous can be through self-identification. The World Bank includes in its definition of Indigenous "self-identification" and "subsistence-oriented production." The World Bank's definition follows:

> The term Indigenous Peoples (also often referred to as "Indigenous ethnic minorities," "tribal groups" and "scheduled tribes") describes social groups with a social and cultural identity distinct from the dominant society which makes them vulnerable to being disadvantaged in the development process. Key characteristics identifying Indigenous Peoples:
>
> 1. Close attachment to ancestral territories and their natural resources.
> 2. Self-identification and identification by others as members of a distinct cultural group.

3. An Indigenous language, often different from the national language.
4. Presence of customary social and political institutions.
5. Primarily subsistence-oriented production.

However, "subsistence-oriented production" does not realistically describe the work of some self-identified Indigenous peoples who hold jobs in modern factories, corporate agriculture, or in other professional and business occupations.

Over the last century, Indigenous peoples struggled to restore traditional education methods after attempts by some colonialists to use Western forms of schooling to eradicate their cultures. In some cases, Indigenous peoples were denied schooling as a method for excluding them from entrance into dominant economic and political organizations. Consequently, many Indigenous nations are trying to restore their control over education and ensure recognition of traditional educational methods.

Indigenous Education World Models

1. Indigenous nations control their own educational institutions.
2. Traditional Indigenous education serves as a guide for the curriculum and instructional methods.
3. Education is provided in the language of the Indigenous nation.
4. Education reflects the culture of the Indigenous nation.

The above represent the four competing world models of schooling. These models do overlap with some religious education using progressive methods and teaching for social justice. The human capital world model and the Indigenous education world model can also utilize progressive methods to accomplish their goals. However, and this is important to stress, the goals of these models are different. There is a major difference between educating students to function in the global marketplace and educating students to become active in fighting for social justice and changing the global marketplace. Religious spirituality, in some cases, can be considered an antidote to the materialist objectives of the human capital models. Indigenous models can reject both the concerns of human capital and progressive models for adapting traditional ways of life to modernity. What is your choice of models to guide global school systems?

CONCLUSION

There continues to be a struggle over the content of textbooks, state standards, the goals of the curriculum, and access to the Internet. These struggles are an inevitable part of a system of education designed to reach all members of the public. Self-interest along with religious and political convictions are the driving forces in these disputes. Different types of businesses ranging from the dairy industry to advertising want to be treated in a positive light by textbooks and in the school curriculum. Religious groups are concerned that their fundamental beliefs not be disparaged in textbooks and the school curriculum. Those supporting or attacking differing political causes, such as environmental regulations and national health plans, are concerned about how these issues are treated. There are also competing world models of education that have different objectives.

The democratic processes of a civil society are reflected in the continual challenges to textbooks, curriculum, and Internet usage. (By "civil society" I mean nongovernment organizations.) In the case of education, civil society is constantly attempting to influence in different ways the knowledge taught by schools. On the other hand, it could be argued that action by a civil society means the influence of those organizations that are most active or have the most money. The most active, such as religious groups, organize and devote time to campaign to change what is taught in schools. Without this type of organization, the average citizen has little voice in a civil society. Money can also buy influence of the type that is not available to most people.

The questions raised by the influence of a civil society lead directly to the larger questions: Who should control knowledge in a democratic society? Should control be given to the most active and those with money? Should voters decide directly on what is taught in public schools? Should the decisions be made by politicians acting as representatives of the voters?

Suggested Readings and Works Cited in Chapter

American Library Association. *Intellectual Freedom Manual.* Chicago: American Library Association, 2005. This publication contains the library association's definition of intellectual freedom.

——. "*It's Perfectly Normal* Tops ALA's 2005 List of Most Challenged Books." Available on the association's Web site, http://www.ala.org, this article lists the top 10 challenged books in 2005.

The Associated Press. "Group: Re-Evaluate School Computers." *The New York Times on the Web* (12 September 2000). http://www.nytimes.com. This article discusses the demand by the Alliance for Children for research to assess the educational value of classroom computer use. The organization believes too much money has been spent on school computers without a knowledge of their benefits.

BEALE, HOWARD. *Are American Teachers Free?* New York: Scribner's, 1936. This is a study of the political pressures placed on teachers and textbook publishers in the 1920s and 1930s.

BLAIR, JULIE. "Kansas Primary Seen as Signaling Shift in Evolution Stance." *Education Week on the Web* (6 September 2000). http://www.edweek.org. This article discusses the continuing political struggle in Kansas over the issue of evolutionary theory in the state science standards.

BLAIR, JULIE, and DAVID HOFF. "Evolution Restored to Kansas Standards, but Called 'Controversial' in Alabama." *Education Week on the Web* (21 February 2001). http://www.edweek.org. This article covers the continuing controversy over the place of evolution in state standards.

BORJA, RHEA R. "Internet Filtering Is Balancing Act for Many Schools." *Education Week on the Web* (16 January 2002). http://www.edweek.org. Borja discusses the techniques used by various school districts to filter the Internet.

BROWN, DEE. *Bury My Heart at Wounded Knee: An Indian History of the American West.* New York: Henry Holt and Company, 1970. This is an excellent example of a U.S. history book written from the perspective of a non-European American.

CAVANAGH, SEAN. "Ohio State Board Removes Language in Standards Questioning Evolution." *Education Week on the Web* (15 February 2006). http://www. edweek.org. Cavanagh discusses the decision by the Ohio State Board of Education to remove from state science standards the requirement that a critical approach to the teaching of evolution be used.

DELEFATTORE, JOAN. *What Johnny Shouldn't Read: Textbook Censorship in America.* New Haven, CT: Yale University Press, 1992. Delefattore studies textbook censorship in the United States.

DIEGMULLER, KAREN. "Standards for World History a Tough Task." *Education Week* (1 June 1994): 1, 10. This article reports the problems in establishing standards for the teaching of world history.

——. "Model Exam in Calif. Is Target of New Attacks." *Education Week* (4 May 1994): 1, 12. Diegmuller discusses the political controversy over the California Learning Assessment System.

——. "Removal of Literary Works from Calif. Test Stirs Flap." *Education Week* (9 March 1994): 11. This article describes the controversy over the removal of stories by Alice Walker and Annie Dillard from the California Learning Assessment System.

DILLON, SAM. "Publisher Pulls a Textbook in Furor on Sexual Content." *The New York Times* (17 March 1994): B10. This article reports on the 1994 furor over health textbooks in Texas.

DWORKIN, MARTIN, ed. *Dewey on Education.* New York: Teachers College University Press, 1959. This collection of Dewey's writings includes Dewey's 1952 statement on the effect of progressive education on the public schools as quoted in this chapter.

Education Week. "Technology Counts 2002." http://www.edweek.org. This report discusses the latest advances in e-learning.

Fight Crime: Invest in Kids. "Ten Steps for Families to Stop Cyber Bullying." http://www.fightcrime.org/cyberbullying/10stepslong.pdf. This organization offers a program to stop cyber bullying.

FITZGERALD, FRANCES. *America Revised: History Schoolbooks in the Twentieth Century.* Boston: Little Brown, 1979. Fitzgerald depicts the major debates and changes in content of public school history texts.

GALLEY, MICHELLE, "News in Brief: Texas State Board Sued after Rejecting Textbook." *Education Week,* Vol. 23, no. 10 (5 November 2003): 26. A group of lawyers sues Texas for rejecting a science book for being too radical.

GLUCK, CAROL. "Let the Debate Continue." *The New York Times* (19 November 1994): 23. Gluck presents the debate over history standards.

HOFF, DAVID. "New Ohio Draft Ignores Alternative to Evolution." *Education Week on the Web* (18 September 2002). http://www.edweek.org. Hoff details the controversy in Ohio on the place of evolutionary theory in the state's science standards.

——. "And Congress Said, 'Let There Be Other Views', Or Did It?" *Education Week on the Web* (12 June 2002). http://www.edweek.org. Hoff discusses whether the No Child Left Behind legislation intended to include evolutionary theory in state science standards as a controversial theory.

——. "Exemplary Texts Withdrawn from California Adoption Process." *Education Week on the Web* (18 October 2000). http://www.edweek.org. Hoff examines the effect of California skill-and-drill math legislation on math textbooks.

——. "Kansas to Revise Standards Without Citing Evolution." *Education Week on the Web* (20 October 1999). http://www.edweek.org. Hoff discusses the removal of evolutionary theory and the origin of the universe from the Kansas state science standards.

KELLER, BESS. "Mich. Pupils Could Face Online Rule." *Education Week on the Web* (8 February 2006). http://www.edweek.org. Keller discusses the proposed online course requirement for graduation from Michigan high schools.

KLEINFIELD, N. R. "The Elderly Man and the Sea? Test Sanitizes Literary Texts." *The New York Times on the Web* (2 June 2002). http://www.nytimes.com. This article deals with the censorship of literary excerpts included in the New York Regents exam.

KLIEBARD, HERBERT M. *The Struggle for the American Curriculum, 1893–1958.* Boston: Routledge and Kegan Paul, 1986. Kliebard's history of curriculum in the twentieth century stresses the conflict among social-efficiency advocates, humanists, social meliorists, and developmentalists.

MANZO, KATHLEEN KENNEDY. "N.J. Standards Beginning to Alter What Is Taught, But Not How." *Education Week on the Web* (3 May 2000). http://www.edweek.org. Manzo discusses the effect of state standards on classroom instruction.

MCMANUS, TERRY. "Home Web Sites Thrust Students into Censorship Disputes." *The New York Times on the Web* (13 August 1998). http://www.nytimes.com. This article surveys the increasing cases of school censorship of student Web sites.

Olweus. The Olweus Bullying Prevention Program. http://www.fightcrime.org/cyberbullying/10stepslong.pdf. This is a widely recognized program to counter school bullying including cyber bullying.

PANARESE, THOMAS. "Commentary." *Education Week on the Web* (2 July 2008). http://www.edweek.org. Discussion about censorship regarding the Clovis, New Mexico, high school yearbook, which contained a spread on students who were lesbians.

People for the American Way. "Press release: Harry Potter and the Censors' Menace" (3 March 2003). Available on The People for the American Way's Web site: http://www.pfaw.org. The organization reacts to the banning of *Harry Potter* books by an Arkansas school district.

"Plan to Teach U.S. History Is Said to Slight White Males." *The New York Times* (26 October 1994): B12. This article discusses Lynne Cheney's reactions to the proposed history standards.

Report Roundup. "Internet Use." *Education Week on the Web* (10 August 2005). http://www.edweek.org. This is a report on the number of youth using the Internet in the U.S.

SPRING, JOEL. *Conflict of Interests: The Politics of American Education,* fifth edition. New York: McGraw-Hill, 2005. Chapter 2 discusses the politics of publishing and testing. Quotes from the 1986 Texas Textbook Committee are taken from this chapter.

——. *Globalization of Education: An Introduction.* New York: Routledge, 2009. This book discusses, among other things, the competitive global education models; human capital, progressive, religious, and Indigenous.

STILLE, ALEXANDRA. "Textbook Publishers Learn to Avoid Messing with Texas." *The New York Times on the Web* (29 June 2002). http://www.nytimes.com. This article discusses the struggle over the content of history and science textbooks before the Texas State Board of Education.

STOKES, PETER. "How E-Learning Will Transform Education." *Education Week on the Web* (13 September 2000). http://www.edweek.org. This article describes the range of possibilities for e-learning to enhance education.

Technology Update. "Virginia Tells Schools to Teach Internet Safety." *Education Week on the Web* (26 April 2006). http://www.edweek.org. This article reports on law requiring Virginia schoolteachers to give instruction on Internet safety.

Texas Education Agency. *Proclamation 2002 of the State Board of Education Advertising for Bids on Instructional Materials: Contains Amendments Dated July 11, 2003; September 12, 2003;*

and February 27, 2004. Austin: Texas Education Agency, 2004. These are the guidelines for publishers who want to have their books approved by the Texas Education Agency.

TONN, JESSICA L. "Kansas Board Primaries Seen as Win for Moderates." *Education Week on the Web* (9 August 2006). http://www.edweek.org.

——. "Kansas's New Schools Chief Sparks Conflict." *Education Week on the Web* (14 December 2005). http://www.edweek.org. New Kansas education commissioner favors restrictions on the teaching of evolution.

TROTTER, ANDREW. "Internet Access Has No Impact on Test Scores, Study Says." *Education Week on the Web* (4 September 2002). http://www.edweek.org. Using data from California and U.S. Departments of Education, researchers conclude that Internet access has no measurable impact on student achievement.

——. "FCC Issues Rules for Filtering Access to Internet Sites." *Education Week on the Web* (18 April 2001). http://www.edweek.org. This article discusses rules governing the filtering of the Internet in schools and libraries.

——. "Rating the E-Rate." *Education Week on the Web* (20 September 2000). http://www.edweek.org. Trotter reports on the effect of federal financing on the wiring of schools for the Internet.

United Nations News Service. "United Nations Adopts Declaration on Rights of Indigenous Peoples." Retrieved on 14 September 2007 from http://www.un.org/news/printnews.asp?nid523794. United Nations declares the rights of Indigenous peoples.

WALSH, MARK, and CAROLINE HENDRIE. "High Court Upholds Law on Internet Filtering in Libraries." *Education Week on the Web* (9 July 2003). http://www.edweek.org. U.S. Supreme Court rules that the Children's Internet Protection Act of 2000 is constitutional.

WILLARD, NANCY. "Filtering the Internet." *Education Week on the Web* (27 March 2002). http://www.edweek.org. This is a discussion of the continuing problems associated with Internet filters.

World Bank. Indigenous Peoples, "Key Concepts." Retrieved on 18 April 2006 from http://web.worldbank.org/WBSITE/EXTERNAL/TOPICS/EXTSOCIALDEVELOPMENT/EXTINDPEOPLE/0,,contentMDK:20436173~menuPK:906311pagePK:148956~piPK:216618~theSitePK:407802,00.html. World Bank's definition of Indigenous peoples.

ZERNIKE, KATE. "Georgia School Board Requires Balance of Evolution and Bible." *The New York Times on the Web* (23 August 2002). http://www.nytimes.org. The second-largest school district in Georgia requires teachers to present Biblical interpretations on the origins of life along with evolutionary thought.

CHAPTER 10

The Courts and the Schools

Can public schools require urine samples from middle- and high school students enrolled in extracurricular activities such as band, choir, and Future Homemakers of America? Can publicly funded school vouchers be used to purchase an education at a religious school? The answer to both questions is yes! These are just two examples of court decisions that affect every aspect of schooling.

Constitutional issues are involved in school activities ranging from student publications to the selection of books for the school library. One result is the involvement of the courts in the control and regulation of public schools. Only a limited number of constitutional issues involving the school are discussed here. Each day court decisions are made and legal issues become more complex. Anyone planning a career in teaching should investigate the rights and responsibilities of both teachers and students. Education law is now a whole field of study, and many lawyers are becoming specialists in education issues as school systems spend increasing amounts of time in the courts.

Many court cases involve the First and Fourteenth Amendments to the U.S. Constitution. The Fourteenth Amendment guarantees that states cannot take away any rights granted to an individual as a citizen of the United States; this means that although states have the right to provide schools, they cannot in their provision of schools violate citizen rights granted by the Constitution. The wording of Section 1 of the Fourteenth Amendment is extremely important in a variety of constitutional issues related to education:

> All persons born or naturalized in the United States, and subject to the jurisdiction thereof, are citizens of the United States and of the State wherein they reside. No State shall make or enforce any law which shall abridge the privileges or immunities of citizens of the United States; nor shall any State deprive any person of life, liberty, or property without due process of law [Due Process Clause]; nor deny to any person within its jurisdiction the equal protection of the laws [Equal Protection Clause].

These few lines are important for state-provided and state-regulated schools. For instance, "no state shall make or enforce any law which shall abridge the privileges or immunities of citizens of the United States" means that the courts can protect the constitutional rights of students and teachers particularly with regard to freedom of speech and issues related to religion. The Due Process Clause is invoked in cases that involve student suspensions and teacher firings. Since states provide schools to all citizens, they cannot dismiss a student or teacher without due process. As we shall see later in this chapter, the courts established guidelines for student dismissals.

All the protections of the Fourteenth Amendment depend on the states making some provision for education. Once a state government provides a system for education, it must provide it equally to all people in the state. The Equal Protection Clause is invoked in cases that involve equal educational opportunity and is central to cases that involve school segregation, non-English-speaking children, school finance, and children with special needs. Recall from an earlier chapter that the famous *Brown v. Board of Education of Topeka* decision in 1954 centered on whether segregated schools provided equal educational opportunity for all students. Before that decision, the Supreme Court had ruled that segregated schools were constitutional; the importance of the 1954 case was the decision that the educational opportunity provided in segregated schools was inherently unequal.

Clearly, the Fourteenth Amendment allows for constitutional protection in the schools. What is important, and generates controversy, is the protection of the rights granted in the First Amendment:

> Congress shall make no law respecting an establishment of religion [Establishment Clause], or prohibiting the free exercise [Free Exercise Clause] thereof; or abridging the freedom of speech [Free Speech Clause], or of the press; or the right of the people peaceably to assemble, and to petition the Government for a redress of grievances.

The Establishment Clause of the First Amendment is important for decisions involving school prayer and religious exercises in the schools. The section dealing with laws prohibiting the free exercise of religion, the Free Exercise Clause, is important when religious groups claim that public schools interfere with their religious practices or that public schools are teaching something that is offensive to their religious beliefs.

There is a thin line between not allowing the establishment of religion and interfering with the free exercise of religion. As we will see later in this chapter, the U.S. Supreme Court prohibits school prayer because it involves the government in the establishment of religion. On the other hand, groups defending school prayer claim that the Court's decision interferes with their free exercise of religion.

The same problem plagues the issue of freedom of speech. On the one hand, the courts recognize the importance of protecting the free speech of students and teachers; on the other hand, the courts recognize the necessity for maintaining order in schools and for school boards to exercise control over teachers. This dilemma also exists in the interpretation of the Eighth Amendment, which reads: "Excessive bail shall not be required, nor excessive fines imposed, nor cruel and unusual punishments inflicted." But when does punishment of a student become cruel and unusual punishment? This, as we will see later in the chapter, is a major issue in court cases dealing with corporal punishment. The first issue I discuss is students' rights.

DRUG TESTING OF STUDENTS

Let's begin considering students' rights in the framework of the 2002 U.S. Supreme Court ruling on drug testing. The case, *Board of Education of Independent School District No. 92 of Pottawatomie County et al. v. Earls et al.*, involved a 1998 Student Activities Drug Testing Policy of the Tecumseh, Oklahoma, school district, which required students to submit to a urinalysis for illegal drugs—for example, amphetamines, marijuana, cocaine, opiates, and barbiturates—prior to participating in competitive extracurricular activities. The extracurricular activities included in the school district policy were the Academic Team, Future Farmers of America, Future Homemakers of America, band, choir, pom pom, cheerleading, and athletics.

Two students at the Tecumseh High School, Lindsay Earls and Daniel James, and their parents, claimed that students' Fourth Amendment rights to protection from "unreasonable searches" and the requirement of "probable cause" were being violated. In other words, was the urinalysis an "unreasonable search"? Was there a "probable cause" of drug usage by students engaged in competitive extracurricular activities?

The Fourth Amendment states that:

> The right of the people to be secure in their persons, houses, papers, and effects, against unreasonable searches and seizures, shall not be violated, and no warrants shall issue, but upon probable cause, supported by oath or affirmation, and particularly describing the place to be searched, and the persons or things to be seized.

Regarding "unreasonable search," the U.S. Supreme Court identifies the right to privacy as a key issue. Is the invasion of personal privacy by the urinalysis an "unreasonable search"? The Court's decision states that students in school are in "temporary custody of the state" and a "student privacy interest is limited in a public school environment." The Court also argues that students participating in extracurricular activities, such as athletics or those requiring travel, involve "communal undress." In addition, the manner in which the school district collects the urine samples is not an invasion of privacy. The U.S. Supreme Court decision provides the following description of the Tecumseh school district's collection of urine samples:

> A faculty monitor waits outside the closed restroom stall for the student to produce a sample and must listen for the normal sounds of urination in order to guard against tampered specimens and to insure an accurate chain of custody. The monitor then pours the sample into two bottles that are sealed and placed into a mailing pouch along with a consent form signed by the student.

> This procedure . . . additionally protects privacy by allowing male students to produce their samples behind a closed stall.

Based on the school's custodial care of the student, "communal undressing," and "given the minimally intrusive nature of the sample collection," the U.S. Supreme Court concludes "that the invasion of students' privacy is not significant."

Is there a "probable cause" requiring drug testing? Are students using drugs while engaging in extracurricular activities? First, the U.S. Supreme Court decision declares, based on previous cases, "that a warrant and finding of probable cause are unnecessary in the public school context because such requirements would unduly interfere with the maintenance of the swift and informal disciplinary procedures [that are] needed." In other words, school authorities do not have to prove "probable cause" before searching a student's possessions as long as the search is conducted in a reasonable manner. Also, school authorities can test for drugs even though there is no suspicion that the student has actually used drugs.

In addition, the Court felt that the Tecumseh school district had identified a drug problem in the school district. The following evidence of drug usage is given in the Court's decision:

> Teachers testified that they had seen students who appeared to be under the influence of drugs and that they had heard students speaking openly about using drugs. A drug dog found marijuana cigarettes near the school parking lot. Police officers once found drugs or drug paraphernalia in a car driven by a Future Farmers of America member. And the school board president reported that people in the community were calling the board to discuss the drug situation.

Based on the preceding reasoning, the U.S. Supreme Court ruled that the Tecumseh school district's Student Activities Drug Testing Policy is not a violation of the Fourth Amendment's prohibition of "unreasonable searches" and the requirement of "probable cause." The result of this decision means that any public school district can legally adopt a drug policy modeled on that of the Tecumseh school district.

Following the Supreme Court decision, John P. Walters, the director of the White House Office of National Drug Control Policy, sent a booklet to local school districts urging the use of drug testing. He writes that drug testing had "enormous potential benefits" and that concerns about privacy were "largely unfounded." "Already," he contends, "testing has been shown to be extremely effective at reducing drug use in schools and businesses all over the country. As a deterrent, few methods work better or deliver clearer results."

The Supreme Court decision was not supported by many groups, including the National Education Association and the American Academy of Pediatrics. These groups were concerned about privacy issues involved in requiring all students participating in extracurricular activities to be drug tested. Some communities have divided over the issue. For instance in New Buffalo, Michigan, there were weekly meetings in August 2002 to hammer out a drug policy. The superintendent, Michael Lindley, stated, "It cuts deep down to how one sees the world, and people have different views. Some say it's invasive and you're assuming my child is guilty until proved otherwise. Others say if kids have nothing to hide, it's not invasive."

Many school districts adopted the Tecumseh school district's stated policies to avoid any future legal problems. "I tell districts," said Paul Lyle, a lawyer representing 50 Texas school districts, "that if they adopt the same verbatim policy as Tecumseh, that would be safe. But I tell them, if you change a comma, it could open the door to something." Raymond Lusk, superintendent of the Lockney, Texas, school district, commented, "We'll probably get 85 percent of the kids in extracurriculars. I think it would be fairer to test everybody, because why are some kids more important than others?"

STUDENTS' FREE SPEECH RIGHTS

In addition to the Fourth Amendment, students' rights are affected by the Free Speech Clause of the First Amendment, which, as previously stated, provides that "Congress shall make no law . . . abridging the freedom of speech." *Tinker v. Des Moines Independent School District* (1969) is the landmark case involving free speech rights for students.

The *Tinker* case originated when a group of students decided to express their objections to the war in Vietnam by wearing black armbands. School authorities in Des Moines adopted a policy that any student wearing an armband would be suspended. When the case was decided by the U.S. Supreme Court, clear recognition was given to the constitutional rights of students. The Court stated that a student "may express his opinion, even on controversial subjects like the conflict in Vietnam. . . . Under our Constitution, free speech is not a right that is given only to be so circumscribed that it exists in principle but not in fact."

One extremely important condition is placed on the right of free speech of students and that is the possibility of disruption of the educational process. The Court does not provide any specific guidelines for interpreting this condition and limitation. What it means is that school authorities have an obligation to protect the constitutional rights of students and, at the same time, an obligation to ensure that there is no interference with the normal activities of the school.

In recent years, student rights were limited by claims of interference with the educational purposes and activities of schools. A federal appellate court ruled that a school administration can disqualify a student campaigning for student body president because of remarks about the vice principal and school administration. The appellate court reasoned that the administration's educational concerns allowed it to censor comments that might hurt the feelings of others. This form of censorship taught students to respect others.

In *Hazelwood School District v. Kuhlemier* (1988), the U.S. Supreme Court ruled that school administrators have the right to control the content of school-sponsored publications because they are part of the curriculum. The case involved a newspaper published by the journalism class at Missouri's Hazelwood High School. The newspaper contained articles about student pregnancies and students from divorced families. False names were used to protect the students interviewed for the articles. The school's principal objected to the articles because the interviewed students might be identifiable to other students, and he considered the sexual discussions inappropriate for high school students. The authors of the articles responded that both divorce and pregnancy were appropriate topics for modern youth and that they were widely discussed among students.

The right of school administrators to censor student publications was expanded to include all school activities. School administrators have the right to refuse to produce student plays, to prohibit student publication of articles that are poorly written and vulgar, and to ban student expression that advocates drugs, alcohol, and permissive sex. In censorship cases of this type, the legal test is whether the school administration's actions are based on legitimate educational concerns.

School authorities are also allowed to punish student speech that they consider to be lewd and indecent. In *Bethel v. Fraser* (1986), the U.S. Supreme Court ruled that school administrators in the Bethel, Washington, school system could punish a high school senior, Matthew Fraser, for giving a nominating speech at a school assembly that used an "elaborate, graphic, and explicit sexual metaphor." The Court said that school officials have the right to determine what is vulgar and offensive in the classroom and at school activities and to prohibit vulgar and offensive speech. This decision did not apply to speech about political, religious, educational, and public policy issues; it was limited to the issue of indecent speech.

GAYS, BOY SCOUTS, AND THE NO CHILD LEFT BEHIND ACT OF 2001

In the 1990s, the decision by the Boy Scouts to deny membership to homosexuals was extremely contentious. In 2000, the U.S. Supreme Court ruled in *Boy Scouts of America v. Dale* that it was a private association with the right to set its own standards for membership and leadership. As a result, school districts across the country banned the Boy Scouts from using school facilities. For instance, when the Minneapolis school district denied the Boy Scouts access to school buildings, Carol Johnson, the superintendent, contended, "We are an inclusive organization. It would be very difficult to continue to partner with them [Boy Scouts] and be consistent with our nondiscrimination policy." Evan Wolfson, a senior staff lawyer with the Lambda Legal Defense and Education Fund, a gay-rights group, asserted, "Schools, as public entities, cannot be accomplices to discrimination, especially discrimination that hurts our kids."

The issue of Boy Scout access to schools was resolved in the No Child Left Behind Act. In a special section titled "Boy Scouts of America Equal Access Act," the legislation states:

> Notwithstanding any other provision of law, no public elementary school, public secondary school, local educational agency, or State educational agency

> that has a designated open forum or a limited public forum and that receives funds made available through the Department shall deny equal access or a fair opportunity to meet to, or discriminate against, any group officially affiliated with the Boy Scouts of America.

SEXUAL HARASSMENT AND DISCRIMINATION

In *Franklin v. Gwinnett* (1992), the U.S. Supreme Court ruled that students who were victimized by sexual harassment and other forms of sexual discrimination by school officials could sue for monetary damages. The case involved a Georgia high school student who was sexually harassed and abused by a teacher. This decision was made in the context of Title IX, which bars discrimination based on gender. In making its decision, the U.S. Supreme Court relied on a previous decision barring supervisors from sexually harassing a subordinate. The Court extended this ruling to include teachers and students.

In contrast, the U.S. Supreme Court in 1996 let stand the decision by the U.S. Court of Appeals for the Fifth District that school systems were not liable for sexual harassment of students by other students. The case involved two eighth grade girls in Bryan, Texas, who were sexually harassed on a school bus. The decision by the U.S. Supreme Court not to review the Texas case left school officials in a state of confusion.

At the other extreme, in a California decision, a state court jury awarded $500,000 to a family of a sixth grade student who was tormented by other students calling her "slut" and "bitch." Alarmed at the possibility of other suits, school officials in North Carolina and New York City punished first and second grade boys for kissing female classmates. These punishments caused a great deal of public criticism. Until the U.S. Supreme Court clarifies the issue, school officials will continue to worry about potential suits over sexual harassment between students.

STUDENTS' ACCESS TO BOOKS

A First Amendment case involved balancing the right of students to have access to books in the school library with the right of the school board to decide which books should be in the school library. The case *Board of Island Union Free School District v. Steven A. Pico* (1982) concerned the removal of books from the school library by the board of education because the content of the books was considered unsuitable for high school students. The issue originated when several members of the board of education attended a conference of a politically conservative organization of parents concerned with educational legislation in the state of New York. While they were at the conference, the board members received a list of books considered morally and politically inappropriate for high school students. Upon returning from the conference, the board members investigated the contents of their high school library and discovered nine books that had been on the list. Subsequently, the board ordered the removal of the books from the library shelves. The books included *Best Short Stories of Negro Writers* edited by Langston Hughes, *Down These Mean Streets* by Piri Thomas, *The Fixer* by Bernard Malamud, *Go Ask Alice* of anonymous authorship, *A Hero Ain't Nothin but a Sandwich* by Alice Childress, *Naked Ape* by Desmond Morris, *A Reader for Writers* by Jerome Archer, *Slaughterhouse Five* by Kurt Vonnegut, Jr., and *Soul on Ice* by Eldridge Cleaver.

In its decision the U.S. Supreme Court gave full recognition to the power of school boards to select books for the school library and to the importance of avoiding judicial interference in the operation of local school systems. On the other hand, the Court recognized its obligation to ensure that public institutions do not suppress ideas. Here, there was a clear intention to suppress ideas by making decisions about book removal based on a list from a political organization.

The Supreme Court's method of handling the preceding dilemma was to recognize the right of the school board to determine the content of the library, if its decisions on content were not based on partisan or political motives. In the words of the Court, "If a Democratic school board, motivated by party affiliation, ordered the removal of all books written by or in favor of Republicans, few would doubt that the order violated the constitutional rights of the students denied access to those books." In another illustration, the Court argued, "The same conclusion would surely apply if an all-white school board, motivated by racial animus, decided to remove all books authored by blacks or advocating racial equality and integration." Or, as the Court more simply stated, "Our Constitution does not permit the official suppression of ideas."

On the other hand, the Court argued that books could be removed if the decision were based solely on their educational suitability. The Court also limited its decision to apply only to books removed from school library shelves, not to decisions about books added to the shelves. In summary, the Court stated:

> We hold that local school boards may not remove books from school library shelves simply because they dislike the ideas contained in those books and seek by their removal to prescribe what shall be orthodox in politics, nationalism, religion, or other matters of opinion.

STUDENT SUSPENSIONS

A student's "property interest" in education is the result of a state statutory entitlement to a public education. The right to attend public schools is usually conferred on children by state law. This law, of course, can vary from state to state.

Property interest and the right to an education were major considerations of the U.S. Supreme Court in dealing with due process and suspensions from school in *Goss v. Lopez* (1975). This case dealt with suspensions from school of junior and senior high school students. The Court ruled that due process "requires, in connection with a suspension of 10 days or less, that the student be given oral or written notice of the charges against him and, if he denies them, an explanation of the evidence the authorities have and an opportunity to present his side of the story." The Court based its decision on "legitimate claims of entitlement to public education" as given in state law. What this meant was that a student's right to an education could not be taken away in an arbitrary manner.

The *Goss* decision established a precedent that due process is required before a school-dismissal decision. R. Lawrence Dessem, in a 1976 article in the *Journal of Law and Education,* "Student Due Process Rights in Academic Dismissals from the Public Schools," argues that in the future the due process requirement might be applied to cases involving dismissal from school for academic reasons. The *Goss* decision dealt only with suspension for disciplinary reasons. In either case, there may be a clear obligation upon school authorities to guarantee due process for all students.

Dessem outlines in his article the basic procedures that must take place to ensure due process for students. First, there must be an attempt to decide the basis of fact. Second, there must be some provision to guarantee future review of any decisions. And third, just procedures must be followed in reaching any decisions.

In practice, these three procedures mean very specific things. A student must be provided with a notice detailing the charges, and the notice must be received in sufficient time for the student to prepare answers to the charges. A student must be given the chance to present answers to the charges in a hearing before an unbiased group. Dessem argues that schools cannot be required to have groups outside the school conduct the hearings because of the expense. Dessem states: "A hearing before a panel of disinterested teachers and school administrators would seem to strike an acceptable balance between the right of the student to an impartial arbitrator and the school's interest in keeping the expense and inconvenience of such hearings to a minimum." Students do have a right to have the decision based only on the evidence presented.

In *Goss,* the U.S. Supreme Court did place a limit on the procedural elements of due process by refusing to require that students be given the right to call witnesses and have legal counsel. "The Supreme Court's rationale," states Dessem, "for refusing to mandate this and several other procedures was that since 'brief disciplinary suspensions are almost countless, to impose in each such case even truncated trial type procedures might well overwhelm administrative facilities in many places."

The *Tinker* decision has provided some protection for the freedom of speech of students in public schools, and the *Goss* decision has provided protection from arbitrary dismissal of students from public schools. Both decisions represent the continuing expansion of civil liberties granted under the Constitution of the United States. Teachers and other school authorities have a duty and an obligation to ensure that these rights are protected. Teachers also have an obligation to protect their constitutional rights, thereby serving as models for students and setting an example for interpreting the meaning of civil liberties in the United States.

DO SCHOOL AUTHORITIES HAVE THE RIGHT TO PADDLE CHILDREN?

Consider the following situations and compare your opinions with the decisions of the courts. Assume the following set of circumstances: The family of a child cannot afford private schooling. Due to compulsory-education laws, the family is forced to send the child to a local public school where the primary means of discipline is corporal punishment. The parents do not believe in the use of physical punishment, have never used physical punishment at home, and do not want the public school to use physical punishment on their child. In this situation, can school authorities spank the child? Can the child be forced to attend an institution that gives its personnel the right to use physical punishment, contrary to practices in the child's home?

Part of the answer to these questions was given in the U.S. Supreme Court decision *Ingraham v. Wright* (1977). A junior high school student, James Ingraham, in Dade County, Florida, refused to let the principal of his school, Willie Wright, paddle him for not leaving the stage of the school auditorium promptly. (Ingraham claimed that he had left the stage when requested by the principal.) When Ingraham refused to be paddled, Principal Wright called in his two assistant principals, who held Ingraham's legs and arms. The student was hit 20 times on the buttocks with a two-foot-long wooden paddle. His mother examined him when he arrived home and immediately took him to a local hospital, where the doctor prescribed pain pills, ice packs, and a laxative, and recommended that Ingraham stay home for a week.

At a Florida trial court hearing, many other students complained about beatings at the school. Children described being pushed up against urinals in the boys' bathroom and being beaten on the legs, back, and across the neck. One boy described how he refused to take a whipping because he felt he was innocent and was beaten across the head with a board. Within a few days of the beating, the student underwent an operation to have a lump removed from his head; he claimed a subsequent loss of memory.

After a weeklong trial, the Florida court granted the defense a motion for dismissal, arguing that there was no showing of severe punishment and that corporal punishment was not unacceptable according to the standards of contemporary society. This ruling was overturned by the Fifth Circuit Court of Appeals because the punishment at the junior high school violated the Eighth Amendment's prohibition against cruel and unusual punishment. A further appeal reversed this ruling and set the stage for a decision by the U.S. Supreme Court.

On 19 April 1977, the U.S. Supreme Court ruled that the Cruel and Unusual Punishment Clause of the Eighth Amendment does not apply to corporal punishment, nor does the Due Process Clause of the Fourteenth Amendment require that notice be given to students before they are subjected to corporal punishment. The Court argued that corporal punishment is the traditional means of maintaining discipline in the public schools and that although public opinion is divided on the issue, there is not any trend to eliminate its use. The Court found no reason for extending the Eighth Amendment to the schools.

The Court felt that community pressure and common-law safeguards should be used to ensure that corporal punishment be used in a reasonable manner. This argument paralleled the lower court's argument that here criminal charges could be brought against the junior high school principal and assistant principal. In other words, public school authorities can beat children, but the extent of the punishment must be reasonable.

Determining what is reasonable creates a difficult problem for courts and the community. A teacher or administrator who inflicts one or two spankings a year without causing any lasting physical damage would be considered reasonable. But what about the teacher or principal who paddles so violently that students are left with black-and-blue marks? A principal of a Kentucky high school, in a recent lecture at my university, argued that administrators and teachers who use corporal punishment excessively exhibit behavior usually associated with child abusers.

What if parents object to the use of corporal punishment? A decision regarding this issue was made by the Fourth Circuit Court of Appeals on 9 May 1980 in *Hall v. Tauney*. Thomas Flygare describes this case in the September 1980 issue of the *Phi Delta Kappan*. A West Virginia grade school student was, in Flygare's words, "repeatedly and violently struck on the hip and thigh by a teacher using a homemade hard rubber paddle about five inches in width. She alleged that because of this paddling she was hospitalized for ten days and has received the treatment of specialists for possible permanent injuries to the lower spine."

Since argument about the Eighth Amendment's Cruel and Unusual Punishment Clause had failed in the *Ingraham* case, Hall's lawyers decided to use a different tactic. The lawyers argued that the paddling, as Flygare states, "violated the right of her parents to determine the means by which she could be disciplined."

The Fourth Circuit Court ruled that parents had no constitutional right to exempt their children from corporal punishment in the schools. The statement of the court raised a whole host of issues regarding the power of parents versus the power of the school. Reflect on the statement by the court that "the state interest in maintaining order in the schools limits the rights of particular parents unilaterally to except their children from the regime to which other children are subject."

COMPULSION AND RELIGION

Since their founding, public schools have been in conflict with religious groups. The Establishment Clause of the First Amendment to the U.S. Constitution states that "Congress shall make no law respecting an establishment of religion, or prohibiting the free exercise thereof." The problem is that many religions believe education cannot be separated from religion. Both education and religion are concerned with the moral and social development of the individual. Religion, education, and the First Amendment conflict when certain religious groups are forced to send their children to public school and conform to the practices of the school, and when religious groups demand that the public schools engage in certain religious practices, such as school prayer. In the first case, forced attendance and compliance with school regulations can be an infringement on an individual's right to practice religion, if school practices conflict with religious beliefs. In the second case, religious activities in public schools can mean that the government is giving support to particular religious practices.

VOUCHERS AND RELIGIOUS SCHOOLS

In 2002, the U.S. Supreme Court issued a landmark decision on school vouchers and religious schools. In *Zelman v. Simmons-Harris,* the primary issue was the use of government-funded vouchers by students to attend schools with religious affiliations. Was the use of these government vouchers a violation of the Establishment Clause ("Congress shall make no law respecting an establishment of religion") of the First Amendment?

The state of Ohio's Pilot Project Scholarship Program provides tuition aid vouchers to families residing in the Cleveland City school district. These vouchers can be used to attend any accredited private school or public schools in other school districts adjacent to the Cleveland City school district. The Establishment Clause became an issue because, as stated in the U.S. Supreme Court decision, "82% of the participating private schools had a religious affiliation, none of the adjacent public schools [in other school districts] participated, and 96% of the students participating in the scholarship program were enrolled in religiously affiliated schools." Clearly, religious schools were receiving the bulk of the voucher money provided under the Pilot Project Scholarship Program.

In the decision regarding Ohio's Pilot Project Scholarship Program, the U.S. Supreme Court relied on a previous decision, *Mueller v. Allen* (1983), which dealt with a Minnesota law that allowed state taxpayers to take deductions from gross income for expenses incurred for "tuition, textbooks, and transportation" for dependents attending elementary and secondary schools. The majority of beneficiaries (96 percent) of the Minnesota law were parents of children attending religious schools. In *Mueller,* the U.S. Supreme Court argued that the law did not violate the Constitution because "the deduction is available for educational expenses incurred by all parents, including those whose children attend public schools and those whose children attend nonsectarian private schools or sectarian private schools." The Court reasoned that the intent of the law was primarily secular, it did not advance religion, and it did not cause an excessive entanglement between the government and religion.

What about the fact that under both the Minnesota and Ohio laws the majority of the government benefits went to parents sending their children to religious schools? Wasn't this a violation of the Establishment Clause? No, the

U.S. Supreme Court answered, because the intent of the law was secular. The fact that the majority of benefits went to religious institutions was the result of the choices made by parents. In the words of the U.S. Supreme Court decision regarding Ohio's Pilot Project Scholarship Program, "The amount of government aid channeled to religious institutions by individual aid recipients was not relevant to the constitutional inquiry."

Based on the preceding reasoning, the Court concluded that Ohio's Pilot Project Scholarship Program was not a violation of the Establishment Clause. However, the decision left many questions unanswered.

In reality, Cleveland parents were limited in choice to private schools because none of the surrounding school districts were willing to participate in the program. This fact highlights the efforts by suburban school districts to protect their educational advantages.

CHILD-BENEFIT THEORY

The now-famous voucher decision in *Zelman v. Simmons-Harris* followed previous attempts to distinguish between religious and secular intents of laws. One approach is referred to as the **child-benefit theory.** The child-benefit theory was articulated by the U.S. Supreme Court in *Cochran v. Louisiana State Board of Education* (1930). At issue was a Louisiana law permitting the purchase and distribution of textbooks to all schoolchildren. Under this law textbooks were provided to children attending private religious schools. The U.S. Supreme Court affirmed the Louisiana Supreme Court ruling that the law did not sanction the support of religious schools. Taxpayers' money was spent to purchase books that went directly to schoolchildren. The law existed for the benefit of children, not for the support of religious institutions.

The same reasoning was involved in the 1947 U.S. Supreme Court decision *Everson v. Board of Education,* which allowed public support of school transportation for parochial students. Here, the support again went directly to the child and not to a religious institution. The Court stated, "We cannot say that the First Amendment prohibits . . . spending tax-raised funds to pay the bus fares of parochial school pupils as a part of a general program under which it pays fares of pupils attending public and other schools."

One difficult issue is the participation by religious schools in federally funded programs, such as Title I programs for remedial education. In 1978, a group called Public Education and Religious Liberty (PEARL) argued that the presence of publicly funded teachers, such as Title I teachers, in religious schools was a violation of the Establishment Clause of the First Amendment. In 1985, the U.S. Supreme Court in *Aguilar v. Felton* agreed with PEARL; as a result, Title I teachers at religious schools were housed in off-campus mobile classrooms or other facilities. In 1997, the U.S. Supreme Court in *Agostini v. Felton* reversed the 1985 decision arguing that there was no reason to think that Title I teachers would give religious lessons in their classrooms. For many teachers, such as Maxine Bender, a New York public school teacher, it was a pleasure to be able to teach remedial reading inside the Sacred Heart Catholic school. "It makes a tremendous difference," she said, "to be back inside the building."

A 1971 U.S. Supreme Court case, *Lemon v. Kurzman,* established a three-part test for determining the constitutionality of government programs that benefit religion. The case involved laws in Rhode Island and Pennsylvania that provided salary supplements to teachers in private religious schools. Under the *Lemon* test, government aid to religious schools

- Must have a secular purpose.
- Must not inhibit or advance religion.
- Must not cause excessive entanglement of government in religion.

In 2000, the U.S. Supreme Court ruled in favor of a federal program that provided computers and library books to religious schools. This decision reversed an earlier decision barring the federal government from giving maps, charts, overhead projectors, and other instructional materials to religious schools.

CAN STATES REGULATE PRIVATE SCHOOLS?

The issue of state regulation of private schools appeared in the U.S. Supreme Court case dealing with the conflict between compulsory schooling and religious freedom. In *Pierce v. Society of Sisters* (1925), the Court ruled on Oregon's Compulsory Education Act (1922), which required every parent, guardian, or other person having control or charge or custody of a child between 8 and 16 years of age to send the child to a public school. The act was clearly an attempt to close parochial schools by forcing all children to attend public schools. Two private schools in Oregon immediately obtained injunctions against Governor Pierce and Oregon state officials.

The First Amendment was not directly involved in the case because the law affected both religious and nonreligious private schools. The Supreme Court did indirectly support the guarantee of religious liberty, however, by maintaining the right to choose a religious school instead of a public school. The Court stated that the "fundamental theory of liberty upon which all governments in this Union repose excludes any general power of the State to standardize its children by forcing them to accept instruction from public teachers only."

The Supreme Court ruling in *Pierce v. Society of Sisters* was based on an earlier ruling involving a Nebraska law that required all subjects in private and public schools be taught in the English language. The purpose of the law was to curb German nationalism during World War I by limiting the use of foreign languages. In *Meyer v. Nebraska* (1923), the Court declared the law unconstitutional. Nevertheless, the Court did recognize the right of the teacher "to teach and the right of parents to engage him so to instruct their children." The importance of the *Meyer* decision was the recognition of the parental right to direct the upbringing of their children within the reasonable limitations of the law.

In *Pierce v. Society of Sisters,* these rights were again confirmed in declaring the 1922 Oregon law unconstitutional. The Court stated, "Under the doctrine of

Meyer v. Nebraska . . . we think it entirely plain that the Act of 1922 unreasonably interferes with the liberty of parents and guardians to direct the up-bringing and education of children under their control." But the Court did not recognize the complete control of the parents and guardians over the education of their children; it very clearly defined the power of the states regarding education.

Probably the most important part of the *Pierce* decision, besides declaring that children could not be forced to attend public schools, was the recognition of the power of the state to regulate education and compel students to attend school. The Court stated, "No question is raised concerning the power of the State reasonably to regulate all schools, to inspect, supervise and examine them, their teachers and pupils; to require that all children of proper age attend some school." Besides recognizing the right of regulation and requirements to attend, the Court also recognized the right of the state to certify teachers and regulate the curriculum regarding citizenship studies. The Court ruled that the state had the right to require "that teachers shall be of good moral character and patriotic disposition, that certain studies plainly essential to good citizenship must be taught, and that nothing be taught which is manifestly inimical to the public welfare."

These qualifications to the *Pierce* decision placed important limitations on the right of parents and guardians to direct the education of their children. The state had the right to force attendance at an educational institution that met state requirements concerning teachers, curriculum, and other reasonable standards. The only right recognized for parents was the choice between public and private schools, and this right was limited by the ability to pay for private schooling. The unresolved issue was what would happen if the state standards used to regulate public and private schools differed from religious practices and the state required attendance at a state-accredited school. This is the problem that the Amish encountered.

RELIGION AND STATE SCHOOL REQUIREMENTS

The Amish are a subgroup of the Anabaptist-Mennonite tradition that has refused to be assimilated into the mainstream of American society and the modern urban and industrial world. They first came to America in the eighteenth century and settled in eastern Pennsylvania in compact communities. They retained in America their original European dress-style of men wearing black clothes and wide-brimmed hats and women wearing capes and aprons. In areas of Pennsylvania, Ohio, Indiana, Iowa, and Wisconsin, communities of Amish continue to exist with traditional religious practices, clothes, and community living. The Amish continue to use horse-and-buggy transportation and avoid the use of electricity and telephones.

One major threat to the Amish way of life is the public school and compulsory education. The public school threatens the destruction of the Amish community by the teaching of values contrary to its traditions and by the introduction of the children to modern lifestyles. For the Amish, this threat can occur in areas that might seem unimportant to other people. For instance, one objection of Amish parents to compulsory high school attendance is the requirement that young women wear shorts for physical education, which is in serious violation of Amish beliefs. In the nineteenth century, the Amish began to object to the rise of public schools. In an article entitled "From Erlanback to New Glarus" in a book he edited titled *Compulsory Education and the Amish,* Albert N. Keim quotes a nineteenth-century Amish leader: "The righteousness that counts before God is neither sought nor found in the public or free schools; they are interested only to impart worldly knowledge, to ensure earthly success and to make good citizens of the state."

The Amish particularly object to public high school because of its broader curriculum and preparation for a vocation or college. The Amish do their own vocational training within their communities. Amish education stresses following instructions, respecting authority, and mastering basic information. The Amish disapprove of modern education that stresses critical thinking and asking questions. They see obedience to authority and tradition as essential for the survival of the community.

New Glarus, Wisconsin, was the scene of the final confrontation between the Amish and compulsory-education laws. In 1968, public school authorities insisted that the Amish community comply with a Wisconsin law requiring school attendance until 16 years of age. The county court upheld the decision of the school authorities. The Amish appealed the case to the Wisconsin Supreme Court, which rejected the lower court's decision and ruled that compulsory schooling of Amish children beyond the eighth grade was a violation of the free exercise of religious rights. In 1972, the U.S. Supreme Court in *State of Wisconsin, Petitioner v. Jonas Yoder et al.* upheld the Wisconsin Supreme Court decision.

In the *Yoder* decision the U.S. Supreme Court placed some limitations on the right of a state to compel school attendance, as recognized in *Pierce v. Society of Sisters.* The Court stated in the *Pierce* decision that there was recognition given that the "values of parental direction of the religious upbringing and education of their children in their early and formative years have a high place in our society." In addition, the Court argued that a state's interest in universal education should not be at the sacrifice of other rights, specifically those of the First Amendment. In the words of the Court, "We can accept it as settled, therefore, that however strong the State's interest in universal compulsory education, it is by no means absolute to the exclusion or subordination of all other interests."

The *Yoder* decision also placed limitations on state educational requirements. The Court stated that there were two primary arguments for maintaining a system of compulsory education. One argument was the necessity for citizens to be prepared to participate intelligently in an open political system. The other argument was that education was necessary to prepare people to be self-reliant and self-sufficient in society. The Court clearly stated concerning these two arguments: "We accept these propositions." The Court then went on to argue that the requirement that the Amish attend school beyond the eighth grade did not aid in the achievement of these educational goals. The Court stated that the Amish community was a highly successful social unit and its members were productive and law-abiding. Education within the community therefore appeared to fulfill the state interests in education.

The importance of the 1972 *Yoder* decision is in the placing of First Amendment religious freedoms above those of the state's interest in education. This would mean that in the future the courts would decide any conflict between religious practices and compulsory schooling in favor of individual religious freedom. The decision also requires that, in any future cases dealing with compulsory schooling, the state must show some relationship between its educational requirements and standards and its interest in educating self-sufficient and intelligent citizens. State standards cannot be arbitrary and unrelated to these objectives.

The U.S. Supreme Court also protects First Amendment rights when required practices in the schools conflict with religious beliefs. This decision involved objections of Jehovah's Witnesses to saluting and pledging allegiance to the flag. The case began in the early 1940s when the West Virginia Board of Education ordered that the flag salute become a regular part of the school program and that all teachers and pupils be required to salute the flag and say the Pledge of Allegiance. Refusal to participate was to be viewed as an act of insubordination, and pupils who failed to conform were to be expelled from school. Pupils expelled from school were considered delinquent and could possibly be sent to juvenile reformatories.

Jehovah's Witnesses object to the flag ceremony because they believe that the obligations imposed by the law of God are superior to the laws of government. One law of God taken literally by Jehovah's Witnesses is "Thou shall not make unto thee any graven image, or any likeness of anything that is in heaven above, or that is in the earth beneath, or that is in the water under the earth; thou shalt not bow down thyself to them nor serve them." Jehovah's Witnesses believe that the flag is an image and refuse, for religious reasons, to salute it.

The U.S. Supreme Court ruling in *West Virginia State Board of Education v. Barnette* declared the West Virginia School Board ruling unconstitutional because of its abridgment of First Amendment freedoms. In its decision the Court went beyond the issue of protection of religious practices to the issue of protection within public schools of all constitutional privileges. The Court argued: "That they are educating the young for citizenship is reason for scrupulous protection of Constitutional freedoms of the individual, if we are not to strangle the free mind at its source and teach youth to discount important principles of our government as mere platitudes." Within the same framework, the Court emphasized that patriotic exercises should not be made compulsory. In the words of the Court, "To believe that patriotism will not flourish if patriotic ceremonies are voluntary and spontaneous instead of a compulsory routine is to make an unflattering estimate of the appeal of our institutions to free minds."

Another controversial issue is religious practices in schools. There is a great deal of pressure to introduce religious practices such as Bible reading, prayer, and meditation into schools. All three practices conflict with the Establishment Clause of the First Amendment.

SCHOOL PRAYER, BIBLE READING, AND MEDITATION

Many religious groups were outraged by the 1962 school-prayer decision in *Engel v. Vitale*. The decision denied the right of a public school system to conduct prayer services within school buildings during regular school hours. Those groups of people whom the decision angers argue that it made education godless, and they seek an amendment to the Constitution that would allow for prayer ceremonies in the school. The Court decision against school prayer was primarily based on the argument that school prayer involved the state in the establishment of religion. This is considered a violation of the Establishment Clause of the First Amendment.

The school-prayer case began when the New York Board of Regents granted a local school system the right to have a brief prayer said in each class at the beginning of the school day. The prayer, considered denominationally neutral, read, "Almighty God, we acknowledge our dependence upon Thee, and we beg Thy blessings upon us, our parents, our teachers and our country." The New York courts granted the right of local school systems to use this prayer. The one requirement was that they could not compel students to say the prayer if they or their parents objected.

It was the decision of the New York courts against which the U.S. Supreme Court ruled in *Engel v. Vitale*. One major objection of the Court was the fact that government officials wrote the prayer. This seemed to put the government directly in the business of establishing religion. The Court stated that "in this country it is not part of the business of government to compose official prayers for any group of the American people to recite as a part of the religious program carried on by government." The Court reviewed the early history of the United States, and the struggle for religious freedom and the ending of government support of churches. The Court argued: "By the time of the adoption of the Constitution, our history shows that there was a widespread awareness among many Americans of the dangers of a union of Church and State." The writing of a prayer by government officials ran counter to this long-standing struggle in the United States.

The Court rejected the argument that the school-prayer law did not violate any rights because it did not require students to recite the prayer and the prayer was nondenominational. The Court argued that this confused the right of free exercise of religion with the prohibition against the state establishing and supporting religion. Excusing students from reciting the prayer might protect their free exercise of religion, but the very existence of the prayer involved the establishment of religion. In the words of the Court, "The Establishment Clause, unlike the Free Exercise Clause, does not depend upon any showing of direct governmental compulsion and is violated by the enactment of laws which establish an official religion whether those laws operate directly to coerce nonobserving individuals or not."

In 1963, the Court applied the same reasoning to the issue of Bible reading in the public schools. In *Abington School District v. Schempp*, the issue was a

Pennsylvania law that permitted the reading of 10 verses from the Bible at the opening of each public school day. The verses were to be read without comment, and any child could be excused from reading the verses or attending the Bible reading, upon the written request of the parents or guardians. Like the school-prayer issue, the Court felt that a Bible-reading service of this type involved the state in the establishment of religion. The Court made it clear that it did not reject the idea of Bible reading as a part of a study of comparative religion or the history of religion. Nor did the Court exclude the possibility of studying the Bible as a piece of literature. What the Court objected to was the reading of the Bible as part of a religious exercise.

The courts are somewhat ambivalent on the issue of meditation in schools. Massachusetts passed a law requiring a moment of silence "for meditation or prayer" in public schools. Here, the Court said that meditation could refer to any subject because the law used the word *or,* which inferred a secular intent for meditation. Therefore, a student might be expected to meditate on anything, including schoolwork or family life. In this situation, the law was not violating the Establishment Clause.

A Louisiana law allowing meditation was struck down as a violation of the Establishment Clause. Here, the law included the permission for teachers to ask students if they were interested in praying. An Alabama law allowing for meditation or voluntary prayer and for teachers to lead classes in prayer was also ruled as violating the Establishment Clause. The argument then was that the law lacked a secular purpose and that it was intended to support school prayers.

In 2000, the U.S. District Court in Alexandria, Virginia, ruled that the state's law requiring students to observe a "minute of silence" did not violate the ban on government-established religion. During the minute of silence, students are allowed to "meditate, pray, or engage in any other silent activity."

The test in all these cases is whether the intent is secular or religious. If the intention is religious, then it is a violation of the Establishment Clause.

STUDENT PRAYERS

In 1992, the U.S. Supreme Court, in a dispute originating over prayers given by a rabbi at a middle-school graduation in Providence, Rhode Island, ruled that prayers conducted at a public school graduation were unconstitutional. Writing for the majority of the Court in *Lee v. Weisman,* Supreme Court Justice Anthony Kennedy declared:

> The Constitution forbids the state to exact religious conformity from a student as the price of attending her own high school graduation. No holding by this Court suggests that a school can persuade or compel a student to participate in a religious exercise. That is being done here, and it is forbidden by the Establishment Clause of the First Amendment.

Student-led graduation prayers were also declared unconstitutional by the U.S. Court of Appeals in 1996. The case involved a 1993 graduation exercise at

New Jersey's Highland Regional High School. Before the graduation ceremony, a majority of seniors voted to have a graduation prayer. A student sued and won an injunction against the prayer. The Appeals Court argued that the religious rights of students who did not want a prayer could not be compromised by a majority vote.

On the other hand, an Appeals Court ruling in 1998 approved the Madison school district of Rexburg, Idaho, policy of allowing the top four graduating seniors to speak on any topic including the reciting of prayers and singing of religious songs. In *Doe v. Madison*, the U.S. Court of Appeals for the Ninth Circuit Court argued that in this case the control of religious content was in the hands of the individual student as opposed to the school. The Appeals Court cited the following factors:

- Students and not clergy delivered the prayers.
- Student speakers were selected on academic standing.
- School officials allowed the students to choose the content of their speeches.

In 1996, the U.S. Supreme Court let stand a ruling barring voluntary student prayers during school events. At issue was a 1994 Mississippi law allowing "nonsectarian, nonproselytizing student-initiated voluntary prayer" during student events. The Mississippi state legislature passed the law in protest of the firing of a Jackson, Mississippi, high school principal. The principal, Bishop Knox, allowed students to pray over the school's intercom. "A state policy of prayer at school," states the Fifth Circuit Court ruling upheld by the Supreme Court, "tells students that the state wants them to pray. The school-prayer statute is an unconstitutional endorsement of religion." This decision was upheld in 1998, when the U.S. Supreme Court rejected an appeal by Governor Fob James, Jr., of Alabama, who sought to restore the right to student-led prayers in Alabama schools.

Do religious groups have the right to use public school facilities for religious services? New York City allows the rental of schools for community activities including religious discussion. It does not allow their use for religious services. A coalition of Christian and Jewish religious groups sued demanding equal access to public schools for conducting religious ceremonies. In 1998, the U.S. Supreme Court, by rejecting an appeal of a decision by the U.S. Court of Appeals for the Second Circuit, let stand a decision that public schools are limited forums rather than public forums. It is difficult to limit free speech in public forums, such as on sidewalks or in parks. However, they argued, public schools are limited forums and, therefore, school officials can limit free speech for the purpose of not being identified with a particular religious service.

In 2000, the U.S. Supreme Court ruled that student-led prayers at football games violated the Establishment Clause. In this situation, the Santa Fe, Texas, school district authorized a student vote on whether to have a prayer before football games. The U.S. Supreme Court ruled that this amounted to district sponsorship of a religious activity.

SCHOOL PRAYER AND THE NO CHILD LEFT BEHIND ACT OF 2001

A special section of the No Child Left Behind Act of 2001 titled "School Prayer" gives the U.S. Department of Education an active role in ensuring that school districts allow for school prayer within the boundaries of the law. The legislation orders the U.S. Secretary of Education to provide guidance in writing and on the Internet to local schools "on constitutionally protected prayer in public elementary schools and secondary schools."

More importantly, under this legislation, local school districts must certify in writing "no policy of the local educational agency prevents, or otherwise denies participation in, constitutionally protected prayer in public elementary schools and secondary schools." Consequently, this legislation directly involves the federal government in monitoring prayer issues in local school districts.

SECULAR HUMANISM AND THE RELIGION OF PUBLIC SCHOOLS

An interesting set of court cases in the 1970s and 1980s involved claims that the public schools taught a religion, **secular humanism**, which could be a violation of the rights of those not subscribing to secular-humanist values. The issue arose over state regulation of private schools. During the latter part of the 1970s and into the 1980s, the fastest-growing private schools were those identified as Christian. These were usually associated with a fundamentalist Christian organization. At first, people outside the movement assumed the growth of Christian schools was a result of white flight from desegregated school systems. But when Christian schools began to multiply in rural areas of Wisconsin and Alaska, where segregation was not an issue, it became evident that the movement was a result of strongly held religious values.

Problems began in the Christian school movement when state authorities demanded that the schools conform to state minimum educational standards. Most state minimum standards are not a small list of requirements but a vast set of statutes and regulations covering everything from the design of the water fountain to the curriculum. Christian schools did not have any problems with regulations related to the safety of school buildings, but they did object to curriculum requirements that interfered with the Christian objectives of their schools.

Of primary concern were state regulations that required the schools to teach ethical values that the Christian schools called secular humanism. The simplest definition of secular humanism is that it comprises a set of ethical standards that places primary emphasis on a person's ability to interpret and guide his or her own moral actions. This is against the Christian fundamentalist viewpoint, which holds that the sources of ethical and moral values should be the Bible and God. Secular humanism relies on the authority of human beings, while Christian fundamentalism relies on the authority of the Scriptures.

One of the earliest and most famous cases dealing with the issue was decided by the Ohio Supreme Court in 1976 in *State v. Whisner.* The case originated when Levi Whisner opened the doors of the Tabernacle Christian School in Bradford, Ohio, in 1973. The issue for Pastor Whisner was not whether the school met minimum state standards, but whether he should even apply for a charter from the state. Keep in mind the fact that compulsory-education laws in most states require attendance at a school approved by the state. If the student does not attend an approved school, the student can be considered truant and the parents and student can be held liable for the truancy.

James Carper of Tulane University reported in a paper delivered at the 1980 meeting of the American Educational Studies Association that after reading the 149-page *Minimum Standards for Ohio Elementary Schools, Revised 1970,* "Whisner and the governing board of the school concluded that as a matter of religious principle they could not conform to all of the standards and, therefore, decided not to initiate the prescribed procedures for obtaining a charter." The consequence of that action was immediately felt by the parents and their children when, within a month of the school's opening, the local probation officer sent out letters informing the parents that if their children did not attend a school that met minimum standards, a complaint against the parents would be filed in the local juvenile court. In November, two months after the opening of the school, 15 parents were indicted by the county prosecutor's office for not sending their children to school. After some negotiation, the trial date was set for 7 May 1974. Professor Carper wrote: "The trial court proceedings revealed again that to the state the primary issue was the noncompliance with state law while the defendants believed that free exercise of religion was at the heart of the matter." One point revealed in the first trial was that the Ohio Department of Education required total compliance with state minimum standards and that one of those standards was a written statement of philosophy of education. The interesting question raised by this standard was how conflicts between a school's statement of philosophy and other department standards would be resolved. It was revealed during the trial that "if the statement of a school's philosophy of education, a mandated standard, ran counter to other minimum standards and made it impossible fully to embrace them, the department would not approve the school."

In August 1974, the trial court found the 15 parents guilty; after an appeal, the Supreme Court of Ohio agreed to hear the case in October 1975. On 28 July 1976, the Supreme Court of Ohio reversed the lower court's decision and argued that Pastor Whisner and the appellants had "sustained their burden of establishing that the 'minimum standards' infringe upon the right guaranteed them by the First Amendment to the Constitution of the United States, and by Section 7 of the Ohio Constitution, to the free exercise of religion."

This decision gave legal recognition to the argument that the state minimum standards did require the teaching of a philosophy, secular humanism, which differed from the religious values of the appellants. To understand this conflict it is best to review some specific points in the state's minimum standards objected to by Pastor Whisner.

Alan Grover, in his book *Ohio's Trojan Horse: A Warning to Christian Schools Everywhere,* provides a detailed summary. For our purposes, I will deal with only a few of these objections, for highlighting the issue of secular humanism. In Grover's words, "The 'Minimum Standards' philosophy points to the wisdom and self-sufficiency of man in finding solutions to all of society's problems." This, of course, is contrary to the belief that humans need the Scriptures and God to deal with social problems. As examples of the Ohio minimum standards' emphasis on the wisdom and self-sufficiency of humans, Grover cited the following statements from the standards:

> Problems are solved by group discussion and decisions. Man's comprehension of the present and his wisdom in planning for the future depend upon his understanding of the events of the past and of the various forces and agencies in society that influence the present. Through all time and in all regions of the world, man has worked to meet common basic human needs and to satisfy common human desires and aspirations. The health of the child is perhaps the greatest single factor in the development of a well-rounded personality. [The objection to this is the belief that the spiritual condition of the individual is more important.]

What should be remembered is that the state required compliance with *all* standards and, consequently, Pastor Whisner considered compliance a violation of his religious beliefs. This case has opened the door to similar cases in other states and has made it possible to argue that compulsory attendance at a public school might be a violation of religious freedom. And it was certainly clear in the mind of Pastor Whisner that the public schools taught the religion of secular humanism.

A 1987 ruling by the Eleventh Circuit Court of Appeals brushed aside parental claims that 45 books approved for Alabama schools taught secular humanism. Alabama's Governor George Wallace supported the parents in declaring, "I don't want to teach ungodly humanism in the schools where I'm governor." The case required the plaintiffs to prove that secular humanism was a religion and that secular humanism was being imposed on children in public schools. Testimony was presented in the trial that teaching independent thinking regarding moral issues was a religious position and, therefore, violated the Establishment Clause. Initially, Judge Brevard Hand ruled that secular humanism was indeed a religion and books based on secular humanism should be removed from the schools but Judge Hand's decision was reversed by the Eleventh Circuit Court of Appeals. The Appeals Court ruled that the books did not violate the Establishment Clause. The court stated:

> Rather the message [in the books] is one of a governmental attempt to instill in Alabama public school children such values as independent thought, tolerance of diverse views, self-respect, maturity, self-reliance, and logical decision-making. This is an entirely appropriate secular effect.

EVOLUTION AND CREATIONISM

Evolution theory challenges a basic premise of many religions about the creation of life. Some Christians believe evolutionary arguments deny the divine authority of the Bible. In March 1996, presidential candidate Pat Buchanan told ABC, "I think [parents] have a right to insist that Godless evolution not be taught to their children or their children not be indoctrinated in it." Antievolutionists are pressing for public school science courses to expose students to creationism along with evolutionary theory. Creationism maintains that humans did not evolve but were created as part of an intelligent design of the Universe. Creationist ideas are also called abrupt appearance theory or intelligent design theory.

In 1982, the Louisiana legislature passed a law requiring that any public school teaching evolution must give equal time to explaining creationism. The Creationism Act did not require the teaching of either theory unless the other was taught. The legislation defined theories as "the scientific evidences for [creation or evolution] and inferences from those scientific evidences."

In 1987, the U.S. Supreme Court in *Edwards v. Aguillard* declared the legislation unconstitutional. In the majority opinion, Justice William Brennan, Jr., wrote, "The Act impermissibly endorses religion by advancing the religious belief that a supernatural being created humankind. The legislative history proves that the term 'creation science,' as contemplated by the state legislature, embraces this religious teaching."

Applying the *Lemon* test to the legislation, the U.S. Supreme Court found that the Creationism Act did have a religious intent. Justice Brennan argued, "Teaching a variety of scientific theories about the origins of humankind to schoolchildren might be validly done with the clear secular intent of enhancing the effectiveness of science instruction. But because the primary purpose of the Creationism Act is to endorse a particular religious doctrine, the Act furthers religion, violating the Establishment Clause."

PARENTS' RIGHTS

Debates over censorship, secular humanism, and evolution highlight the issue of parents' rights. Do parents have the right to protect their children from exposure to school services and educational materials that the parents consider objectionable? In 1989, Jason Newkirk's father refused permission for his son to receive school counseling. Authorities in an East Lansing, Michigan, school district found Jason had difficulty interacting with other children and sent him to see a school counselor. The parents claimed the psychological tests administered during counseling caused Jason to have panic attacks and separation-anxiety disorder. The Newkirks sued, contending their parental rights were violated because the school acted without their permission. A federal district court rejected their arguments. In 1995, the U.S. Supreme Court, by declining to review the case, let the lower-court decision stand.

In 1991, the Falmouth, Massachusetts, school district adopted a policy of making condoms available to junior and senior high school students. The school nurse distributed the condoms along with AIDS-prevention pamphlets. Condom vending machines were placed in high school restrooms. Some parents protested the policy contending that their constitutional rights to direct their children's upbringing were violated; they also argued that the policy was a violation of the Free Exercise clause.

Ruling against the parents, the Supreme Judicial Court of Massachusetts maintained, "Parents have no right to tailor public school programs to meet their individual religious and moral preferences." The court argued that students were not compelled to accept a condom and that the parents could instruct their children not to accept condoms. In 1996, the U.S. Supreme Court rejected the parents' appeal.

The Chelmsford, Massachusetts, High School required students to attend an AIDS-prevention assembly featuring comic Suzanne Landolphi of the Hot, Sexy and Safer Productions. Two parents sued claiming they were not given an opportunity to remove their children from the assembly. They lost the case in the federal district court and in the U.S. Court of Appeals for the First Circuit. The U.S. Supreme Court rejected the parents' appeal on 4 March 1996.

The U.S. Court of Appeals' written decision in the Chelmsford High School case reflects the general policy of courts to deny parental control of the public school curriculum. The Appeals Court stated:

> If all parents had a fundamental constitutional right to dictate individually what the schools teach their children, the schools would be forced to cater a curriculum for each student whose parents had genuine moral disagreements with the school's choice of subject matter.

TEACHERS' RIGHTS

During the nineteenth and early twentieth centuries, schoolteachers were expected to be models of purity. Pressure was placed on teachers to be circumspect outside the school regarding dress, speech, religion, and types of friends. Within the school, a teacher's freedom of speech was abridged at the whim of the school administrator. Some school administrators allowed teachers to discuss controversial topics freely within the classrooms; others fired teachers who spoke of things within the classroom that were not approved by the administration. Very often, teachers were fired for their political beliefs and activities.

During the last several decades, court actions, the activities of teachers' associations, and state laws granting teachers tenure expanded academic freedom in the public schools and protected the free speech of teachers. The expansion of academic freedom in the United States first took place at the college level and later in elementary and secondary schools. The concept of academic freedom was brought to the United States in the latter part of the nineteenth century by scholars who received their training in Germany. The basic argument for academic freedom was that if scientific research were to advance civilization, scholars had to be free to do research and to lecture on anything they felt was important. The advancement of science depended on free inquiry. In Germany this was accomplished by appointing individuals to professorships for life.

The concept of academic freedom was not immediately accepted in institutions of higher education in the United States. Many professors were fired in the late nineteenth and early twentieth centuries for investigating certain economic problems and for backing reforms such as child labor laws. College professors found it necessary to organize the American Association of University Professors (AAUP) to fight for academic freedom. The major protection of academic freedom in American universities is provided by tenure. The idea behind tenure is that after individuals prove they are competent as teachers and scholars, they are guaranteed a position until retirement, if they do not commit some major act of misconduct.

Tenure and academic freedom are supported by the NEA and AFT as ways of protecting the free speech of public school teachers. Many states adopted tenure laws for the express purpose of protecting the rights of teachers. Court decisions also played an important role in extending academic freedom. But there are major differences between the way academic freedom functions at the university level and how it functions at the secondary and elementary levels. The organizational nature of public schools and the age of children in them places some important limitations on the extent of teachers' academic freedom.

Before they teach in the public schools, teachers must understand their rights and the limitations of their rights. There are three major types of rights about which teachers must be concerned. The first deals with the rights and limitations of speech and conduct of teachers in relationship to administrators and school boards. The second deals with rights and limitations of the speech of teachers in the classroom. And the third deals with the rights of teachers outside the school.

The most important U.S. Supreme Court decision dealing with the rights of teachers in relationship to school boards and administrators is *Pickering v. Board of Education of Township High School* (1967). The case involved an Illinois schoolteacher who was dismissed for writing a letter to the local school board criticizing the district superintendent and school board for the methods being used to raise money for the schools. The letter specifically attacked the way money was being allocated among academic and athletic programs and stated that the superintendent was attempting to keep teachers from criticizing the proposed bond issue. In Court it was proved that there were factually incorrect statements in the letter.

The U.S. Supreme Court ruled that teachers could not be dismissed for public criticism of their school system. In fact, the Court argued in *Pickering:* "Teachers are, as a class, the members of a community most likely to have informed and definite opinions how funds allotted to the operation of the schools should be spent. Accordingly, it is essential that they can speak out freely on such questions without fear of retaliatory dismissal." Here, the participation of teachers in free and open debate on questions put to popular vote was considered "vital to informed decision making by the electorate."

The Court did not consider the factual errors in the public criticism grounds for dismissal; it did not find that erroneous public statements in any way interfered with the teacher's performance of daily classroom activities or hindered the regular operation of the school. "In these circumstances," the Court stated, "we conclude that the interest of the school administration in limiting teachers' opportunities to contribute to public debate is not significantly greater than its interest in limiting a similar contribution by any member of the general public."

The *Pickering* decision did place some important limitations on the rights of teachers to criticize their school system. The major limitation was on the right to criticize publicly immediate superiors in the school system. In the words of the Court, immediate superiors were those whom the teacher "would normally be in contact with in the course of his daily work." The Court, however, did not consider the teacher's employment relationship to the board of education or superintendent to be a close working relationship. One could imply from the decision that teachers could be dismissed for public criticism of their immediate supervisor or building principal. But what was meant by close working relationship was not clearly defined in the decision. The Court stated in a footnote: "Positions in public employment in which the relationship between superior and subordinate is of such a personal and intimate nature that certain forms of public criticism of the superior by the subordinate would seriously undermine the effectiveness of the working relationship between them can also be imagined."

There is a possible procedural limitation on a teacher's right to criticize a school system if the school system has a grievance procedure. This issue is dealt with in a very important book on teachers' rights published under the sponsorship of the American Civil Liberties Union (ACLU). The question is asked in David Rubin's *The Rights of Teachers:* "Does a teacher have the right to complain publicly about the operation of his school system even if a grievance procedure exists for processing such complaints?" The answer given by this ACLU handbook is "probably not." The handbook states that this issue has not been clarified by the courts, but there have been suggestions in court decisions that if a formal grievance procedure exists within the school system, a teacher must exhaust these procedures before making any public statements.

The Rights of Teachers also argues that a teacher is protected by the Constitution against dismissal for bringing problems in the school system to the attention of superiors. But, again, the teacher must first exhaust all grievance procedures. The example in the ACLU handbook was of a superintendent who dismissed a teacher because her second grade class wrote a letter to the cafeteria supervisor asking that raw carrots be served rather than cooked carrots, because of the higher nutritional value of the raw vegetable. In addition, when the drinking fountain went unrepaired in her classroom, her students drew pictures of wilted flowers and of children begging for water, and presented them to the principal. The ACLU handbook states that the Court decision found "the school policy was arbitrary and unreasonable and in violation of . . . First and Fourteenth Amendment rights of free speech and freedom peaceably to petition for redress of grievances."

Concerning freedom of speech in the classroom, one of the most important things for public elementary and secondary teachers to know is that the courts seem to recognize certain limitations. The three things that the courts consider are whether the material used in the classroom and the statements made by the teacher are appropriate for the age of the students, related to the curriculum for the course, and approved by other members of the profession.

An example of the courts considering the age of students, given by the ACLU in *The Rights of Teachers,* is a case in Alabama where a high school teacher had been dismissed for assigning Kurt Vonnegut's "Welcome to the Monkey House" to her eleventh grade English class. The principal and associate superintendent of the school called the story "literary garbage," and several disgruntled parents complained to the school. School officials told the teacher not to use the story in class. The teacher responded that she thought the story was a good literary work and felt she had a professional obligation to use the story in class. The school system dismissed her for insubordination. The first question asked by the Court was whether the story was appropriate reading material for eleventh grade students. In its final decision, the Court found that the teacher's dismissal was a denial of First Amendment rights, since it had not been proved that the material was inappropriate for the grade level or that the story disrupted the educational processes of the school.

Another important issue is whether the classroom statements of a teacher are related to the subject matter being taught. One example given in *The Rights of Teachers* is of a teacher of a basic English class making statements about the Vietnam War and anti-Semitism, although the lessons dealt with language instruction. The Court found that his remarks had minimum relevance to the material being taught but might have been appropriate in courses such as current events and political science. What is important for teachers to know is that their freedom of speech in the classroom is limited by the curriculum and subject being taught.

Whether the method used by the teacher is considered appropriate by other members of the teaching profession might be another consideration of the courts. In a case in Massachusetts, an eleventh grade English teacher wrote an example of a taboo word on the board and asked the class for a socially acceptable definition. The teacher was dismissed for conduct unbecoming a teacher. The teacher went to court and argued that taboo words are an important topic in the curriculum and that eleventh grade boys and girls are old enough to deal with the material. The ACLU handbook states that the Court ruled that a teacher could be dismissed for using in good faith a teaching method "if he does not prove that it has the support of the preponderant opinion of the teaching profession or of the part of which he belongs."

In addition, officially stated school policies can limit the free speech of teachers in a classroom. A 1998 Colorado Supreme Court decision involved school regulations requiring teachers to get the principal's approval before using controversial materials in the classroom. A Jefferson County, Colorado, schoolteacher failed to get approval before showing the Bernardo Bertolucci film *1900* to his high school logic and debate class. The Colorado court upheld the firing of the teacher because the film depicted "full frontal nudity, oral sex, masturbation, profanity, cocaine abuse, and graphic violence." These scenes, according to the court, clearly fell under the school district's controversial-materials policy.

In another case, Cecil Lacks, a Missouri high school teacher, was fired for not complying with the school district's policy prohibiting profane language. She allowed students to use street language in writing plays and poetry dealing with sex, teenage pregnancy, gangs, and drugs. Other teachers defended her methods as being student-centered but the Eighth District Circuit Court supported the school district's firing of Lacks because she had willfully violated school board policies against the use of profane language in school.

Besides the question of academic freedom regarding curriculum and instruction, there is the issue of teachers' freedom of conscience. For instance, a New York high school teacher was dismissed from her job for refusing to participate in a daily flag ceremony. The teacher stood silently while a fellow teacher conducted the ceremony. In *Russo v. Central School District No. 1* (1972), a federal circuit court ruled in favor of the teacher. The U.S. Supreme Court refused to review the case and, therefore, the circuit court decision was allowed to stand. The circuit court ruled that the teacher's actions were a matter of conscience and not disloyalty.

Although teachers do not have to participate in flag ceremonies or say the Pledge of Allegiance if it is a violation of their conscience, they cannot refuse to follow the curriculum of a school because of religious and personal beliefs. In *Palmer v. Board of Education* (1979), the U.S. Court of Appeals decided, and the decision was later upheld by the U.S. Supreme Court, that the Chicago public schools had the right to fire a teacher for refusing to follow the curriculum because of religious reasons. The teacher was a Jehovah's Witness and she informed her principal that because of her religious beliefs she refused "to teach any subjects having to do with love of country, the flag or other patriotic matters in the prescribed curriculum." The court declared, "The First Amendment was not a teacher license for uncontrolled expression at variance with established curricular content."

Can school districts require urine testing of teachers? In 1998, the U.S. Court of Appeals for the Fifth District struck down two Louisiana school districts' drug policies on testing teachers. The court argued that there has to be some identified problem of drug abuse before requiring tests. The ruling stated, "Despite hints of the school boards, the testing here does not respond to any identified problem of drug use by teachers or their teachers' aides or clerical workers."

In summary, teachers do not lose their constitutional rights when they enter the classroom, but their employment does put certain limitations on those rights. Important is the requirement that teachers follow the prescribed curriculum of the school. In addition, they must comply with any school policies regarding controversial materials and profane speech. Teachers have freedom of speech in the classroom if their comments are related to the curriculum but when exercising the right to freedom of speech, teachers must consider whether their comments are appropriate for the age of the students and would be considered appropriate by other educational professionals. While teachers are required to follow a prescribed curriculum, they do not have to participate in flag ceremonies and other political ceremonies if it is a violation of their personal beliefs.

TEACHERS' LIABILITY

Is a teacher liable for monetary damages if a student is seriously injured by rocks thrown by another student? The answer in some situations is yes! In this example, Margaret Sheehan, an eighth-grade student, was taken along with other female students by her teacher to an athletic field. The teacher told the students to sit on a log while she returned to school. During her absence, a group of boys began throwing rocks at the girls, resulting in serious injury to Margaret's eye. In *Sheehan v. St. Peter's Catholic School* (1971), the Minnesota Supreme Court declared: "It is the duty of a school to use ordinary care and to protect its students from injury resulting from the conduct of other students under circumstances where such conduct would reasonably have been foreseen and could have been prevented by the use of ordinary care."

In *Teachers and the Law*, Louis Fischer, David Schimmel, and Cynthia Kelly state that teachers can be held liable for student injuries under the following conditions:

1. Teachers injure the student or do not protect the student from injury.
2. Teachers do not use due care.
3. Teachers' carelessness results in student injury.
4. Students sustained provable injuries.

The issue of teacher liability for student injuries is extremely important because of the potential for the teacher being sued for monetary damages. To protect themselves in these types of situations, teachers should carry some form of professional liability insurance. Often, this insurance coverage is provided by teachers' unions. In some cases, teachers might want to contact their insurance agents about coverage.

Now consider whether school districts should be liable for a teacher's sexual harassment of a student. In a small Texas school district, a high school teacher was fired after district officials discovered he was having an affair with one of his students. The student, Alida Gebser, testified that the teacher, Frank Walrop, began giving her special attention in 1991 when, as a 14-year-old, she attended an after-school Great Books discussion group. She stated that the 52-year-old teacher acted as a mentor; however, she became "terrified" when he made sexual advances. The following year, the teacher and student began having sexual relations until the police discovered them having sex in a wooded area. The teacher was barred from school and lost his state teaching certificate. The student and her mother sued the school district. The plaintiffs argued before the U.S. Supreme Court that the school district was responsible for the conduct of the teacher and that they should be awarded monetary damages under Title IX, which prohibits discrimination based on sex in any school receiving federal funds. Ruling that the school district was not liable in *Gebser v. Lago Vista Independent School District* (1998), Justice Sandra Day O'Connor stated in the majority opinion that school officials are liable only if they have "actual knowledge of discrimination . . . and fail adequately to respond."

Can gay or lesbian teachers inform students of their sexual orientation? In 1998, U.S. District Judge Bruce Jenkins ruled that Wendy Weaver could not be fired from coaching high school volleyball because she answered yes when asked by a student, "Are you gay?" The judge said her free speech and equal protection rights were violated. "Although the Constitution cannot control prejudices, neither this court nor any other court should, directly or indirectly, legitimize them," Judge Jenkins stated.

TEACHERS' PRIVATE LIVES

Another concern is teachers' activity outside the school. A controversial issue is whether a teacher's membership in a radical political organization is grounds for dismissal or denial of employment. The two most important U.S. Supreme Court decisions on this issue both originated in cases resulting from New York's Feinberg Law. The Feinberg Law was adopted in New York in 1949, during a period of hysteria about possible communist infiltration of public schools. The law ordered the New York Board of Regents to compile a list of organizations that taught or advocated the overthrow of the U.S. government by force or violence. The law authorized the board of regents to give notice that membership in any organization on the list would disqualify any person from membership or retention in any office or position in the school system.

The first decision concerning the Feinberg Law was given by the U.S. Supreme Court in *Adler v. Board of Education of New York* (1952). This ruling upheld the right of the state of New York to use membership in particular organizations as a basis for not hiring and for dismissal. The Court argued that New York had the right to establish reasonable terms for employment in its school system. The Court also recognized the right of a school system to screen its employees carefully because, as stated by the Court, "A teacher works in a sensitive area in a schoolroom. There he shapes the attitude of young minds toward the society in which they live. In this, the state has a vital concern." The Court went on to state that not only did schools have the right to screen employees concerning professional qualifications, but also "the state may very properly inquire into the company they keep, and we know of no rule, constitutional or otherwise, that prevents the state, when determining the fitness and loyalty . . . from considering the organizations and persons with whom they associate."

The *Adler* decision underwent major modification when the Feinberg Law again came before the U.S. Supreme Court 15 years later in *Keyishian v. Board of Regents of New York* (1967). Here a teacher at the State University of New York at Buffalo refused to state in writing that he was not a communist. This time the Court decision declared the Feinberg Law unconstitutional. The reasoning of the Court was that membership in an organization did not mean that an individual subscribed to all the goals of the organization. The Court stated: "A law that applies to membership, without the specific intent to further the illegal aims of the organization, infringes unnecessarily on protected freedoms. It rests on the doctrine of guilt by association which has no place here."

The *Keyishian* decision did not deny the right of school systems to screen employees or to dismiss them if they personally advocated the overthrow of the U.S. government. What the *Keyishian* decision meant was that mere membership in an organization could not be the basis for denial of employment or for dismissal.

Whether a teacher's private life can be a basis for dismissal from a school system has not been clearly defined by the U.S. Supreme Court. The ACLU argues in *The Rights of Teachers* that courts are increasingly reluctant to uphold the right of school authorities to dismiss teachers because they disapprove of a teacher's private life. Examples given by the ACLU include an Ohio court ruling that a teacher could not be dismissed for using offensive language in a confidential letter to a former student. The Ohio court ruled that a teacher's private actions are not the concern of school authorities unless they interfere with the ability to teach. The California Supreme Court ruled that a teacher could not be dismissed because of a homosexual relationship with another teacher. The court could not find that the relationship hindered the ability to teach.

It would appear that the major concern of the courts is whether teachers' private lives interfere with their professional conduct as teachers. But the difficulty of establishing precise relationships between private actions and ability to teach allows for broad interpretation by different courts and school authorities. Teachers should be aware that there are no precise guidelines in this area. The best protection for teachers is to develop some form of agreement between their teachers' organization and their school district regarding the use of private actions as a basis for dismissal and evaluation.

One limiting condition applied by the U.S. Supreme Court is that teachers' and students' actions cannot interfere with normal school activities. For instance, in *Board of Education v. James* (1972), the U.S. Supreme Court upheld a lower-court ruling that a teacher could not be dismissed for wearing an armband in class as a protest against the Vietnam War. The lower court reasoned that the wearing of the armband did not disrupt classroom activities and, therefore, there was no reason for school authorities to limit a teacher's freedom of expression.

THE LANGUAGE OF THE SCHOOLS

Court rulings are quite clear that the primary task of the schools is to teach standard English and that other languages and black English are to be used as a means to achieve that goal. On the other hand, schools must provide special help to students who have limited use of English. The landmark case is the 1974 U.S. Supreme Court decision in *Lau et al. v. Nichols et al.* The case was a class-action suit brought for non-English-speaking Chinese students in the San Francisco school district. The complaint was that no special instruction for learning standard English was provided to these students. The complaint did not ask for any specific instructional methods to remedy this situation. In the words of the Court decision: "Teaching English to the students of Chinese ancestry who do not speak the language is one choice. Giving instructions to this group in Chinese is another. There may be others." This point created a good deal of controversy in 1980, when the federal government issued regulations for a specific remedy to *Lau*. It was argued that specific remedies were not defined under the *Lau* decision. Those regulations were withdrawn in 1981.

The claim in *Lau* was that the lack of special instruction to help non-English-speaking students learn standard English provided unequal educational opportunity and therefore violated the Fourteenth Amendment to the Constitution. The Court did not use the Fourteenth Amendment in its ruling, but relied on Title VI of the 1964 Civil Rights Act. This law bans discrimination based on "race, color, or national origin" in "any program or activity receiving Federal financial assistance." The Supreme Court ruled: "It seems obvious that the Chinese-speaking minority receives fewer benefits than the English-speaking majority from the respondents' school system that denies them a meaningful opportunity to participate in the educational program—all earmarks of the discrimination banned by the regulations." Although the Court did not give a specific remedy to the situation, its ruling meant that all public school systems receiving any form of federal aid must ensure that children from non-English-speaking backgrounds be given some form of special help in learning standard English so that they may have equal educational opportunity.

The problem that was not addressed in *Lau* was that of specific remedies for the situation of children from non-standard-English backgrounds. A decision regarding this issue was made by the U.S. District Court in 1979 in *Martin Luther King Junior Elementary School Children et al. v. Ann Arbor School District*. The court was quite clear that the case was "not an effort on the part of the plaintiffs to require that they be taught 'black English' or that a dual language program be provided." As the court defined the problem, it was the ability to teach standard English to "children who, it is alleged, speak 'black English' as a matter of course at home and in their home community." The plaintiffs introduced into the case the testimony of expert witnesses who argued that attempts to teach standard English without appreciating the dialect used by the children at home and in the community could cause the children to be ashamed of their language and hinder their ability to learn standard English.

The court gave recognition to the existence of a bilingual culture within the African American community, in which individuals would speak African American English with peers and standard English with the larger community. In the words of the court, the African American children "retain fluency in 'black English' to maintain status in the community and they become fluent in standard English to succeed in the general society."

After reviewing the evidence and the expert testimony, the court argued that there was a possible relationship between poor reading ability and the school's not taking into account the home language of the children. This prevented children from taking full advantage of their schooling and was a denial of equal educational opportunity. This argument was based on the reasonable premise that knowing how to read was one of the most important factors in achievement in school.

The court gave a very specific remedy to the situation, a remedy that might be used as a guide in future cases. The court directed the school system to develop within 30 days a plan that would "identify children speaking 'black English' and the language spoken as a home or community language." Second, the school system was directed to "use that knowledge in teaching such students how to read standard English." The language of the school is one aspect of providing equal educational opportunity. Another aspect is equality of funding of schools.

SCHOOL FINANCES

Equalizing school finances is an important step in providing equal educational opportunity. The problem is that how much money spent per public school student varies between school districts because of differences in local property taxes. There are differences between school districts in the value of the property to be taxed and the amount a community is willing to tax its property. For instance, some communities have several large industries and expensive residential and commercial areas that can be taxed for support of schools. Other communities are composed of modest residential areas and do not have any large industries. Both communities might levy equal taxes. This would not result in equal revenue, due to the unequal value of property in the two communities. This could mean, for instance, that a homeowner in one community could pay the same amount of taxes on a house as a homeowner with a house of the same value in another community, but very different sums might be spent on the education of their children because of the disparity in total value of property between the two communities.

The disparities that exist between school systems in the same state is illustrated in a report in the 5 March 1990 issue of *The New York Times,* which compared the schools of East Orange and Millburn, New Jersey. Millburn spends \$6,247 on each schoolchild while East Orange spends \$4,867. The difference in per-pupil expenditures is almost \$1,400 and reflects differences in property values. Millburn is a community of spacious homes and quaint country lanes. In 1988, the median sales price of a home in Millburn was \$370,000. On the other hand, East Orange is an urban school district with a median sales price for a home in 1988 of \$80,000.

The differences in school expenditures are evident in both systems. When Scott High School in East Orange needed a new library, a gymnasium was converted. Millburn built a new high school library in a large courtyard. East Orange's teachers average 14 years' experience and earn \$35,000 a year. Millburn's teachers average 20 years' experience and earn \$41,520 a year. The pupil-teacher ratio in East Orange averages 27 to 1, while in Millburn it is 18 to 1. Millburn offers 14 advanced-placement courses; East Orange offers none. *The New York Times* explained that Millburn High has plenty of classroom space, but

> Scott High [East Orange], built here 52 years ago for 800 students, is bulging now with 1,200. The other day, Deborah Mayes's American history class was squeezed into the music room, next to the piano. Ester Lundy was teaching a

first-year business course in the typing room as her students tried to balance their open texts atop typewriters.

The first major judicial decision dealing with school finances was made by the California Supreme Court in *Serrano v. Priest* (1971). This case involved the two sons of John Serrano, who lived in a poor, mainly Mexican American, community in Los Angeles. The local school in the area had rapidly increasing class sizes and a consequent shortage of textbooks and supplies. Local school authorities told John Serrano that the financial situation in the schools would not improve. According to Charles Tesconi and Emanuel Hurwitz in their book, *Education for Whom?,* the family was forced to mortgage their property and move to another community to provide a better education for the two sons.

The case presented before the California Supreme Court put the situation of the Serrano family in the following terms: "Plaintiffs contend that the school financing system classifies on the basis of wealth. We find this proposition irrefutable. . . ." The court went on to assert that this was a direct result of the method of financing the schools. The example given by the court: "Baldwin Park citizens, who paid a school tax of $5.48 per $100 of assessed valuation, were able to spend less than half as much on education as Beverly Hills residents, who were taxed only $2.38 per $100."

The California Supreme Court ruled in the *Serrano* case that the California school financing system, with its dependence upon local property taxes, violated the Equal Protection Clause of the Fourteenth Amendment. The court stated: "We have determined that this funding scheme invidiously discriminates against the poor because it makes the quality of a child's education a function of the wealth of his parents and his neighbors."

Serrano was a landmark decision for action within state court systems. When the issue finally reached the U.S. Supreme Court, a major setback in the legal struggles occurred. In 1973 the Supreme Court ruled in one school financing case, *Rodriguez v. San Antonio Independent School District,* that the right to an education was not implicitly protected by the Fourteenth Amendment and was not entitled to constitutional protection. The Court declared: "The consideration and initiation of fundamental reforms with respect to state taxation and education are matters reserved for the legislative processes of the various states."

The *Rodriguez* decision meant that school financing cases would have to be argued within the courts of each state under state constitutions. This would mean a long struggle within each state to achieve a method of providing equal financial support to the schools. One cannot predict whether this will occur in all states in the country, but it is one important part of the attempt to achieve equality of educational opportunity in the United States.

CONCLUSION

The courts continue to play an essential role in protecting individual rights within the public schools. Because public schools attempt to educate a large population having a variety of backgrounds and beliefs, there is always the danger that minority rights will be lost or forgotten within the school. In addition, public schooling is a property right and in most states is compulsory. These conditions mean that some institutions must exercise vigilance in the protection of rights in education. This is the important role that the courts have assumed and will continue to assume in American education.

Suggested Readings and Works Cited in Chapter

COONS, JOHN E.; WILLIAM H. CLUNE; and STEPHEN SUGARMAN. *Private Wealth and Public Education.* Cambridge, MA: Harvard University Press, 1970. This is the book that provided the basic arguments for the school finance cases.

DELEFATTORE, JOAN. *What Johnny Shouldn't Read: Textbook Censorship in America.* New Haven, CT: Yale University Press, 1992. This book contains discussions of court cases involving claims of secular humanism in textbooks.

DESSEM, LAWRENCE. "Student Due Process Rights in Academic Dismissals from the Public Schools." *Journal of Law and Education,* Vol. 5, no. 3 (July 1976).

FISCHER, LOUIS, et al. *Teachers and the Law,* 5th edition. New York: Addison-Wesley, 1998. Written in a question-and-answer format, this is a very useful and up-to-date guide to laws that affect the teaching profession.

"Gay Teacher Faced Discrimination." *The New York Times* (26 November 1998). http://www.nytimes.com. This article describes how the court supported a schoolteacher who told a student that she was a lesbian.

GROVER, ALAN. *Ohio's Trojan Horse: A Warning to Christian Schools Everywhere.* Greenville, SC: Bob Jones University Press, 1977. The book contains a description of the *Whisner* case and the arguments regarding secular humanism.

HANLEY, ROBERT. "New Jersey Schools: Rich, Poor, Unequal." *The New York Times* (5 March 1990): B1, B4. This article describes the disparities between the school systems of Millburn and East Orange, New Jersey.

HILL, DAVID. "Counter Evolutionary." *Education Week* (20 November 1996). http://www. edweek.org. Hill reviews cases that involve the teaching of evolution.

KEIM, ALBERT N., ed. *Compulsory Education and the Amish.* Boston: Beacon, 1972. This book contains articles about the Amish and their struggle against compulsory education.

LAPATI, AMERICO. *Education and the Federal Government.* New York: Mason/Chapter, 1975. The last section of this book reviews all the major U.S. Supreme Court cases regarding education.

LEHNE, RICHARD. *The Quest for Justice: The Politics of School Finance Reform.* New York and London: Longman, 1978. This is an excellent analysis of the movement for equitably sharing the cost of school finances.

LEWIN, TAMAR. "With Court Nod, Parents Debate School Drug Tests." *The New York Times on the Web* (29 September 2002). http://www.nytimes.com. Lewin presents a survey of the reaction of local school districts to the U.S. Supreme Court decision to allow drug testing of students involved in extracurricular activities.

PORTNER, JESSICA. "Federal Court Upholds Va. Minute of Silence." *Education Week on the Web* (8 November 2000). http://www.edweek.org. Portner reports on the federal district court decision that the Virginia law requiring a minute of silence in public schools is not a violation of the Establishment Clause.

RUBIN, DAVID. *The Rights of Teachers.* New York: Avon, 1972. This is the American Civil Liberties Union handbook of teachers' rights.

"Supreme Court on Aid to Religious Schools." *Education Week on the Web* (6 September 1995). http://www.edweek.org. This article reviews cases that involve government aid to religious schools.

TESCONI, CHARLES, and EMANUEL HURWITZ. *Education for Whom?* New York: Dodd, Mead, 1974. This book contains essays about the school finance cases.

WALSH, MARK. "Court Allows Vouchers in Milwaukee." *Education Week* (17 June 1998). Walsh reports on the Wisconsin Supreme Court decision that declares the Milwaukee voucher system, which allows students to attend private religious schools, constitutional.

——. "Appeals Court Rejects Employee-Drug-Test Policies." *Education Week* (10 June 1998). Walsh reports that a federal appeals court struck down two Louisiana school districts' policies for drug testing of teachers.

——. "Appeals Court Allows Student-Led Graduation Prayers." *Education Week* (3 June 1998). Walsh reports on the U.S. Court of Appeals decision that allows student-led graduation prayers when students are allowed the choice of speaking on any topic at graduation.

——. "Court Clears Cleveland's Voucher Pilot." *Education Week* (7 August 1996). This is a discussion of the lower-court decision stating that the Ohio voucher law is not unconstitutional.

——. "Bills in Six States Address Student-Led Prayers." *Education Week* (23 February 1994): 10. This article describes the continuing effort to get prayers back into the schools.

WALSH, MARK, with LAURA MILLER. "White House Backs Wider Drug Testing in Schools." *Education Week on the Web* (11 September 2002). http://www.edweek.org. This article discusses the booklet issued by the White House Office of National Drug Control Policy urging drug testing of students involved in extracurricular activities.

——. "Scouts' Ban on Gays Is Prompting Schools to Reconsider Ties." *Education Week on the Web* (25 October 2000). http://www.edweek.org. This article discusses the school districts' reactions to the Boy Scout ban on gay leaders and members.

——. "Education and the Supreme Court: The 1999–2000." *Education Week on the Web* (12 July 2000). http://www.edweek.org. Recent educational rulings of the U.S. Supreme Court are reported.

——. "Supreme Court Lets Stand Rulings on Drug Tests, Teaching Materials." *Education Week on the Web* (14 September 1998). http://www.edweek.org. Walsh reports on the U.S. Supreme Court decision to uphold the right of school districts to perform random drug tests on students participating in extracurricular activities.

——. "Teachers Fired over Classroom Practices Lose Appeals." *Education Week on the Web* (7 August 1998). http://www.edweek.org. Walsh reports on how the courts upheld the firing of teachers for using a film and class methodologies that violated school policies on controversial materials and the use of profane language.

——. "Religious Schools Welcome Back On-Site Title I Services." *Education Week* (8 July 1998). This article discusses the U.S. Supreme Court decision to allow federally funded programs to be conducted on the site of religious schools.

——. "High Court Rejects Two Appeals on Religion in Schools." *Education Week on the Web* (8 July 1998). http://www.edweek.org. This article deals with the U.S. Supreme Court's refusal to overturn a federal district judge's rulings that struck down a state law allowing student-led prayers in public schools.

——. "High Court Limits District Liability on Harassment." *Education Week on the Web* (24 June 1998). http://www.edweek.org. This article describes how the U.S.

Supreme Court denies parents the right to sue the school district for monetary rewards in a case involving sexual relations between a teacher and student.

——. "High Court Lets Stand Ruling on Religious Uses of Public Schools." *Education Week on the Web* (29 April 1998). http://www.edweek.org. This article reports on how the U.S. Supreme Court upholds the right of school districts to bar the use of school facilities for religious services.

——. "Supreme Court Declines to Accept Student Sexual-Harassment Case." *Education Week on the Web* (16 October 1996). http://www.edweek.org. This article tells how the Supreme Court avoids clarifying the legal issues involving a public school student sexually harassing another student.

——. "Court Upholds Drug Tests for Student Athletes." *Education Week on the Web* (12 July 1995). http://www.edweek.org. The recent ruling on drug tests for school athletics is reported.

——. "High Court's Ban on Graduation Prayers Disappoints Districts." *Education Week* (5 August 1992): 1, 41–43. This article discusses the U.S. Supreme Court case *Lee v. Weisman* (1992), which banned prayers from public school graduation services. The article contains lengthy excerpts from the decision.

——. "Students Claiming Sex Harassment Win Right to Sue." *Education Week* (4 March 1992): 1, 24. This article discusses the U.S. Supreme Court ruling in *Franklin v. Gwinnett County Public Schools* (1992), which provides students with protection from sexual harassment by teachers.

WEEKS, J. DEVEREUX. *Student Rights under the Constitution: Selected Federal Decisions Affecting the Public School Community.* Athens: University of Georgia Press, 1992. This is a guide to student rights under the U.S. Constitution.

Text Credits

P. 79, Quotation from American Federation of Teachers, "Resolution on Inclusion of Students with Disabilities," © AFT 1994, used by permission.

P. 103, Quotation from Audrey Singer, The Brookings Institution in *The New York Times* online, "Census Shows Growth of Immigrants," 8/15/06. Reprinted by permission.

P. 156, Quotation from National Education Association, "Vouchers," 2006. Used by permission of the NEA.

P. 163, Quotation from the AFT Charter School Achievement on the 2003 National Assessment of Educational Progress, © AFT 2004, used by permission.

P. 166, Quotation from National Education Association report, "Can Corporate Management Solve the Challenges Facing America's Public Schools?" Used by permission of the NEA.

P. 184, Quotation from W. James Popham, "Standardized Achievement Tests: Misnamed and Misleading." First appeared in *Education Week*, 9/19/01. Reprinted by permission of the author.

P. 225, Quotation from People for the American Way, "Harry Potter, and the Censors' Menace," 3/3/03. Used by permission.

Index

Italicized page numbers refer to figures and tables.